SIMONE WEIL

SIMONE WEIL

AN INTELLECTUAL BIOGRAPHY

by Gabriella Fiori

translated by Joseph R. Berrigan

The University of Georgia Press

Athens and London

© 1989 by the University of Georgia Press
Athens, Georgia 30602
All rights reserved
Simone Weil: biografia di un pensiero © Garzanti Editore s.p.a., 1981
Originally published in Italian in 1981 by Garzanti Editore, Milan
Designed by Mary Mendell
Set in Galliard

The paper in this book meets the guidelines for permanence and
durability of the Committee on Production Guidelines for Book
Longevity of the Council on Library Resources.
Printed in the United States of America
93 92 91 90 89   5 4 3 2 1

Library of Congress Cataloging in Publication Data
Fiori, Gabriella.
Simone Weil, an intellectual biography.
Translation of: Simone Weil, biografia di un pensiero.
Bibliography: p.
Includes index.
1. Weil, Simone, 1909–1943. 2. Philosophers—
France—Biography. I. Title.
B2430.W474F5613 1989   194   88-20536
ISBN 0-8203-1102-2 (alk. paper)
British Library Cataloging in Publication Data available

To three women whom I fondly love:
my mother, Ave, and my daughters,
Stefania and Francesca

Contents

Preface

_____

_____

_____

This book resulted from my need to rediscover Simone Weil, as a woman, a person, and a character, in the fullness and complexity of her reality. I wanted not so much to analyze and study biographical details and writings, though they are examined with as much depth and rigor as I could command, as to listen to them, to grasp them in an intuitive synthesis, in an effort to bring back to life a way of thinking and of living in its manifold facets.

So I based my work solely on evidence provided by people who knew her and upon her works. I have often subordinated chronological order to thematic; so, in the same way, I have allowed the witnesses to appear on stage. The notes complete the text; they contribute to a biography which I have designed as a mosaic reconstruction or, even better, an organism of living cells.

This book of mine, which I have conceived and wished for as a vivid reconstruction of the life and thought on earth of Simone Weil, could never have been born without the recollection, testimony, and documentation of those who have known her or just met her for a short time, or discovered her through her works.

I express my gratitude to them for their precious help, beginning with André Weil, who has ever encouraged me with trustful attention. In one or more conversations, or by letters, I had an opportunity to receive the help of many: Susy Allemand, Mr. Andrews, Père Arrigoni, Colette Audry, Denise-Aimé Azam, Marcelle Ballard, Charles G. Bell, Dom Beissart, Claire Claveyrolas, Pierre Dantu, Marie-Hélène Dasté, Malou David, Marie-Magdeleine Davy, Victor-Henry Debidour, Elisa de Jager, Jean-François Detoeuf, Jean-Marie Domenach, Adèle Dubreuil, Jean Duperray,

Berthe Ergas, Charles Flory, Eugène Fleuré, Mr. Frank, Robert Gaillardot, Léon-Gabriel Gros, Madame Herlin-Besson, Jeanne Hersch, Georges Hourdin, M. and Mme. Isambert, Père Jobert, Gilbert Kahn, Jean Lambert, Marcel Lecarpentier, Madame Lectourneux, Jacques Loew, Camille Marcoux, Marianne Monestier, Abbé Etienne Ostier, Aimé Patri, Leslie Paul, Père Joseph-Marie Perrin, Simone Pétrement, Clémence Ramnoux, Mère Germaine Roussel, Soeur Saint-Maur, Maurice Schumann, Lucienne Sigel, Vernon Sproxton, Soeur Thérèse de la Trinité, Albertine Thévenon, Gustave Thibon, Henri Thomas, Jean Tortel, Iris Woods.

To those of my dear interlocutors who are no more among us, I send the message of my grateful memory. I remember: Suzanne André, Jean Ballard, Pierre Bost, Mère François Copeau, Alida de Jager, Denis de Rougemont, Thérèse de la Marguette, Lanza del Vasto, Stanislas Fumet, Louis Goubert, François Le Lionnais, Madeleine Marcault, René Nelli, Jean Oswald, Jacques Redon, Déodat Roché, Lella Rosin, Boris Souvarine, Edoardo Volterra, Jean Wahl, Eveline Weil.

To the following individuals, I owe special thanks for their permission to reproduce unpublished documents of Simone Weil: Marcelle Ballard, René Nelli, Mère Germaine Roussel, André Weil. For photographic documentation, I thank Denise-Aimé Azam, Marcelle Ballard, Robert Gaillardot, Gilbert Kahn, Camille Marcoux, Leslie Paul, Mère Germaine Roussel, Lucienne Sigel, Boris Souvarine, Albertine Thévenon.

For its genial cooperation, I thank the "Association pour l'étude de la pensée de Simone Weil," namely, André-A. Devaux, vice-president; Jean Tavernier, to whom we owe the first idea of a group studying the thought of Simone Weil in 1970; as well as members Georges Charot (now president), Patricia Little, Adriano Marchetti, Emmanuel Nguyen Van Tu and Gérard Perrodo. Last but not least, I am warmly grateful to Bernadette and Mathieu Capitant for the friendly hospitality at their home in Paris.

Gabriella Fiori

SIMONE WEIL

1

The News

On August 31, 1943, a Thursday, the newspaper "Tuesday Express" of the little town of Ashford in Kent published on its first page this notice:

French professor starves herself to death.

There followed, in all of its particulars, the chronicle of the inquest conducted by the coroner at Grosvenor sanatorium.

"When I think of my fellow citizens who are dying of hunger in France, I cannot eat"; this was Professor Weil's response to the doctor who tried to get her to eat.

The chief nurse of the sanatorium, Mrs. Wilks, said in the course of her deposition that . . . the patient ate very little and was very thin. Miss Iris Woods, for twenty years the linen attendant at the Grosvenor, had never seen her but declared that "Everyone knew about her, because she was such an interesting case, and that they could not give her nourishment because she was so thin."[1]

The deposition of Dr. Henrietta Broderick, the head of the Grosvenor, was the following (as the newspaper provided it): "On her arrival Professor Weil was utterly convinced that we would be able to cure her. We judged that her tuberculosis was not very far advanced and so with proper nourishment the patient had a good chance of recovery. Dr. Roberts[2] of Middlesex Hospital in London had already informed me in his letter that Professor Weil was allowing herself to die of starvation and repeated insistently that we should send her food to the French prisoners of war . . . I believe that her death was due to a cardiac collapse brought about by the weakness caused by her deprivations, and not by pulmonary tuberculosis. The verdict of the coroner was that of 'suicide in a state of mental disturbance.'"[3]

The official death certificate, which was issued in Ashford on August 27 by the vice-coroner of the county, Mr. A. K. Mowll, speaks of "Cardiac cessation due to the weakness of the miocardium, in its turn caused by deprivations and pulmonary tuberculosis. The deceased condemned herself to death and killed herself by refusing to eat, in a state of mental disturbance."[4]

She was buried in the New Cemetery, or Bybrook Cemetery, on a little hill alongside the premises of the Grosvenor. The burial certificate, in the pseudo-Gothic offices of the New Cemetery, records the ceremony on page 169. The date given is August 30, 1943; there is an error in her name: Weil Adolphine Siome (for Simone). A French refugee, she was considered a Catholic and buried in the section reserved for Catholics. Why? The superintendent of the cemetery, who has held the position for only ten years, speaks of her as "an atheist."[5] She appeared to entertain "bizarre" ideas on religion, ideas that were entirely her own. She said that "she did not have a religion."[6] On her admission form to the Grosvenor the place reserved for *Religion* remains blank, at the wish of the patient. She would have said to Dr. Broderick, "I am a philosopher and am interested in humanity."[7] And then she would have told one of the two doctors in charge of the sanatorium, but we are not sure which one, "I am Jewish; but I want to become a Catholic, although there is still a point not settled."[8]

Was she baptized or not? Who had asked that she be buried in *dedicated* ground, as contrasted with the *consecrated* ground for Protestants? Perhaps it was simply a question of an emergency. "The Hebrew cemetery was far away, some fifty miles from here," explains Miss Woods. "The arrangements were to be expedited and so they sent her to Bybrook." "There were a good number of Frenchmen, of the Free France forces, in the sanatorium, soldiers and airmen. Perhaps, since she was French, too, they naturally considered her a Catholic," asserts Mr. Frank,[9] for long years in charge of the office at the Grosvenor and an old friend of Dr. Roberts. And yet, he insists that he could not give me any second-hand information, because "there wasn't any." Do you know the priests who were detailed for the ceremony? "Of course, they were Fr. Gilligan and Fr. Miller, but they are dead." This is what Iris Woods tells me.

A German Franciscan answers on the telephone from Canterbury quite sharply, "She was not baptized." A Scottish priest, Fr. McKay, tells me so; he lives in South Africa and is on temporary duty at St. Theresa of the

Child Jesus. He is a weary, disappointed sort of person and he adds that the Franciscan does not like to talk about the past, about the war.

Simone Weil sinks amidst all these denials and disappears. She reappears but with a mistaken name. For yet another time, this one the last, she is cancelled out by her destiny of anonymity and yet she is made vivid as in dreams by the perplexity about her story. Who was she, what kind of person was she, what did she do?

The "Tuesday Express" speaks of her "slight mental disequilibrium," in contrast with Dr. Broderick, who asserts that the French professor had "preserved her complete mental clarity intact. Her glance was luminous, she read and she wrote. At the same time she seemed to have achieved a detachment from everything, in the consciousness that she had to die."[10]

She had loved her room, on the first floor of the Grosvenor, in the building intended for patients. Constructed of brick and mortar, it looks like a house on the sea, with its little white columns featuring and prolonging its profile. "Here the wards faced south, so that the patients could be in the sun," Iris Woods tells me. The rooms, like so many cells, opened on a terraced balcony. From her room Miss Weil looked into the distance, towards France. Beyond the first meadow and beyond the second large meadow bordered with trees, on an English horizon delicately moulded with hills, "at definite times there billowed the columns of smoke from the London-Dover trains."[11]

"What a beautiful place to die." Apparently she said this upon her arrival.[12] And her smile must have brought a little comfort to Madame Closon, her French friend, who had accompanied her and Mrs. Jones, the mother-in-law of the administrative director. Mrs. Jones, herself a Frenchwoman by birth, had labored mightily to have her admitted to this rural sanatorium, intended primarily for laborers.

She was so exhausted that her admission form reads, "Too ill for adequate examination." This was August 17. She had seven days to live. The most serious problem for the doctors was to get her to eat. She said that she could not bear any solid food or even milk. She would try, "with great effort, to take some liquid (a rich broth of chicken, the yolk of an egg, beaten in sherry, a very ripe peach) that she could digest."[13] And a purée of potatoes, but made in the French fashion, the way her mother had cooked them. She said this on August 21 to Madame Closon, who promised to return in a week and cook such a purée for her.

On August 22, a Sunday, she received the visit of a woman friend. Monday was a pretty good day for her. Tuesday, the 24th, had a rather good beginning, in which she "had a quite lively conversation." Around five in the afternoon she sank into a coma, from which she never regained consciousness. "She must have died between ten and ten-thirty, in her sleep. She appeared very serene."[14]

Her parents were in New York. On August 26, they had received their last letter from their daughter. It carried the date of the 13th and the usual address of 31 Portland Road, Holland Park, London W. 11. There Professor Weil had lived in the boardinghouse of Mrs. Francis, in an atmosphere "pure Dickens."[15]

As tender as ever, the short letter, more than anything else, was a message that warned:

> I have little time or inspiration for letters now. They will be short, rare and infrequent. But you have another major source of comfort.
>
> When you have received this letter (unless it is especially fast) you will already have received the expected cable. (Nothing for certain! . . .)
>
> Good bye, darlings. Thousands and thousands of caresses.
>
> Simone[16]

It was Madame Closon who sent the telegram with the news of her death to André Weil, Simone's brother, who taught at a university in Pennsylvania. A letter, dated the 27th, followed to André's wife, Eveline. André decided to go to New York; he asked Dr. Bercher, their old friend, who happened to be in Philadelphia at the time, to join him as soon as he could. On his first visit to his parents, when he realized that they knew nothing, "he did not have the courage to tell them the news." It was another friend, Louis Rougier, who called the Weil parents the next day to find out "if Simone was really so seriously ill." They were dumbfounded and, now on their guard, were preparing to send a telegram. "Dr. Bernard had come down to go to the post-office. He had hardly gotten off the elevator when he met his son, this time accompanied by Dr. Bercher. They told him the terrible news and all three of them went up together to bring it to Mme. Selma."[17]

2

Loneliness in London

She was buried in space 79, in the third row from the hedge that surrounds the cemetery, against the background of a grove in which ash trees predominate. For fifteen years there was no sign, no inscription concerning her; only that number 79, cast in relief on an iron shield. "A pauper's grave," was the comment of the citizens of Ashford.[1] It is not a simple emotional comment; it is a juridical fact. A *pauper* is someone without means, someone who belongs to no one, whom no one inquires after. Such a person has no juridical character; he depends on the state, which offers him a grave six feet deep. For a certain number of years he has the right to that little sign, to that number. Then, he is erased forever because someone else can be buried above him.[2]

On that thirtieth of August seven persons accompanied her to the cemetery: Suzanne Aron, an old friend from the lycée and the wife of Raymond Aron, the sociologist and politician; Thérèse Closon, the wife of Louis Closon, of the French government in London; Professor Fehling, rediscovered by Simone after years of separation (they had known each other in the long-distant days of vacationing at Montana); Mrs. Rosin, a German painter, likewise a friend from years earlier; a Frenchwoman of her own age in service with the French forces; Maurice Schumann; and Mrs. Francis, Simone Weil's landlady. The Catholic priest who had been asked to come missed his train or got lost; for whatever reason, he did not come. Schumann had a missal; he knelt down and read some prayers; Thérèse Closon recited the responses.[3]

Mrs. Francis was not rich. The hours she lost from her work as half-day help and the expenses for the train from London represented a real sacrifice for her. But she had to do it; she was overwhelmed by an invincible impulse of tenderness towards a woman who had always tried to understand all, a woman "of such a sweet, such a quiet voice."[4] A mysterious woman with a secret vision to realize, doing her nightly task at the writing desk, under the lamplight.

Miss Simone was alone. On April 15, a fellow worker had found her on the floor in her room, unconscious. "At first Simone objected; she wanted her to swear that she would tell nothing to anyone. Then she understood that she would have to yield, that they would have taken her to the hospital anyway. She telephoned Schumann in tears."[5] It was hard for him to console her and to convince her about what had to be done.

At the Middlesex, Dr. Bennett diagnosed granulitis, or numerous small lesions in the two lungs, but "with good possibilities of recovery." Complete rest and good food should allow the patient to enter a sanatorium. After improving in her appearance after a few days, she soon stopped her progress because "she ate too little." Since she could "hardly lift a spoon" in her extreme weakness, from the very beginning she was assisted in feeding herself. "But she did not like being helped."[6]

She had received permission for daily visits, as long as they were brief. She made her friends promise never to tell her parents about her condition. From April 17 until her death she would write them letters that bear the address of her room on Portland Road and describe London, her work and her companions.

Her correspondence with her parents was the only activity the doctor allowed her. As for the other writings that date from the London phase of her life, they were all probably composed between the middle of December, 1942 and the middle of April, 1943. They constitute so great a mass of work that it seems unbelievable. "She must have written day and night, with hardly any sleep. More than once she spent the whole night in her office, where she had been locked in at her own request."[7]

The exhaustion resulting from such effort helped precipitate a latent state of illness. Her wish not to eat and her by now chronic inability to digest certain foods (such as milk) prevented the patient, although she was under care, from achieving any improvement. Conflict with her attending physician, Dr. Bennett, became unavoidable. He called her "the most difficult patient I have ever had" and when he learned, both from Simone and her friends, that she had eaten little even before entering the hospital, he concluded that her fate was to die of hunger in a garret.[8] This was also the reaction of Dr. Roberts, at the sanatorium in Ashford. As his friend Mr. Frank says, even today he has a bitter memory of the anorexia that prevented any definite cure and ended in causing his patient's death.[9]

Another sign of her noncooperation with her doctors was her refusal to accept a pneumothoracic operation. Bennett made the suggestion quite brusquely, perhaps to shake her. Simone's reply was to leave the Middlesex for a sanatorium in the country. Did she really want to die? Her friend Thérèse Closon, with reference to this, declares that Simone refused the operation both because of her wish to leave London and "the hospital atmosphere,"[10] and because she felt that sort of intervention inappropriate for her case. She asked herself, in fact, "if it would be a good idea to give up one lung when the other, still untouched, might wind up one day in just as bad a state."[11]

During her last days in London, her digestive crisis grew worse and her exhaustion so extreme that she had to be brought to the Grosvenor on a stretcher, as Miss Woods explains.[12]

Did she really want to die? The coroner's inquest and his conclusion set forth a reasoning process dictated by everyday logic and express an opinion on an objective fact. What did her friends say about her, those friends who went to visit her often? Mrs. Rosin always found Simone happy and smiling. She says that she was "very lucid and remained so until the end. She was also very beautiful, ethereal, transparent. Everything material seemed destroyed in her."[13] She felt, however, and she is the only one of Simone's London friends to do so, that she wanted to die, even if she never said so, even if she never utterly refused to eat and ate only a little, saying that she was not hungry. Suzanne Aron has said that "both the coroner's inquest and his conclusion seemed absurd to all those who knew Simone in London. Admittedly, Simone was desperate; she revolted against the thought that she had not received a mission to France."[14] But it is impossible that she could have decided upon her destiny on her own. For Suzanne Aron this does not seem to coincide with her spiritual attitude, after she had turned to religious doctrines. "It would have been easy for her to commit suicide, if she had wanted to, since she had access to sleeping pills in the hospital," someone else said.[15] Furthermore, she often spoke of the future, even of a brief future in a free France.

In postwar France, the news of her death arrived after several months. "Necessarily; she never ate. She was the only one to be rationed; everyone else had coupons to spare. If one does not eat enough, one gets ill and dies." These are the words of Déodat Roché.[16] For René Nelli, Simone was fated to die in "endura" (which means in Provençal privation, fasting), a mystical suicide in which the soul leaves the body, its mortal remains, to the earth, freeing itself at length from "a world that is at the mercy of the prince of darkness."[17]

For Madeleine Marcault, Simone was "so absolutely unhappy that she desired to die."[18]

Albertine Thévenon, in her desperation, at first said, "If I had been beside her, I would have convinced her to eat, to take care of herself; she would not have died." Then she remembered this, "Simone knew how to be happy, yes she did, especially when we were together, but she never sought happiness. And she had always told her mother she wanted to be left alone at the moment of her death. Nobody could have done anything for Simone."[19]

"Speaking of her death does not have the same sense as speaking of someone else's death. I do not any longer remember how I heard the news. I immediately thought of this. Simone Weil could not have lived much longer than the length of Christ's life. That was written at the bottom of her heart." This is the thought of Camille Marcoux, a companion of hers at the Ecole Normale.[20]

So the mystery of her death begins to raise questions about the meaning of her life. As the writings of Simone Weil gradually appeared, like twinkling lights, like hidden treasures—letters of confessional autobiography, notebooks entrusted to friends or still remaining in a drawer, essays, poems, a tragedy, testimonials (sometimes lost and then found years later)—a woman's project came clearly into view.

The London writings contain hardly any cancellations. The handwriting, small, patient, and clear, spreads over the pages in all clarity. It traces powerful ideas with a sternness that indicates full consciousness. In a letter to her mother, Simone writes:

I am experiencing, increasingly, a sort of inner certainty that there exists in me a deposit of pure gold to pass on.

But she adds:

Experience and the observation of my contemporaries are forever persuading me more surely that there is no one ready to receive it.[21]

She clearly knows she is speaking in the desert. She senses the practical ineffectiveness of her work as an editor, a pointless labor in comparison with the mission of total sacrifice, a mission she had begged to achieve for herself. Her writings, which strive to evaluate the most distant motives in historical situations and to foresee the future resonances of human actions, in order to formulate laws from within, seem "a perseverance in the generic." André Philip asked her, "But why do you never take up concrete matters, the problems of the unions?"

She had the unbendable concreteness of the truth to speak. And she knew it well. Looking at herself from the outside, she gives a self-portrait. Her intelligence, which she defines as "middling," is one of those intelligences "entirely, exclusively abandoned and dedicated to the truth" and so

of no use to any human being, even the one in which it resides.

Simone declares:

It is an intelligence which uses me, which obeys without any hesitation—or at least I hope so—what appears to it as the light of truth. It obeys day by day, hour by hour, and my will does not exercise any power over it.[22]

And the truth is not heard. It is like the good. It is mysterious. To receive it one must remain loyally turned towards it; it abides in a reality lodged outside the world, beyond time and space, beyond the mental universe of man. Bound to this reality, man has at

the center of his heart the ever present thirst for an absolute good which finds no object in this world.[23]

To reach that reality in which the good and the true shine together in satiating splendor, one must follow this thirst, without lying to oneself; and to experience it fully, one must grant it space and accept it in the emptiness of a detachment from things which is

the real and lasting consent to death and to the loss of all transitory goods without exception.[24]

To bring her obedience to perfection and to transform her will into this "consent" to the law of necessity that weaves death and suffering into the reality of things, this unknown Frenchwoman has traveled a long conscious road. Why?

For me personally life does not have and has never had any other meaning than the expectation of truth.[25]

And death

is the instant when for an infinitesimal fraction of time pure, naked, certain and eternal truth enters the soul.[26]

This certainty lives at the center of Simone Weil, the woman who wanted to find the secret map where the points of intersection between the soul and things are marked, to learn the proper orientation for the eternal journey of each creature. This certainty unifies her actions, her choices and, above all else, the opening of her entire existence. She says:

I have always believed that the moment of death is the norm and the goal of life . . . even when I was a child and thought that I was an atheist and a materialist, I always feared this, not that I would fail in life, but in death.[27]

But it is not a question here of failing to make the grand gesture, in which one affirms one's egotism and imposes oneself in a certain sense on reality. Because

death is not a suicide. One must be killed; to experience the heaviness, the weight of the world.[28]

═══════

This definitive despoilment took place in the loneliness of London. Simone Weil had resigned from the Free French Forces; she remained without means of sustenance. Many times in her letters to her parents she declared that she had no part in events, either for good or for bad ("I would prefer to sleep under bridges").[29]

She had reached the essential. Not by chance does she compare herself with the *fools* of Shakespeare, whose unbearably tragic character she has only now discovered. It is searing how they are not heard; and yet they alone have the chance to say "the pure and simple truth," because they have plumbed the depths of humiliation and find themselves far inferior to beggars, not only deprived of all social consideration but regarded by all as beings lacking the prime human dignity, reason.[30]

They praise Simone for her intelligence; in haste they heap praise on her, so that they will not have to hear her or reflect on her words.

It is well known that a great intelligence is often paradoxical, even at times a little extravagant . . . The principal *goal* of the praise showered on me is the avoidance of the question, "Is she saying the truth or not?" My reputation as an "intelligent person" is the practical equivalent of the badge of folly given to those fools. How much I prefer the latter.[31]

In such a way is she even more silenced by the dull banality of the world. But that is the way it had to be. She had to depart in this way, alone, exhausted out of compassion, her body frail and innocent, her soul sincere to the pitch of coarseness of the "mendicants of the spirit."[32]

The first sign of this was that little plate with the number 79 above a pauper's grave. The inhabitants of Ashford knew that well.

3

Infancy and Childhood

Simone Weil, born in Paris[1] on February 3, 1909, was the second child of Bernard Weil, a doctor, and Selma (diminutive of Salomea) Reinherz.

Bernard, a Jew of Alsatian origin, had been born at Strasbourg in 1872, of the second marriage of Abraham Weil. He was the only intellectual in a family of businessmen and commercial agents. His mother, Eugénie, had been born in 1839; she came to Paris when she was seventy and lived to be ninety-three as a widow; she never learned to speak French. She was fiercely devoted to Jewish rites, to the extent of "a certain fanaticism."[2] They provided her with a means of defense in her psychological solitude as an Alsatian.

Selma, born in 1879 in Rostov on the Don, was the daughter of Adolf Reinherz, a native of Galicia, and of Hermine Sternberg, a Viennese, also of Galician origin. She had left Russia for Antwerp in 1882. There, Adolf Reinherz became very successful in the field of exports; Selma became a naturalized Belgian along with her whole family. Simone used to tease her mother about her diverse origins and repeat with a smile, "You are of suspect nationality."[3]

Selma had had a Cossack nurse and the various, free and stimulating ambience of a rich, cultured family. In Russia, the Reinherz household had seventeen servants; guests would arrive almost every afternoon at four and remain till the next morning. Conversations lasted into the night. Adolf, an able and energetic merchant, was, at the same time, a poet; he composed verses in Hebrew, a language he knew well; he also collected Hebrew texts. André Weil remembers seeing volumes of his poetry in his childhood.[4] Hermine was a very talented pianist; she cultivated the dance and Greek. Selma played the piano, too, with fine taste and great musical culture; she learned to sing so well that a celebrated professor who had taught her said good-bye with these words: "I have nothing more to teach you." Unlike the parents of Dr. Bernard, the Reinherz family maintained no religious practice, although they may have been deists.

Within the family, Dr. Bernard was called Biri, a nickname created by his wife and his two children, André, born on May 6, 1906, and Simone. He was a thin little man, whose face charmed others with an expression at once kind and penetrating. It is possible to trace in portraits, photographs and reality a line of similarity that runs from his mother, Eugénie, to him, to Simone and André, to Raymonde, the daughter of Oscar Weil and a first cousin of Simone: "the same dark look, the same mouth, curved with a light smile, and a straight, slightly aquiline nose." These are Raymonde's words; she adds, "Bernard was a good man, a man who was too considerate of others; he was easily devoured. His wife had the upper hand and so his personality seemed less distinct than it really was. His wife would have preferred a more brilliant life, one more socially alive. Not from the point of view of money; they were not at all eager for that."[5] He was a very fine doctor, a general practitioner, "of the type which is disappearing fast; he truly loved his profession and dedicated his whole self to it; he left to my mother the direction of the family, especially the supervision of our studies. On this basis they were very happy together. Later, with the war, circumstances hindered him from practicing medicine. From then on, his life became essentially unhappy, even apart from the fact that my sister died prematurely."[6]

Selma, who did not like her name (which came from a grandfather named Salomon), whether full or abbreviated, was called affectionately Mime. "An intelligent and passionate woman, she was not very objective; endowed with an abundance of talents, she had not succeeded in channeling her brilliant abilities in one particular career."[7] In her youth, in Belgium, she had wanted to study medicine, but her father had not allowed her. Smaller than her husband, she was more vigorous than he in appearance. "She had something of the violence of the Tatar about her, which the children inherited."[8] Busy, creative in arranging the details of daily life, she took an interest in everyone and everything; she was tireless in giving advice and assistance." She had a kind of "practical genius."[9]

Simone was born a month early; for the first six months she developed normally. In August of 1909, her mother, suffering from appendicitis, was forced to restrict her diet and to take more rest, but she continued to nurse Simone. Probably because her mother's condition had made her milk bad, the baby began to waste away. Simone would later playfully complain about this early poisoning. "This is why I am so incomplete a being,"[10] she would say. But from London, on July 12, 1943, she would write with tenderness,

> I prefer having had a mother like mine (not to mention my fa-
> ther . . .) despite the bad milk.[11]

Simone was weaned in the following January, at the insistence of Grandmother Reinherz, who was living with them; a very serious illness ensued, for the child, too, suffered from appendicitis. She did not grow at all; at sixteen months she still wanted only the bottle. With the advice of a specialist they continued using it, even for solid foods, by making holes in the nipple.

Every day the mother would take Simone, André and their nurse to the Luxembourg Gardens for fresh air. They would take the tram and always sit on the top deck, to avoid the crowds and microbes, which Selma feared, especially for the baby. André learned to read at this time, by observing the signs in front of the businesses along the rue de Strasbourg. They then gave him rose-colored books for children, with stories of the Greeks and Romans. Simone, three years of age, would listen. One day, when they had left one of those books on the bed for her to look at the pictures, they heard her say: "The Romans, are they really here? I am afraid of the Romans!"[12]

At three-and-a-half years, after a violent attack of appendicular colic, they had to operate on her. The surgeon Goldmann, who had listened to the discourses of the little child under the effects of chloroform, later confided to Selma Weil that he had feared for her. It seemed to him that a child like that could not continue to live. Unlike her brother, who had recovered from the same operation in a few days, Simone needed three weeks for convalescence. For a long time she had a real horror of doctors; she would flee from the room as soon as she saw someone she did not know enter it.

Simone seems to have been constantly encumbered with precarious health, despite the attentive care of a modern mother. Perhaps, even this early in her life, her body was becoming extraneous to her, more impediment than means. She soon tends to exert her will over it, to train it, to make it her servant. In the accidents that happen to her she reacts at times with a patience out of character with her usual vehemence.

October, 1913: after a bout with influenza she begins to limp. She has grown too suddenly and is tired from it; she has to remain on her back for long periods. She does so "without any complaint whatsoever," as her dumbfounded mother observes.[13]

November, 1914. It is during the first months of the war. Bernard is stationed away from home as a military doctor at Neufchâteau. Expecting to join him shortly with the children and his mother, Selma spends several days in the apartment in Paris without heat. It freezes. Simone, five-and-a-half years old, is shivering as her mother bathes her. Suddenly, she strains herself and says, "Why are you trembling, you carcass?" Selma is speechless; she did not know the exclamation of Turenne. It had surely been André who had taught it to his sister.

André and Simone: a magical and informative solidarity unites them. They are enclosed in their own universe, with their own set of symbols and games. "Two instruments tuned to the same note," says André.[14] "Only their mother was allowed to come into that world," remembers their cousin Raymonde, a little younger than Simone, who lost her mother in 1916 and came to live with the Weils. Although happy and emotionally satisfied in the company of her cousins, she found that their universe was impenetrable; it inevitably separated them from other children, too.

Summer, 1913: a holiday at Ballaigues, in Switzerland. Selma writes to Mlle. Chaintreuil, André's teacher at the Lycée Montaigne: "Simone has grown in an incredible fashion. She follows André everywhere; she is interested in his every movement. She has become like him; the days are not long enough for her . . . he protects her, he helps her clamber out of tight spots, he often yields to her; since she is with her brother all day from morning to night, she is becoming more active, more spry, more enterprising . . . Their favorite game is one they call 'voyages of exploration.' Their greatest happiness is in reaching a place so far away that they have the illusion of being alone in the wilds of nature."[15]

At Menton, in 1915, they discover a precious little gazebo of their own in the garden of an abandoned hotel. Every evening when they leave, there are scenes of desperation; they want to stay until night and look at the moon. They exchange everything, this love for nature, as well as knowledge. André shares with Simone everything he learns at school. One day, on the tram, he explains astronomy to her. And they speak with such precise questions and answers that a woman gets off the tram with an angry exclamation that she could not bear two such wise parrots!

It is André's decision: Simone will learn to read; it will be a New Year's Day present for Biri. It is early December, 1914, at Neufchâteau, where the family is living secretly, close to Health Lieutenant Bernard Weil. André makes Simone work for hours; when their father is visiting, the two children continue their studies tirelessly under the dining-room table. On New Year's Day, André asks, "Papa, would you like Simone to read you the newspaper?" Simone shows her ability, but is exhausted.

They are partners in wild pranks, real expressions of ironic inventiveness. Holidays at Jullouville, 1914. Holding each other's hand, the two children knock at the door of several houses. They beg the person who opens the door, "We are dying of hunger; our mama and papa are letting us die of hunger." "Poor babies!" the people exclaim and they hasten to stuff them with candies and sweets. André and Simone return home fat and full. The poor Weils almost burst with shame and indignation.

Another time, Paris, the winter of 1916. André, ten years of age, decides not to wear socks to make himself stronger. Simone copies him. Passersby notice them; their mother begs in vain that at least Simone put on her socks; they cry and cry. One day, on the street, a big woman notices that Simone's legs are almost blue with the cold; she goes up to Mme. Weil and exclaims, "You wretch!" So, too, on the tram, their teeth chattering, they exclaim in a chorus, "I am cold, I am cold! Why won't mama and papa buy us socks?" Fierce glances are shot at Selma, who must endure them, powerless.

One had to keep them amused constantly; when they became bored, they were unbearable. At times they would fight. Here is Selma's description of these battles: "they would fight in the deepest silence, so as not to catch our attention and so be separated. We heard only a shuffling; never a shout. When one came in the room, they would have each other by the hair, they would be pale and shaking each other."[16] It was a sort of magical duel of honor. Simone was proud of her brother and admired him, but she was not afraid of him and she would not yield to him when she was convinced that she was right.

This family comprised a unified body, joined together by the bonds of a zestful emotionality, refined but not weakened by a great taste for culture. It was a happy family, in which there existed "a joyful creativity in mirth."[17] They presented comedies, they created games, charades, poems with the most outlandish rhymes. André and Simone were inexhaustible in this kind of activity. The game of families, with the names of their purveyors and trades, became the game of grand personages: poets, dramatists, orators. They would recite whole scenes from Corneille and Racine; between André and Simone, whoever made a mistake or missed the beat, risked a slap. This in 1916. Their language, nourished with literary allusions, set the Weil children apart from their contemporaries but they were still full of "extreme courtesy, affability and modesty," as their comrade Yves Barnéoud clearly remembers.[18]

In general, Simone was little interested in the amusements and conversation of other girls of her own age; according to her nurse, Ebba Olsen, Simone never played with dolls. At home, the only toy was a ball. Furthermore, she did not want to learn how to sew. Ebba succeeded in getting her to embroider a handkerchief with a little border, as a present for her mother. According to Ebba, this was the only thing she sewed in her life.[19]

Simone's hands were small, compared with the rest of her body, and not adroit. With the cold they would swell and become red with chilblains. For this reason, she wrote very slowly as a child, and when her parents decided reluctantly to enroll her in the second grade of public school, in October, 1917, Simone could not keep up with her comrades.

In her first contact with school, Simone is docile and hardworking but she shows a lasting fear of making a mistake. She changes; she is no longer the indomitable Simone of a short time ago, who would oppose her parents with a merry obstinacy but who knew how to win forgiveness with winning graces, a "real little lady."[20]

In the enchanted realm of the provincial houses where Selma Weil, utterly in love with her husband, had made her family live during the war, to stay close to him, Simone could express in a free and happy fashion the clear streak of her feistiness. This trait goes hand in hand with a taste for independence, heroism, and deeds of bravery. As a child of four, she cannot hear enough of Elie Metchnikoff, an old friend of the Weils, an anarchist with regard to the education of children. He loved her intensely and predicted that she would be a great actress with "many lovers." He also told her stories from the crime pages, above all the story of a Madame Claire, who had killed her husband. "More Madame Claire," Simone would demand as soon as she saw him.[21] At six years of age, her passion was Cyrano. She would recite it along with André, with an emphasis that would make everyone laugh until they cried. "For the tirade of the (nose), we put her standing on the table."[22]

This feistiness would reappear at school, in a paper she wrote for her favorite teacher, Sapy. The subject was, "What would you like to do in your life?" Simone's list was so long that Mlle. Sapy was dismayed. "Remember, Simone," she told her, "plants not only have to grow in height, they also have to increase in girth."[23]

One gathers that even as a young child Simone wanted to create herself with the tautness of a will that is the violent impulse of her whole being. The incandescence of a stalwart psyche struggled to overcome the hindrances of a frail organism. Life in a family, which, although ever hospitable and generous to its friends, had its own area of development within its own emotional limits, tended to detach her from others and make her unique. There were, furthermore, some hygienic beliefs that had a powerful influence upon her emotional makeup. Their friendship with the Metchnikoffs, along with medical science, created in the Weil household a veritable phobia with regard to microbes. Selma did not want her children to kiss; they had to wash their hands before meals and keep them scrupulously clean. Once André had washed his hands, he would open doors with his elbows. In Simone, this caused certain habits of disgust which led to an alienation from her body; she did not want to be kissed, "even by her parents,"[24] nor would she eat certain foods nor often even touch what someone else had touched.

Even their studies, pursued at home until they were eight years of age and then, but only partially, in public school, contributed to their isolated development. This was due, for Simone in particular, to her prolonged illnesses as a small child, but for both Weil children to the constant dislocations of the family. André remarks: "Our studies were, one might say, greatly disturbed, essentially greatly accelerated, by that process. Instead of following the regular classes, we took lessons mostly by correspondence, taking a class here, a class there, for short periods. So we quickly got through all the stages without being retarded by the routine."[25]

For André, everything went exceptionally well. At eight years of age, in the house of a maternal aunt, he found a geometry book and began to study it by himself, for entertainment; he was soon able to solve difficult problems. His worried family "took away paper and pencil; he began to

write on the bare cement."[26] Here was a very early forecast of his mathematical genius. In the third grade of grammar school, he was too far advanced in mathematics, so he took only courses in literature. As far as Greek is concerned, he initially taught himself, at ten-and-a-half, by linking Greek words together with the help of his Latin dictionary; he then had private instruction, first with Charles-Brun at Chartres and later with Sinoir, who had to admit that this twelve-year-old boy was reading Plato fluently. At this time André was also studying the violin; later he would take singing and dancing at the Dalcroze school in Paris; for a while Simone studied the piano and also took the Dalcroze course. But while her brother rose rapidly and even became a "star," Simone, especially in these activities that involved the body and the ear, was quite slow.

The two adolescents differed in their attitude towards things and their mother, ever intent upon shaping her children, noticed this with concern; she compared them constantly. André has a consuming passion for algebra: "Completely on his own he has reached the stage of solving equations of the first and second degree . . . Simonetta is satisfied with her passion for patriotic poems."[27] André is always placid. For him questions and assignments in class are a real joy, "since without being the least vain, when he knows that he knows, he is sure of himself . . . Simone, on the other hand is always inclined to mistrust herself."[28]

Simone still possesses patience in great abundance and this helps in forming the force of her will. It was a fierce patience, spurring her on, together with her affection, to imitate her brother. Using a German word, Grandmother Reinherz said she was a real *Kopiermaschine!*[29] She practiced sports, played soccer with him on the beach, and swam; she also learned to ride the bicycle "quite" well; she was able to ride for forty kilometers along the Mayenne with her parents and André, an excellent cyclist. This was in 1917.

In her relations with others, outside the immediate family circle, Simone was fond of Mlle. Chaintreuil, "Aunt Gabrielle," who taught her for three months at the Montaigne in Paris in 1916; she was fond and protective of her cousin Raymonde. She had a war godson, to whom she wrote and for whom she made sacrifices. He would stay with them several days in 1917 and would later be killed.

Still in 1917, she suffered the trauma of a cruel joke played on her by some of her schoolmates. During a long absence of her mother, who had to undergo an operation—an absence that caused Simone much suffering

("I fervently desire your return")[30]—these schoolmates wrote her a letter, according to which her teacher did not want to bother with her anymore. But Simone did not cry; as her cousin Raymonde says, she did not allow herself tears. When she did cry, she would explain her tears in this way: "I am not weeping, I am bursting with rage."

How did Simone Weil appear to the girls of Section A, Fénelon grammar school, when she entered public life on October 3, 1919?

Geneviève Mathiot gives us this picture: "Physically she was a little child, unable to use her hands but of extraordinary intelligence. She had the appearance of a diverse origin, of a mind that did not belong to our age or our milieu. She seemed to have lived for a much longer time."[31]

She was two years younger than the others and seemed smaller than her age. At first she could not endure a discipline she did not understand and did everything wrong. The idea of going to school made her unhappy; she would often sit at home with her head between her hands, in the grips of discouragement. But then her lessons became a joy for her. She was far advanced beyond her comrades; according to Mlle. Sapy, Simone "overheated" the class. She would often receive a small group of her friends at home. The Weils granted absolute freedom of initiative to the girls, who soon decided to form an association: The Knights of the Round Table. The knights had their uniform and swore an oath of fealty. They had to defend the innocent, if wrongly accused, and practice charity. Each girl chose a character from the British legend to recreate. Simone wanted the role of a bachelor, the uncle of King Arthur, his constant counselor. She had as her task the protection and guidance of a group of schoolmates who were not well-endowed intellectually. Evidently, there flowed together in this project the heroic dreams of daring and loyalty which had dominated her childhood.

At the age of fourteen (between 1922 and 1923), this girl, "inclined by nature to roam among general ideas, foreign always to every aspiration, even embryonic, to the femininity of the world and to the pleasures of mediocre living,"[32] fell into a bottomless crisis of despondency.

There were two immediate causes of this prostration: the success of André in his studies and the attitude of one of her teachers at the Fénelon. After completing both phases of his classical matriculation examination before he was fifteen,[33] André presented himself at sixteen for admission to the Ecole Normale Supérieure and was allowed into the scientific section, after only one year of preparation and a special dispensation due to his very young age. Mlle. P., who employed with all of her students the same method of constant and negative criticism, had had a depressing influence upon Simone for a trimester of her third year and her entire fourth year at the grammar school.

> I thought seriously of dying, because of the mediocrity of my natural abilities. The extraordinary gifts of my brother, who had a childhood and a youth worthy of Pascal, forced me to become conscious of it.

She will herself define this crisis as one of adolescence, but she takes it up, examines it, and pays attention to it. It is the message from the infinite.

> I regretted, not external successes, but the fact that I could not hope for any access to that transcendental realm which only men of authentic greatness enter and which is the home of truth.

It is as though she suddenly saw the essential reality: life oriented towards truth. And this is everyone's calling; they have only to recognize it. Such a life is not limited to common morality but

> consists for everyone in a strictly personal succession of acts and events which is so necessary that anyone who passes by without seeing it misses his goal.

The certainty that such a destiny of truth is reserved for "every human being, even for those who hardly have any natural abilities," took root in her "after months of interior darkness."

There are three roads by which a human being can reach this realm: *desire for the truth*, ceaseless effort of attention to achieve it, and *obedience to one's own calling*. How should one discern the actions required by one's calling? Simone sees them as flowing from

> an impulse which is clearly and essentially different from the impulses which originate in the senses or the reason.[34]

Henceforward, her recognition of this unifying calling will make her bring together every aspect of her being, every crumb of defect, *disgust* and fatigue, in what she will call her *dressage:* the training of her entire being to the clarity of *attention:* both a personal and impersonal vision of herself, other human beings and reality.

She has thus established the limits for the project of a manifold life, rendered straightforward by her coherence and tenacity. The desire to be prevails over the desire to have, the will to understand, over the will to dominate.

At the center of Simone Weil there has been kindled the light of a noble hope. It will be *her* light, scoffed at, smothered, misunderstood now and then by the weaknesses of her body, the awkwardness of her temper, the ambiguities deriving from her being a woman, the necessary opaqueness of good sense, the limits of mediocre moderation and the leaden sectarianism of ideologies. Simone Weil, beautiful as she is, will become fatally ugly according to the widespread canons of the banal; impassioned, she will assume the character of the inhuman; indestructibly young, she will seem to reject youth; universal, she will seem to betray everyone. Fascinated and angered at the same time, other people will approach her with some dread, they will not dare to call themselves her friends, they will feel inferior to her and with an inner, more or less conscious satisfaction, they will feel that they are fortunately more normal than she is. Or they will detest her, so prickly, so intractable. Or they will soon forget her, so unusual, so different. Or, finally, they will love her, even though they will be powerless before her in her unreachability as a person.

4

The Birth of a Thinker and a Style

Three photographs exist of Simone at twelve-and-a-half; they are amazing. A photographer at Baden-Baden took them in the summer of 1921. The Weils were in the Black Forest, on an excursion which they made mostly on foot.

Simone's head is turned and foreshortened, on bare shoulders. Her face is more intense than those twelve-and-a-half years. In the first two shots the smile is full, her lips soft and well-shaped. The girl is gazing at us from her own world, solid and content. In the third photograph the look thrills you with its blazing brilliance. This was the period when Bernard and Selma Weil heard, "What would you say of letting your daughter be in the movies? She is so beautiful; a real Murillo!"[1]

A happy, satisfied childhood is thus expressed in that face: the fruit of an intelligent protectiveness in which Simone had grown up, without ever being forced to go against her inclinations to fit into social or academic requirements of the conventional sort.

At the same time she was always offered the best in the field of knowledge. On different occasions, Mme. Selma even had her children transferred "from one section to another of the lycée, so that they would have a more intelligent teacher"[2] and she herself followed some of the courses with joy. The Greek of Charles-Brun, "a very original man, different from other professors, who explained marvellously the *Crito* and the *Phaedo*";[3] the Romance philology of Bédier, who held his courses at the College de France. It was 1924. Simone was preparing herself, as far as she could, for the first part of her examination for admission to the lycée.[4]

The Weils were inspired by no laws or rituals other than those of their strong emotional feelings. There were never any indications of a religious or political creed. Dr. Bernard was an agnostic, or rather a convinced atheist, even though he respected with great sensitivity the religious attitudes of his mother. As a young man, he had sympathized with the anarchists but had later turned, always as a sympathizer, to the Radical party. Mme. Selma, who had suffered considerably from anti-Semitism, in agreement with her husband had never explained to her children the difference between Jews and gentiles. This was part of her "profound desire to integrate herself in French society and in her love for Paris";[5] Bernard Weil, an Alsatian, had chosen French nationality. In the climate of that house, generosity and the absence of materialism, together with a love for intelligence and a respect for culture, had formed the basis for a moral soundness, a noble ambition and a free expansiveness of ideas. This intellectual ease was also evident in their emotional lives, in which a considerate tenderness alternated with a rough, playful acerbity.

How did the woman emerge from the child? Her mother certainly did not encourage in her a traditional femininity. Simone belonged to the myth of the unrealized Selma. Her violent, Tatar, barbarous background impelled her to love force and clarity. She preferred boys, "honest and noisy"; she detested girls of the conventional types, with their "levity, their poses and frivolity in public." So, as she wrote Mlle. Chaintreuil: "I am doing my best to encourage in Simone, not the graces of a little girl, but the straightforwardness of a boy, even if she risks the appearance of rudeness."[6]

In her anxiety about the weak points of her daughter, she regretted that Simone had not had the same basic education as her brother. The girl's first teacher, in fact, concerned herself exclusively with her memory, without caring for "reason and the critical spirit . . . I am truly sorry that Simone will always have this burden of inferiority . . ."[7]

She wanted to provide both children with the same strengths, from the point of view of their physical, moral or intellectual lives. She wanted a Spartan education for them. She showed a sense of modern hygiene in her choice of vacation places, in her concern with sports and health, which was not completely French: mountains in the summer and the winter, from Auvergne to Switzerland to Germany, hikes, bicycling, rugby, dance courses. The Weils were very much taken with gymnastics. Every morning the entire family got together to do exercises. "She had the ideas of a naturist," says André, explaining their childish jokes (going barefoot in the winter, for example) as a kind of humorous revenge against those ideas.[8]

In keeping with this same method of education, the Weil children soon learned quite naturally what the English call the facts of life. When some little girls asked her, "And where were you born, under a cabbage or under a rose?" Simone at eight years of age replied tranquilly: "I was born in the belly of my mother."[9] At that time this was something unusual.

Sport was a training for courage and the mastery of one's movements; in Simone they nurtured her taste for self-sufficiency and her tenacity. After the sports of childhood with André, Simone would continue gymnastics and rugby at the Elisabeth Stadium: during her years at the Normale she would also practice racing and jumping. "She was incredibly awkward" but profoundly respected by her comrades, all of whom were students and workers, "for her indomitable courage." "Neither swift nor able, she races at the rear . . . Even at the starting line, she loses ground . . . Jokes are made and run the course with her . . . She stumbles, you realize that her exhaustion is dimming her sight . . . The spectators begin to call her by name in a friendly fashion and to encourage her. Only after crossing the finish line does she stop . . . out of breath, while the spectators shout their sympathy and their admiration."[10] Simone found in noncompetitive sports one of the "pure pleasures" of life.[11]

The love of nature, so strong in the Weils, was made concrete when they bought some land at Chevreuse in 1920. Mme. Selma designed the plans for a small house they called "La Guinguette." From 1923 on, they spent a part of every summer there. The garden they left to itself, full of plants and wild bushes, since they loved it that way.

If Mime "had excellent taste in the house, the same cannot be said for clothes," observes André. "So she never taught my sister what girls usually learn from their mothers: dressing properly, using a little make-up, and such things. Certainly, my sister never learned this, from my mother or from anyone else."[12]

Throughout her childhood and early youth Simone principally identified with her brother; she approached life with the ways of a boy. And even later "she was always more at ease with men than with women,"[13] with manners which were simple, direct and concrete like a man's.

Like André, Simone could not endure social gatherings. When she was eleven and he fourteen, they were invited to a wedding. After the ceremony there was a dance. "Ridiculous, how those adults behave!" commented Simone; on his part André swore that, given the boredom, he would never go to another wedding, not even his own.

"She never cared the least about clothes," says Raymonde. "And as we grew up and I liked more and more to see people, to dress well and to dance, I could not even speak about this with her."

At the root of this carelessness there lay her taste for what is essentially masculine, a taste unwittingly and unconsciously cultivated by her mother, and her first interpretation of life, which had taken place through her brother. There was also another element, natural to Simone and at the base of her thought: her visceral instinct for equality. She would be equal with others, so as not to hurt them. She used to say, when she was a little child: "It would be better if everyone dressed the same way and for the same amount of money. So we would work and nobody would see the difference."[14]

Working, studying, thinking. Already, Ebba Olsen says of Simone at eleven years of age that "she thought a good deal and this took up a good bit of her time."[15] Adèle Dubreuil speaks of an adolescent Simone who wrote late into the night. "I have to finish," she would say repeatedly. "And the next morning, Mme. Selma asked me to check, without being seen doing so, that she did not leave the house with unmatched socks, as had happened before."[16] Later, as a student at Henri IV, between 1925 and 1929, she would show the legendary distraction of someone who is always sunk in her own thoughts; on the street, it was only miraculously that she was not hit by cars; she used to say that she was protected by a spell. In 1936, while teaching philosophy at Bourges, to a friend who advised her in a kindly fashion to change her blouse, Simone would reply, almost in tears, "I c-can n-not."[17]

"She thought being born a woman was a singular misfortune."[18] This conviction of hers would slowly be reinforced as she determined the key pattern of her life. For this reason she clung to the image her mother had made of her, when she called her *Simon* and *notre fils n° 2*; she signed her letters of 1925–28 as *ton fils respectueux*.[19] This was not just a joke; it was also a profound desire. Gradually as her life would proceed, as the pattern of Simone as "a different person" would become more definite, Selma would remain, it is true, perplexed, a little alarmed, but she would not take away either space, esteem, confidence or support.

Simone was *la trollesse*. This enchanting nickname, invented by André,[20] became hers around the time she was eight or nine. This definition of a free, magical, androgynous being came more and more to correspond with the reality. For her family it meant above all that Simone was unable to look after herself in practical matters and so had to be looked after, protected to the greatest extent she would allow. For others she seemed indescribable in terms usual for a woman. For herself, since she did not want the gentle screens of social appearance between herself and reality, this was the only way to be.

She approached the world with an aggressiveness and a creative spontaneity in manners. Even today this is difficult, if not impossible for a woman. A man who is an artist, a scientist, or a thinker can, in fact should, have his odd quirks, his peculiarities, his eccentricities. Einstein would usually wear his sweater inside out. A woman may not do so; it irritates. She is more tied to her envelope, in which we expect her to go through certain tranquil patterns of behavior, to provide certain signs by which we can recognize her and find acceptable. You can either see her or not see her, as you prefer. Simone, however, appeared as an unbearable provocation. She did not understand moderation, because she could not conceive of any sort of compromise. And in the eyes of her comrades she appeared inhuman; inhuman in the sense that she did not show any human weaknesses, nor did she seem to have needs and desires or forms of feminine patience characteristic of girls of her age.

She would arrive at school in a large cape or a khaki overcoat, her bare feet in sandals even in the depths of winter, her hands and legs purple with cold, her hair a black cloud. Someone said she was "inedible."[21] Another said, "Ah, but that is not a girl."[22] For Camille Marcoux, Simone Weil was simply a "hippy *ante litteram*."

For Jacqueline Cazamian, a comrade of school and lycée, Simone had "a sort of archangelic character: a transcendence of intellect which admitted no compromise of a physical or emotional order. Never has a more splendid soul appeared to me to be less embodied."[23]

"With regard to love . . . she did not have the slightest sense of reality; she would protect those in love, excuse them, help them but she never saw clearly in the area of relations between a man and a woman, above all from the physical and psychological point of view. She had the attitude of a 'dear nun,' says Raymonde.

Alain, her great teacher, nicknamed her "the Martian," because, as he wrote later in his *Journal,* "she was nothing like us and she judged us all in a sovereign manner."[24]

Alain, as he signed himself in his books, was Emile Chartier,[25] a professor of philosophy, who taught the preparatory course at Henri IV for the Ecole Normale Supérieure. In student slang the course was called *cagne* or *khâgne* (with a more pompous spelling) which stands for *paresse* (laziness). It lasted two years. Simone went into it because she was attracted by the reputation of Alain. He was the sole polarizing model of her education, the Socrates of her thought and her style.

It was during the second year that women were admitted to the course. Lucienne Cervières, Simone Pétrement and Simone Weil, the only three women in a class of thirty, sat next to each other in the front row beneath the teacher's seat. The room was an old amphitheater on the ground floor with two doors that opened onto two courtyards, one to the right and one to the left. The door to the right was used by boarding students, the other by day students and professors. The platform upon which the teacher's chair rested was close to the door on the right. The ceiling of the room was supported in the middle by a whitewashed arch, not very thick, which ran from one wall to the other parallel to the rows of seats. In that year 1925–26, the first of Simone's attendance, the arch was reinforced by large horizontal boards of roughly hewn wood, supported at both ends by other boards which formed a brace. The ensemble of the arch and the solid boards had its own beauty and gave the room the appearance of a shipyard. Simone loved "her beautiful classroom of boards," and spoke of it to her friend Edi Copeau, who then wanted to become a philosopher.[26]

The lecture proceeded in this fashion. At the center of the wall, in front of the girls, there was a large blackboard. Sometimes "Alain entered the class . . . without even looking at us and would sit down with three-quarters of himself the other way, even his shoulders were turned from us. He would write, in a brusque manner, a Sybilline formula which served as his starting point; then again in a brusque manner, after a series of extravagant word games, he would reassert the thought, illustrate it with a thousand examples, overturn all possible points in opposition and let it echo in our minds over a long period of time."[27]

Sometimes, with a privilege associated with the oldest tradition of the courses, it would be the students who would write. They would put on the blackboard a favorite quotation, which they wanted Alain to comment upon. The teacher would often begin his remarks by saying, "I do not understand." Like all strong intellects, he would not allow himself to be swayed easily. He tarried, created a distance between himself and the idea and then confronted it. "'I do not understand,' he repeated. Then like a cold engine which warms up with difficulty, his thinking gradually began to turn and to pick up speed . . . Chartier would speak: seated firmly in the chair, his elbows on its arms, his eyes half-shut, drawn into himself . . . : he was like a fighter who leans over his opponent. Finally, his voice, which was usually very quiet, was raised in all its resonance. The idea had surrendered, we felt it. Chartier's face cleared. We breathed again."[28]

These were unforgettable improvisations. Actually, Alain always improvised. "He would arrive with the lecture prepared but he never used it," recalls Louis Goubert. "As he spoke, he created an entirely new one; finally, at home, he rewrote it; and this was its third draft, the one you can find in his published works. If someone had never heard his lectures when he gave them orally, he would never know the splendid inventiveness of that second, spoken draft."[29]

The teacher would then return the dissertations or the so-called *topoi* which the students had turned in the previous time. The dissertation, assigned every three weeks, dealt with a theme chosen from a series of titles provided by Alain at the beginning of the trimester. It was assigned a numerical grade. The *topos,* on the other hand, was a random essay, usually short (thirty or forty lines), entirely on the initiative of the student. Alain insisted that his students write as much as possible; he was convinced that "learning to write well means learning to think well"[30] and that writing is more honest than speaking because "it does not have to take account of the listeners." He wanted his students to express universal truths in simple and clear language. "The ideas of all in the language of all: that is what I have always sought."[31] And he would read even the most mediocre of these essays word for word.

Above all else, he would read with confidence. "He gave confidence to everyone of us. He sought most scrupulously the point which revealed the positive feature characteristic of each of us. Alain bet on man."[32]

Some students never turned in an essay of this sort, the more active did so often. Simone was among the most active; she must surely have liked them, for they are the assignments she kept in the largest number.

Furthermore, Alain, who in class was very formal, addressing his students as Mister or Miss and leaving them to themselves, "as is appropriate to men,"[33] established a deep friendship with those men whom he profoundly admired, particularly through those careful annotations placed at the end of the essays.

Men, all of them, even his beloved girl-students. Alain must have seen in them, not women in flesh and bone, but splendid and noble intellects; he must surely have breathed a sigh of relief in not having to treat them as women, a thing which definitely annoyed him.

How beautiful, not being forced to be disturbed by desire but living a life of limpid friendship, one which contains "marvelous joys . . . "[34] "Love is not natural and neither is desire, by a long way."[35] "Desire and passion bind and deform; liberty is as indispensable as the air for the construction of the self." A happy couple is rare, because of "certain distinctive traits that often make the two sexes inimical the one to the other . . . The one is emotional, the other active . . . " Above all, the man is soon bored, constrained as he is to the "idleness of complacency." The only remedy for the couple's crisis: public life. Action and the relations of friendship and affinity impose upon the couple, from the outside, a "habit of civility, absolutely necessary to check all those whims of feeling which have too many occasions to make an appearance." And it was this man, so radical in his independence and such a mocker of his own authority, who finally said: "It is the institution that saves feeling."[36]

Robust, clear-eyed, with the complexion of a Norman and the voice of a peasant, Alain surprised his students, to whom such a vigorous appearance was unthinkable for a philosopher. There also existed in him that clear division, so typical of men, and even clearer in those days, between the life of the body and the life of thought. He despised the ladies of the salon. He called them, with impatience, "corset-crushed insects";[37] in him there prevailed the joy of intellectual activity; in love relationships harmony and serenity, created by reason, had to prevail. "True sentiments are works of art."[38] In his private life, he married in his last years a woman who was always beside him, with admirable devotion. They can still be seen together on a gig, out of focus in the bright sunshine of a yellowed photograph.

Thought as labor; writing, painting, composing music: labor. One learns and achieves results as a carpenter learns to work: only by doing. And to do so, one must be free; being really free means acting according to one's will and not abandoning oneself to desire or to passion, which enslave a person. Will consists neither in one's intention nor in one's decision, but in action. The will does not have the function of selecting but of modifying, making good, actions which have already been begun, situations. For the will is always for the good: it is born in the conscience and conscience is a single power, which is manifest as soon as we pose a moral problem to ourselves. Confronting situations, employing errors committed in the past, always overcoming something, in a word, acting with full consciousness, every man can create moral and intellectual values. "We must believe in the good," says Alain, "because it does not exist. For instance, in justice, because it is not present. We should not believe that it is loved and desired, because this leads to nothing; but we should believe that we shall create it."[39]

Labor is what reveals us to ourselves. Alain was convinced that everyone is able to get from himself more than he believes and that there does not exist a labor for which we do not have the aptitude. Persevering, we shall discover it.

Knowing reality with clarity, knowing our relationship with reality and with ourselves, knowing our own passions to control them and living with them in harmony, transformed into true feelings. These are the fruits of a control exercised over ourselves, essential for the survival of everyone. Since war is unleashed by passions, the lot of all mankind depends on the degree to which a child learns to control himself. The goal of all public instruction is that of "restoring to everyone his own spirit and of training it in its principal use, that of not paying attention to money or to force, but only to what is true and just."[40] The teacher has the great responsibility of keeping alive "centers of humanity" which will fight against prejudices, violence, and injustice.

To this end, the principal nourishment is found in the great, whom Alain taught his students to love deeply, in a relationship of daily conversation with their works: reading them, rereading them, committing them to memory, beginning with children and poetry. For, if Alain taught his students to reject and refute the weak and false ideas which filled the manuals and rendered dull the courses of so many professors, he never resorted to sterile polemics and disdain "which does not nourish the soul."[41] He cultivated in the young, upon whom he principally based his innate confidence in the nobility of man, the admiration of the great. Homer, Plato, Tacitus,

Balzac . . . have not need for proof. Everyone sees himself in them "and finds in a certain sense the human spirit guaranteed by a long succession of admirers."[42]

The great works of art, literature, and music speak an absolute language, the language of beauty, which awakens our thinking and guides man towards the truth about himself and his own condition. Everyone should have access to the understanding of this beauty and be equal in the possibility of constructing the autonomy of his own mind.

A great admirer of Socrates, he made use of the midwife's skill in two ways: by retracing the journey of a thought to its origin by way of words and by questioning every philosophical maxim. Towards the first goal, there was an exercise in which students and teacher began by looking for the most precise definition for a group of words and then organizing them in different series according to their most natural philosophical order. In the second case, he encouraged the personal response. Before accepting or rejecting an idea, we must always examine it, even if it is widely asserted. Only in this way do we rise above "trembling fanaticism."[43]

We must maintain our freedom even in the face of an idea which satisfies our judgment or acts as a sophism to cloud our minds on which moral action to take. This means accepting thought as a "violent state" of battle which requires you to separate the soul from the body. Yes: "The outside invades and thought stands on the ramparts."[44] Man must overcome himself. "There exists no other truth of ourselves except the Good, the idea which must change."[45] Transforming ourselves means living on the dividing line between the two orders Descartes posits for things: extension and thought, force and virtue.

It is upon a similar dividing line that "there passes the faith of the unbeliever, something new and always, note this well, something opposed to force, which is here called with its own name, stripped, and put on trial."[46]

Faith, "entirely of will and courage," is directly opposed to credulity. "Faith denies its destiny." Credulity commits itself to the winner, to the rich, to the number thirteen. One has faith in Jesus, in Plato, in Mozart.

We must break away from temporal things. "Faith, considered seriously, consists absolutely in not believing in anything that wants to be believed in, like flatterers, power, money, knowledge. God is the negation of all these values of pomp."[47] It is the harsh law of the spirit that opposes the soul and the world: one cannot serve two masters. The choice is clear. Liberty and truth coincide on the Cross, the supreme sign. "A free man on

a cross . . . : this execution at least proves that virtue is not an instrument
of power."[48]

Unlike many distinguished students shaped by Alain (we think for example of André Maurois and of Paul Bénichou), Simone Weil wrote nothing
about her impressions as a student at Henri IV. But this should not surprise us: Simone Weil never describes her life, her childhood, the persons
she met from the point of view of an autobiographical account. She does
not linger on memory, whether to develop the traits of a human figure or
the characteristics of an ambience. Everything for her happens in the
spaces of the soul and has ethical dimensions.

Simone Weil absorbed Alain's thought eagerly and put it into practice
with "an immediate and total admiration,"[49] which did not exclude at any
time a loyal and constructive discussion of it. In her own impulse towards
the useful, in the passion for urgency which will inspire her in her every
line of investigation, Simone must have sensed in Alain the teacher who
could really instruct her in a method that she could live with all her being.

Aimed as she was towards action, in 1924 (she was fifteen), she found
herself undecided between preparing for the Normale and going into a
factory, between the two ways of understanding the truth of her time: the
deepening of her knowledge and concrete contact with the most painful
condition of the age. She had to bring the two things together: Alain gave
her the method to do that. He offered her the one harbor in which she
could prepare to set sail and provided her with maps which she learned to
trace for herself with the guidance of old experiences.

The compass that oriented her was thought as labor. Labor on ourselves
and on things, beyond all schemes, all prearranged itineraries; labor which
neither trusts magical powers nor is satisfied with illusions nor makes
imaginary predictions of results by sliding into whimsy. It obeys the laws
of time, lives it and completes it minute by minute, patient in its fatigue. It
realizes that there are no stages to shun and that we do not lie to ourselves.

There were simple rules to follow; genius or not, one should sit at the
desk two hours a day and write on large pages in a beautiful hand; one
should leave wide margins and not make cancellations but rewrite. With a
craftsman's tools, made by oneself, one should continually be renewed and
renew. One should relive the thoughts of the great and have nothing but
scorn for manuals, summaries and outlines, which were, according to Alain, sad stuff for the autopsy of humanistic materials. "Do not take

notes . . . what you do not understand, reread even twenty times: you may err in your citation but you will have gone straight to the heart of the thought."[50]

The thoughts of the great are made for life; true ideas do not exist in themselves, but rather true thoughts, true men. Alain held that the great philosophies cannot be explained on the basis of historical causes, and history is learned above all by reading original works, memoirs, diaries. He professed a metaphysics of liberty and of interest in the individual. It was not by accident that his students called him "the Man."

"The Man," ironic to the point of mockery, anticonformist in the face of official moralism, was the prey of skepticism when confronted with morality. "He admired with ingenuity and passion good actions, fine actions and knew how to speak of them without emphasis, as usually no one can." To her friend Edi Copeau, Simone synthesized her teacher's doctrine: "For Chartier, all greatness is moral."[51]

It was thus that, by being nurtured by a set of thoughts naturally in tune with hers, by finding at last an expression of the ideals of honor and autonomous heroism born in her childhood and always present in her, from Cyrano to Julien Sorel—a beloved character of her years at Henri IV— Simone Weil slowly matured her own moral doctrine and her own style as a writer.

Her starting point was a way of composition which presented "perspectives on the whole less clear than her analysis, which was crisp and prompt." Abundant in inventiveness, she had at first a style somewhat less developed than her ideas. She drank so deeply from the great authors that she derived from them "an original method." At first she presented "meditations, a little dense, in an almost impenetrable style." Then, "by detaching herself from the subtleties of abstract thought, a game for her," she devoted herself to a direct analysis in a style both "sound and strong."[52] For her handwriting, which at first was messy and ill formed, Simone set herself to forming each letter, one by one; she even used matches on occasion.

Two essays in particular betray the first clear imprints of her inner journey. We are drawn to them; we should turn to hear these phrases in which her moral meditation takes form in poetry.

The first is a commentary on the story, "The Six Swans" of Grimm. It carries the date of November, 1925, and was the first written by Simone that Alain judged "excellent." Six brothers were transformed into swans by their stepmother, a witch. To regain their human form, their sister had to spin and sew six shirts made of white anemones, without saying a word until she had finished her task. Six years pass for the girl and in this long time her silence puts her in great danger, because it forbids her to defend herself against unjust accusations. At last, when she is about to be executed, six swans appear in the sky and swoop towards her. She throws the shirts on them; the swans regain their human form. The girl is saved.

Simone commented upon the story in this fashion:

> Acting is never difficult; we always do too much and waste ourselves in disorderly actions. Making six shirts of anemones and being silent: that is our only way of acquiring power . . . it is almost impossible to sew anemones together and turn them into a shirt and the difficulty is such that it prevents any other action being added that would alter the purity of that silence which lasts for six years. In this world purity is the only force . . . it is a fragment of truth . . . Refraining from action: here lies our only force and our only virtue.

This is the first expression of Simone's idea of 'radiation,' (*rayonnement*); the perfectly pure being, whom she identifies more than once, for example, with Saint Francis, will 'radiate' a force stronger than any physical violence. She begins here her meditation on thought and action; for her they should coincide. Thought should find its proof in action; action should make thought concrete without compromises. We realize that this is almost always impossible on the level of earthly circumstances. Pure action will flow forth as a result, on another plane, in unexpected ways, unbeknownst to him who performs it. Man can only submit his thought to daily labor, which is humbling and purifying. On most occasions, as for the girl in the Grimm story, true efficacy will be found in the renunciation of action.

A similar inspiration animates the other essay, of February, 1926. It is entitled, "The beautiful and the good"; Alain wrote at the bottom, "most beautiful." It is perhaps this essay upon which Simone worked those long nights.

Here moral action is even more tightly connected with the person who performs it; it springs forth from his whole being as a work of art: "a free, unforeseeable act . . . not in keeping with this or that rule . . . a gesture of purity and of loyalty to ourselves."

The theme of the meditation is an episode in the life of Alexander the Great. He was with his men in the desert. During their long passage, they brought him water from afar, water contained in a helmet. Alexander, who was as thirsty as his soldiers, poured the water on the ground, so that he would not be more favored than they. Simone observes:

> No one, and Alexander least of all, would have dared foresee this surprising action; but once the action was finished, everyone felt that it had to be that way.

If Alexander had drunk the water, his happiness would have separated him from his men.

> Everything takes place in the soul of Alexander and for him it is only a matter of treating himself like a man . . . We must then save ourselves, save ourselves in the Spirit, of whom the outer man is the myth . . . Every saint has refused the water; every saint has refused all happiness which would have separated him from the suffering of mankind.[53]

Remarks like these form the basic fabric of a life that she was beginning to express externally in actions which were often disconcerting, obstinate and provocative.

Simone Weil was the young woman who made "impossible" the class already considered odd enough by the authorities. An official with responsibility for observing discipline called her a *monstrum horrendum*; she came to blows with another. He had decided that men and women should sit in separate areas. Simone prepared two cards with the inscriptions, "Men's side" and "Women's side." The official caught her as she was putting them up. He tried to snatch the cards from her; she defended herself and they came to blows. That same year (1927–28; her third at Henri IV) Simone was suspended for eight days; the reason: she had smoked in the men's courtyard. But all the courtyards were for the men. Simone did not understand these differences and showed it with actions which were natural to her. "In triumph she announced her suspension to her parents."[54] And again, the principal encountered Simone in the Luxembourg Gardens and admonished her on her bad conduct: unimaginable attire, masculine actions, nonconformity.

Simone was delighted to find herself on bad terms with the administration. This was part of her loyalty to Alain. In the demanding vehemence of her youth, she, who found it so difficult to find reasons which would prompt her admiration, lived to the fullest her absolute respect for her teacher. Alain pointed to the administration as one of those powers which a free man obeys with detachment, without trusting it too much. Simone exaggerated the contrast between Alain and the powers of bureaucracy, which were actually more cautious than hostile in his regard. The *chartiéristes*[55] were admitted, especially to the Normale, with good scores without betraying their teacher's instruction. Simone, however, was convinced that the philosophy taught by Alain was regularly boycotted on the examinations. So she thought "that a good policy was to sprinkle here and there in the essay idiocies which agree with the official philosophy."[56] This kind of shrewdness was permitted for the students of Alain, who were naturally conspiratorial. As far as the truth is concerned, if Alain preferred the reading of original sources, "he never deprived his students of supplementary material for preparing for the competition." Simone refused to study and to attend classes, so she failed the first time to gain entry to the Normale (1927), above all because of this material.

In reality, there was no split between the substance and the appearance of this young woman. Her external appearance showed "a restlessness and a refusal to take her place in life";[57] on the page these qualities appeared in dense formulas which later turned out to be milestones on her journey. Thinking, writing, and living coincided. By nature, she and her soul were a unity.

Keen in discerning her substance, quick in seeing beyond her slothful attire, her thick glasses, her awkward manner and her incessant smoking, Alain encouraged her to be faithful to herself. He was the only one not to limit her to preordained ideas. He gave her space from the start; Simone soon began to publish articles in his review, "Libres Propos"; she taught for a long time (French, sociology, political economy) in courses for workers, courses organized by a railwayman, Lucien Cancouët, a fellow militant and friend of Alain; she was the only woman always in the front ranks in the pacifist campaign between 1928 and 1929. Alain considered her "superior, and by a great margin, to all the others of her generation."[58] To reward his student Maurice Schumann for an excellent paper, Alain made him sit next to Simone Weil,[59] by then a student at the Normale. In fact, once she was admitted to the Normale, she would continue to attend the lectures of her teacher and hand him her essays, which he would correct with the same care and pleasure. Then there would come the moment of the *grand œuvre*, the essay *Oppression et Liberté*.[60]

Alain would think it so fine and definitive that he would consider it the first of a series of "Cahiers de Critique" he would assign completely to her. The essay goes back to 1934. Simone would submit it to her teacher's judgment in 1935. Here is his reply:

"Your work is most excellent; it deserves a sequel . . . Your example will inspire courage in generations deluded by ontology and ideology. Criticism awaits its laborers. Could you formulate a plan for your work? . . . The 'Libres Propos,' which have grasped only fragments of ideas, could become the 'Cahiers de Critique' in the near future. Consider that . . . I am sure that works of this sort, in the form which is proper to you, serious and rigorous, endowed with continuity and solid enough to have its own volume, are the only ones that will open the future and true Revolution . . . I am not succeeding in explaining myself well; but then, I do not have anything to explain to you.

"I know only this, that the sole thing that could prevent you from fulfilling your mission is indignation. Keep in mind what I have always said: whatever is misanthropic is false . . . Fraternally, Alain."[61]

5

The Youth of a Different Kind of Woman

How did Simone Weil appear to people of her own age? When Simone Pétrement met her, in 1925, this is what she looked like. "A narrow little face, obscured by hair and glasses. A sharp nose, dark eyes which fixed you with boldness, and a neck thrust forward gave the impression of passionate curiosity, even to the point of indiscretion, but her mouth with its thick lips gave an impression of sweetness and goodness . . . it was a face at once insolent and tender, bold in questioning but shy in its smile, which seemed to mock itself."[1]

From her whole self there shone through an eagerness to live the life of friendship, to share the bread of common hours, studies, and enterprises, as well as a lucid, instinctive critical judgment which set her apart from others. There was an initial incandescence, more of a collision than an encounter between her and another person. Simone chose people with impetuosity, provoked and excited the intellect with the tenacity of her questions, aided and defended her friends with excessive ardor, especially when they were outmatched; then, at times, she would suddenly end the relationship.

Friendship would reach the threshold of saturation. The friend would feel emptied of his existence in front of her. Then there was always the question of how actual the friendship really was, even from the beginning. "She seemed to love no one," observes Raymond Nathan. "She spoke of you in an abstract fashion, as though of another. For this reason, even though I loved her, I found it difficult to overcome a sense of separation from her, as from a person who lived on another planet," declares Camille Marcoux.[2]

How did they get to know one another? She came up to the *turne,* the dining room of the young men of the Normale. It was after supper. She addressed him abruptly, "Are you Marcoux? Follow me." And Marcoux followed her. There ensued a year of long walks, especially at night, of extended sessions of conversations in cafés, of the joint courses for the railwaymen in rue Falguière.

Even today the memory of a magnetic attraction, fused with the perplexity of which we have spoken, makes her image both obsessive and fleeting. Simone Pétrement: "I was soon a friend of Simone's; I don't know how it happened, because there was nothing about me that could attract her and I had to strain to understand her."[3] And again, Marcoux: "You could not speak of friendship. I always felt the drama of the impossibility of a placid friendship between us. For others, the rudeness of her bare manners, her unusual appearance and, above all, the battering of those ruthless judgments led to a refusal. "All around her there was turmoil, confusion and disorder. She always had to be giving orders, involving you in demonstrations, urging you on to get signatures, sending you out with leaflets. I withdrew," says Clémence Ramnoux.[4]

This violent desire for action, which she expressed with youthful impatience, flowed from an almost psychic sensibility to the ills of the world. At the news of a famine in China, Simone Weil had broken into sobs. When Simone de Beauvoir heard this, she wanted to meet her. She often saw her cross the courtyard of the Sorbonne, always in the company of other *chartiéristes;* she would have a copy of *L'Humanité* stuffed in one pocket of her coat and *Libres Propos* in the other. "I envied a heart able to beat across the world," writes Simone de Beauvoir. In their conversation, young Weil was implacable. "I don't know any longer how we started. She said in a piercing tone that only one thing counted in the world today: the Revolution that would give all something to eat. In no less peremptory a tone I replied that the problem did not consist in allowing men to be happy but in letting them find a meaning in their existence. Simone Weil gazed at me from head to toe and said: 'One can easily see that you have never been hungry.' Here our relations ended. I understood that she had classified me (with the petite bourgeoisie of the spiritualist type) and I was angry."[5]

She would wound you with her aggressiveness. Louis Goubert recalls, "One time she told me, 'You are living outside life; you cannot understand the world, because you are in a position of privilege.' I was upset, even a little angry, since I had lost my father when I was very young and I had seen my mother, a *première de modes,* work very hard to help her family forward. But Simone Weil, at that time, was mounting the barricades to teach workers."6

Marie-Magdeleine Davy used to spend Sunday mornings with Simone. They would station themselves in front of Sacré-Coeur, Montmartre, to sell *L'Humanité* for two old women news-vendors who were so infirm that they could not leave their homes to sell their papers. "We never had much success, in fact we didn't have any. To comfort ourselves, we used to stay at a table in a café, to chatter. At first, I did not understand her. Simone was too deep for us . . . She was all of a piece, with a nasty character. We used to argue, to fight with each other. We both liked politics but she had a social sense that I do not have, have never had, and shall never have."7

While Simone de Beauvoir "believed that she had been emancipated from her class and did not want to be anything other than what she was,"8 Simone Weil sought an identity that coincided with the universe. For her, being herself meant freedom from all belonging. Loyalty to her own inner scheme corresponded to a road of liberation from the idols of the cave and the idols of the tribe. One must finally emerge from the cavern of the point of view, which imprisons us and thwarts our "pure perception" of others and reality. Already at seventeen Simone was yearning for such a perception.9

The viewpoint of an epoch coincides with the ideas of the dominant class. Simone hurled herself savagely against the commonplaces, the set phrases, the presumptions of the bourgeoisie. She wanted to smash the dangerous filters they used to judge facts, live politics, and measure beauty.

She was excessive in her vehemence. "Simone had a prejudice in favor of whatever was not bourgeois," remarks Marcoux. "She dumped upon the middle class, and upon the intellectuals in the first place, every responsibility. So wealth, talent and spirit were all betrayals or potential betrayals." With fanaticism she savored those who were different, apart, or outside the law. "One time she dragged me into the darkness of a shady café. She wanted me to meet a strange, tattooed individual. He fascinated her; he was a genius for her," says Camille.

In her search for eternal beauty, beyond the time and modes codified by one class, she was very attentive, even with a sort of stubbornness, to the ugly and the ridiculous in the faces, clothes and circumstances of the bourgeoisie. One day, on the Metro, she pointed to some workers and said to Simone Pétrement, "You see, it is not just in a spirit of justice that I love them. I love them naturally, because I find them more handsome than the bourgeoisie."[10]

She was remorseful that there were lower classes and she wanted to create in them a sense of their rights and their honor. From the urgency of such a feeling developed an episode at the resort hotel of Challes-les-Eaux. It was a place for taking the waters, a place for the haute bourgeoisie; among the guests was Senator Lisbonne, whose physician was Bernard Weil. At sixteen, Simone struck up a friendship with the whole staff: maids, doorman, cashier. They would meet in the garden in the evening to discuss their problems, heavy schedules of work and salaries; she suggested that they form a union. Another time: in 1927, she spent most of the last trimester in the school of Mme. Letourneux[11] in Charente, where she was preparing for the admission examination for the Normale. How did she spend her days? She could not make friends at all with the other girls of her own age but alternated a schedule of tireless study in her own room (on the table an enormous ashcan almost filled with cigarette butts) with meetings with the gardener. She invited him to discussions in her room and was unaware that his wife entertained jealous suspicions of them; she offered him cigarettes. "The day of the local elections, she walked to the city hall, arm-in-arm with him and other workers."[12]

She thought that she was too privileged. "But why was I not born to poor parents?" These words she repeated to Adèle Dubreuil, as she would later say to Marcel Lecarpentier when she was on his fishing boat, seeking to appreciate the sea as work, as a daily task. Before inviting Camille Marcoux of Poitiers to her house, she hesitated to introduce him to her family; she feared that the young man, who had come from the provinces to study bravely, would suffer from their comfort and ease.

The *point of view* is the hotbed of injustice. Patriotism, experienced as the point of view by which a nation or a civilization holds perfection, can become one of the most lethal causes of this injustice. Even here she tried to welcome and respect the diverse. Still a child, at five years of age, she declared with ardor, "For me, you are a pure-blooded Frenchman!" in reply to a Syrian student who told her he was grieved by the cold treatment he received from the French. One day, on the street, she blushed violently. Students were selling a newspaper and shouting that it was "Anti-métèque et anti-youpin!" She had to explain with a shudder to her friend Pétrement the disparaging meaning of the word *youpin*, Jew.[13] A "beautiful inquiry by Louis Roubaud on the condition of the Indo-

Chinese, their wretchedness and enslavement, the perennially unpunished insolence of the whites"[14] of October, 1930, she found so powerful she could hardly bear it. This is when she began to consider colonies as a profound injury done by France to other peoples, to other human beings. And it will be in this spirit that she will visit l'Exposition Coloniale of 1931, as she brings to maturity her clear admonitory vision of French colonial policy, a vision that she will maintain as long as she lives.

The swollen bladders of rhetoric were her target. Alain had trained his students to aim straight. Simone was among the freest and most disposed to this exercise: there was her family training, her youthful anarchism, her feminine sensibility which more easily grasped the concrete detail apt to overthrow the useless abstraction. She was always zealous in her observations and associations; she would hit home hard. She was ironic and cutting; at times she would burst into great gales of laughter. She loved a *canular,* a practical joke of acts or words, in vogue with students at the Normale. Every week she would read with eagerness *Le Canard Enchaîné,* a satirical paper that still appears in Paris; its true successors today are such papers as *Charlie Hebdo* and *La gueule ouverte.* The *Canard,* like the other papers cited, is an expression of the spirit of Gavroche,[15] which uses *argot* to deflate, to cleanse, and to upset the reassuring appearances of news and ideas. It goads you to emerge from yourself, it forces you to be on the alert, it makes you doubt your certainties. Such papers are not hypocritical, nor are they the product of emotional vulgarity. One must go beyond their shocking appearances and discover the questions they pose in secrecy.

The investigation of all that appeared suspect was part of Simone's being, it was one of the ways in which she expressed her restless curiosity. She wanted to understand, to go beyond the often smooth and soothing surface of circumstances. One of her comrades at the Normale, Huguény, is emphatic in stating that "Simone loved to fish in troubled waters."[16] For this reason they were always quarreling and then they would look each other up again, only to start arguing once more. In his second year at the Normale (1928–29), Huguény wanted to establish a union to bring together the students of the Normale Supérieure and those of the normal schools for primary teachers. His intention was to lessen the distance between primary and secondary education and, at the same time, to battle the inferiority complex of the primary teachers. Simone was very much in favor of the project; according to Huguény, her interest was primarily due to her vision of the project as an instrument for agitation and anti-militarism.

It was in the area of pacifism that Simone Weil found her most precise zone of action. In September, 1928, Alain had written: "There exists a more beautiful sight than the one who does not like to obey: he who does not like to command. This noble type is spreading."[17] At the beginning of the academic year 1928–29 some of the most troublesome *chartiéristes*, including Simone, gave concreteness to this idea of Alain in a brave document: the petition concerning military service for the students of the Normale. Written by Chateau and commented upon by Ganuchaud in an article which appeared in the pacifist monthly, *La Volonté de Paix*, the petition requested for the students of the Normale an optional, rather than an obligatory type of service. Up to then, they had been favored with a shorter period of military service and an automatic promotion to officers' rank. They demanded the freedom of not being officers insofar as that meant "belonging to the army. We wish to enter under constraint, as soldiers."[18]

Simone, as a woman, could not sign it but she was the only woman to support the petition with tireless requests for signatures and lively reproofs for those who did not sign. Bouglé, infuriated, told her to mind her own business.[19] There were eighty-three signatures, about half of the students.

The press of both the right and the left criticized the students with harshness and sarcasm. "Late-arriving Tolstoyism" (*L'Action Française*); "a hateful document" (*Echo de Paris*); "the singular mentality of these anarchists is neither normal nor superior" (*L'Ami du Peuple*). Only a few papers, like *L'Oeuvre, La Volonté, Le Progrès Civique*, supported them. What most saddened Ganuchaud was the basic attitude of the public, which reduced the gesture to "a joke of urchins to escape a task."[20]

This affirmation of nonviolence was extremely unpopular. Why? Sartre tells us in describing the climate of the era. "My contemporaries and I had known two acts of sacred violence between our childhood and adolescence. In 1914, the war; they told us it was just and that God was with us. In 1917, the Russian Revolution . . . We were intoxicated with the violence of our fathers . . . When I entered the Normale, not even a *thala* would have dared to say that one should reject violence. We thought above all of limiting it, channeling it. A violence with a content, a violence that pays.

Although most of us were of very meek disposition, we had become violent, because one of our problems was: is this an act of revolutionary violence or does it exceed the violence justified by the revolution? That is still our problem today: we shall not manage to solve it."[21] We shall see Simone Weil grappling with this contradiction for her whole life.

The petition had followed two other acts of pacifism by the *chartiéristes:* a petition in support of the historian Georges Demartial and the circulation of a manifesto published by *La Volonté de Paix* in September, 1928. Demartial held that Germany was not the only nor the principal party responsible for the war of 1914. The manifesto, in support of the Kellogg Pact signed in Paris on August 27, 1928, according to which war had been outlawed, demanded complete and immediate disarmament, "the destruction of the materiel of war and the termination of all arms industries, both public and private."[22]

Alain's students had created a whole climate. The manifesto awakened the slumbering activity of the Ligue des droits de l'homme, which, in accord with the impetus of some of its rank and file members, actually presented a protest against the budget passed by the Chamber in 1929, because it included an increase in military spending. The *chartiéristes* decided then to join the Ligue *en bloc* and to present a pacifist motion in January, 1929. Simone even got her parents to join; Simone Pétrement became a member, too; they dragged the railwaymen of rue Falguière to the meetings.

In the motion, the Ligue was defined as the "organ of defense against all powers"; now that it was "mobilized against war," it demanded that the government immediately take "real initiatives towards peace, such as the acceptance of absolutely universal and obligatory arbitration . . . a sincere attempt at disarmament, at least analogous to that of Germany . . . the realization of the Franco-German union."[23] On February 4, the motion was passed in the fourteenth *arrondissement*, despite the opposition of the mathematician Hadamard and even of the president of the Ligue, Victor Basch. Both men were opposed to a pacifism which they considered favorable to exaggerated vindication and to a systematic opposition to power and authority. Simone felt the impulse of justifying to Basch the position she and her comrades had taken.

A piece she wrote in those days, between February and April, 1929 ("Congress of the Ligue at Rennes") says:

What should the Ligue be? . . . Some hold that, considering the positions of the people and the government, the Ligue should be an impartial arbiter between citizens and power. But . . . the government is the only one that has the possibility of acting on the State . . . It is impossible to control the arguments of the government. To remain loyal to its own name and origin, the Ligue should not be impartial but, remaining deaf to the argument of those who govern, it should systematically support the people.[24]

Here is the key element of her social doctrine: proceeding to a maturing of the people from within, by reinforcing the clarity of their observation and their capacity for criticism.

It is already clear that the only action she is interested in finding and then gradually refining is action which is nonviolent in practice but profoundly revolutionary in substance, one intended for the transformation of the fabric of human relationships.

Beyond all schemes, she lives in what will be more and more a contact between souls. She is unaware of the carnal character of daily life as she is of the conventions and rites of social classes; thus, even on the social plane, Simone Weil will be perceived as inhuman. The "good comrade" Simone Weil, who would upset you with her wild and paradoxical ideas: this is how the railwaymen of the rue Falguière considered her at the time. The activity of the Groupe d'Education Sociale, founded by Cancouët in 1927, was intended to prepare its students, on the one hand, for a promotion test in the railways and, on the other, to develop in them a critical sense and a consciousness of their problems. Inaugurated with lessons given by Château and Ganuchaud, and with some courses in mathematics by André Weil, the school was gradually entrusted above all to Simone Weil and Camille Marcoux. On Sunday mornings there were always from twenty-five to thirty students. The topics of instruction dealt, in the context of sociology and political economy, with the use of machinery, property, the role of intellectuals in society, war.

Lucien Cancouët, the Breton railwayman, was, for Simone, the image of the people. She had become great friends with him and with his wife. "We used to go together to see them often," remarks Marcoux, "and Cancouët thought we were something other than friends; he would look at us in a suggestive manner. I was embarrassed; Simone did not even notice it." She remained involved in her fervent discussions, in which she never lost the thread of the argument; with calm inflexibility she would examine it in all of its complexity. Because of those discussions, Cancouët nick-named her "the terrible." At Auxerre, during her year of teaching (1932–33), humble employees and laborers will call her a 'pistolet,' an odd and tedious type. After conversations with her, a plumber, nicknamed by her Robinet, could not sleep the whole night. Simone compelled you to polit-ical reflections vexing for their abrupt evidence. Renunciation, responsibil-ity, overcoming the *idola tribus,* resistance to ready-made phrases, examina-tion of the party's passwords: always the same requirements, irrefutable, but hard to accept.

A human being must feed on his or her loyal inquiry into the truth, without supports or shelters of any kind. Simone loved to wander in the harsh freedom of the essential.

She had one habit which sums her up. Simone used to study her geom-etry on the bank of the Seine,[25] near a pillar of the Austerlitz bridge. At that spot on the right bank, barges unloaded large blocks of stone. She loved those stones, which were associated with geometry. This was her explanation to her friend Marcoux, who had come to get her and saw her studying from the bridge. She was kneeling down, as was her habit, and immersed in the book, with her exceptional capacity for concentration. From time to time, she would pull a lock of her hair.

6
The Growth of a Vocation

When, in the summer of 1928, Simone intended to join her friends Château and Ganuchaud in the factories opened in Liechtenstein by the International Civil Service,[1] she was merely proceeding in accord with the primary direction of her life: *intervening in the real world through labor.* Manual labor, contact with matter that resists you, provides you with proof of both your and its existence. She wanted to be a common laborer, like her friends, but she was not accepted. Women, defined as "sisters," were assigned to the kitchen.

The Service offered a model of actively pacifist cooperation, beyond all differences among men. Simone proposed to write an article on the enterprise, which struck her as the best way to achieve peace. In a sketch which has been rediscovered, we read:

> Religion makes love manifest but work sheds light on right, respect for the human person, equality; that is why cooperation creates a rough friendship for which there is no substitute. Such friendship builds peace.

Labor in common is the only just form of cohesion. For other bonds, such as family ties, the love of lovers, certain types of friendship, and the religion that links fellow worshipers, are nourished and are pleasantly nourished "by that seductive accord that engenders all wars."[2] She had always loved cooperation even in her studies; Simone Pétrement and other comrades at Henri IV used to meet at the Weil house around a blackboard Simone had had installed, to develop together the outline of an essay. Marcoux recounts how it had been Simone who wrote, within a few hours, a lesson intended for a correspondence course in the École Universelle, another activity that involved them both. "I am slow at writing; I proceed by stages. She even had to read texts by Helvetius and

D'Holbach on that occasion, as I remember, but she still rapidly wrote an excellent paper."

And yet one must always deny oneself that seductive agreement; it is a difficult matter not to desire it; but "if we do not protect ourselves against seductive agreement, every friendship perishes." For this reason, even with Marcoux, the rigor of objectivity triumphed over the tolerance suggested by affection. One should not hide the truth about a friend from him because there is one truth only, which must never be betrayed. Camille remembers: "I erred in a presentation on Proudhon. I used a text by Bouglé, the vice-director of the Normale, a sociologist and the author of brilliant but superficial essays on French economists. At the end of the presentation, we left, and Simone abused me. Later she told my comrades that for her 'I was dead.' In fact, I continued to spend musical afternoons in the Weil household . . . Mme. Selma would invite me to stay for a meal and then she would sit at the piano and I would accompany her on the violin: Mozart, above all else. But Simone would not even look at me; she would take her place at table without a greeting and would leave before the end of the meal. We proceeded like this for two or three years: we were shadows to each other."

For her the most beautiful form of manual labor, since it was most suited for bringing men together, was labor in the fields. She had a chance to share in it for the first time in 1927 at La Martinière Farm in Normandy, owned by the Letelliers. Pierre Letellier, perhaps her most beloved comrade at Henri IV, was the son of Léon Letellier, who was a peasant by birth, but at sixteen had been a fisherman in Newfoundland. After being a sailor for a long time all over the world, in his thirties he had studied philosophy in Paris. He had then returned to the fields to farm and raise cattle. For Simone he represented "the complete, truly human man,"[3] since he was a thinker and a manual laborer at the same time.

Léon Letellier had died at the beginning of 1926. During her time at the farm, Simone also devoted herself to making copies of his writings, with the goal of producing an anthology. At the same time, she shared in the farm chores in a much more arduous and bold way than she wrote to her mother. She wanted to share in all the work; one time she insisted on picking up a great bundle of thistles with her bare arms. "Why can they do it and not me?" she replied to Michel Letellier, who told her not to do it.[4] She had long conversations with everyone, owners and laborers. These "labors" made her happy. She wrote her mother:

I am living in a situation which I shall never find again, together with people I love, people who interest me, people with whom I am much better acquainted after scarcely three weeks than I am with others I have known for a long time.[5]

And in the summer of 1929, as the guest of a maternal aunt in the Jura, she again expresses this joy of being together with people, of getting to know the people of an area.

What interests me about a village are not the old stones nor the fine panoramas. I am happy here because I have become friends with the people of the place. Their chores, their fairs and their festivals are all occasions for cultivating this friendship by sharing their life.[6]

The time was drawing near when, after finishing the École Normale, Simone could realize her "great project," her cherished dream since 1924, as she would later say in a letter to Martinet: becoming a worker. It had arisen in Simone when she was fifteen and it was the inspiration at the center of her life. It was associated with her instinct for equality, which always compelled her to come out of herself, and with any sort of adjustment to a comfortable set of protective circumstances. This inspiration was certainly *her* way of reaching the realm of truth. It was a difficult course, almost impossible because of her poor manual dexterity and before long, because of her basic physical problem, migraine headaches. On the one hand, it meant confronting the impossible, not measuring the real dimensions of the situation. On the other, it was the only road along which Simone succeeded in grasping the truth of her own and our time. Her profound cultural preparation, from Plato to Marx, from Sophocles to Racine, from Tacitus to Machiavelli to De Retz, from the Pythagoreans to Galileo to Evariste Galois, permitted her to find the points of intersection between theory and practice, between thought and reality. She did not love knowledge as an end in itself nor did she take refuge in books; eager as she was for them and suffused with their words of beauty and truth, she used them to understand men and facts.

I read, as far as possible, only what I am hungry for, when I am hungry and then I don't read, I eat.[7]

This will be her explanation to Father Perrin. And for this her one teacher in flesh and blood remains Alain, the ethical man.

In the first two years of the Normale, her theoretical reflections on labor express her personal philosophy. They explain to us her way of establishing her relationship both to herself and to the world. These reflections are found in two articles published in *Libres Propos* in 1929, in May and August respectively.

The first article, "De la perception ou l'aventure de Protée," defines labor as a

> series of actions that have no direct relationship either with the primal emotion or with the end pursued, or the one with the other.[8]

It is, then, indirect action par excellence, which needs means which are indifferent to one another and indifferent to your desires; so it can teach you how to proceed with detachment from your end, without confusing levels and values.

The second article, "Du temps," examines labor as a power exercised over the one who labors or over oneself.

> To act is nothing else, for me, but to change myself . . . a change that I will, but it is not enough for me to will it to have it. I can only obtain it indirectly.[9]

In this type of action, the exigencies of which coincide with the material difficulties which the labor encounters and which it has to resolve, I learn to know myself. And at the same time I learn the world.

> Only through the experience of labor do I meet, always together, time and space, time as the condition, space as the object of my action.[10]

Here Simone affirms her primary exigency: the search for the detachment between what we are and what we do, to place ourselves and our works in a real, not imaginary, space and time.

She understood her inspiration of becoming a worker as an attempt to discover space-time, the relationship of man with the world through the form of labor at the center of our era, industry.

For this reason she felt with her whole being that, until she followed this inspiration, she was merely spinning around things. Hence we find, among the first notes in the *Cahiers*,

You live in a dream. You are waiting to live.[11]

At the same time her manner of expectation, which is a preparation, explains the impossibility for her of belonging to a political party and the concept of religion which was her own at this epoch.

―――――――――

At school Simone had declared, "I am a Bolshevik."[12] By that she meant revolutionary. After the first world war, she sided directly with the conquered foe, who had been unjustly humiliated, she felt. Revolution meant for her a struggle against an unjust form of government. She developed within herself a strong sympathy for the Communist party, dictated by her desire to defend the "most despised strata of the social hierarchy."[13] She was then convinced by the teaching of Alain, for whom revolution was the resistance of the individual thinker to those in power; Simone thus devoted her political passion above all else to the defense and empowerment of the individual in his dignity and autonomy. Hence her antimilitarism and the ripening of a critical spirit that challenged organizations and learned to discern the obtuse and unjust actions of the left as well as the right. So, although she drew the hammer and sickle on her cards, letters and notebooks and frequently read *L'Humanité,* her sympathy never reached the point of making her join the party. André Weil recalls seeing, in his sister's bedroom, a letter which began, "Animated by a strong feeling of solidarity . . ." "She was perhaps eighteen when she wrote it," he says. "But the letter was never finished."[14] According to Simone Pétrement, this impulse to join the party must have welled up at a moment of indignation, only to sink back again very quickly. "I find it impossible for her to have accepted any limitation on her liberty of thinking, speaking and acting."[15]

Like Alain, but even more than he, she was opposed to parties. A representative, if he wants to fulfill honestly and effectively the task of representing the people, must be free of the power games connected with the necessary expansion of a party; he must be a stranger to all interest groups. For this reason he would never be a general, a banker, an industrialist, or a priest who defended the temporal power of the church. For he must be vigilant in guaranteeing respect for the law or respect for the human person. The laws impose limits upon the eagerness to deceive of the government and other powers (the rich). The good deputy must be sought and selected

> from among those who neither have nor desire any power; one must take into account their firmness of character and judgment and the absence of any political passion.[16]

Here, too, the need for detachment reappears; it coincides with the need for freedom in the management of one's own life.

There exists a duty, there exists a happiness in understanding the design that is impressed upon us and in bringing it to light. One must follow one's calling or

> have before one's eyes one's whole life and take the firm and constant resolution to make something out of it, to orient it from one end to another in a determined sense by means of the will and labor.[17]

The only life that seemed decisively oriented in the sense of a calling was that of Edi (Edwige) Copeau. The daughter of Jacques Copeau[18] and a Danish woman, Edi speaks of having lived until she was twenty years old "divided in half" by the religious fissure between her Catholic father and her Protestant mother. "When my father, after long years of not practising his religion, devoted himself completely to it, I did, too. Instructed by the Benedictines of rue de la Source, I took my first communion on June 12, 1927." She was twenty-two. She remembers her meetings with Simone Weil especially after that date. "We would see each other when I came to Paris from Burgundy, where I lived after 1925. We used to speak a lot about religion; this would happen at the house of Suzanne Gauchon-Aron, who had introduced us, or along the street. I remember Simone, who would ask me questions without end, sitting on the floor at Suzanne's house; she seemed to expect something important from me. I felt that she was much superior to me and was astonished at her intense manner of listening to me. And then she knew the Holy Scriptures much better than I."

For Easter of 1930, Edi went with her father to Assisi. In November of the same year she became a Benedictine, taking the name of Mother François, in the monastery of Vanves, at the gates of Paris.[19]

She told Simone about this in a letter. Camille Marcoux remembers it well. "I had never seen her so upset. We walked along the fence of the Luxembourg in silence, as was our habit. Simone had her hands thrust in her pockets; one knew they were rolled into fists. Finally she took out a crumpled envelope, Edi's letter. With her face inflamed, she said in three words that Edi had become a nun. But she did not manage to show me the letter: it was too much for her."

It was complete dedication, setting out for a life of action, involving both body and mind, with nothing left out. And this was not for flight but for life to the fullest. At the center of things there was a connection with God. God. How did she think of God at that time?

She felt a great sympathy for Christianity, especially for Catholicism. One has only to read her essays. She cites the Old and the New Testaments, Pascal, Saint Augustine and she invokes Christian dogmas. She tries to find the true sense of these words and dogmas and to agree with them. There is a yearning for a personal religion, for a religion that would confirm her own freedom and her own salvation.

> Our first duty, one could say our only duty is that of "allowing the dead to bury the dead," as Jesus says, that is to leave things in their proper order, which is mechanical necessity, and to dedicate the mind only to the ceaseless assurance of our own freedom.

With regard to sin:

> Sin is sleep; the sinner is only conscious of it when he repents; this expresses the Catholic doctrine that repentance saves . . . So our life becomes beautiful and a symbol of God, along with our passions and our sins, as Catholicism has seen with such force.[20]

She loved to visit churches and to attend religious services; she believed (as did Alain) that beauty and quiet have a good effect upon the soul through the body. For this reason she found that the Protestants, in their rejection of many aspects of beauty in worship, neglected the union of the soul and body. Once, while she was listening to music in Notre Dame with a comrade, she grew very angry with him because he misbehaved during the ceremony in his anticlericalism.[21] Another time, however, she was the one, in a small group of Normale students, to join in a series of anti-religious remarks that offended Clémence Ramnoux. Saddened, Clémence slowed her pace to separate herself from her comrades. Simone noticed it and suddenly darted in front of her; she said, "Perhaps one day I will be the one to become a nun."[22]

What was God for her at this time? In a discussion, Raymonde, who considered the conversion of Pascal a weakness, made the remark, "I do not understand how one could believe in God." Simone declared, "I, on the other hand, do not understand how one could not believe in Him."[23]

Later she will write:

> Since my adolescence I have believed that the problem of God is a problem for which we lack data here below; for this reason, the only sure method for avoiding a mistaken solution, something I thought the worst possible evil, was not to pose it as a problem. So I did not pose it. I did not affirm and I did not deny.[24]

Simone did not want a God-problem, a God-object. She felt that there was a God who involves you in all your being, who teaches you to read within things, who teaches you love in the true way. Here she begins her road towards this God with a noble assertion of herself as a being free to do the good, in as much as

> The good is . . . the motion by which we break away from ourselves as individuals or as animals to affirm ourselves as men, that is, sharers in God.[25]

It is in an overcoming of ourselves, "rejecting and leaving behind ourselves what is material," that we shall find God, that we shall make Him exist.

> Action is the affirmation of God.[26]

Then He can coincide with our liberty, be and exist every time this liberty is made manifest in ideas or movements.

> But this is merely a matter of words and I am always alone, whether with this God or without Him.[27]

The only certainty, and the only tangible relationship with the infinite, remains our calling, which we must obey.

One must "decide for oneself, no matter what it may cost"; we do not have the "right" to subject ourselves to someone else's authority. One must seek the truth solely through one's own life. For this reason, "the most necessary thing is to pardon oneself."[28] Simone quoted this phrase of Alain to her friend Pétrement. They were talking together about their lives as they boated in the Bois de Boulogne. It was May, 1931.

They wanted to remain together even for the subsequent reception of their degrees, on August 1 of that year. It was Simone Weil who told the inspector of public instruction, when he hesitated to receive them together, "We do not have secrets from each other."[29]

That day, however, Simone did not make any request of the inspector. She nurtured her real desire and waited. It was in September that Simone Pétrement learned what follows:

My grand project has been abandoned because of the depression.[30]

She had asked, in compensation, for a teaching position "in a port city (if possible, le Havre), or in an industrial city of the central or northern part of the country."[31]

They sent her to Le Puy, in Auvergne, "something that did not correspond at all to her desires."[32]

7

The Beginning of a Quest

During the summer of 1931, Simone, at twenty-two years of age, confronted work at sea. She wanted to share in the life of fishermen, to study the relationship between the constellations and navigation, between the efforts of man and the resistance of nature, between labor and profit.

At first her request appeared strange to the inhabitants of the few houses along the road (then more a path than a road) that led between large ponds and reeds to the point where the lighthouse of Réville stands in Normandy. She boarded with the Passilly family, at first along with her parents, then by herself.

Her parents were there to support her in her request and finally, after many refusals, Marcel Lecarpentier, who owned a four-man ship along with his brother, accepted her. "I decided to please Dr. Weil when I saw his daughter running along the beach like a crazy woman. She would go into the sea in her large skirts; she was getting soaking wet, without a slicker. I had already departed but I turned around and picked her up. I borrowed a set of oilskins to wrap her in from a ship that was returning to port. She had a little book and a pencil with her; she spent a good part of the night drawing the constellations and writing."

Marcel squints his eyes to see her better in his memory. "She was not pretty and she would not take care of herself. She was a real ragamuffin. Her parents suffered from this, Passilly told me. And someone else, one of my village, who later became an admiral, kept telling me, 'Don't have her come to your house. She is a Communist and will bring you trouble.' I didn't mind at all; she had a right to my table, along with my wife Yvonne and my child, also called Yvonne. And then, too, she was not a Communist. She used to teach catechism to my child." When the weather was too bad to go out, Simone would teach Marcel. "For six months, I continued my studies of arithmetic and French. I would send her the notebooks and she would correct them and send them back to me. 'Do not be selfish,' she would write me. 'Share what I send you with your comrades.' And she continued to send me books, when she was working for Renault. *Gold Seekers of Alaska*, for example. Here's one of them here." On the oilcloth of the table was *La peine des hommes* of Pierre Hamp (Gallimard 1934). "She wanted to know our misery. She wanted to free the worker. This was the goal of her life. I would say to her, 'But you are the daughter of rich people.' 'That's my misfortune; I wish that my parents had been poor,' she would say. 'You would not know so much, you would not have studied so much,' I answered. 'No, no, we'd get to the same point; I would want to share what I know with everyone.'"

"She still made a strange impression," said Mme. Yvonne with great effort.[1] Today she appears wild and exhausted.

"Ah, she was indeed different. She hated clothes and jewelry, for all the wealth of her family. She would glide like this, glide above what they thought of her. She did not pay them any attention; if she had, she would have made herself look better. She loved solitude and the sea. 'The sea inspires me,' she used to say. She always had a headache; once she lost a watch because of a headache; they would come on her like waves of emptiness. Another time she really frightened me. There was a terrible storm and I asked her to tie herself down; she refused: 'I am ready to die, I have always done my duty.' She said that."

Even the countenance of Yvonne grows more lively, at least a little, as these memories flow back to Marcel, significant and so much richer in life than his present days. And yet the road to the lighthouse is today a real road, the tourists flock there in large numbers and the inhabitants of Réville own four hundred and sixty automobiles.

"Simone followed the work with a medicine-dropper. She watched the price of fish and calculated the proper divisions. 'Why don't you form a cooperative, Marcel?' She was always afraid that I would become an exploiter and warned me of this danger. I had four men; I made them some concessions. On Saturdays, the families would be paid on the basis of the total sales. The other captains did not understand this. They wanted their men to work only for a percentage of the sale of the fish; they would have their salary and that's all. Ah, another thing. She used to ask me all the time if there were any families that needed aid; I did not tell her, because I did not want her to be penniless."

Marcel is sorry that he no longer has the notebooks with Simone's corrections. "It was the war; I was afraid, because she was Jewish and here in Normandy we were in the midst of the battle. Simone Weil carried off my notebook of soldiers' songs, those of the Legion, marines, men condemned to military prison.[2] They were from my period of military service and I had annotated them. There were about forty of them. She was especially fond of the antimilitarist songs; love-songs did not interest her. She had eyes only for misery."[3]

On September 30, 1931, Simone Weil arrived at Le Puy, a picturesque little city, clerical and conservative, in Haute-Loire, to take up her first position as a teacher of philosophy. With this date there began the phase of her life that may be termed *euphoric*. Euphoric in the sense of dedicated activity on the union level; in the sense of a comradeship warmly shared, if not with many; in the sense of generous and innovative teaching, both of her students in three female lycées where she taught (Le Puy: 1931–32; Auxerre: 1932–33; Roanne: 1933–34), and of the miner-students in a true workers' university expanded by her at Saint-Étienne; in the sense of traveling to learn about contemporary reality. This is true above all of her trip to Germany in 1932.

The same themes reappear, from her years in the Normale in Paris: concrete participation in the life of the workers by way of the direct experience (even if only sporadically at present) of manual labor; crossing the threshold of the difference among classes; sharing the results of her study and her thought above all with workers.

These themes, in a Simone who is now playing a public role, result in actions that cause scandal in the narrower and less enlightened ambience of the provinces. They are real monstrosities, which engender fear; they are all the more inconceivable because they are done by a woman, and emphasize her "difference."

In her year at Le Puy, the year of her most confident euphoria, her political activity was threefold: the organization of an inter-union group "among all the laboring elements of the city, without distinction of party, including the Communists";[4] the development of a workers' university at the *Bourse du Travail* at Saint-Étienne; solidarity with the unemployed of Le Puy. Her actions for the last-named were considered the most subversive, inasmuch as they broke with the patterns of social and feminine behavior in an obvious way. A woman, a teacher of philosophy, who went to a café with the unemployed and paid the bill? And again: right in the middle of Place Michelet, didn't she shake hands with a stone-breaker? These were the most glaring particulars in a police report, to which Simone was asked to give her reply by the office of the inspector of instruction. The events took place between December 1931 and February 1932. On two occasions she led the unemployed in presenting demands to the mayor of the city; she wrote, in their name, clear and decisive articles for *La Tribune;* she demonstrated in processions. A real public dispute blazed up between her detractors and her defenders, who confronted each other in a press campaign. Viewed with suspicion by the authorities, Simone was on the point of being fired. At Le Puy, in Lyon, even in Paris, the more reactionary papers called her from time to time "a handsomely paid functionary who mobilizes the unemployed of dubious intentions to corrupt the other workers and to create agitation in the city";[5] "a militant in the pay of Moscow, with a strange idea of her mission as an educator, she is trying to poison the girls of French race who have been entrusted to her by their families";[6] "the Jewish Mlle. Weill [sic] . . . who should begin by splitting the salary they say is handsome with the forty unemployed of Le Puy."[7] Right in the cathedral, a priest preached against her; on a train, Mme. Anthériou, the mother of a colleague with whom Simone shared her apartment, was heard to say: "It seems that the Antichrist is in Le Puy; it is a woman, who goes around dressed like a man."[8] On the other side she was defended: by Professor Villard of the boys' lycée, who termed her activity "generous, replete with fervor and humanity, an activity that no man in her position would have dared perform";[9] by the syndicalist Vidal, who wanted to vouch for the disinterest of Simone "in the face of the hypocrisy" of the campaign against her . . . [10] The union council appointed him to appeal to the Ligue des droits de l'homme to defend Simone against the threats of being fired. Cancouët, even though he did not share her way of impulsive action, "like Joan of Arc," wrote an article to support her in Paris.[11] Alain wrote Villard: "I am very much pleased with the child Simone Weil." And to his friends he said, "She's the only one who could have brought about a strike by the unemployed!"[12]

A letter of solidarity, for which Villard had gathered the signatures (nine in all) of his colleagues at the two lycées, showed, for the actions of Simone, "the respect that is due to convictions that are sincerely expressed in the fullness of her rights."[13]

As she will always want it in her life, Simone had placed herself at the epicenter of discomfort, where she felt the most pressing need of justice.

To join forces, to find the energy and the dignity necessary for non-violent action, this had been indispensable for the unemployed. Simone had given voice to this conscious solidarity. In the same sense, with an enormous amount of labor, she will give life to the intersyndical union of Le Puy. This regional group would remain loyal to its decisions at the same time that in Paris the CGTU[14] would declare, in its national congress, complete opposition to any type of intersyndical unity (November 8–14, 1931).

Simone believed in union among the syndicates, because there she saw

the only real bond created by the community of productive activity and not an imaginary bond created by the community of opinion,[15]

as happens with parties. Since the hostility of the organizations had become obvious, it was necessary for the working class to realize its unity without their support or even in spite of the organizations.

This problem that seems insoluble must be solved by the working class or they will condemn themselves to disappear as a revolutionary force.[16]

This political action was one of her answers to the central question she asked herself in this period: "Under what conditions could a revolution be truly effective?" Another answer must be sought in the profound direction of her instruction.

———

How did Simone look at Le Puy? And how did she live?

Despite "the silk stockings, a soft sheath for her slender legs,"[17] which a reactionary paper thought it had to invent, at first Simone was mistaken for a student. When she arrived at the lycée, with her mother accompanying her, the woman porter asked her which class she wanted to be enrolled in. Vexed by the gloves she had to wear for the occasion, she kept her fingers comically extended; she would not wear them again.

From the very beginning she decided to spend on herself only six hundred francs of her salary, that of a teacher with a first appointment. Loathing individual acts of charity, as her colleague Simone Anthériou, who shared her life at Le Puy, has said of her, she distributed the rest of her salary to welfare funds, assistance agencies, newspapers and reviews; in particular, she gave considerable sums to the Solidarity Fund of the miners of Saint-Étienne.[18]

The personal life she had been leading since her adolescence was a disciplining of her body until it became "a thing" to control (her refusal of rugs and heater for her room).[19] Her complete control of her life is expressed in her increasing indifference to her own health, in the even more unbelievable absent-mindedness of an inept "trollesse," in an urchinlike taste for not setting times for rest and meals. There continued that *self-dilapidation,* which is bound up with the eternally young appearance of her deepest nature.

Mme. Selma, with her practical sense and justified apprehension with regard to her daughter, accompanied her and set her up in one of the finest and most comfortable apartments at Le Puy, with the use of a large garden and the exceptional presence of a bathroom. She provided her with a companion, also a first-time teacher and a student of Chartier. These two young women will become quite close; during those three years of Le Puy, Auxerre and Roanne, Simone Anthériou will be Simone's only friend in the same profession.

All those rooms: there was trouble in persuading her to live there. Too much bourgeois luxury: the salon was done away with, immediately becoming a sort of wardrobe-laundryroom. From the very first day, lines criss-crossed it from one side to the other. In her bedroom, the wallpaper with little designs was gotten rid of (perhaps too bourgeois, perhaps too ugly) and replaced with paper of a single color; for furniture, they tolerated a sofa, a large worktable, bookcases and a lovely old sideboard for the linen. From the very first, the half-time servant (also providentially supplied by Mme. Selma) was absolutely forbidden to clean the room. The floor was covered with books and notebooks. Simone preferred to study on her knees and to go from one book to another. In the eyes of strangers, the place was to look uninhabitable. Some officials, who visited the apartment for taxation purposes, were already shocked by the salon but when they came to the bedroom, they exclaimed: "And what is this? A cleaning room?"[20]

Mme. Selma set up the kitchen and thus put off the day when the two women would survive on boiled potatoes and tea. At Simone's wish, the kitchen maid was paid at union rates, probably two or three times as high as the wages other maids received. In gratitude for this salary that seemed enormous, the poor woman went on bringing sacks of pine cones to light the fire. Actually they could have had excellent heating, beginning with a heater in the entrance hall, and Selma Weil had already provided a supply of coal. Simone, to share the sacrifices of the unemployed, refused to heat her room (she slept with her window open, studied wrapped up in a sweater, and lit the fire only if she expected company) and then discovered to her surprise that the unemployed always found some way to have their houses heated. The bags of pine cones usually served as seats.

Thereafter, between one wearisome trip to Le Puy and another (thirteen hours on the train), Mime continued to send packages of food. Simone complained about their weight because she had to carry them from the station to her apartment; they were unbearable because they were things destined for her, and not the big parcels of books which she would then soon request from Paris for her pupils or for the miners of Saint-Étienne. Those would never seem heavy.

Too much stuff: "As if I were a soldier in wartime!" she exclaims in a postscript to a letter.[21] And yet, the good Dutch cheese, the bacon, the spaghetti helped nourish Simone when she was not having headaches. Then she did not eat, even for five or six days. An effort like chewing would cause her to vomit. "She tolerated only grated apples."[22] At home she was forced to lie in bed, face down, her head thrust between the pillows, to avoid every motion. But she continued to teach. The other Simone accompanied her. She had literally to hold her up when she stepped up to the sidewalk; as they walked along, Simone Weil leaned on her for support.

=====

So strange! At first we laughed at her. She dressed badly and her gestures were awkward and graceless. She hesitated when she spoke. Her method was as odd as her appearance. She told us that we should never miss a class and that the texts should be avoided; they were badly done. We would make do with her lectures. She would give us brief essays to write on all kinds of subjects; she would correct, with special care, the logic of the argument and the preciseness of the expression. She would thrust those papers in her pocket and return them the next day, beautifully corrected and often pocked with cigarette burns."

These are the words of Claire Claveyrolas and she continues: "She would give her explanations in a monotonous tone and was often utterly lost in her thoughts. Then she would ask a question and no one would answer, simply because it was difficult to answer someone who had asked us to be more precise, to distinguish, to clarify again and again, until we were practically drained by so much thinking."[23]

Hers was a presence, however, in which "the awkwardness of gestures . . . the strange facial expressions when she was concentrating, the piercing glance behind her thick lenses, the smile, everything exuded a total frankness, a forgetfulness of self, revealing a nobility of mind which was at the root of the sentiments she inspired in us but of which we were not immediately conscious."

"Her negligence in dress did not shock us; she was neither affected nor masculine."[24] It was the negligence of someone who is continually immersed in other interests and thoughts. She was very generous with her students, furnished them with extra books, which she ordered in sufficient numbers and paid for in advance, since she wanted the girls to benefit from the discount received by teachers. "What a joy it was to see her come into the courtyard of the boarding school, the courtyard which teachers entered so rarely, especially on their free day!" It was Thursday and here she was, loaded down with books, "which she carried with great fatigue."[25] Even the little girls, whom she taught Greek, protected her maternally, since they sensed that she was defenseless in practical life. "One time she arrived in class with her sweater inside out. The little girls told her and arranged for her to go behind the blackboard and put the sweater on properly. One of them stood guard, to give warning if the principal arrived."[26] This woman had never been very friendly to Simone and became even more glacial and stiff than the other authorities (inspectors, the superintendent of Clermont-Ferrand) in her dealings with Simone the "agitator."

Worse will follow at Auxerre, where Simone will indulge in the most exasperating insolence; given the scanty results on the official level (at Le Puy, only two students out of fifteen were given the certificate of graduation; at Auxerre, only three or four out of twelve, with most of the best students failing the examination), the principal, Mme. Lesnes, decided to end the teaching of philosophy to her students. As far as colleagues are concerned, at Le Puy, as we have seen, she had some she could rely on, but at Auxerre she was detached from them all. In her report of December 15, 1932, the principal wrote: "Quite different from her colleagues, she systematically isolates herself from the rest of the staff, whom furthermore she does not care to know, since she has found no echo there of her own political opinions, which are extremely advanced."[27]

A teacher in the boarding school at Roanne gives a picture of her that is involuntarily a caricature. "She was of a very distinctive type; I remember that we had instinctively very little sympathy for that young woman. We did indeed admire her intelligence but she was always a stranger among us, even in the most common matters of everyday life. This was true even of our meals in common. It seemed that she was not even there. She would read Karl Marx directly from the original text and continue to eat; every now and then she would direct a completely dull look from behind her thick glasses; the look was even more hidden by the locks of hair that fell over her eyes. It was a look that seemed not to see us."[28]

Everywhere she went, she created confusion, she broke the customary rules established in stable situations, especially in organizations, from the most official and precise, such as schools and city government, to those of workers' groups. She was always striving to come out of herself, to understand, to create open situations that would develop harmoniously on the basis of their real reasons for existence.

=====

Already, some years earlier, in Paris, Simone had made contact with the group that animated *La Révolution Prolétarienne*, a monthly founded in 1925, with the original subtitle of *A Syndical-Communist Review*. Its principal figures were Monatte and Louzon, "both revolutionary syndicalists of a libertarian bent."[29] Around it clustered syndicalists who had been members of the party, in their enthusiasm for the October Revolution, but had then either been thrown out or voluntarily left it. This independence pleased Simone, who generously supported the review and begged her parents to do the same; she called it the only publication "that contains historical studies of the first order on social problems."[30] It will be *La Révolution Prolétarienne* that will publish her most important political essays in these years.

In the meanwhile, Monatte, born at Le Puy, introduced her to the political life of the region, especially through Claudius Vidal, the secretary of the teachers' union at Le Puy itself, and Urbain Thévenon, a teacher, an eminent and courageous syndicalist of Saint-Étienne.

On October 7, 1931, Simone went to Saint-Étienne to meet him. Albertine Thévenon, his widow, remembers with great precision the brusque and startling way with which Simone introduced herself forcibly into the dark entrance of their house. When she rang the bell, Albertine was about to do some darning, so she went to the door with one hand inside a sock. "Is M. Thévenon here?" asked the unknown young woman. When she received an affirmative reply, she brushed past Albertine with her shoulder and went straight to the room where Thévenon was sitting; she actually just burst in. Albertine did not even have the time to close the door. This action of Simone is understandable on the basis of some of her earlier experiences. "Often the wives of her syndicalist comrades were not sympathetic towards her or did not trust her; so they tried to keep her from seeing their husbands."[31]

Their conversation lasted so long that the Thévenons set up a cot for her in the parlor and Simone returned to Le Puy the next day, a Thursday, in the afternoon. From November 18 on, Simone would repeat this trip ("three hours on the train in freezing cars!" her mother would write) at least once a week, principally to work with the study center established at the *Bourse de Travail*. She would attend meetings, take part in demonstrations, complete the work of the secretariat of the miners' union, a task that Pierre Arnaud, one of her most fraternal friends, gladly allowed her to perform.

An initiative for a school for miners already existed at Saint-Étienne. In 1928, the departmental union and the local union of the CGT had created *Collèges du Travail*. In 1931 Urbain Thévenon and another teacher, Gustave Claveyrolas, were in charge. Simone insisted upon expanding the teaching as much as possible. The courses began on December 5, after careful preparation since November 18, and would continue from one week to the next (these days were for Simone her life, a festival): there was a course in French taught by Simone and a course in political economy taught by Simone and Thévenon. This involvement flowed from her dearest conviction, already put in practice in the Parisian courses for railwaymen and, personally, in her friendship for Marcel Lecarpentier: giving workers access to knowledge and culture. This was for her one of the principal conditions for a true revolution. Teaching should be conducted on the basis of equality. Among the experiments conducted for teaching workers, it was important to distinguish those managed in a way that reenforces the ascendancy of the intellectuals over the workers from those managed in a way that frees the workers from such an ascendancy.

It was necessary to reject manipulation but not to deny the positive contributions of intellectual culture in time.

Since the days of primitive society men who possessed the almost miraculous power of employing words and of expressing the essence of things have had an ascendancy, and consequently a power. It is true that those who have joined words together, priests and intellectuals, have in general used this power to set themselves apart from men who work only with things and have, ordinarily, been on the side of the dominant class. And yet it is also true that respect for language and for the men who have the ability to use it has, over time, favored the evolution of human thought in its entirety. Thus, it is not by instilling in the workers a disdain for culture, "tendentiously defined as bourgeois," that we must free them from the domination of the intellectuals. Even if the superiority that until now has been accorded to the latter by convention should be rejected, this does not mean that workers should also reject the heritage of human culture. They should rather prepare themselves to take possession of it.

This taking of possession is the Revolution itself.

The abolition of the "degrading division of labor into manual labor and intellectual labor," frowned upon by Marx and by Simone along with him, should and can be prepared for at the present time.

For this purpose, it is necessary first of all to give to the workers the power of handling language, and in particular, written language.[32]

=====

Her *visit to a mine* was influential in discovering another side of the same problem. She yearned for this visit, she begged for it and she finally obtained it (in a way extraordinary for a woman) thanks to Guillot, a friend of Thévenon, on March 10, 1932. They allowed her to use a pneumatic hammer and a compressed-air drill. If they had not stopped her, she would have continued, despite her headache, to make herself shudder with the drill until she fell over in a faint. She asked to be employed. Guillot made her understand it was impossible. "An infernal job," Simone wrote on a card to her parents on March 12. After this experience Simone turned her attention specifically to the relation between man and his tools, which is the relation between science and its application.

What type of tool is the drill? It is a

> machine . . . not modelled upon human nature but upon the nature of coal and compressed air: [its] motions follow a rhythm profoundly foreign to that of life; [it] bends a human body violently to its service.

For this reason, it will not be enough for the miner to expropriate the companies to become master of mining.

> The political revolution, the economic revolution will not be realized unless they are prolonged by a technical revolution which will re-establish concretely, within the mine and the factory, the dominion which the worker maintains over the conditions of labor.[33]

She wrote this in *L'Effort* of March 19. In the same paper, an organ of the *Cartel Autonome du Bâtiment* of Lyon, which often accepted her work, there had appeared, on March 12, "Le capital et l'ouvrier," in which Simone criticized automation in general, as the most concretely oppressive aspect of capitalism. A profound transformation of technology is therefore necessary, but "without destroying the collective form which capitalism has imposed upon production,"[34] a form which has formidably increased the efficiency of human labor. And again: we must find the means for coordinating labor without subordinating one type to another. The elevation of the level of consciousness and of culture of the proletariat must be accompanied by theoretical research on the problem of the relationship between science and technology. This key problem would otherwise re-emerge after the revolution and render it vain. And the anxiety which torments Simone is the thought of a revolution which is vain, willful and bloody. The question she now asks herself is this: how are we to find a way of organization by which it would no longer be necessary to have a revolution? To this end, there is need for reflection, for concentrating all our thinking. The first indispensable step: analyzing the real causes of oppression.

In another article, of January, she wrote:

> As long as the exploited exist, revolutionaries exist. These revolutionaries have killed and been killed. They have neither destroyed nor,

often, even lessened the exploitation. It is not enough to rise up against a social order founded on oppression; it must be changed and it cannot be changed without being known.[35]

Simone Weil is always pursuing the road of reflection. Knowledge, the work of thought, must save us from hasty action, from clouded imaginations, from inflamed opinions, from violence against others. Her deepest desire is to succeed in applying to the vicissitudes of history the luminous objectivity of true science, not as an end in itself, but as a means to make clear the actions of man. In the articles we have cited, she has taken the first steps in that *science of society*, whose laws she will research by analyzing the past and the present. In the name of the respect due to the individual, as we have seen up to now: the revolutionary fallen at the barricades, the miner shaken by the drill, the unemployed without a voice at Le Puy. And this is what we shall always see.

A series of lectures on Marxism dating from the period at Roanne show a maturing of her method. The general conclusions which she drew from these lectures were the following: social movements are determined by economic relations; men and their thoughts are determined by the social situation; what is determined cannot pretend to change what determines it. So only the individual who is in a position to escape social determinism can use a science of society, either to put it at the service of the masses and under their control or, in an opposite manner, to enslave them and to suppress any democracy. She comes to the decisive role of the individual in society: "the individual, the sole true revolutionary leaven." To achieve control of the instruments of labor and an understanding of the web of relations determining them, the proletariat must be aided in acquiring the capacity for breaking that web. It will be necessary to reestablish the autonomy of industrial enterprises and restore their more human dimensions. The worker will then have the power to "distribute *his own time* freely between reflection and action"[36] in his private life and on the job.

Simone would bring with her to Saint-Étienne the books she used and "would never make a quotation without presenting it, underlined in the text, to her students."[37] She would be very careful in her preparations, as she always was at the lycée, working until late at night. For the courses, she at first went on Saturday for the Sunday classes; from March on, she would sometimes leave at five in the morning on Sunday and had to get up at four. In the year 1933–34, when she shuttled between Roanne and

Saint-Étienne, she often preferred to work at a table in a bar across from the *Bourse du Travail*. She refused the hospitality of her friends; that would have distracted her. For the few hours of sleep she allowed herself in her weariness, the bar owner allowed her to rest on a little leather sofa in the establishment.

The unification of her ideals on the level of action and of thought, which always had to coincide for her, came in the optional courses on *the history of science* she invented for her students in the lycée. A letter, in which she replied to an inquiry by a scientific publication on the usefulness of such instruction, and a text, in which she presented the method to her comrades as a way towards a socialist culture, show us the results of the experience.

It was a pedagogical success. Even the weakest students in mathematics benefited from it. Their interest became enthusiastic. Becoming aware of the bonds that exist between the various sciences and the methods that have gradually allowed their development, the students came to understand

> that the sciences are a product of human thought and not an assemblage of dogmas.[38]

Knowledge as the personal work of the mind was the only one worthy of the name. And it provided for the autonomy of the students. Simone, who had in Paris refused to give a talk on feminism, with the declaration, "I am not a feminist,"[39] saw in her students "whole" persons to develop, and she was interested more than in anything else, in their thinking. This intention of hers was unconscious to the degree that it perfectly coincided with her, with her orientation of life.

For her comrades, to achieve a true socialist culture, which must be a "synthesis of theory and of practice," Simone suggested the following method.

> In my thinking, the teaching of the sciences, to constitute a culture, should include: (1) instruction, at least in part historical, in each science, with a reading of the original texts and, for physics, the reproduction of the experiments made by its discoverers, whenever possible; (2) instruction in the history of the relations between science and technology; (3) apprenticeship in and practice of a productive

trade, connected with more detailed instruction in the history of that trade in relation to science and the full array of technology.[40]

The need for equality with the proletariat on the pedagogical level, a sign of profound respect for the intelligence and the life of the learner, became in her on the practical level a personal expression of that amorous impulse we have seen in her early youth. And it continued to have those aspects of naïveté and fanaticism characteristic of adolescent love. As lucid and exacting as she was in her writings, as inflexible as she was in debates, establishing all the points of the question without looking anyone in the face, so involved was she inwardly and emotionally with the sufferings, the humiliations and the inability to defend themselves she sensed in the humblest. She wanted to make herself one of their number by eliminating her privileges, from the heating of her house to her position as a professor of the lycée (she immediately joined the syndicate of the schoolteachers and used only the fraction of her pay which corresponded to theirs).

Men, all of them, were gradually moved to admiration and ready to follow her; or they were irritated; or they were protective. Her mother wrote: "It is unreal to see the authority this child has assumed with the greatest naturalness over teachers, workers, etc. . . . and one feels the confidence she has inspired in them."[41] In the hot period of the campaign against her at Le Puy, workers' delegations waited for her at every little station along the line between Le Puy and Saint-Étienne, to show her their solidarity.[42] Albertine Thévenon recalls: "In the Loire, those who felt attracted by her could be counted on the fingers of one hand. She absolutely never tried to please anyone." But she adds: "The miners of the group at Saint-Étienne were tough men, hard types, battlers; some had been in the Foreign Legion. So, you see, among them, she did not have to fear anything. She was as safe as if she were in a fortress. And she did quite well for herself there."[43]

Pierre Arnaud says: "One felt in Simone the deep joy of being with men who earned their livelihood with the strength of their arms." She wanted to know everyone in her "circle of studies." She liked strong types. On the wall of her room she showed her friends the photograph of "a strong, handsome young man," and exclaimed, "Such are the kind who please me."[44] "Beauty in the face and the body, in men, women and children," she will later say, "are *echoes* of God on earth."[45]

Simone had made copies of many workers' songs; she knew them by heart, but she was tone-deaf; she would recite them rather than sing. Or she would sing, in an impossible way, student songs to evoke them for her friends. Sometimes she would just listen and say in a sad voice, "I don't know how to sing." She would also tell tales of her nocturnal wanderings, in Paris, on the night of July 14, from one popular dance to another, without ever dancing. "I don't know how to dance," she would repeat. Late at night, she would start reciting verses, whole pages of Greek tragedy from her prodigious memory.[46]

What she wanted most was to carry the red flag in a demonstration. The first time she did so was on May 1, 1932, for a very short time, after having trotted behind the man who was carrying it; then for a longer time, officially, on December 3, 1933, for the "grand march of the miners," in which Pierre Arnaud assembled more than three thousand men of the department. She bounded into the first row to claim it, since she had been promised it. She kept in step quite seriously. During one pause of the trumpets, she was heard to exclaim, "And so? The miners don't know how to sing?"[47]

The press of Roanne attacked her with violence.

8

The First Test: The Situation in Germany

Not to be an accomplice, not to lie, not to remain blind.

Simone wrote this in her *Cahiers*,[1] notebooks of conversation with herself; we believe she began them around 1933–34. From that time onward they will be the story of her thought and her soul. With this warning she pointed to the sole form of responsible action in the rush of events. She had come to this view after a journey of reflection she had begun in August, 1932, with her personal observation of the situation in Germany, where she stayed for a month, mostly in Berlin, boarding with a worker's family. This visit marks a break in these three years, her most active from the point of view of politics.

Her euphoria, never unconscious or excessive, but still present in the confidence which animated her actions and publications during her year at Le Puy, begins to wane, until it vanishes altogether. We shall see it in her prophetic brightness of a fresco on Germany, on the threshold of Hitler's power, in her constant opposition to every obtuse dogmatism and every form of sectarianism. And, finally, in her two essays, "Perspectives" and "Oppression et Liberté, in which the objectivity of social science intends to prevail over every political hope, which would now be only a lethal illusion.

When Simone left for Germany, at the end of July, 1932, she had decided upon the trip "to attempt to understand what the force of Fascism rested on."[2] She had prepared herself, as we can see from her commentary on Trotsky's essay, "Et maintenant?" (What now?), which in part concerned the internal situation in Germany. Monatte had given her a letter of recommendation to a Zurich comrade, a Communist, but "not of the strict party line,"[3] who would help her attend "even" illegal meetings. The Trotskyite Raymond Molinier had given her the task of finding, in Berlin, Leon Sedov, Trotsky's son, who was apparently in great danger.

Those whom she called her "adoptive fathers," and especially Cancouët, discouraged her from making the trip; they were afraid of the urban guerilla warfare and of murderous attempts they had heard of in the German capital. The Weils were distressed at the idea of their daughter traveling in a disturbed country, already controlled to a great extent by a violently anti-Semitic party. When they learned that Dr. Bercher of *La Révolution Prolétarienne,* one of their most trusted friends, would neither accompany her nor meet her in Berlin as planned, they followed her, but stayed mostly in Hamburg, so as not to be intrusive in their desire to protect her.

═══════

With her antennae ever alert, Simone pokes through the entire city, to learn all about it. She is enthusiastic about her human contacts.

> I am falling in love with the German people . . . Everyone (on the train, the street, in businesses, on the tram, etc.) has been gracious with me . . . As far as the situation is concerned, one is less worried about it here than in Paris.

The news about murders are put into the context of normality; one reads about them as one would about automobile accidents . . . there are no longer any riots on the streets.

> Nothing indicates a special situation, unless it is this calm itself, which involves, in a certain sense, something of the tragic.

There is a contrast between the anti-Semitic and nationalistic influence exercised by the Nazis through their propaganda, especially against the Communist party and, once again, the absence of "anti-Semitic and nationalistic feelings . . . in personal relationships."[4]

This is the point upon which Simone's reflection concentrates: the difference which exists between public expressions and private expressions of needs, feelings and reactions proper to man. Real fears, discontents and resentments dwell in the individual together with a courage, a soundness, and a need not to allow oneself to become brutish, which are also real. Instead of catalyzing the soundness and nobility of man, propaganda catalyzes his rancors and misery. It lumps together confused dreams of revenge in phantasms on which hatred and love rest, from which an insatiable illusion draws its nurture. Collective bewilderment is on the rise; every day men lose more of their ability to look at the facts with lucidity. And facts are what one should always refer to. Simone Weil constantly returns to them and never omits one of them, because none is irrelevant. Bound together with one another, facts explain the course of actions and express the moment; if we listen to them, we might find a solution.

Almost as soon as she returns from Germany, she turns what had been the first and decisive impressions in her letters to her parents into dense and compact articles; among them are the portrait "L'Allemagne en attente" and the series of ten articles, entitled "La situation en Allemagne," in which the themes of her portrait are deepened and expanded.

With an immediacy provoked by their urgency, but with a concomitant fullness that takes into account the complexity of life, these essays focus on the situation in a country where the fate of the age is taking shape. They intend to inspire action in three senses: to launch a campaign of solidarity with the German proletariat, who are to receive a fraternal welcome when Fascist terror, of which she more than all others saw the proximate realization, will force them across the frontier; "to make the French people understand that France, with her aggressive imperialism and attachment to the Versailles system, has been directly responsible for the movement of Hitler"; to criticize, without reservations, the behavior of the German Communist party, which, bound hand and feet to its own top-heavy bureaucracy and to the interests of the Russian state-machine, has not known how to sustain and employ the marvelous force of young German workers.

What is happening in Germany? Coming from France, one gets the impression that one is passing "from a retreat, secluded from the world, to the real world." Here politics is not a skirmish of ideas or the subject of discussions in cafés, withdrawn from the true interests of everyone. Here, where the Depression has smashed the protective framework of habit, tradition, and everyday stability, and has closed every prospect for the future of a man as an individual,

> the political problem is for everyone the problem that touches him most closely . . . whatever is most intimate in the life of the individual can only be expressed within the problem.

Man's dependence on society entraps him and distorts him in all of his relationships; with himself and the dignity of his life; with himself and his plans for the future; with his family.

Ex-engineers get to eat only one cold meal a day and rent benches in public parks; old men in celluloid collars and derbies beg at the exits of the subway or sing in their cracked voices along the street.

Students have abandoned their studies and sell matches, nuts, or shoe-laces along the streets; their more fortunate comrades know that, given the poor chances of finding a job at the end of their studies, they can one day wind up the same way. As for . . . getting married, having children, the majority of young Germans cannot even think of it.

An unemployed person who lives in a family, with a father or a mother, a husband, or a wife who works, has no right to support. The same happens to an unemployed person who is younger than twenty. Such a dependence . . . exacerbates relationships . . . ; often, it becomes unbearable because of the scoldings of the parents . . . it pushes the young people out of the family house and force them to become vagabonds, beggars and sometimes suicides.

The most tragic element is that no one, however vigorous or resolute, can escape this misery with his own efforts alone. Utterly at the mercy of the play of economic forces, he is at the same time shut up in an impotent solitude. The constant collision with the problems created by the Depression does indeed generate revolutionary impulses, but the energy expended in them remains latent. And revolution is not a myth: "it is a practical task" . . . In the present situation the task, huge but basic, is that of "rebuilding the entire economy on new bases." Only an organization could succeed in uniting the masses around the workers devoted to this task. How do union organizations appear? What are their relations with the masses on the one hand and the parties on the other? The largest and most important union organizations, insofar as they comprise the majority of qualified workers in business enterprises as well as those who are best prepared and conscientious, are the reformist unions. These remain inert because they are internally unbalanced by the factions the Depression has produced in the mass of the population, factions that are divided into those who cling, despite everything, to the regime, those who blindly desire something else, those who get through each day without any hope.

On the other side, the problem of deciding upon an action becomes acute in relationship to the

only two elements capable of acting in a methodical manner: the revolutionary segment of the proletariat and the grand bourgeoisie.

All three of the mass-parties, the Social Democrats, the Communists and the National Socialists, proclaim the revolution and call it *socialist*. The force of their attraction and influence upon the workers, the petit bourgeois, the unemployed, and consequently their ability of involving them in action, depend upon their manner of convincing those factions, awakening their fears or their hopes, and upon their manner of using these elements.

The Social Democrats have always been, in the first place, the parliamentary channel between the reformist unions and the state. The workers' movement, born and alive in France between 1792 and 1871, found a sort of homeland in Germany after the defeat of the Commune; there it has assumed a prudent, methodical, and almost always legal form, with notable results for the welfare of the workers. At the moment, the security of four million members, the majority of the workers in key industries, depends upon the maintenance of these organizations. They have functionaries, the so-called "bonzes" of social democracy, who sit in splendid offices and preside over institutions that have become ends in themselves and have as their central goal the maintenance of peace with the government. How can the regime be toppled and why? Although the reform workers are in latent contrast with their bureaucratic union officials, they are strangers to polemics and do not like taking chances. They are opposed to the demagogy of Hitler. At the same time they do not trust the Communists and refuse to form a common front with them. Why?

Simone asks this question with sorrowful perplexity. The German Communist party is the vanguard of the proletariat, with apparently considerable power (six million votes in the elections of November 1932— 330,000 members). Even with its halo of heroic prestige, it has not yet been able to inspire confidence in the most responsible and vigorous forces of labor. In reality, this party has followed a policy both counterproductive and full of errors. It has created red unions with revolutionaries expelled from the reformist unions; it has indulged in fierce and constant criticism of the Social Democrats and has made any common front impossible. Indeed, it has practiced a kind of common front with the Nazis.

These errors derive from the weakness of the very structure of the party. More than ninety percent of its members are unemployed; more than half of them lost their jobs within the past year. Its internal regime is a bureaucratic dictatorship without any control by the rank and file. It is committed to a policy of adventurism, which makes the workers in the business enterprises quite nervous. It makes life impossible for its conscientious members, forced to keep their true thoughts secret. It hinders the serious education of its most recent members, often recruited by accident.

> Such a party is in a position to spread sentiments of revolt but not to set the revolution as a task.

And yet its impotence does not reflect the impotence of the German proletariat, simply because this party

> is not the organization of German workers determined to transform the regime . . . it constitutes an organization of propaganda in the hands of the bureaucracy of the Russian state.

And the interests of German workers do not coincide with those of such a bureaucracy. For the workers, it is vital to stop fascist or military reaction; for the Russian state, whatever regime prevails in Germany, the essential thing is to hinder any Franco-German bloc against Russia. A revolution which opened future prospects for German workers would constitute a dangerous competition for Soviet heavy industry; a serious revolutionary movement would give notable support to the struggle of the Russian opposition against its bureaucratic dictatorship.

The National Socialist movement (not party, according to the astute definition of its leaders) is the strongest by far. Why? Because it takes advantage of the weakness of "those who blindly desire something different," using a revolutionary, amorphous mass of men who are both non-conscientious and irresponsible. On the other side, it takes advantage of the fear and the greed of the grand bourgeoisie and turns that amorphous mass into armed bands against Communism. It attracts all those who feel the weight of the regime without being able to count upon themselves to transform it. It gives the illusion of force through violence; it gives the

illusion of order through defending the family, private property and religion; it gives the illusion of protection with its promise of dignified comfort for all. Its fundamental character is inconsistency. Since it is the "reflection of the very inconsistency of the German people in their present
circumstances," its language is understandable to all those desperate men
who flock to National Socialism: intellectuals, the petite bourgeoisie of
the city and the country, almost all farm laborers, the majority of the unemployed in the cities, among whom there are many adolescents.

To the romantic young it offers the mirage of noble deeds, to the brutish
the implied promise of beatings and killings. It promises high prices to the
farmer, low prices to the consumer. In its substance, it is nationalist fanaticism rooted in a feeling which the Germans have experienced, whether
they are right or wrong: the certainty that the capitalism of the victorious
Allies is crushing them much worse than German capitalism. This embit-
tered nationalism has seized the petite bourgeoisie in particular;

> sometimes their women become almost hysterical against conscien-
> tious workers.

Nazi workers make fun of the illusion of international solidarity cham-
pioned by Communists, with whom they hold frequent and almost
friendly discussions. Overwhelmed by their hatred of the "system," they
believe that they are more sincerely revolutionary than the Communists
themselves; they will surpass them in their revolution, insofar as they will
no longer be proletarian. Hitler attracts them with a vision of an "idyllic
regime," which will make them independent with the possession of their
own piece of land and secure under the protection of an "omnipotent and
thoughtfully paternal state." They do not concern themselves with an economic program.

They have entrusted everything to the man they call "the leader." Hitler
has given them the illusion of force as he has the intellectuals and the petite
bourgeoisie. It is a force that overflows, in its tawdriness, in the parades in
uniform, the assassinations, the planes used for propaganda;

> and all these weak people flock towards force like moths towards the
> flame.[5]

The force they cling to is, in reality, the force of great wealth, which,
through Hitler, is using them for the sole purpose of bringing the revolutionary movement to its destruction.

As we have seen, the other two parties which promise a Socialist revolution are bound to powers at least extraneous to the German working class, which then stands there "with bare hands," or worse, since

The instruments it has fashioned and believes that it holds in its hands are in reality managed by others.

The principal source of weakness for the revolutionary movement is an ignorance, "shameful for materialists who claim to descend from Marx," of economic phenomena. This ignorance is common to all, capitalists, parties, and unions, which are not in the least position to foresee the developments of the economic situation. The turn of the economic circumstances of the world, overcoming the Depression, is one of the three unknown factors which could avoid the violent imposition of fascism. The other two are the outcome of diplomatic efforts with France, which could satisfy the nationalism of the petite bourgeoisie, and the determination of the German workers.

In them Simone discovers what will always be her one source of confidence, the values of the individual:

It is impossible to despair of the German workers, once one comes to know them.

After years of unemployment and of misery, there are few thieves and murderers among them. They have remained, to a great extent, outside the Nazi movement. Nationalist propaganda has had little hold on them. In the situation in which they find themselves, one in which there is no exit, they are conscious of their tragic lot but they do not allow themselves to be crushed by it. They do not seek to dull their senses, but have preserved "their dignity as human beings with a sound life and an elevated culture." They always manage to save a little money for their sports organizations, for their trips with boys and girls to the lakes and forests; they take bread from their mouths to buy books. They spontaneously create circles for "writing and discussion."

Their passiveness is due to their repugnance to involvement in adventures; it is then "a sign of courage, not of desperation." Simone looks forward, with a secret hope, to the moment when this treasure of a true workers' force will find a way to show itself in a spontaneous uprising, like that of Paris in 1871, like that of St. Petersburg in 1905, perhaps even more moving:

But who can say if such a struggle will end in a disaster like those that have crushed spontaneous uprisings up to now?[6]

La Révolution Prolétarienne omitted this last anguished question, which concluded the article "L'Allemagne en attente." Simone was angry over it.

If that groan expressed the only hope that Simone had been able to draw from her human contacts, it did not have to be a rhetorical hope. From the daily news she had been able to fashion a story that was not an ideological mask for reality but an inquiry into the objective elucidation of facts. It was objective, but not cold. Impersonal, but at the same time participatory, it sought to use reason to hamper the fraudulent devices of a policy more or less intentionally in the dark about the real causes of events.

> I want to strip away all pretence and finally learn to pose the problems with honesty.[7]

This desire is at the center of her subsequent actions.

═══════

At home, when Simone returned from Germany, she wept.[8] It was at this time that Jean Duperray met her for the first time. He had been in Germany, too, and the thin girl in a long blue skirt was at first eager to know what his impressions had been; then she began to tear them apart with her insistent questions. She was visibly disappointed by their banality. Duperray found himself with scraps of his "anecdotal trash" in his hands. "Alas, what a difference between the two ways we saw Germany. I only succeeded in acquiring some clichés on the "coming revolution."[9]

What she wanted above all else was action to renew socialism. And that meant being at the side of the working class in an effective way. She went from the National Union of Teachers to the Unified Federation of Instruction, which "maintained its revolutionary tradition, . . . the spirit of independence thanks to which it alone opposes the Stalinists, and . . . the level of theory." At Auxerre she found that she was automatically a member of MOR,[10] a union loyal to the Communist party. She wrote to Thévenon, "I have entered waving the banner of opposition" in an attempt to open their eyes to the Communist International.

> The principal goal to pursue is once again that of agreement, for an objective reflection in common.

It is the moment for everyone to come to terms: members of unions, Communists, those in opposition, and even sincere orthodox believers in the ranks . . . It is the moment above all—and above all for the young—to commit themselves to a serious revision of all ideas.[11]

At the beginning, her relations with the union and with the Communist cell were good (the cell asked her to give courses on Marx), although Simone did not miss any chance to criticize the Communist International; but before long, her articles on Germany provoked violent objections.

The first appeared in *Le Travailleur de l'Enseignement* of February, 1933. The protest went as follows: "While our brothers in Germany are striving with superhuman effort to align the German proletariat against Fascism and are falling by the dozens in the front lines . . . our direction finds it the proper time to insert in the *École émancipée* a series of articles by Mlle. Simone Weil, in which the action of the German Communist Party is odiously distorted."[12]

On March 19, it was the turn of two normalists, J. Daudin and P. Lussiaa-Berdou: they wanted to protest insofar as they were students of the same school as Simone. *L'École émancipée,* with a gesture of impartiality, published the article. "We consider that excessive space has been devoted by our journal to an article of mere impressions . . . among diverse omissions and inexactitudes . . . it tends to justify the most cowardly sense of panic. Among the petite bourgeoisie there are some men who have been demoralized by the provisional success of Hitler."[13]

Finally, on April 30 (it should be noted that on March 23, 1933, the Reichstag had granted Hitler full powers and had been adjourned sine die), the MOR, in the name of the "confederated majority of the Union of Hérault," published an article entitled, "On the situation in Germany, a few words of correction." It opened like this, "Finally, the grand, the very grand analysis of S. Weil on Germany has been concluded: it is grand in its number of pages, grand for the rage of destruction it breathes, grand for the accumulation of errors and lies, grand for the pretense of the author to suppress, with her crushing report, the Communist International through its German section, grand finally for the sadistic pleasure of the author in burying for good the organizations of revolution." After a series of general affirmations, which took the place of a point-by-point discussion of the facts, the article concluded: "This is not the time for defeatist reports, but for action."[14]

This time Simone replied, observing that despite the charge that there was an accumulation of errors and lies, the MOR had not shown the slightest inaccuracy in the articles it intended to refute. Comrades interested in knowing the truth, she hoped,

> will understand fully the mortal danger in which the revolutionary movement is involved because it is in the hands of men who prefer to base their thoughts and their actions upon myths rather than a clear vision of reality or believe that not all truths should be spoken . . . Today, in all important questions, the labor movement is utterly abandoned to illusion and lies . . . The best organized, most powerful and advanced proletariat of the world, that of Germany, has capitulated without resistance . . . The importance of such a disaster reaches far beyond the frontiers of Germany.[15]

History has certainly shown us to what degree the drama of Germany influenced the whole world. What Simone had noticed was the failure not only of organizations but of revolutionary theories.

An inability to learn from the two earlier experiences, the Commune of 1871 and the October Revolution of 1917—the first suppressed in blood, the second eventually reinforcing the military and bureaucratic machines—"demonstrates the insufficiency of revolutionary thought." For herself, Simone comes to this decision:

> For some time I have believed that, since it is impossible to take a position outside the fray, I will always share the misfortunes of the workers and not the victory of the oppressors, even where the issue is one of sure defeat. But when it comes to closing my eyes out of fear of weakening belief in victory, I do not want to do that for anything.[16]

9
The Heretic

She conducted her action securely and openly in two directions: aid to the German refugees and support for the dissident Communist minorities.

After Hitler came to power, many Germans opposed to Nazism chose exile to avoid prison, concentration camps, torture, and possibly death. There was an exodus of republicans, people of the left, syndicalists and Jews. Simone sought to help especially those who, not belonging to either of the two Internationals, received assistance of no kind. The USSR had shut its doors to safeguard its foreign policy interests, which were leading to a rapprochement with Germany. Simone's help was tangible in many ways: statements on behalf of the refugees before congresses, sums of money, assistance in looking for positions of employment and, first of all, hospitality in her own house, always joined in this by her parents.

Her support of the dissident Communist minorities, which often coincided with her aid to German refugees, expresses the maturing of her political vision.

Her principal goal was uniting all revolutionaries who were disposed to "honestly" critical thought, that is independent, and helping them overcome their respective divisions. Of the three actions the laboring class should conduct at the same time, "struggle, thought, construction,"[1] Simone held that the first was possible only to a slight degree, the third for the moment impossible. There remained thought: an action carried out so as not to be blind any longer. "Revolution is a *task*"[2] and if men are blind they cannot prepare for it.

The problem Simone set at this time was what kind of organization to create?

> an organization that does not generate a bureaucracy. For a bureaucracy *always* betrays.

On the other side,

> unorganized action remains pure but fails.[3]

She continued to proceed more deeply into her special area of inquiry: the character of the proper group, larger than the individual person, but providing ample space for personal action and allowing cooperation with other individuals without indulging in prevarications.

Simone made a significant appearance, supporting the creativity of the minorities, at the so-called *Conférence d'unification* in the spring of 1933. This was a small meeting, the initiative for which was due to a small Communist group separated from the party, "the autonomous group of the banlieue Ouest." It had invited not only similar groups but also individuals, among whom was Simone.

At the first session, the spokesmen of the Trotskyite delegation asked for the immediate expulsion of those participants who held that Russia was not any longer a true workers' state, that there had to be a rupture with the Third International directed by Moscow, and that there should be preparations undertaken to found a Fourth International. Simone was among these opponents. When they did not obtain their expulsion, the Trotskyites withdrew.

In the conduct of the meetings, two tendencies became clear: the partisans of a break with the Third International and others less distant from the Trotskyites, who had the following slogan, "Let us correct the Third International."

The meetings took place at the Café Augé in rue des Archives. In both the first and second sessions, Simone held that the events in Germany required a revision of all theories and that thinking of a "historical mission of the proletariat"[4] meant clinging to a senseless mythology. Some people felt profoundly injured by this denial of their dogmas and their hopes.

The second meeting, on April 9, 1933, ended with a schism. On April 22, Simone, Patri, Rabaut, Treint, and others held a conversation, at the end of which they signed a declaration written by Simone. "She drafted it, with the comment that only in that way was she sure to be in agreement with the text."[5]

The document wanted to express the common attitude which several comrades had reached at the end of a course of reflection "pursued independently by each of them." Since they could not regard the present Rus-

sian state as a "state of the workers directed towards Socialist emancipation," but rather saw the bureaucracy working "towards a constant
increase in the power of the state, they believed that their duty as conscious militants was to break morally with the Third International. This
was intended to prepare a "new type of revolutionary organization on the
national and international level," which would assemble conscious revolutionaries "outside any relationship with the bureaucracy of the Russian
state."[6]

Even if the Fourth International was not named in particular, it was
prophesied in a clear way, as an end towards which to direct political activity. This idea circulated from the last months of 1932 in various little
groups of young revolutionaries and also among militants in charge of the
FUE.[7]

Simone found herself in agreement with all of them but the sentiment
that was becoming dominant in her and that would slowly bring her to
break with syndical organizations and even with small groups was her
certainty that she would express ideas "which were heretical in respect to
all orthodoxies."[8]

The impossibility of an understanding was made clearer and clearer
both in practice and in theory.

In September, 1933, at the Congress of the CGTU, the union most
closely associated with the Communist Party, the minorities were subjected to a hatred "that reached paroxysms of rage . . . Comrade Simone
Weil, who was supposed to intervene on German events, was not able to
speak."[9] An even more serious matter was that she was at first officially
forbidden and then forcibly prevented from distributing, along with her
comrade Charbit, leaflets with an appeal for contributions to the committee for the relief of imprisoned German workers and their families.

Her article, "Perspectives," where her heretical ideas flow into her
urgent social analysis of

> this current, novel age of ours . . . in which it seems that only the
> body has life and that the mind continues to move in a world that
> disappeared with the war[10]

was opposed by violent criticism.

It seems that she wrote it in only one day, from the morning until late that
night, without interruption and without touching any food. With the

subtitle, "Allons-nous vers la révolution prolétarienne?," the article appeared in the August 25, 1933, issue of *Révolution Prolétarienne*. It consists of a synthesis of her reflections upon the failure of the Russian Revolution as the liberation of the proletariat. It is dictated by her desire to achieve an objective analysis of the world situation, to ascertain the real possibilities of a successful socialist revolution.

The mythical vision, simplistic and in some instances intentionally distorted, of those militants shaped by Bolshevism uses the term *class warfare* both for the evolution of capitalism in the economy and in its productive technology and for resistance to it. And class warfare is seen superficially as a duel or game between two conscious players; in this duel, every event, whether social or political, is only a *maneuver* of one or the other player. An orthodoxy, both prejudicial and dogmatic, is prevalent according to which

> presently there can only exist two types of state, the capitalist and the workers'.

Taking as her basis, instead, the facts of the present age, slothfully defined as one of transition, Simone tries to clarify the two phenomena of contemporary society that are entirely new and difficult to analyze, insofar as they do not have a role in the schemes of classical Marxism: the actual Russian regime and Fascism.

To avoid having to reflect upon them, the two phenomena are catalogued in a hasty manner. The regime of Stalin is defined by Trotsky as "the workers' state with bureaucratic abnormalities"; on Fascism there is the commonplace that it is "the last card in the hand of the bourgeoisie before the triumph of the revolution."

In reality, the regime of Stalin, except for its exclusion of capitalist property, is as repressive a regime as any other; what makes it run are not the democratic organizations of the working class, but

> exclusively the pieces of a centralized administration from which the entire economic, political and intellectual life of the country depends.

And Fascism is actually a mass movement which the great financiers, the powerful industrialists, and the reactionary politicians are in no position to create, hinder or direct. It has established a political regime quite similar to the Russian regime in Tomsky's definition, "One party in power and everyone else in prison." It tends to resemble the Russian regime also on the economic level. It wants to concentrate all economic and political power in the hands of the head of state. It is a state apparatus which must centralize everything. Other movements of the postwar period tend in the same direction, as for example the group of technocrats around Roosevelt which calls for an economic dictatorship run exclusively by technicians.

In establishing the existence of these novel tendencies, Simone states that the supposed guiding principle of our time,

> the idea of a society directed . . . by the cooperation of workers, does not practically guide any more mass movements, whether spontaneous or organized.

Since this happens at a time when everyone is speaking of the failure of capitalism, it would be well to look society in the face and ask what the true successor of capitalism will necessarily be. Perhaps we shall be present at the establishment of a new oppression, "oppression exercised in the name of function."

Today, the decisive moment of enslavement does not occur when the worker sells his own time to the owner but when, "once he has crossed the threshold of the factory, he is devoured by the enterprise."

To the discrimination created by money between the buyers and sellers of labor power has been added another discrimination in the orbit of labor itself, created by the very means of production: *the machine.*

The machine has become an "insurmountable barrier" between *passive performers,* the manual laborers who specialize in the use of one type of machine, and *inactive guides,* the operators who set out the machines necessary to a given task. The *rationalization of labor* has caused almost the complete disappearance of skilled workers, those who understand and use the machine with the same intelligence and initiative as craftsmen.

In the management of factories, the development of joint-stock companies has created another barrier, even if it is not as clear, between the owner and the director of the enterprise. In this way the administrators, who at the time of Marx were employees in the service of the capitalist captain of industry, have become ever more numerous and indispensable in their role as "technicians of direction."

This establishment of bureaucracy in industry is the most characteristic aspect of a general phenomenon: *the accentuation of specialization.* In almost every field, the individual finds himself confined within the limits of restricted competence and engulfed in an aggregate that submerges him.

> The rationalized factory, in which a man is deprived of whatever is initiative, intelligence, knowledge or method for the benefit of an inert mechanism, is a kind of picture of present-day society.

Given the evolution of the productive system in the sense of a ruthless subdivision of tasks, *coordination* becomes the most important function. Since, throughout history, the power of one class over others depends on the difference of efficiency between a dominant social function and one or more subordinate functions, we can expect only one thing: *the dictatorship of a bureaucratic caste.* During the primitive phase of production, the necessity of defending the fields with armed force created feudal power; with economic transformations, it was discovered that power depended on production; in this way, the capitalist regime arose. With the evolution of such a regime, war returned as the essential means in the struggle for power. Military power presupposes superiority in production. If, in the hands of capitalists, power has as its goal the game of competition, in the hands of organized technicians of a bureaucracy of state, it would necessarily have as its end the preparation for war.

Simone foresees "the moral atmosphere" of a similar regime. In the name of a

> religion of the state which would choke all individual values or all true values,

the bureaucratic machine, which excludes all geniality and all capacity for judgment, would look for a structure of total domination. It would eliminate every manifestation of inventiveness and free examination and, in so doing, destroy "what is precious and still survives in the bourgeois regime." What would we have? An official opinion from which it would be forbidden to depart, a carefully developed fanaticism to change misery from an unwelcome burden to an accepted sacrifice, a mixture of mystical devotion and bestiality without limit.

What prospects lie before us? The present Russian regime, clearly, is not a stage on the way to socialism. As for capitalism in other countries, will it be able to perish without passing through expropriation but simply by transforming the sense of property? Here, the facts give a less clear response.

Still, in the face of a similar evolution, the worst "calamity" would be for us to forget the goal that we set for ourselves; it is a calamity that has already "ruined many comrades . . . and menaces all of us."

Simone persists in the direction she had taken since her first essays on work, her first articles on workers' culture, her courses on the history of the sciences. We shall see the same motif in her *"grand œuvre," Oppression et Liberté,* in the remarks of the *Cahiers* and, finally, in her project for a society based on different prospects, in *L'Enracinement.*

> Let us not forget that we want to place the individual and not the collectivity as our supreme value. We want to make men complete by suppressing this specialization which maims everyone.

In what way?

In vain will we look for an answer in Marxist literature. Simone lists the reasons for despair. The capacity for free judgment is becoming rarer and rarer, especially in intellectual circles; specialization compels everyone, in the fundamental questions asked in every theoretical inquiry, to believe without real knowledge. In the field of pure theory, individual judgment declines in the face of results achieved by joint effort. As far as the working class is concerned, its condition as a passive instrument in the hands of production has surely not made it capable of taking its own fate in its hands. Present-day generations, first decimated and demoralized by the war, have been further damaged by peace and prosperity in two ways: on the one side, luxury and the fever of speculation have profoundly corrupted all levels of society and on the other, technical changes have taken away from the laboring class their principal source of power: skilled workers. Finally, unemployment has lasted so long that it has become habitual and, where it is more extensive, it has reduced the proletariat to considering itself a parasitic class.

Will organizations be able to give the proletariat the force it is lacking? Simone again poses the same question she had asked in her letters to her friends the Thévenons, a question that has become more urgent since her trip to Germany. The answer seems difficult, because spontaneous struggle has always shown itself powerless, while organized action automatically secretes a directive structure which sooner or later becomes oppressive.

Today, aggression comes from ties with the apparatus of states, national and Russian.

Militants cannot substitute for the working class. The emancipation of workers will be the achievement of the workers themselves or it will not happen. The most tragic fact of our era is that the Depression falls more pervasively upon the proletariat than upon the capitalist class, for which reason it appears not as . . . the crisis of a regime but as the crisis of our entire society.

Simone foresees that she will be accused of defeatism. This, in fact, would happen.

But the problem was no longer that of preserving religiously for socialism what Simone calls the vocabulary of the High Command. The only question to ask was: "Should we continue to struggle or not?"

Simone's reply was in the affirmative. But we should continue the struggle with our eyes open. We should preserve intact on the plane of action precisely that hope which upon critical examination has been shown to have the slightest foundations.

This is the very essence of courage.[11]

There are two reasons for hope. The first rests on "the mere fact that we exist, that we conceive and will something different." The second is that we can still trust in workers of value, rich in that vitality of mind and soul that is the treasure of the proletariat. In our period of expectation we should help them to educate themselves and to think, to assume an influence in the workers' organizations that still remain intact in France: the unions.

"A brilliant article! There have been none like it since Rosa Luxemburg." This is what Marcel Martinet told Urbain Thévenon. Boris Souvarine, who considered Simone "the only brain in the workers' movement for years,"[12] saw in "Perspectives" a proof of his judgment. Except for these two, among the very few eulogies full of enthusiasm, the criticism of the article was harsh and especially charged with a violence that obscured comprehension.

With the title "What is all this pessimism?," Roger Hagnauer wrote: "Simone Weil views the world from above . . . her attitude reminds one of Pascal's story of the 'thinking reed.' What is there in common between such an elevated intellectual resignation and our revolutionary syndicalism?

"Would that adventurous intellectuals, of generous inspiration and doctrinal strength, cease thinking about the weakness of the proletariat! They should rather assure themselves that they do not have the ability to direct it."[13]

A similar critique, which for the rest only repeats earlier criticism of her articles on Germany, shows a completely mistaken comprehension of Simone's ideas. The error rests, on the one hand, on an ignorance of Simone's life and, on the other, on an understanding of politics as ideology to impose by means of particular tactics upon the social group we wish to lead forward. This is the most banal conception of politics, as different from Simone's as a silhouette is from a fully rounded sculpture. With every article, every letter, every discourse and lecture, Simone was intensifying politics as the intelligent reflection on reality, to the end of searching for the greatest possible balance on the earth. This will be the theme of *L'Enracinement*. In the meanwhile, she continued giving her comrades her lucid and sad reflections, completely free of the blur of opinion, clear of the complacency of illusion, and untouched by the concerns of personal ambition.

She had never wanted to please anyone, not even her favorites in the name of justice, the workers, the miners. She had always wanted to involve herself in manual labor to understand their experiences from the very foundation, just as she had wanted "to raise them in their own eyes,"[14] so that they would walk alone and alone take up their life. Simone combined an absolute independence of judgment, linked with her rebellious nature and nurtured by Alain, with the practical good sense of a woman, ready to determine the source, the development and the harmful results that derive from blind and unconscious activity. She will write in her *Cahiers:*

My essential idea of 1934: it is not the end that matters but the implicit consequences of the mechanism of means we put into operation.[15]

And yet, she was considered abstract, intoxicated with intellectualism, a defeatist, corroded with deluded ambitious desires. This, because the concrete reality of "political syndicalism" in the eyes of Hagnauer and the majority was the ability to lead the working class with a type of calculation unknown to Simone. With the honesty of her true scientific analysis, she studied the facts in their interrelationship and their capillary influences upon the daily life of men; she was considered abstract because she did not galvanize men to senseless action.

Even Trotsky was coarse in his reaction. He declared that the opposition of the left, the Trotskyites, did not have to wait for Simone Weil, Souvarine and their comrades to discover the insidious damages of bureaucratization. He added in a note: "Despairing of the unhappy 'experiences' of the dictatorship of the proletariat, Simone Weil has taken comfort in a new mission: defending her own personality from society. A formula of old liberalism, refreshed by the cheap exaltation of anarchism . . . the most reactionary prejudices of the petite bourgeoisie."[16]

Here the charge against Simone is complacent solipsism; her loyalty to the ego is misunderstood. She proceeded from the nucleus of her own personality and the deep respect that is due it, to regard as sacred the respect due to everyone else. Quite properly Aimé Patri has said of her: "I do not believe that any other human being has carried as far the respect for the higher side of oneself."[17] It is on this side that one must place one's reliance, since, in all circumstances,

> being a man means to separate the *ego* from the *me*, a task that must be pursued incessantly.[18]

These are Simone's words to her students.

Nothing can exempt you from directing all of your faculties towards conscious thought. Nothing, not even the impulse of the most justified generosity. And much less such things as ambition, calculation, human respect for men or ideas. For this reason, the Dutch independent socialist, Jacques de Kadt, who took part in a secret meeting of the Trotskyites at the Weil home, found Simone's articles strong with a particular sort of effectiveness. It was the effectiveness of intelligence linked with a "moral courage that does not stop in the face of conventions and sometimes even dares to accept conventions which are generally condemned, when they seem just to her. And above all else, a moral purity and disinterest carried to the highest pitch of elevation."[19] And yet de Kadt declared at the same time that he did not at all share Simone's ideas, which were drawing ever closer to Gandhi's. The nonviolent editors of the Dutch monthly, *Liberation*,[20] published a translation of her articles in the form of a booklet. They had quickly discerned her detachment from every separatist scheme and from all factionalism.

And from all personal rancor. The harsh criticism of Trotsky amused, rather than upset her. She was only afraid that she would now not get to meet him, as she had desired for a time. In October, 1933, she wrote her mother:

Daddy[21] has done me the honor of firing at me, with an abundance of insults . . . 'vulgar liberalism,' 'cheap exaltation of anarchism,' 'the most reactionary prejudices of the petite bourgeoisie,' etc. Common conduct. The only thing is, alas! I no longer have any hope of seeing him.[22]

Ready as she always was to help even those with whom she did not agree, if they were persecuted, she begged her parents to offer their hospitality to Trotsky, who was living under surveillance at Barbizon, for a clandestine meeting. "Doctor Bernard Weil did not concern himself with politics. He limited himself to accommodating the wishes of his daughter Simone."[23] The meeting was set for December 31, 1933, in the second apartment of the Weils, on the seventh floor of rue Auguste Comte, 3 (they lived on the sixth floor). Lev Davidovich, unrecognizable without his moustache and goatee, his thick hair brushed flat with brilliantine, visited with his wife Natalia from December 29–30,[24] so that Simone had a long conversation with him. It soon became an argument, punctuated with shouts by Trotsky. (Simone was always very composed in her conversations.)[25] She recorded it immediately afterwards. These notes contain, above all, the phrases of Trotsky, who, disconcerted by the many doubts and reproofs of his interlocutor, concluded by saying, "But why did you welcome us, if this is the way you think? Do you perhaps belong to the Salvation Army?"[26]

She would accept the point of view of others and listen to them but she would at the same time remain detached from everyone on the plane of objectivity. Ever since the period of Le Puy, at the center of her most euphoric activity, she remained a spectator of the game of politics, as though it were all a matter of moving pawns. On November 9, 1931, she wrote her parents:

Now that the preparatory work for the intersyndical meeting of the day after tomorrow is finished, I am beginning to breathe more easily. I do not know if anything will come of it. At this point all I am doing is watching, as if it were a spectacle, and my only reaction is curiosity.[27]

And again, in the following May:

> I am under full sail in the sciences (for the logic of the sciences), and
> with joy. Politics is completely forgotten.[28]

"To eliminate every doubt about her sense of humor, you had to hear
her tell about her meeting with Trotsky, to hear her describe syndical meetings. You would die of laughter," says André.[29]

Her most deeply felt involvement was with the real sufferings of individual lives, overwhelmed by persecution and intolerance. In February of
1934, she heard the awful news that four young men of the SAP[30] had
been turned over by Holland to the Nazis; she begged her mother to send
her *immediately* the names of the young men.

> Until then I shall live in mortal anguish, so as not to lose the habit
> . . . I would set fire to the Dutch embassy in Paris.[31]

She was most severe in her judgment of the person who forgot about
the individual, erased him, exploited him for political ends. So she harshly
scolded Jakob W., a leader of the German SAP, who had been a metal-
lurgical worker. Living in the Weil household like a prince, he was a jolly
bird of no scruples; he behaved quite bluntly. Selma Weil even darned his
socks, and his girlfriend would find fault with the darning. Jakob intended
to send back to Germany a twenty-year-old man who was also living with
the Weils, Emil. He had been tried in absentia and been found guilty of a
capital charge. If he returned home, he would meet certain death. Simone
opposed Jakob violently and then gave Emil the money necessary to go to
Scandinavia.

She did not want martyrs; at a meeting of a group which included
German political refugees and French militants, someone remarked: "German parties are the best because they have had martyrs." Simone replied
that martyrs are not the justification of a party and probably some parties
intended to have as many martyrs as possible for propaganda purposes.[32]

═══════════

How and why should we want a revolution? At Le Puy, Simone had asked
herself, "What are the conditions for a truly effective revolution?" And she
had begun studying the real motives and the profound cause of the inferiority and the oppression which conditioned the working class. Then,
after her visit to Germany, she saw the increasing weight that the bureau-

cracy, national, international or syndical, was exerting in connection with her idea of the state as a machine; so she asked herself, "How can we form a workers' organization that will not generate a bureaucracy?" At the end of "Perspectives," without indulging in illusions, but as a last hope, she proposed action inspired by the confluence of investigations and groupings of single individuals. This is what nourished her attraction for the small opposition groups, independent in their questioning; but even these she approached from the side; she was always alone. In her flight from the *seductive accord* she could not become a full member.

We find a synthesis of this attitude of hers, which is also an action, in her relations with the *Cercle communiste démocratique,* presided over by Boris Souvarine.[33] There she met Georges Bataille. On the contrast between their totally diverse conceptions of revolution, we may pose the question, "What is the meaning of a revolution?", a question that coincides with the last phase of Simone's "political" life.

In a torn and tattered letter to the *Cercle,* Simone explained why she could not become a member, as Bataille had invited her to do; and she advised them to dissolve such a *Cercle,*

> a psychological phenomenon, composed of mutual friendships, of obscure affinities, and especially of unclarified inhibitions and contradictions between the various members and within each of the members.

Why?

> When the question of action is taken up, the presentation of real problems will quickly lead to its dissolution.

For Bataille, "the revolution is the triumph of the irrational"; for Simone, it is the triumph of the "rational." What for him is a "catastrophe," for Simone is "a methodical action for which we should strive in every way to mitigate the damage." While for him the revolution is a "liberation of the instincts, especially those considered currently to be pathological," for Simone it means the need for "a superior morality."[34]

The dissolution of the *Cercle* would not imply an absolute rupture; it would rather find its meaning in occasional meetings dictated by a concrete common goal, to which each one would bring the results of his own time of solitude and silence.

It is again the question of the shaping of the individual, a shaping that excludes narcissism and every sort of mutual complacency. There is a text, intended for Souvarine's review, *La Critique Sociale,* in which Simone examines *La Condition Humaine* of Malraux; opposing the type of praise Bataille had given it,[35] she warns us of the grave danger posed by revolution as a flight from ourselves.

Here Simone disapproves of revolution as a sublimation or a compensation.

If it is a matter of flight from ourselves, it is simpler to gamble or to drink. Or even simpler to die.

It is self-hatred, self-destruction.

Like every form of *'divertissement'* revolutionary action of this type is a masked form of suicide.

Revolution demands love for life. It has no value except as a *means* of struggle against everything that "hinders" life. In a general sense,

Nothing has value when human life does not have it.[36]

Therefore: no to revolution as blind heroism or useless bloodbath; no to revolution engineered by the powerful for their own ends; no to revolution as a drug.

This signifies for her the progressive withdrawal from every type of militancy.

Around March 20, 1934, she wrote to her friend Pétrement:

I have decided to withdraw from every kind of politics, except for theoretical research. This does not absolutely exclude my eventual participation in a great mass movement (in the ranks, as a soldier), but I do not want any responsibility, no matter how indirect, no matter how slight, because I am sure that all the blood which will be shed will be shed in vain and that we are beaten in advance.[37]

Her profound affirmation now turned to the daily adventure in the heart of reality: work in a factory.

10

The Completion of the Design

... my dream for about ten years. Perhaps you can understand what I anticipate from a similar experience ... It's hard to explain in a letter. This I can say: only thinking about it brings me great joy.[1]

These are Simone's words to Marcel Martinet, in July of 1935, when she was twenty-five years old.

It was during this summer that she decided to request a leave "for personal study-goals," so as not to risk putting off further, perhaps forever, the essential project of her life, to defeat the menace of her precarious health and to overcome the dead point where her researches on contemporary society had settled. From these months, too, must date her decision to kill herself if she did not stand the test.[2] The reasons for her leave request, dated June 20, 1934, are these:

It is my desire to prepare a philosophy thesis on the relation between modern technology, which is the foundation of our great industries, and the essential aspects of our civilization: on the one hand, our social organization and, on the other, our culture.[3]

On Tuesday, December 4, 1934, Simone Weil was taken on as a hand at the presses by the Société de Constructions électriques et mécaniques Alsthom. Her position had been obtained for her by her great friend Boris Souvarine, who knew Auguste Detoeuf, an administrative delegate of the company.[4]

"She was so little and thin. She had the air of a Catholic schoolteacher, with her cape and beret. At work she wore a white blouse, while the other workwomen wore either pink or blue. She had an eager, intrusive curiosity. She had poor eyesight, so she leaned over the machines until she grazed them with her hair. She wanted to know everything. At first we did not trust her; we thought she was a spy. Then we all adopted her. She was interested in everything, the births of babies, accidents. Above all, she was a woman, full of feeling. She was pretty, too, yes, pretty! The only thing was that she could not think of marriage, with that ascetic sense of hers of loving life to the limit, as she did."[5] These are the words of Jacques Redon (the Jacquot of *La Condition Ouvrière*), whom Simone describes several times in her *Journal d'usine* as a calm, understanding man, ready to give instruction with kindness. He had the post of foreman (*régleur*); he had to deal with assigning the machines and tools necessary for the individual workers and then he had to follow their progress.

Simone had wanted to enter a factory because she felt that only direct knowledge of that life, as an experience of her own, would allow her to "enter intimately into the relations between workers and their work."[6] So writes Albertine Thévenon, who had been harsh in discussing this decision with her. She saw Simone as ill-equipped, awkward and thought that it would be impossible for her to get what she wanted. "A worker's situation is not a matter of choice, it is a matter of fact, with an influence upon one's attitude, upon one's way of perceiving life. I thought that her experience would be inevitably falsified because of her poor health, too. The worker does not know how to express the consciousness of what she is doing; in fact, she does not even have such a consciousness. Simone did stop to listen and my words even made her suffer, but she continued right along her path; she was sure of herself."[7]

She knew that she had been given the duty of becoming the conscience and voice of the moments of weariness, fear, meanness, suffering, deafness, joy, solidarity which composed that life. She achieved this through the pages of her *Journal d'usine*. Here she recounts to the minute the exhausting hours and the pitiful wages of work by the piece ("and she does not miss a count!" says Redon); here she records her physical reactions and her rapid perceptions of others, encountered for a second and forever. The *Journal* is both lean and emotional. Brief moments of meditative synthesis alternate with her narrative, which, in its dryness, is never arid because tenderness, the light of intellect, the love of life and her sense of humor are incessantly twinkling from an adjective, a little scene, a comment on the season. In some of her letters her meditation becomes ample; in the pages of the *Cahiers*, it is shaped into thoughts of universal resonance.

═══════

She had rented a little room on the top floor of a building at 228 rue Lecourbe, XVème, quite close to her place of work. She wanted to live in complete independence; when she went to dinner with her parents, she would put on the table the amount of money she would have spent at the restaurant and she made her parents accept it. Beyond her frequent inability to eat because of headaches, which increased now because of her exhaustion and the noise of the machinery in the factory, and despite her desire to deprive herself to control her body, Simone really wanted to live within the amount she was making. Sometimes her wages barely reached the prescribed three francs. Then she would eat very little. "It was a much harder time then; one must eat a sandwich without interfering with one's work; she did not even eat that."[8] Sometimes she agreed to share it with the workers who had taken a liking to her, and that was all of them, even the redhead, Josephine, "carrot-haired," who was the most cantankerous of them all and never looked anyone in the face.

The only one who knew who she was was Mouquet, the head of the factory; he never told anyone. Mouquet was at times demanding in useless ways (he forced her to a dangerous task at the fly-press; he refused another woman worker, the Italian, the use of an easier machine); he was "just but capricious" in his evaluation of the piece-work. He would remain for Simone the most interesting of all the heads and bureaucrats she would know in her factory experience, not only at Alsthom, but later at Carnaud and Renault.

A sculptured, tormented head—like that of a monk—always tense— "I shall think about it tonight" (he would say this when confronted with a difficulty)—I have seen him happy only once.

Another fully developed figure—"he expresses himself quite well . . . he knows the machines"—is the storekeeper, Pommera.

Born in the country—one of twelve children—at nine, the keeper of cows . . . at twelve, graduated from elementary school . . . no other learning, either technical or general, except for what he has acquired for himself in evening classes.

A skilled worker: the only one Simone would meet who was happy to stay in the factory, excepting one other, the young man at the furnace, "the one who is always singing." Pommera gave her "luminous" advice. Between him and the operators, especially Léon, the most mediocre, there is a "notable distance." Léon gets angry, yells, is a little mean; he is at the center of avoidable dramas, caused by his anxiety and rage. He never explains anything. If Simone wants to see the design of the orders she is filling, he begins to rail at her. He does not trust her. He thinks that she wants to corner the best pieces. Robert, who had at first been a little sharp, becomes

courteous, attentive to making her understand the task. He is decidedly friendly. The importance of the human qualities of an operator.

Fellowship, solidarity are shown in a smile, a glance, which become precious. The fifth week: at the furnace. They had to install copper spools on trams.

The pain of the searing heat, the weariness and the pains in my head make me lose complete control of my movements.

Every time that my face contracts with pain, a welder . . . blue eyeglasses, serious face, gives me a sad smile, full of fraternal sympathy. It does me an incredible amount of good.[9]

Later, at Renault, when she is painfully transferring bolts with her hands in a box, a man, "a foreman of positive goodness," will watch her . . .

Never forget that man.

A fine experience is that of teamwork at welding.

The furnace. A completely different angle, even if it is next to our shop. The heads never come there. A free and fraternal atmosphere, without anything servile or mean. The lively young man who is the operator . . . the welder . . . the young Italian with blond hair . . . my "fiancé" . . . his brother . . . the Italian girl . . . the big young man with the hammer . . . Finally, a joyous place of work.

Later, after she is exhausted from having spent the whole day on her feet, she turns a tin box around in her hands and experiences a "great pleasure in thinking that her comrades have welded it." She will write to Albertine:

It was a unique experience in my life in the factory . . . I would return there at once, to that little work place, if I could (or at least, as soon as

I have recovered my strength). Those evenings I experienced the joy of eating bread I had earned.[10]

Despite her violent headaches, which sometimes force her to weep even in the course of the work itself (December 19), despite her toothache, which forces her to endure sessions with the dentist before coming to the factory, despite her eczema, on the Wednesday of the thirteenth week she writes:

> This evening, with my papers, a migraine. But at the same time I feel the sense of having physical resources. The noises of the factory, some of which now are full of meaning (the blow of the hammer of the metal-workers, the sledge-hammer) produce both a profound moral joy and a physical pain. A very strange impression.

Joy, for her, strikes in unison among human beings. It is the joy that comes from perfect equality. So it will happen on a Wednesday, a "divine day," when she finds herself, as she is looking for a new job, talking with two fitters:

> One is 18. One is 58, "very interesting, but very reserved. A man in every sense, to look at him. He lives alone (his wife has jilted him). A "secret vocation," photography . . . At his age, he says, he is disgusted with work (work in which, as a young man, he was passionately interested). But it is not a question of work in itself, it is a question of subordination . . . Even the young man is interesting. We pass by Saint-Cloud; he says: "If I were in shape (which he is not, unfortunately, because he has not been eating), I would make designs." . . . The young man asks me, "And you, what passion do you have?" Embarrassed, I reply, "Reading." "Yes, I understand. No romances. Rather philosophical stuff, right?" . . . Both of them have revolutionary tendencies (a very inadequate expression—no they have a class-consciousness and the spirit of free men) . . .
>
> Complete camaraderie. For the first time in my life, after all. No barrier, not in difference in class (which is here suppressed), not in difference in sex. Miraculous.

Yes, miraculous. In fact,

> disdain of men for women, reserve of women in the presence of men . . . are much more pronounced among workers than elsewhere.

Women. After a week of work, Simone writes to Urbain Thévenon that the women in the factory are unhappy and that there is "little or nothing" that can be done with them.

> Some are resigned to an impotent desire for revolt; and if they dream of anything, it is on the level of individual good fortune (winning a lottery, etc.).[11]

Their life as workers is more tiring, more humiliating and more degrading than that of men. Although the storekeeper has told her that there are specialized cutter positions for women, Simone has only seen women employed as hands. Those who have been in the factory for years have learned only from experience the snares of each machine (the dangers each machine presents of ruining the pieces). And they have to sharpen their wits, for, if they do not maintain their time and ruin too many pieces, they are the first to be fired. For this reason there is more competition among them than among the men and for this reason they are more harsh and more gloomy than the men.

> I know only three or four who are completely agreeable.

There are great inequalities among them. Those who have husbands and are working to attain a higher standard of living feel more secure and criticize the proud attitude of a tubercular worker, who has been fired for ruining too many pieces. They feel for her a mixture of "pity and 'it serves her right' of schoolgirls . . . 'When you have to earn your living, you have to behave as you should, period.'" In some factories they do not want women.

With the women, the men are coarse. Once, in search of a new job,

> the bird in charge of hiring . . . looked us all over as he would horses. "Her, the most robust." His way of questioning the young woman of twenty who three years earlier had had to stop working because she was pregnant . . .

What saves them is their vitality, their spontaneous earthiness; just like little girls.

> Eugénie interrupts her work to come over and tell me in all happiness that at the Versailles gate she has seen the wild animals of a circus (2 francs a ticket), and she had petted a leopard.

One day, in the dressing rooms,

> a beautiful girl, fresh, strong and healthy, exclaims, "We are fed up, after a day of ten hours! Long live the fourteenth of July and its dances." "After ten hours you can think of dancing?" She: "Sure. I would dance all night, etc." (laughing) Then, gravely, "It has been five years since I have danced. I really want to dance, even while I do the laundry."

On the other side, an old working woman

> who had gone to Russia in 1905 . . . "who was not bored when she was by herself, because she read in the evening" . . . she had a passion for Tolstoy ("ah, he really understood love").

It is the same woman, Eugénie, and Simone calls her "the admirer of Tolstoy."

The consciousness of weariness, the desire to escape so harsh a life are expressed through their children. Nénette, perhaps thirty-five, has a son of thirteen and a daughter of six-and-a-half. She is a widow.

> Her conversation consists almost exclusively of jokes and confidences that would make a guard-room blush. Extraordinary vivacity and vitality. A good worker . . . *But:* an immense respect for learning (she speaks of her son "who reads all the time") . . . She says of him, "The idea of sending him into the factory makes me feel, I don't know how to say it . . ." (and yet a superficial observer could believe that she is in the factory quite willingly).

One Tuesday, in the rain, Simone is looking for another job. A working woman speaks of her son of thirteen; she keeps him in school. "If he didn't go to school, what could he expect? A martyr's life, like ours."

Life is especially hard for women. Jacquot recalls: "I never spoke with them; they could not wait; they had to rush home to cook, to look after the children. So, I spoke little, even with Simone Weil."

> Louisette's friend had an abscess in her throat and was out for five days—then she is back. "The children, they never ask if you are not feeling well." She, although she is always happy, says that she is becoming nervous and cannot put up with the noise of children . . .

A little boy of nine comes to meet his mother. "Does he work, too?" "Would that he were old enough," the mother answers; she works at the drill. Her husband has just returned from the hospital . . . there is nothing to be done . . . there is also a little girl of ten months at home.

Eugénie has lost a son and "luckily" her first husband, who had suffered from tuberculosis for eight years. Simone will tell this story to her students at Bourges.

Consciousness surfaces, but in spurts. Mimi, twenty-six, has been married for eight years to a man who is now unemployed . . . she has spent six months acquiring a rhythm fast enough "to earn her living"; she has cried often, she believed that she would never make it. To a remark of Simone, exasperated because she does not understand what she is doing, she responds with this observation.

"They take us for machines . . . others must think for us . . ." (the same idea as Taylor's, but with bitterness).

Even the women take no pity on one another. "Simone Weil did not defend herself, she did not quarrel with her comrades; her language was so different from theirs. They played dirty tricks on her, like stealing the box where she was to put a certain number of pieces; but they did not do it on purpose, against her. That's the way work went." Jacquot tells this story. Simone, in her notes on the practical details of the factory, will observe that there are not enough boxes.

A collection for a pregnant worker provokes comments of irritation and disdain. "Carrot-haired" Josephine protests that she thinks it unfair that single workers and those with children are exempt from unpaid rest periods. But:

In this type of life, those who suffer cannot complain. They would not be understood by the others, perhaps they would be ridiculed by those who do not suffer, considered tiresome by those who, in their own suffering, have had enough suffering. Everywhere, the same harshness as on the part of the heads, with rare exceptions.

Simone observes the processes of the factory in all of their practical details. There is a great difference in temperature from one area to another.

At times, she finds herself so cold that work slows down. You pass from a machine installed in front of a furnace to another exposed to air currents. In the dressing rooms, "it is freezing."

Orders can be dangerous or impossible to execute, because they have no relation to the product requested. At times they differ from one operator to the next. Above all, there is an inability to understand the machine on the part of the operators themselves, for whom the slightest trouble is a drama. Simone investigates "the mysteries of the factory."

> First. The mystery of the machine; the worker has not done mathematics and the machine is a mystery for him, since he does not see in it a relation of forces and so he lacks a sense of security before it . . . Jacquot and the broken press: "It's not going . . ." As though the machine refused.

The second mystery is the "mystery of manufacture." The worker does not know the use of every piece, the way in which it combines with others, the succession of operations completed on the machine, the final end of the entire process. The third is the "mystery of 'training the hand.'" An expression suitable for defining the essential principle of manual ability does not exist.

And she asks her questions of the storekeeper, she examines the relations between tools and machines; three specializations exist, on a declining scale: of workers, of machines, of areas of the factory. The great enterprise has a character "scarcely adaptable"; a large number of tools exist along with too many machines, each one specialized in one particular task. Simone thinks of "desirable transformations"; different machines next to one another in the same work area and "the arrangement of the factory to give the worker a sense of the whole." She notes that there are no "stools, boxes, oilcans." The result: one dies of exhaustion for 2 francs an hour. And not because the task demands it; no, only because of the negligence and the whim of the timekeeper, who is also bound too rigidly to periods of time, because the variations associated with circumstances have not been considered. One dies, then, without any result, either subjective (salary) or objective (finished work), corresponding to the energy expended.

This is why one feels like a slave, humiliated in the depths of oneself.

And at times it would take so little. Some devices, for example, to let the workwomen know that they can acquire some safety.

For every task, there exists a limited and small number of possible errors, some which would break the machine, others which would ruin the piece.

Simone makes lists of innovations which would increase, on the one hand, the solidarity of the workers and, on the other, their understanding of the logic of their work: two matters which actually coincide. Simone has always found that, among workers,

generosity of heart and aptitude for general ideas go hand in hand.

So, technical and organizational innovations should proceed together with a solidarity which is not anonymous; the workers should "have the sense of giving something of their own." There should be prizes to prevent waste and, at the same time, preparatory classes.

The total ignorance of what one is working on is the source of un-bearable demoralization. One does not have the sense of a *product* resulting from the energy expended on it . . . Activity appears arbitrarily assigned and arbitrarily compensated. One feels like a child whose mother gives her beads to string to keep her good, with the promise of caramels.

The principal problem is that, at work, "the worker cannot think of anything else, so he thinks of *nothing*."

Forced to rest with a case of ostitis, Simone writes to Albertine and tries to express the essence of the organization of an enterprise. She finds it "something inhuman" on two accounts: "the merely bureaucratic organization" of relations between the various elements of the enterprise and the various operations of labor; the compulsion imposed upon the mind "to concentrate, moment by moment, upon a paltry problem," always the same, with variations: making fifty pieces in five minutes rather than in six, or suchlike . . .
From this flows but one feeling with regard to one's lot: "sadness": and it is a sadness which squats down in resignation.

The situation itself destroys every impulse to revolt; doing a job with irritation would mean doing it badly and condemning oneself to death by starvation.[12]

Three moments, in the *Journal d'usine,* punctuate the story of Simone's transformation in contact with factory life.

The Tuesday of the seventh week (January 15, 1935) she notes:

> Exhaustion finally makes me forget the very reasons why I am in a factory, it makes almost invincible the temptation this life brings with itself: no further thinking.

Only on Saturday afternoon and Sunday "do memories and fragments of ideas" reemerge in her. Panic seizes her when she realizes how dependent she is upon external circumstances. Work without weekly rest would soon make her become "a beast of burden, docile and resigned."

> The only things remaining intact are my sense of fellowship and my indignation in the face of injustices experienced by others—but for how much longer?

The salvation of a worker's mind, but also "the salvation of his soul," depend in great part upon his physical strength.

> I do not see how those who are not strong avoid falling into some form of desperation: drunkenness, vagrancy, crime, lechery, or, simply and most often, brutishness.

In her second job, a harder one, at the forges of Carnaud, "a true prison (frantic rhythms, fingers cut off in profusion, firings without scruple)," despite her weariness she returns on foot along the Seine.

> I sit on a stone close to the water; I am worn out, exhausted. My heart is seething with impotent rage and I feel emptied of all my vital substance. I ask myself if I were condemned to this life forever could I pass every day by the Seine without throwing myself in.

At Renault, her third position, in the May of 1935, she records a strange experience she had when she got on a bus.

> What? I, a slave, can get on this bus and use it for 12 centimes, like everyone else? What an extraordinary concession! If they were brutally to make me get off and tell me that such commodious means of transportation are not for me, who should walk, it would seem the most natural sort of thing. Slavery has made me lose completely my sense of having any rights . . . The moments when I am not forced to

endure any type of brutality are like the smiles of heaven, a gift of chance.

She has to climb up from the pit of this sensation, to find herself upon the earth, to rediscover herself as a human being uniquely strong. To Albertine she writes:

When illness has forced me to stop work, I become fully conscious of the degradation into which I have fallen. I have sworn to myself to maintain this existence until the day comes when I succeed in becoming myself again despite it. I have kept this promise.[13]

It is a struggle with the real difficulties of existence, which are reflected in real inner difficulties. Obtaining a true sense of reality, of her situation in the world: this seemed to her the fundamental fruit of her experience. So, in the conclusion of her *Journal* she repeats:

What have I gained? . . . The sense of not having any right, of any type, to anything (be careful not to lose it). The ability to survive with moral sufficiency for myself, to live in this state of perpetual, latent humiliation, without feeling humiliated in my own eyes; to taste intensely every moment of liberty and camaraderie, as if it would last forever. A direct contact with life.

This is why she has so loved certain moments of relaxation: as, for example, lingering before a band, "fresh air, delicious. And yet I am tired. But altogether happy"; walking along the fortifications, after a solitary lunch at Prisunic in which she had alleviated her hunger and felt relief; enjoying Italian art on a Sunday; going on a trip to Puteaux, "with a lovely sun, a fresh wind . . . Delicious"; too tired to eat, allowing herself to be suffused with the "sweetest" weariness and to sink into a "delicious sleep"; and discovering that

a smile, a good word, an instant of human contact have here a greater value than the finest friendships among the privileged, great and small. Even if it is little, very little, here alone one knows what human brotherhood means.[14]

She dreaded being corrupted by returning to her life in her parents' house, to her activity as a teacher, to freedom in the use of her time. "I experience the greatest reactions," she writes to Albertine. Letting herself go was very dangerous: it meant settling into privileges "without wanting to think that they are privileges." Simone had verified in the depths of her being that the sense of personal dignity created by society had been "smashed." So there was need of "forging a new one." For:

In the end one comes to realize one's own importance.[15]

———

This forging of her essential self is seen in the meditations of the *Cahiers*. There the deeds and events of her daily life find their profound significance.

Experience echoes there only in the form of reflection. Scenes, things and persons are not described. They send coded messages to be interpreted. One such interpretation is intended, on the one hand, to objectify her. Simone, and her behavior in relation to her ideal of life; on the other, she wants to understand the causes of human bewilderment and of the decadence of the age. Even if its purpose is impartial study, the *Journal d'usine* is a diary of immediate experience. In its pages Simone gives voice to the sensations of her body and the perceptions of her emotions, the sense of abasement, the bitterness of impotent rage, sadness and joy, warm gratitude and solidarity. In the *Cahiers*, on the contrary, she concentrates upon the lessons that are derived from these sensations and perceptions, to find "the equilibrium of man with himself and of man with reality."

There are two principal reasons for disequilibrium:

Modern life is abandoned to immoderation. The absence of moderation invades everything, action and thought, private and public life. (Sport: championship—enjoyment to inebriation, to revulsion—exhaustion to abasement, etc.)

It is impossible to think of the relationship between the weariness of work and work itself, "between the action and the effects of the action, so that even when he acts, man is passive."

Hence, in the training of oneself, one must have *temperance* before his eyes; this quality of life has become unthinkable. It is particularly difficult to live according to temperance in "a moral atmosphere" dominated by intemperance. For this reason, "in many fields we cannot escape except by privation." But privation is dangerous, because it can become an unhealthy self-satisfaction (Simone cites Pascal: "The man who plays the angel plays the devil.") It should not be undertaken as a scrupulous code of conduct but as a provisional remedy, when we are sure that we cannot do without it. Our need to acquire a real, and not imaginary, knowledge of a condition of life requires hunger. When she is unemployed, she notes:

Hunger becomes a permanent feeling.[16]

Privation, which engenders contact with reality, is one of the means, one of the *bridges*, to rediscover the proper dimension of man. The boundaries of this dimension have been erased.

Man has lost the notion of his proper limits and hence the notion of the real possibilities of his body and his mind. He has persuaded himself that he dominates "forces which surpass him in an infinite way"; without limits, he has been turned over to himself. Between him and nature there are too many intermediaries; he has lost "the very notion of necessity," he no longer perceives difficulties in themselves and he does not know how to apply his own movements and thoughts to them through conscious labor. He employs *results* crystallized in things: *machines*. He applies methods crystallized in signs: *algebra*. He acts like a robot, because "what has been learned one time is reproduced an unlimited number of times." It is useless to start thinking again . . . it wastes time . . . Among things that think for themselves, "man is reduced to the status of a thing." *Specialization* transforms him into a cog, which becomes useless junk if it is separated from its mechanical context.

An essential fact: the deskilling of labor is the end of civilization. This is true materialism.

Science, which has become a "mere game" of signs far removed from their meanings, is separate from technology, which now uses the applications of science as so many recipes. The only tangible, but still fleeting, fruit of effort is *money*. This digs the deepest divide between exertion and results, especially by way of speculation, which is money's relationship with itself.

MONEY	}	The three monsters
MECHANISM		of contemporary civilization
ALGEBRA		a complete analogy

We are guided and misled by the value of *quantity*. This is "the trap par excellence." It coincides with our immoderation in desires, in needs, in the number of things which become indispensable for us. Our mind, crushed by quantity, justifies its own discomfort by establishing *efficiency* as the central criterion of the age. Society, which has mastered the method that has eluded the individual, has apparently freed him from enslavement to nature and offered him the satisfaction of his primary necessities. The individual, clothed and fed, finds himself, on the contrary, in the condition of an "everlasting minor," enslaved to collectivity. How can we set him free? Asserting the rights of the individual against society is as ridiculous as sustaining "the rights of the gram in relation to the ton."

> The individual has only one strength: thought. Not as banal idealism understands it—consciousness, opinion, etc. Thought constitutes a strength and hence establishes a right only to the degree that it enters into material life.

> So we must see to it that society has need for the individual. To achieve this, man must become conscious of his own thought as an activity intended to confront the obstacles set in place by nature and its laws. We must then empower thought as a skill of the worker.

> Apply yourself to research, not in a technology that will yield the greatest profit but in a technology that will provide the greatest liberty: *totally* new.

Reach the goal of making man passive in the least possible degree: "multiply the relations between cause and effect," so that the laborer will have a constant perception of his own method and a consciousness of the primary reason for labor itself. The tasks are two:

> individualize the machine;
> individualize science (popularization).

Individualizing the machine means utilizing the appropriate energy in our possession by means of the appropriate machine. To create such a machine, the "machine instrument," imaginable, repairable, not foreign to man, Simone conceives of what we could call a *physiology of labor*. Since labor is the relation between man and the world, we must consider in the first place the "obstacles set in place by the indefinite world" and the "essentially mysterious role played by the body of the laborer." We must recognize the possibilities of transforming energy present in the body, a machine which does not reveal its method. The method begins with the "instruments of transformation *constructed*" by man (pulley, lever, boat). Simone projects a *balance* of everything which in automation is a different element: transformation of energy (engines), transformation of matter (chemistry), excitation of reflexes. She thinks of a catalogue of all the *transformations of movements,* to reach a method to use for the energy present in man as a machine, made for those transformations, but absolutely incomprehensible.

We could obtain two extreme types of machine:

> First, the machine tool, to adapt to all sorts of work; with it the worker would have a relationship similar to the one a sailor has with his boat; second, the automatic machine, with which a man intervenes only in a supervisory fashion.

Simone would hope to eliminate most of the intermediate types of semi-automatic machines intended to perform the various steps in the production line, which is more deadly to the laborer and his labor than the machine itself. Simone imagines a technical revolution as the foundation of an "entirely new civilization," which would have as its basis *"the very notion of equilibrium."* The new civilization would have to be adapted to a "decentralized" world; technical transformation would be realized in cooperative enterprises, without enslavement or domination and without wages in money, as in the first monasteries. At the same time, in the heart of these enterprises a *different* science would find its way. This science would make fruitful that critical inventory "of the technical and theoretical treasures of our civilization," which Simone sets as a task for herself, to discover "the role of reflection" and to create a contact between the laborer of today and the one of the past, in the consciousness of a tradition. The relations between science and its technical applications should be made comprehensible, not to make the labor more efficient, but more conscious and methodical. In popularization, rather than explaining established science with rational method, we should take the concepts of science from their foundation, from technique, and make them intelligible.

In scientific education, we should learn four things:

the *method*
the *exercise of the imagination*

criticism
ascertainment

To acquire them, one must perform manual labor in a particular way; Simone imposes three disciplines, in the first place, upon herself:

> Discipline of concentration . . . no distraction or reverie. No giddiness, though. Always observe what is being done without allowing yourself to be absorbed. A second discipline through comprehension supported by imagination. A third through reflection. You possess only the third. A complete being possesses all three. You should be complete.

An approach to understanding all the moments of labor means finding an equilibrium between labor and ourselves; it means accepting it as our teacher of liberty. For the value of efficiency, Simone substitutes the value of liberty. Which liberty? Not the "liberty of indifference," which is a dream, not the "earthly paradise," in which man would live only for his own passions: liberty would mean "limits," the acceptance of the obstacles set in place by necessity.

> *Escaping* from necessity? Like children? We would lose our precious life in so doing.

The ideal does not lie in the passage from the kingdom of necessity to the kingdom of liberty, but from necessity "undergone" to necessity "methodically managed." The acquisition of an inner discipline diminishes the necessity of external discipline. Living one's thought as attention to a task composed of moments bound together for a precise goal brings us to the consciousness of the liberating function of thought. We have the concrete definition of liberty when "the thought of the action precedes the action."

This liberty we must create. How is it possible to create it in the conditions of industrial society? Simone searches for the realistic bases for an *ethics of labor,* directed towards providing mental health for man. There are two ways to be free: either suppressing overproduction, i.e., returning to savagery, or establishing the foundation for a *"voluntary overproduction."* Overproduction is indispensable to prevent succumbing to other societies; and yet, centralized and collective overproduction is today destroying both man and itself. The problem lies in finding a motivation for voluntary overproduction. It cannot be the need for providing for natural necessities nor the will to power; it can be neither compulsion nor surrender. It has to be "the conscious will."

To achieve it, we must come to a comprehension of our own work, directed towards a determined goal. This comprehension must be awakened in the individual worker, despite the division of labor. It has to be developed and nurtured in habits which are individually forged and in the assimilation of the method, put into practice in *coordination* by various workers.

At the beginning of her diary of the factory, Simone had set this formula for orientation:

> Not only should man know what he is doing—but if possible he should *perceive its use*—understand nature as he has modified it.

A grasp of his own work and a perception of its utility provide a man with the "feeling of creating." Such a feeling should be encouraged by means of "respect for work." It is a respect which implies the search for a method of realization which would be suitable to express a harmonious relation between man and his work.

Simone lays the foundation for an *aesthetics of work*. Art, which for centuries has been connected with human collectivity (the coincidence of Greek art with geometry and athletics; of medieval art with artisanry; of Renaissance art with the beginnings of mechanics . . .), has since 1914 been cut off from it. Reduced to its mere self, it is withering. But:

> Art is knowledge. Or better, art is exploration . . . The triumph of art is bringing to another from oneself, i.e., to life, through a full consciousness of the mind's relationship to the world.

And the greatness of man consists always in "recreating his life." By way of labor which shapes nature to produce the means of existence; by way of science which translates the universe into symbols; by way of art, "the alliance of the body and the soul."

For the ancient law, with its curse, "You shall win your bread with the sweat of your brow," we must seek to substitute the "new law: command nature by obeying it."

"Preparation for this conscious domination" seems to Simone the only thing "worth the effort," the ideal that we "carry within ourselves—new—," *"our"* mission, for this age.

Simone, in her depths, unites herself with the man of her time. In her there is a full *co-responsibility* for the wretchedness, the exhaustion, and the emptiness in which we debate one another, and all of this is shared by her, participated in with love.

> You could not desire to be born in any age better than this one, in which all has been lost.

She does not, however, allow herself to be corrupted by her age; she does not use its weak points in order to influence others; nor does she flee into illusion, isolation, study as an end in itself.

> We must keep in mind two preoccupations: First, *save ourselves*—that is, not go mad in the middle of a world that has gone mad . . . Second, do everything possible to be prepared.

And again:

> Evasion into primitive life is the lazy solution. We must find again the original pact between our spirit and the world through the civilization in which we live.

This means, for her, making an inventory and critique of our civilization.

The road of research passes, in the first place, through her. And yet, without a shadow of programmatic artificiality. There exists in her a precise vision of her inner reality.

The ideal, which coincides with "her clear vision of duty," is part of her essence, runs through her veins as does her blood. Joined with it is her lucid acknowledgement of her own limits: laziness, which she defines as "by far her strongest temptation"; physical and emotional suffering, her cowardice in the face of time. Time is the very image of necessity; for this reason it must be accepted in all its moments, consciously. We should not put things off; we should not blindly submit ourselves to it; we should not flee from it in unconsciousness. We must begin with fidelity in small matters; Simone establishes arbitrary allotments of time, to respect to the minute, throughout the day. If she puts off, she decides to put off, up to a particular moment, when "dealing with her migraine."

> It is a matter of creating a habit.
> Training.

Simone Weil with her father, Bernard Weil, at Mayenne in 1915–16

Simone with her brother, André, at Mayenne

Simone at age 12 at Baden-Baden in 1921

Simone with André on a holiday at Knokke-le Zoute, Belgium, in 1922

Simone in Spain, on her return
from the war front in 1936

Simone and Lanza del Vasto in Marseilles, 1941

Cher ami,

Diverses circonstances ont retardé ma métamorphose en paysanne et mon départ. Ces deux choses se font aujourd'hui. Je vais passer quelques semaines en Ardèche, chez l'ami du P. Perrin (adresse : chez M. Thibon, St Marcel d'Ardèche) ; je serai chez lui quelques jours de travail par semaine ; puis je m'embaucherai pour la vendange ; puis j'aurai (pour un an, je suppose) une vraie place de domestique de ferme à Maillane — à supposer que je tienne le coup, ce que j'espère.

Votre nouveau exposé de la méthode de multiplication par 2 m'a intéressée en me montrant combien je suis loin des modes de raisonnement actuels, à

forcé de me transporter mentalement en
arrière de 25 siècles. Bien entendu, le
jour où on m'a raconté le procédé,
j'avais trouvé la théorie après 10 minutes
de réflexion; je suis mal douée pour les
mathématiques, mais non pas au point d'être
arrêtée par une chose pareille. Je vous avais
posé la question seulement pour vous amuser
et m'amuser. Mais votre exposé algébrique
m'aurait été inintelligible, au moins à
première vue, s'il ne s'était agi d'une
chose que j'avais déjà comprise :

    Voulez-vous remercier votre sœur (je
ne sais plus où lui écrire) de ses interventions
auprès des bénédictins pour les Cahiers du
Sud? (Et plus encore de m'avoir fait
connaître le P. Perrin).

    Quelque autre jour, car je n'ai pas
le temps, je vous enverrai quelques vers.

      Bien cordialement

          Simone Weil

Letter from Simone to her friend Pierre Honnorat in 1941, on the eve of her
peasant experience

Simone in New York, 1942

FRANCE COMBATTANTE

LAISSEZ - PASSER

o. *1663*

Nom *Weil*

Prenoms *Simone*

Grade ou Profession *Redactrice*

Bureau ou Service *C. N. I*

Londres le *30 Mars 1945*

Le Chef du Service de Sécurité

Simone's pass from war torn France in 1943, when she took refuge in London, against her will, with her family. Later that year she died and was buried in a pauper's grave.

A habit is never external, it corresponds to the construction of an inner discipline. This prepares one for action. How should this action be? As far as possible, objective and conscious of its consequences. This implies neither coldness, nor calculation, nor compulsion. How are we to overcome the vehemence, the sensibility, the physical pain, which obscure our clear vision of the duty we must perform and impede the will? The will, inasmuch as it is thought, has only one weapon: it can "embrace the several instants of time." The body is limited only to the "present."

> In conclusion, it is a matter . . . simply of refusing to the passions a role in thought . . . Do not "make resolutions," but have your hands tied in advance.

Let us remember when every step cost her a "special effort of the physical will,"[17] or when her fingers grew bloody at the press, and she succeeded not only in continuing in what she was committed to do, but in analyzing it.

On the threshold of an action, never undertake it without having for a good while "examined carefully" all possible consequences ("responsibilities"); then, once you are in the heart of an action, "*never* hesitate," never stop, never go back. The almost pitiless use of the will is intended to make one loyal to the project of constructing oneself, not to turn one into a zealous activist. We must "avoid all responsibilities which do not correspond to a particular duty." There should be no intemperance in action. The fundamental rule is:

> Avoid to the greatest measure possible situations that risk creating contradictions between the raw reactions of sensibility and higher feelings and the will.

Objectifying oneself is indispensable to the end of the *salvation* for which we are debtors to ourselves and to others. Salvation will come more and more to coincide with a *beauty* similar to the beauty of great art, an unselfconscious perfection on the level of human relations.

She addresses this exhortation to herself:

> Strive always to do for yourself . . . devote yourself, if necessary, to many years of silence . . . but do not teach!

This detachment is essential for her to live in truth the drama of her time and to attempt to find the best remedy for it by way of the lucid disinterest of analysis. Her sense of social responsibility dictates this to her; but her sensibility and her anguished desire to cure the evils of the world blossom from her stoicism, without illusions, given the reality of the circumstances.

> There is no hope that any among us, even the young, will see the fall (of our present civilization). And even more, no hope that we can at least leave our thought as an inheritance to the generations which will witness its fall.

She is without illusions even with regard to her own importance:

> . . . do not believe in a mission. First of all there are all the possibilities of dying before you are heard—and then, even if you are heard . . .

But "at least we shall have lived . . ." Life is "precious," as she has said, especially with its struggle and its effort.

And yet the task appears impossible. Human life is too short to fulfill it and there exists an "impossibility of cooperation and of succession." Are a completely assimilable science and a free technology perhaps beyond our grasp? In that case, "we would not have to worry about society in general." On the level of personal independence, it would be sufficient to live as "honorably" as possible in the framework of our existing society and "life would keep all of its sense." But on the level of *co-responsibility* this cannot happen, for "we must have a tranquil conscience."

Then "we should reflect *by ourselves*." Furthermore, "the machine will function according to its own laws until it breaks down . . . Do not be accomplices . . . Do not lie—do not remain blind."[18]

11

Love

Do not ever forget that you have the entire world and your whole life before you . . . That for you life can and should be more real, more full and joyous than it has perhaps been for any other human being . . . Do not maim it in advance with any kind of renunciation. Do not allow yourself to be imprisoned by any affection. Preserve your solitude. The day, if it ever comes, that a TRUE friendship is granted you, there will not be any opposition between inner solitude and friendship; rather . . . this is an infallible sign by which you will recognize it.[1]

These are Simone's words to herself at twenty-five. It is a passage under-lined in the manuscript, a fervent secret exhortation to herself in the period when her project was being realized. Her vision of love, which she frequently calls friendship, has the same sources as her aspiration for the truth.

Living life with full access to a vocation, as she said to Simone Pétre-ment on that distant boat ride, is the happy task of everyone on earth. For this reason, everyone has the vital need for both an internal and an external space in which to bring his own autonomy to maturity: it would be better not to encounter love when we are "very young," when we do not yet know how we are made or what we want to do with our lives. "Do not flee from it, no, but do not search for it either," Simone writes to a student, because:

Love is a serious matter, in which you may involve your life and the life of some other human being forever.[2]

So, for "time immemorial," when we encounter love which is the "vital need" for another human being, there arises in us a conflict between loyalty to love and the need for liberty.

In Simone, the conflict had been waged in the secrecy of the ego; between herself and her project, between herself and her consuming desire for friendship. Friendship is nourishment, inspiration. At fifteen, Simone fashioned an interior character, "the unknown friend." As far as the idea of love codified in marriage, associated somehow with feminine attraction, dates, clothes, the signals and messages of use and wont, she perhaps never paused there at all.

Her first reference to marriage is the black humor of her eulogy of a woman who had killed her husband, Mme. Bessarabo. After killing him, she had sent his body on a train, in a suitcase. She was condemned to twenty years of forced labor. The poem, which Simone wrote when she was thirteen, has not survived. It was entitled *Saint Bessarabo* and Selma Weil remembered some of its passages: "You of the great heart, you who committed so glorious a crime . . ." The last lines said: "And virgins will come some day to lay flowers on your tomb."[3]

At Auxerre, where her teaching was perhaps even more scandalous, there are echoes in the notes of her students of these evaluations by their anarchic professor. "The family is legalized prostitution . . . The wife is a lover reduced to slavery."[4] At Bourges, once again teaching philosophy in 1935–36, after her time as a laborer, she asserts the superiority of a free union. Unlike marriage, such a union has no need for any social support and is kept alive only by the love between a man and a woman.[5] She understood the desire for motherhood. She fully approved the decision of a girl who wanted a son, arranged to have one in secrecy and then adopted him.[6]

She wanted to be free from the dictates of society and from its patterns. She asserted this symbolically when, for an evening at the opera, she wanted, except for the skirt, a tuxedo of black cloth, "quite an expensive outfit for the evening and requiring a fitting."[7] She was still very young then. She was "Simone, *le fils n° 2*"; that tuxedo was the sign of her determined uniqueness.

She was never shy with young men. She never tried to please. In her intransigence, she lacked moderation and she actually hurt people, without meaning to. One of her great friends was Jacques Ganuchaud: "very tall, with almond-shaped eyes; he was one of the most brilliant of Alain's students; he wrote a very great deal." Then there came René Château; with him Simone had a "fearful" friendship.[8] The three of them, Simone, Ganuchaud and Château, preferred a café on the rue des Canettes and would talk there late into the night. They would often supply sandwiches and cheese; they would drink wine and Simone would force herself to drink it, to show that she could handle it like a man. She would do the same thing later with the workers at Le Puy and Saint-Etienne, but she really never got used to it and did not like it. She took to smoking on the other hand, with great pleasure. She made her own cigarettes, quite awkwardly. And "she would take the cigarette between two fingers, like a piece of bread, the lit end toward the hollow of her hand. Ashes everywhere."[9] Once along the street an urchin yelled, "Women don't smoke!" She blushed violently.[10]

Ganuchaud later wrote of her: "I remember above all her willingness to reach out to others, only to be deceived to the very degree of her own needs. All of this against a background of indifference to her own person. Already evident were her restlessness and her refusal to settle down in life."[11] Suzanne Aron confirms this thought when she says, "Simone had a passionate desire for tenderness, for communion, for friendship, but she never found the way to get what she wanted so ardently." And Suzanne, her fellow student at the lycée, was one of the two or three persons to whom Simone felt bound until she was twenty-five. Then she became more solitary. "But, in a certain sense, she was always that way," adds Suzanne.[12]

=======

Suzanne, G. (probably Ganuchaud), and Boris (or B.) are characters who recur in the *Cahiers*, where friendship is one of the dominant thoughts.

At the end of 1934, after a period of serious concern for the private problems of a friend, Simone reflects on the entanglements that come with friendship. What transformations does it produce in you? How can you live your friendship in such a way that it is both true and positive for you and your friend? The primary value in the life of sentiment is the *responsibility* we have for our own integrity and for that of the other, an integrity that coincides with our own and the other's destiny ("sort").

Friendship should not be sought, dreamt of, nor desired.
Friendship is exercised (it is a virtue).[13]

It simply "exists," like beauty. It is a "miracle," mysterious, like all miracles, and all the same, mounted in the setting of life; hence it is inseparable from it. One should not desire friendship as compensation or as relief from solitude; it should not be fabricated nor based on warped visions of yourself and the other.

There are some "temptations" to overcome, temptations we should be aware of, temptations against which we should subject ourselves to a merciless *dressage:* the temptation of the *"interior life,"* the temptation of *"devotion,"* of *"domination"* and of *"perversion."* You would in fact "sell your soul for friendship"[14] and it is easy both to corrupt and to be corrupted. The interior life is happy to admit an abundance of phantasms and imaginary creations; in our emotional life, however, we must "cut away without mercy everything that is imaginary" and allow ourselves only "what corresponds to real interchanges or is absorbed by thought as inspiration."[15] For this reason we should forbid ourselves those "impulses of the heart" that do not find a similar response in the other and we should not pretend that we are understood when we are not even clear in our own eyes; nor out of misunderstood "loyalty" should we suppress evidence of what the other is really like. The excess of devotion can lead to this, that is, to a subordination of the capacity for judgment, "the subject," to beings and to things. Not being fooled by another also means not fooling the other and not pretending that he can give you more than he possibly can. Never cover him with promises and offers to which he cannot respond. Such gifts may be an imposition, a desire for dominance, an extortion of favors and recognition. And for yourself,

> the more you give, the more you *depend* for your happiness and unhappiness. A word can give you more happiness than you have given in a year of devotion . . . You are putting yourself in the role of a mendicant, of a dog that expects a bone.[16]

By an inevitable mechanism, finally, "one cannot depend upon human beings without aiming at a tyrannical conduct towards them," and this is at the root of "all cruelty, private and public."[17]

As far as giving help to others, this help should be clear and limited to a sober action. You must grasp the reasons for their suffering insofar as they give you the opportunity, without indulging in personal interpretations, and you should indicate the remedies insofar as they are disposed to accept them.

Do not suffer any longer because of them but for their benefit.[18]

The other illusion we should reflect upon is imagining that friendship may exist between one who "condemns himself to life in the kingdom of shadows,"[19] or unconsciously is in the cave, and one who strives to come out from it. You do not have the power to persuade him, to bring him to the light. What words would you use? You should forbid yourself desiring to have such power and be content with having "the shadow of a friend," that shadow that Socrates himself yearned for.

Perversion comes from suffering excessively the evil which others can do to you. One should never "respond to one evil with reactions liable to increase it." So one should not dwell upon one's own suffering nor fuel one's own anger. "Months of inner fury during my years at Henri IV . . . How could I end them as soon as possible? Simone believes that the cure is found in solitude, in the temporary severance of "*all* bonds." That anger is like the "convulsions of children."[20]

Perversion, illusion, surrender, dependence and domination are all pleasures of sentiment. Using oneself and others to excite such pleasures means transforming and being transformed into phantasms; it means no longer living but dreaming. In order that others *exist* as "particular beings, without dominating them and without being dominated by them,"[21] we should live with them in a relationship of equality and detachment. Freedom from the temptations of sentiment analyzed by Simone is "the purity after which we all thirst."[22] The thing most opposed to purity is precisely the search after *intensity* (the provocation of pleasure); and intensity is the same as intemperance. With regard to music, Simone used to say to Marcoux: "And above all, nothing expressive." It reached the point, at the time of their friendship, that Marcoux could listen only to Bach.

=======

What was, on the deep level of her life, a humble and attentive search for an ethical perfection analogous to the perfection of art, found only scanty echoes on the stage of the world. Here, above all in the eyes of her friends, she appeared tired, inept, frenetic in vain, poorly dressed, obstinate rather than tenacious, genial but a little mad. She never managed to reach them and she realized it. "Suzanne . . . Pierre and the others . . . Boris . . . Sentiments that never reach their object, this is not love. And you, you never knew it . . . Why? Not from a lack of generosity, but from a lack of naturalness."[23]

Naturalness, indulging in spontaneity. She who had wanted and would want to use her body as a proper instrument to live again the laws of the world, did not want or know how to use it as an effective means. The embrace, the kiss were unknown to her or very rare. Albertine recalls with emotion one occasion at the movies, when they were seeing Clair's *A nous la liberté*. "I embraced her shoulders and she embraced my waist. Another time, at a worker's café, she came and sat on my knees. We were bound together in a simple, fraternal, flesh-and-blood relationship."

Albertine is perhaps the only friend of Simone to receive tangible nurture from her. She says that "Simone is one of the persons I have most loved in my life." It is perhaps for this reason that Simone emerges more concretely in her description.

Her friend Pétrement remembers December 20, 1934. "I went to get her at the factory. As soon as she saw me, she ran up and hugged me. She usually did not do that ever . . . Thereafter, when I learned of all the sufferings of her life as a worker, I thought that perhaps that hug had been dictated by the great, unexpected joy of rediscovering the world of human relationships.[24]

Loving and being loved: Simone saw in others, with tenderness, the ability and the possibility of living in the daily spontaneity of love. They are those who live in the present: "It is only thanks to them that the chain of days is not an empty sequence lacking any human content." This is how she comforted a friend, who felt unable to imagine a future for herself. And to a friend, sad at being nothing and having nothing to do, she said: "There are persons who can be happy to exist only for the one who loves them."[25] For her, the meaning of existence, which she could not avoid, was:

> Conceiving one's entire life before oneself and directing it all in a sense determined by the will and with one's labor.[26]

=====

Georges Bataille called her with disgust, "the Christian." Perplexed before her, in *The Blue of the Sky* he deforms her into a black-and-white image, the painful fruit of his ambivalence, and at the same time transfigures her. Simone emerges both gigantic and repulsive. He gives her a symbolic surname, Lazare, and calls her that all the time. "Lazare became her macabre looks more than her name. She was strange, even ridiculous. To explain to any extent at all my interest in her, you had to suppose that I was mentally disordered. That, at least, is what my friends said at the Exchange . . . She wore black, ill-fitting, and dirty clothes . . . She did not wear a hat and her hair, short, bristly, and ruffled, gave the appearance of crow's wings around her face."[27] "Everything about her, her jerky and sleepwalking gait, the tone of her voice, her ability to project a sort of silence around herself, her eagerness for sacrifice, helped give the impression that she had made a pact with death. I felt that such an existence would only have sense for men and for a world doomed to misfortune."[28] Fatuously, he thinks: "The women I used to go out with were always well-dressed and glamorous."

But he was stranded in the swamp of sloth and Lazare "was the only person who helped me escape depression." "She was there and I felt less lost" because Lazare "was as calm as a priest in the confessional."

"She spoke slowly, with the serenity of total indifference; illness, exhaustion, misery, or death did not count at all in her eyes. She presumed, a priori, the calmest detachment in others."[29]

She had an "inner" tone of voice. " 'Whatever happens, we must be at the side of the oppressed,' she said. In the name of what? 'One can always save one's soul,' observed Lazare . . . without a movement, without even lifting her eyes. She gave me the impression of unshakable faith."[30]

In his fictional narrative, Bataille saw her participate in the revolutionary events that took place in Barcelona in the fall of 1934. Simone had been there actually in the summer of 1933, along with her parents and Aimé Patri; she had met dissident Communists, fishermen and peasants, and had often swum and taken sun-baths. Never, according to Patri, had she been so close to the joy of living. Once she had put a flower in her hair: how it did become her! Patri was both elated and dumbfounded.[31]

Bataille sees in her "the decisiveness and the firmness of a man at the head of an insurrection"; he loathes his own curiosity, which makes him a spectator of the war; he fears and hopes that he will meet Lazare, his conscience. Stupefied, he realizes that he "belongs to her."[32] He speaks about her with Michel, a character in whom we glimpse Patri; he learns to his astonishment that Lazare was spending her evenings at La Criolla, a bar for transvestites, and wanted to see and understand everything. Michel goes on, "Lazare fascinates anyone who hears her. She does not seem to be someone of this world. There are people here, workers, whom she would discomfort. They admired her. Then they met her at La Criolla.

Here at La Criolla she seemed to be a ghost. Her friends, seated at the same table, were horrified. They did not understand how she could be found here. One day one of them began to drink out of boredom . . . He would have preferred to be killed for her, but never would have asked her to bed. She seduced him . . . but, to his eyes, she was a saint. And she should remain a saint. He was a very young mechanic."[33]

To learn how to endure torture, Lazare asked Michel to drive pins under her fingernails. This is a true episode, which Patri recounted to Simone Pétrement.[34]

Bataille admits, "Fundamentally, I was obsessed with Lazare."[35] And seeing her coming towards him under the plane-trees of the Ramblas, he asked himself for a second "if Lazare was not the most human being he had ever seen."[36]

═════

Tone-deaf and pasty, just about nonexistent, incredibly detached, but at the same time she would "senselessly . . . terrify people with the tenacity of her fixed ideas."[37] She was as curious as a "little pole-cat" and she succeeded in knowing all the secrets.[38]

Among all the stories and legends of her personal folklore, Simone cited one: *The girl with the skull. Her sweetheart fled—she has to leave and wander in solitude, because she disgusts everyone—she cries with joy when she realizes that she does not disgust a lion, whose paw she has healed.*"[39]

She would say to herself: "First of all, do not be vulnerable." But she was, and she suffered too grievously from the criticism of her friends. Boris, for example. She wants to help him, to give him a goal in life through their joint research. She anxiously follows the drafting of his book on Stalin and asks Urbain Thévenon to collect funds for its publication. But . . . from Boris: "Do not expect anything (I do not need anything anyway) . . . I can only help him materially and intellectually but not morally." The real exchange can occur only on the level of equality and Simone feels that this equality does not exist between them, because she cannot reach "the level of little things (the virtue of the good worker)." Up to then, she says to herself, Boris "will not have any confidence in me." "Nor will I. I will be like a baby and at twenty-five, that's too much." She sees Boris as a leader and she asks herself, "Perhaps you are one of those people destined to obey because they do not have the courage to confront responsibility? In that case, Boris would be right to despise you." She is subject to continual rending in two by the force of her aspirations and of her thoughts and the impossibility of realization. "And yet this everlasting physical emaciation of mine comes into the picture . . . not even in a family could you hold down a responsible position because of those long periods in which you are a complete loss."[40]

═══════

What is love? In friendship there is a moral encounter, in love there is a physical one. What does this mean? Work makes you feel within yourself "in all your being the existence of the world." Does love perhaps mean feeling within yourself "the existence of another being"? Yes, it really should be like that, "but with the proviso that there does not exist any desire and even less what we call pleasure."

> To perceive the loved being with all of your own sensible surface, like a swimmer in the sea. To live within his own universe. It is by chance (a providential chance) that this deep aspiration, which has its roots in infancy (gestation), coincides with the instinct we call sexual, which is extraneous to love except for the idea of children. This is why chastity is indispensable to love. And infidelity contaminates it. From the instant that there is *need, desire,* even reciprocal, there is outrage.[41]

The human being is considered a whole, body and soul, with value in itself. The distinction between body and soul is a "rough" one; the true distinction is between "slavery and freedom"[42] as to oneself and to another.

Simone also reflects on the pleasures of the senses: innocent in themselves, they contain two dangers: our own corruption and the exercise of power over another. Using them as compensations, to fill a void (even the pleasurable use of thought can have this function), we turn ourselves over to them, and in so doing we estrange ourselves from ourselves and we destroy others, through excessive cupidity. One tumbles into the first temptation (the strongest, in Simone's eyes): laziness.

> Enjoyment and power . . . Among the enjoyments that stun us, are there any that are not associated with power?
> Certainly not love . . .
> And luxury? . . . *in itself*, it has nothing intoxicating. But it is suffi-

cient to define it in particulars. In clothes: the pleasure of power. In part, this is also true of the food we eat. Clearly in the type of house. Luxury and female pride . . . Intoxication with alcohol, opium, morphine, and the solitary vice . . . the same thing; only that we are dealing with a fictitious power.[43]

We ought not to want to possess. By nature, every love is sadistic; the "sign of humanity" comes from the feeling of respect. We find the same sign at the root of art. Like the love that surpasses itself, art refuses to destroy, to consume, to eat. "The artist's inspiration is always *Platonic* . . . poetry teaches us to contemplate thoughts without transforming them."[44]

One loves the soul from the instant one ceases wishing to appropriate the loved being (possession).[45]

It is "cowardice" to seek in the persons we love, or to aspire to give them, any comfort other than what works of art give us. They exist and that's it. Loving and being loved simply make each other's existence more concrete for the two beings in love. The presence of one for another should be the "source" of thoughts, not an "object": nurture, inspiration . . .

If it is proper for one to wish to be understood, it is not for oneself but for the other, to the end of existing for him.[46]

The existence and the integrity of the other, of everyone, nurtured in the amniotic fluid of love: this is the intuition of her moral genius.

For this reason, the crime that horrified her the most was rape, the extreme manifestation of cupidity and violence. She told her mother that the only instance in which "she might perhaps kill would be to prevent a rape or to defend herself."[47]

Using another, being used by another for pleasure was something she could not bear in her thought, even through the least hints of gallantry. Simone, who already believed that she was guilty of *laziness* in connection with the resolutions she had made with herself, utterly refused to indulge in any kind of surrender with men. There are two telling episodes in this connection: one the refusal of innocent comfort, the other a revulsion, more or less unconscious, at being touched.

It is December, 1933. Jean Duperray, the teacher of the Thévenon group, comes to Roanne to find Simone, to invite her to the miners' festival, which was to take place the next day at Saint-Étienne. The night is beautiful and bright. The two friends speak of popular songs. Suddenly, Simone puts her head between her hands, to get some relief from the daily torture of migraines. Duperray tells the story: "To give her some comfort, I did what my grandfather used to do with me as a baby with his strong weaver's hands . . . I took Simone's head between my cold hands and pressed as hard as I could to break that scorching ring of pain. She told me that yes, the cold of my hands did her good but that it was not worthwhile to use such a momentary comfort and she almost immediately pushed them away."[48]

The second time we are in Saint-Étienne, in February, 1934, in the days when Simone was holding one of her conferences on "historical materialism." Afterwards, the group of the *Bourse du Travail* met, as was their custom, at the house of a comrade, to sing and to talk. The room was bare, except for a few seats and a kind of mattress made out of newspapers. That evening the meeting lasted until dawn. "We had decided to stay, camping out in expectation of a cup of hot coffee and the next day. Simone retired with a girl friend into the next room. We three men remained with our host to sleep on the papers."

A little later, Simone, already awake, silently walked towards the door. "I knew that she had a syndical meeting in Lyon, but she could have left later. I got to my feet, rapidly, and stretched out my arms to hold her. I did not have time to say a word before she pushed me to the side. To get away from me, she hit me under the chin with the edge of her hand, obliquely: a gesture at once brutal and awkward."[49]

When Duperray, dumbfounded, asked her later why she had done so, Simone always avoided answering him.

———

She was particularly interested in the plight of prostitutes. She wanted to get close to them, to speak together, to understand them. It seemed to her that, among the debased and the injured of society, they were at the center of degradation. In the evening, after the meetings, she would want to accompany her worker friends to a brothel, where she knew very well that they were going. It was Thévenon who would accompany her home, with the pretense that he was doing nothing in particular.

Later, in 1937, she convinced a friend, Pierre Dantu, to undertake this strange adventure: together, Simone dressed as a young man in her blue factory overalls and a beret, they went to one of the most infamous brothels, where the women "did" sometimes up to eighty clients a day. "I still remember quite vividly our entrance. The madame took Simone for a boy who was too young; she wanted to avoid trouble with the police, so she asked me if Simone was the proper age. We walked to the counter; leaning up against the wall, several North Africans were waiting. Two fat naked women, their flesh cascading down, came up to us for a drink; they attempted conversation. But after a short time, one of them sensed that Simone was not a man; she snatched the beret from her head, violently insulted her, and began to cuff her. Dreading scandal, the madame intervened; we took to our heels in a hurry."[50]

The only instance in which she would accept the penalty of deportation, which she otherwise opposed with all her force, was for procurers guilty of white-slave trade or for those who exploited prostitutes.[51]

For her the physical side of love was more separation than union. It meant touching the very bottom of vegetative life, beating against a blind wall. She writes for herself: "Ever since the Luxembourg, being the object of desire has created in me a revulsion and a humiliation which are fortunately invincible . . . Wait . . . Do not accept anything impure."[52] André thinks that his sister was referring to an encounter with an exhibitionist in the Luxembourg Gardens, an event of her adolescence.

How the separation between the sexes vexed her! She had instinctively never grasped it; she had erased it in her manner of dressing, in her habits which did not mind another's judgment or prejudice. She would appear in the men's dormitory at the Normale at all hours and see the dawn arrive in a café . . . Even: "For her it was natural to ignore women. One sensed in her a powerful ambition and a consciousness of her intellectual superiority that bordered on conceit." These are the words of Colette Audry. She adds: "I think that Simone Weil both rejected and endured her condition of being a woman. For example, in comparing herself with her brother, she believed that he excelled in the field of mathematics because he was a man."[53]

In fact, Simone always spurs herself to reach "the full maturity of a man." Man had been the ideal of the Greeks; man was the model of will and thought that Alain proposed to his students.

What miraculous spontaneity she showed in that conversation with two unemployed workers, that Wednesday afternoon when she was looking for work! She established a real relationship with them, very rare even in the workers' milieu, where "despite the exchange of obscene remarks,"[54] which seemed to imply a free and easy intimacy, the separation between the sexes was even more marked.

Another afternoon, when she was also unemployed, she was taking a walk with a worker, "a mechanic that does honor to his trade," who brags and lets off steam. They find themselves along the Seine, near the river; the bank is deserted. He makes a pass at her; Simone rejects it and explains her reasons. "An error of interpretation in my regard and his attitude subsequently. On leaving me, he said, 'You don't bear me a grudge, right?'" Simone gave him her address. Two days later she heard knocking at her door early in the morning. Simone did not open the door. "Was he there? I shall never see him again."[55] An interrupted dialogue, regret for an impossible friendship.

In the group of miners at Saint-Étienne, one in particular adored her: François Chapuis, called *le Boul,* a miner who worked far below the surface, an ex-legionnaire who had been condemned to forced labor for desertion. A little sickly body that swam in clothes too big for him, a black foulard swelling around his neck, his wrinkled face thrust up towards heaven as though in ecstasy, his hand clutched in his pocket around his legendary knife, he displayed his tattoos from the Legion. His crew-cut hair was somewhere between the tow-colored hair of a child and the hoary head of an old man. He spoke in spurts: a wild flood of memories, flashes of imagery, words of suffering, torture and humiliation from the basis of which there emerged "the grandeur of a man." And Simone, suffused with this grandeur, would write feverishly in a notebook; "she recorded scrupulously 'the explanation of the world and of life according to *le Boul.*'"[56]

One evening, at the festival of the miners, they had danced. *Le Boul,* with his beret on his head, "full of attention, of pride, and of courtesy," had tried to teach Simone a waltz which, in his desire, would be the choreographic ideal of all waltzes. Yet another evening, *le Boul* wanted to make even more explicit his homage to Simone the woman. There is a Legionnaire song that ends like this, "Je me rappellerai toujours / Thérèse, / Ma petite Française!" *Le Boul* substituted for Thérèse the name that was dearest to him, Simone, and made her a bow. Suddenly Simone was on her feet and froze *le Boul* with a glance. She went away in a hurry. "Did she perhaps grasp in the courtesy of *le Boul* a kind of tattered tenderness, the homage of which she feared? *Le Boul* should not see in her an object of adoration."[57] It was not she, not she personally, who should be loved. She could not *depend* in any way on the thought of another, nor should she do anything to make someone else depend on her in any way.

> During the wait, a remedy: treat men as a spectacle, apart from all fraternal bonds . . . Do not expect anything, except from yourself.[58]

And elsewhere: "Learn to be alone." Because, "since you were sixteen, you have not been alone except for one year, and that was so disheartening! Learn to be so with joy, with serenity. Otherwise you should despise yourself."[59]

In January, 1938, Simone went with her mother to the Mathurins theater. They were presenting a play by Anouilh, *La Sauvage;* she was overcome. As they left, she broke down sobbing.

La Sauvage tells the story of Teresa, an intelligent girl, who has preserved a great nobility of soul in wretched circumstances. Her father, her mother, her mother's lover, and she all play in a little orchestra in a café at a spa. Florent, a handsome, genial, very rich musician, falls in love with her; she loves him too, and he convinces her to marry him, to accept a happiness that is both dear and protected. But this happiness which Teresa convinces herself to favor, "domesticated" by her love for Florent, she realizes is impossible. Teresa cannot and, in the truthfulness of her very self, does not want to forget the misery, the evil, the impotence against which her people struggle. She cannot become invulnerable, unconscious and merciless like Florent's mother, satisfied with her roseries and her knitting for the poor. She cannot do so even for the love of Florent, a naturally happy creature. She has to go away without a word of farewell. Her dazzling wedding gown remains there, abandoned. In the next room, Florent is playing the violin. Teresa whispers to him, "You see, Florent, cheat as I might and keep my eyes tightly closed . . . There will always be, somewhere in a corner of the world, some lost dog that would keep me from being happy." Hartman, a friend of them both, remarks: "There she goes, wandering through the world, small, hard and sharp, to bang into every corner."[60]

So it had to be for Simone. She could never find a refuge or rest her head in the solace of personal happiness. The impossibility of being satisfied with a human union, the multiplicity of her interests directed at a rigorously defined goal, her feeling of rejection, her vulnerability, her unwillingness to accept any role converged in this. Simone was intrinsically repelled by the idea of becoming a "persona," a mask. She wanted to bring to realization her very *substance* and to offer it to everyone upon the earth through the attentiveness of impersonal love. For

> every man is a Proteus. Friendship is the reward you get when you embrace him tightly, without losing confidence, until he resumes his human shape.[61]

12

The Second Test: The War in Spain

True self-value: knowing it and being conscious of it, in the very heart of *necessity* that compels you to the role of a slave, in the whirl of a war, as absurd as all wars are, in the gathering of the totalitarian hurricane. This was the main thought Simone tried to convey to her students in Bourges in the year 1935–36, to workers before and after the victory of the Popular Front in June, 1936, in her reflections on war. The sense of one's own dignity as a human being, despite the loss of all rights, despite circumstances of the maximum constraint. And from the depths of the greatest humiliation that can come from without, not coming to despise oneself, but discovering therein one's true meaning. It is a law engraved upon a reality she had wished to live: her experience as a worker. And this law now unifies her restless and manifold activity, apparently at the very boundary of dispersal.

Her courses in philosophy include ever fewer philosophical abstractions and ever more frequent references to great literary works (from Homer to Goethe to Balzac to Hugo), not only from the classics but from contemporary works (Saint-Exupéry, Claudel), besides examples taken from her life in the factory.

Circumstances condition behavior. In a lecture on the family, Simone quotes the reflections of two of her worker comrades. "At least he might be big enough to work," said one mother of her little boy. And another, of her husband who had suffered tuberculosis for eight years, "Fortunately, he died."[1] Sentiments are fine, but life is hard. A short observation glances at that. "Work and sentiments: love changes with occupations. Examples: the difference between the love of an engineer, the love of a peasant, the love of a miner."[2] What exists in man that is not at the mercy of external circumstances? What are the reactions, the thoughts or the actions which he is really master of? Being able to recognize this subjection to the necessity of things "proves that man has at least the negative idea of another kind of thought."[3]

Becoming conscious of this slavery means becoming a man. Otherwise we remain as children, "even at sixty years of age." Or as adolescents, who fight with the sword in the name of honor. "Feudal honor, that of Corneille, a virtue of the privileged, of adolescents." Our only possible liberation takes place through our obedience to necessity. Attention to all the phases of a task which cause you suffering, and the courage to confront them, create in you a "force of the spirit." Used in this way, *suffering* becomes a factor in one's *training*. In the same way, even money does, inasmuch as it forces you to accept in silence reprimands which are often unjust, since they make you fear that you will be fired.

> Things that test human value: humiliation, degradation, slavery, sin, error. A great idea that is found at the basis of the Catholic religion.

And she adds, in parentheses, "Pascal."

For this reason, she asserts, "Christianity is a religion of slaves."[4]

Her ethical attitude begins to take shape: the good, purity of intention and behavior, yields bad results on the social level.

She takes as an instance *Colonel Chabert* of Balzac: "Humility attracts insolence."[5] Hyacinthe Chabert, a Napoleonic hero who was believed dead in the battle of Eylau, agreed to die a second time so that he would not disturb the new life of his wife. She takes advantage of his nobility with effrontery and cleverly leads him to the decision.

It is naive to believe that bad actions alone harm you or put you at risk. Often doing good can be a much greater risk. She makes more precise the contrast between the individual and society, a contrast which exists within each of us. It is a conflict between an unwritten law, which we cannot help obeying in certain extreme moments, and the law imposed from the outside, which above all codifies the relations of power present in circumstances.

The character of Antigone, whom Simone presents to the workers in an effective essay, is the incarnation of this unwritten law. "I have come to share love, not hatred." This was Antigone's response to Creon, who required her to distinguish between her two brothers, one who had died the friend of the homeland, the other the foe.

The essay, pressed within the limits of a bare presentation, was published in *Entre nous,* a house journal for the workers of the Foundry of Rosières, in the outskirts of Bourges. It represents the only concrete result of a large correspondence which, together with meetings, took place between Simone and M. Bernard, the head engineer of the factory.

The possibility of this correspondence provided the only relief for Simone's restlessness during her year at Bourges. Obsessed by her experience as a worker, in her anxiety to give some help to the sufferings and frustrations she had accumulated, she would wander alone in the evening, along the streets of the little city. By walking fast, her head thrust forward, she tried to soothe her headache. People did not look upon her kindly. "In the city, the attitude of Mlle. Weil provokes consternation." They knew that she lived in poverty, giving away the major part of her salary. She surrounded a sick beggar with all kinds of cures, as he lay in the hospital. On seeing her carrying baby carriages for workers' children, they pointed at her and were scandalized. They said she was a Communist. She was not able to establish lasting and personal rapport with her students, as she had at Le Puy, Auxerre, and Roanne. The girls slipped into her drawer clippings from reactionary papers and reviews of the *Jeunesse Ouvrière Chrétienne,* to make her unhappy. "Her looks are unsatisfactory." At a distribution of prizes, she appeared in an utterly worn out raincoat. She read Homer in French, or better, she recited it, improvising, on first glance, a poetic rhythm from the Greek. She displayed an admirable objectivity in the face of opinions contrary to hers. But "the results would be better if the students could participate more actively in the courses and if the material were presented in a livelier fashion." For the rest, "Mlle. Weil is requesting a position in the north; she is looking for the milieu of workers in which she likes to live."[6]

But the workers understood her no better. A great part of her time was devoted to seeking contact with them, in occasional or repeated conversations. For the whole month of October, 1935, Simone ate at the Monoprix, to get to know the shop girls. Many times she invited workers to eat with her. She abandoned this habit when she saw that the shop girls, satisfied with their three hundred francs a month, did not lack anything and did not think that workers were unhappy in the least. The workers, for their part, did not even understand her words.

As far as the Bellevilles, a couple of small landed proprietors whom Simone periodically visited, are concerned, they became downright "neurasthenic." Simone was very adaptable, not clumsy, but she lacked practice. She was not depressing in character, but what she said was depressing and dark to the Bellevilles. All those questions: "How are you, how much do you make, are you happy, what do you want?" She would eat nothing. They would bring her a fine snack of fresh cheese and cream and she would refuse it with the comment that the little Indochinese were hungry. "Poor girl, so much instruction went to her head!" the Bellevilles said to each other. Simone Weil upset them, because she had broken through the usual barriers between intellectuals and peasants and gotten rid of roles that had always existed and were comfortable because they were known.[7]

The only friends who had the opportunity to share many of her hours were the Coulombs, a young and friendly couple for whom Simone felt fondness. They would come to meet her in her garret and she would offer them vodka in a glass for brushing one's teeth. On Thursdays they would take long walks in the countryside; once they went looking for the estate that was the setting of Alain Taurnier's novel, *Le Grand Meaulnes*. They spoke of music and Simone made the Coulombs listen to records of Gregorian chant, which she particularly loved. They would hold long conversations and Simone told them how she could not belong to any of the groups in which she had worked. Her friends felt her restlessness and realized that her opposition to society was not the fruit of superficial negativism. Simone was in search of a way of communicating and acting among men that would take account of the complexity of circumstances and bring that complexity to the best possible synthesis.

She says so to M. Bernard, in a letter she wrote to clarify her social and political position.

> I look forward with all my heart to a transformation of the current regime that would be the most radical possible, in the sense of the greatest equality in the relationship of forces . . . All political groups that count tend in an equal way . . . to the accentuation of oppression . . . ; some call it a worker's revolution, others Fascism, still others the organization of national defense . . . Two factors are prevalent: on the one hand, implicit subordination and dependence on modern forms of technology, on the other, war. All those who want, on the one hand, an increasing "rationalization" and, on the other, a preparation for war are the same in my eyes and they are everyone.[8]

Her wish, then, was to achieve equality from within, by pointing out ways to be alert to self-knowledge and to communication both with work-

ers and with their directors. She appealed, then, to the whole man, and
with Bernard she did not use diplomacy at all, she did not take advantage
of him, because she dealt with him as a person.

Empowered by her own suffering in the factory, where the humiliation
of living in a situation of inferiority "which is taken for granted" corrodes
the intelligence and "degrades" the whole being, Simone asked Bernard
for a way to penetrate the factory through a paper. She submitted to him
an "appeal" to the workers; the appeal invited them to express "with the
first words that came to their mind" suffering or joy, the feeling of loneliness or comradeship, the monotony or the energy that they found in their
daily work. These letters, addressed to her, would then be modified by her
so that they would not injure their authors. Comrades and supervisors
would then read them, the former to gain courage to express themselves in
their own turn, the latter to discover, perhaps, the necessity of improving
life in the factory. "People never put themselves in others' clothes." "It is
difficult for the man who gives orders and the man who receives them to
understand each other." A more serene knowledge, insofar as it lies outside
the normal routine of work, and a more direct knowledge, insofar as it is
free from the play of command and execution, would give the supervisors
a means of penetrating into the dimensions of the worker. They could then
develop the initiative of making the workers participants in the difficulties
involved in production. "The pitiless law of profit weighs with an inhuman weight upon the whole of industrial life" and the only thing to do, in
truth, is an investigation into the "most human organization compatible
with a given yield."

The appeal was not published. Bernard objected that Simone was in
reality pretending to extend to everyone what was *her* interpretation of the
life of the worker, that educating the workers was a "very difficult enterprise," and that the encouragement to express themselves would end in
fomenting a dangerous class spirit.

Simone replied that, having chosen the point of view of "those who are
at the bottom," she had experienced and seen others around her experience, in silence, all those states of mind which derive from the certainty
that "they do not count for anything," which is part of the condition of the
worker. So she thought that she was speaking of something that was very
real. She suggested that he go see the film *Modern Times,* which described
that life much better than she.

Educating the workers would seem "quite difficult" until contacts were established with them on the human level, in such a way that one would know them in their aspirations and their real capacities. For this reason it was indispensable to make them express themselves, to make them find "the sense of their own dignity." To educate anyone, it is necessary first of all "to raise him in his own eyes."

With regard to class spirit, they are not words which foment it but the real situations in which an inferiority, which is taken for granted, creates uneasiness.

When her attempt at making an appeal failed, Simone requested the chance to sound the situation through questionnaires. An inquiry could elicit the conclusion that one of the obstacles to a more human form of organization was just to be found in the *ignorance of the workers* themselves. This conclusion would be the natural source of inspiration for writing and accepting, in a fruitful manner, a series of articles of *popularization*.

> An investigation of the true method for popularization—a matter completely unknown to everyone today—is one of my dominant preoccupations.

The goal of education is the "moral welfare" of the worker. In her experience, Simone had always discovered, in the "worn-out beings" with whom she lived, "elevation of mind" united with a "generosity of heart." Even in relations between men and women, the only ones "who could speak to a woman without hurting her" were skilled workers. For this reason, work itself should tend, to the degree it is possible, to constitute an education. It is a risk that even a supervisor must run, to the end of assisting

> a progressive passage from total subordination to a certain blend of subordination and collaboration, the ideal being pure collaboration.[9]

It is the project of a "totally new" culture of the *Cahiers*.

The strikes which followed the victory of the Popular Front awakened in Simone "an ineffable sense of joy and of liberation," as she directly asserted in loyalty to Bernard. And their relations came to an end.[10]

On June 10, under the pseudonym of Simone Galois (the surname of the great mathematician she so much admired), she published an article rich in memories. In it she perceived the strike as the possibility of "opening the vise," of standing up, of speaking, of at length feeling like men.

Quite independently of all claims, this strike is a joy in itself.

She returns to Renault.

The joy of wandering through the workshops, of chattering, of having a snack together. The joy of hearing music, singing and laughter, instead of the merciless clanging of machines.

It means finding again "the rhythm of human life," the proper respiration of the organism, the beating of the heart . . . But Simone did not have illusions. "The hard days will return." Certain things have been obtained forever: joyful holidays, the increase of salaries, the possibility of having a voice in the running of the factory. And yet: "the workers go on strike but they leave to the militants to study the details of the claims." This passivity, formed over the years like a second skin, includes a grave danger: not taking account of the real problems posed by the strike, in the first place, the "relation between material claims and moral claims." This means seeing clearly what the increases claimed can correspond to, what they risk creating in the national economy, what they will succeed in creating in the daily life of the factory. Simone urges workers to limit their material claims, to establish rather "the first embryo of workers' control."[11]

Her profound participation in the joy of the strikers did not dim even for a moment Simone's vision; she will again turn it upon industrial life in precise interventions with Auguste Detoeuf, in an investigation of northern factories (Lille, end of 1936—beginning of 1937) and in drafting "Principes d'un projet pour un régime intérieur nouveau dans les entreprises industrielles." The investigation was on her own initiative. She requested and obtained the charge from the CGT. The report deriving from it, with the title, "Remarques sur les enseignements a tirer des conflits du Nord," is outstanding for its impartiality, good sense, and resistance to any demagogic assertion.[12]

In it she highlighted the abuses of certain labor delegates who had departed from their "theoretical mission," and had become rather soon "a power in the factories," with the result that they made employees and technicians pass over to the anti-worker side. She considered and found just some complaints of the industrialists, in particular the right of applying sanctions.

Slavery has to a large degree disappeared, and along with it has disappeared the order connected with slavery. We can only rejoice at that.

But industry cannot live without order. So the problem is posed of a new order compatible with the freedoms of recent acquisition . . . It is not even in the moral interest of the working class that workers should feel irresponsible in the performance of their labor.[13]

She did not want to be paid for this investigation, an attitude that "cheapened her irremediably" in the eyes of Johaux,[14] the director of the CGT.

═══

Now, in the summer of 1936, she feels the pressure of another need for action within herself, one which is also a need for a test: she wanted to participate in the Spanish Civil War. As always, the impulse is stronger than she is in determining her decision. As always, Simone *cannot help but* rush to where she discerns the center of need. She would have the unbearable feeling of "remaining in the rear." Also leading her are her explosiveness (a hundred lives in her, already so spent), her taste for action, and her sympathy for the Spanish anarchists, the last in whom she has any confidence, who seem to express the greatnesses and the faults of "a people whom it is impossible not to love."[15]

Confronted with the decision of nonintervention declared by Léon Blum, Simone understands the reasons of a man at the head of a government and so responsible for the destiny of a people; all the same, for herself, she "does not accept" her own responsibility in this decision and has to leave.

Later, either in Aragon or Catalonia, among militants feeling betrayed who harshly opposed the policy of neutrality, she will defend Blum. Peace is too precious to "sacrifice it deliberately."[16]

From this, all the same, there does emerge one condition: neutrality should also be maintained in the future. Abandoning the Spanish to massacre to avoid a world war and later going to war for any other reason (aggression against French territory or territory protected by France, colonies, treaties with other countries) would be unjustifiable.

Do we or do we not want to look matters in the face, to set the problem of war or peace in its entirety?[17]

This is her anguished question, in which are blended her experience with unions, her investigation of the German reality, her study of the productive machinery of industrial civilization, and her first meditations on man as he is branded and constrained by this type of civilization in all of his behavior.

Ever since her pacifism as a student of Alain, Simone had always opposed war. After the deepening of her social life, as the desire for a more just society had led her to evaluate the real possibilities of a successful revolution, this pacifist opposition is based on new considerations.

She begins with an examination of the relationship between war and revolution and then between war and the labor movement. This occurs in her article "Réflexions sur la guerre" of November, 1933.

She finds that we are strangely and "shamefully" unable to judge a phenomenon which, along with preparations, reparations, and preparations again, and with all the moral and material consequences, "seems to dominate our age and to constitute its characteristic mark." This inability is a little less surprising if we reflect that war has been seen only in the wake of an "illusory tradition" and studied with an extremely defective method.

Until 1918, all revolutionary ideas on war and peace were based on a legendary interpretation of the events of 1792, according to which war, whether offensive or defensive, is per se *revolutionary*, conducted by a people now free from class oppression against foreign tyrants. Thus, in 1870, the International, through Marx, invited the workers of the two countries in the struggle to defend their respective lands. Both Bolsheviks and Spartacists were opposed to this idea. For them all wars, with the exception of revolutionary and nationalist wars for Lenin, revolutionary wars alone for Rosa Luxemburg, are the fruit of imperialist aims. Thus the proletariat must look forward to the defeat of their own country and sabotage the war effort.

The only point in common among the Marxist theories, which were neither clear nor homogeneous, was "the categorical refusal to condemn war as such." Paraphrasing a formula of von Clausewitz (one of Simone's readings), Lenin repeated: war is nothing but the continuation of the policy of peacetime with other means, so a war is to be judged, not by the *violence of the means* employed, but by the *ends* pursued.

But we shall never succeed in judging a war with a method which takes into account only the ends and disregards the means, no matter how violent. For

war represents in every epoch a well-determined form of violence.

We must study its mechanism, analyze the social relations which a military struggle implies in a determined "technical, economic, and social context."

The great error of almost all studies of war and in particular of all socialist studies has been that of considering war a matter of foreign policy.

War is in the first place a matter of internal policy and the most atrocious of all.

In fact, "massacre is the most radical form of oppression."

Modern war differs completely from what corresponded in the past to that definition. In the first place it only prolongs the other war called *competition;* secondly, the entire economic life is oriented towards a future war. In factories, the workers are subject to instruments of labor, which they do not control. In war the soldiers are subject to armaments, "the true heroes of modern wars," directed by those who do not fight. Given that competition does not know any weapon other than the exploitation of workers, it is transformed in the last analysis into the struggle of all owners against all workers. In the same way, the necessity of defeating the enemy is based on sending soldiers to their death. To this they are forced by the apparatus of the state, for which war becomes the definitive war between the apparatuses of states and their armies.

War is to reproduce in the most acute form the social relations which structure a regime. If it is conducted by revolutionary forces, it becomes a factor of reaction, inasmuch as in war the apparatus of state must exercise upon its own armies the maximum of oppression, even unto death.

Revolutionary war is the tomb of the revolution.

This is the reality of the war of 1792 in the France of Robespierre.

The profound affinity between Fascism and war is evident from Fascist texts, with their evocations of the "warrior spirit" and of "socialism to the front." In both cases we are dealing with the erasure of the individual in the face of the bureaucracy of the state in the name of an exasperated fanaticism.

In a general sense it seems that history is more and more forcing every political action to choose between aggravating the oppression of the apparatuses of the state in an unbearable fashion and a desperate struggle directly aimed against those apparatuses to break them.

The struggle is destined to remain impotent until we "discern" how it is possible to avoid this domination of the apparatuses over the individual in the very act of production and of combat.[18]

The war in Spain seemed to her a spontaneous war on the model of the Commune, a war of individuals with whom one should demonstrate solidarity. For this reason she was going there, but without deceiving herself on the universal plane of reality. On page 19 of the *Cahiers,* we find this notation, which expresses the relationship between war and the human psyche.

> The *Iliad*—The mainspring of war is desperation. Violent labor of the soul upon itself, inasmuch as it is forced to conform to a situation in which *all* of its aspirations are purely and simply denied.
>
> . . . The ends of war are forgotten; one is constrained to reach the point of denying *all* ends. They continue to exist not in spite of, but because of their absurdity. This desperation exists wherever man is *sacrificed*.[19]

In June of 1936, Simone Weil came home from a meeting and announced to her parents, "I am leaving for Spain." To calm them, she added, "I am going as a journalist."

Her parents decided to follow her; they would stop at Perpignan. The railway syndicalists approved of their decision ("Simone will surely do something foolish") and they gave them the necessary letters of introduction to the syndicalists of Perpignan.

Simone crossed the frontier at Port-Bou on August 8. In the days that followed she wrote a large number of undated letters and cards. "Barcelona is always the same. I am infinitely less distressed than in Paris; the stay is already doing me good." "I shall go with two French comrades who know Spanish . . . to see villages where they have done the cultivating in common . . . for some days I shall study socialized production."[20]

In reality, she was forming plans which were less reassuring. She went in search of Julian Gorkin, who had taken refuge in Paris after the riots of October, 1934; he had already heard of her from Souvarine and Colette Audry. He was a director of the POUM,[21] composed in great part of dissident Communists. Its founder had been Joaquin Maurin, a brother-in-law of Souvarine. Maurin had disappeared in Galicia during the early days of the war and was probably in the hands of Franco's troops. Simone proposed to Gorkin that she go in search of him. She could not move Gorkin from his rejection of an enterprise he considered useless; it could even compromise Maurin. After a painful discussion, Simone went away discouraged.

She tried to enroll in the militia of the CNT,[22] the central anarchist union, along with other journalists, but she left them to go to Pina, in Aragon. Here, on the banks of the Ebro, she found Buenaventura Durruti, at the head of the most important unit of the anarchist militias: a Franco-international body composed of Frenchmen, Spaniards with French citizenship, Italians, and Germans, charged with dangerous missions. There were twenty-two men and one woman, Simone. At night, two comrades, Ridel and Carpentier, will take turns protecting her, without ever telling her.

On Sunday, August 16, Simone hears an address of Durruti[23] to peasants and notes in her *Journal d'Espagne* this one phrase, "I am a worker. When all of this is over, I shall return to the factory."

For preceding days, there are some notes of a conversation between peasants and militiamen.

Their former life: "Working day and night, terrible food. The majority cannot read . . . They go barefoot." The curate. "We had nothing for alms but we brought chickens to the curate. Loved? Yes, by many. Why? the answer is not clear." Those who speak, of every age, have never been to Mass.

Hatred for the rich? "Yes, but even more among the poor."

Life in the city seems a kind of mirage. Workers in the city are more up to date. One of them, who had gone there to work, "returned after three months with new clothes" . . . During their time of military service, however, they are looking forward to returning. Why? "Bad food, thrashing (if one answered back, executions) . . . The rich do it in other situations." "A very lively sense of inferiority."

On Monday, August 17, she had a rifle: "a fine little musket." Short-sighted, clumsy . . . her comrades made sure they were out of her way during target practice.

An expedition to burn three enemy bodies is the first and *only* time Simone says that she was afraid at Pina. In effect they were shot at by Nationalists, 112 men who were waiting for them at the ford. Durruti gave orders that the peasant family living there be brought to camp. The peasants were a father, a son, and a youth of sixteen "(handsome!)." "Fontana raises his fist. The son replies with obvious distaste. Cruel coercion."

Another time: "Aerial reconnaissance. On the ground . . . I look at the leaves, the blue sky. A most lovely day. If they catch me, they will kill me . . . I will have deserved it. Our men have shed enough blood. I am morally an accomplice."[24]

On August 19, Simone's bad eyesight betrays her. They are all in the underbrush on the right bank of the Ebro. In a hole in the ground there is a fire, over which there is a huge pan of boiling oil. Simone does not see it and puts her foot on it. The whole lower part of her leg and ankle are seriously burned. When Carpentier removes her stocking, the skin comes off with it. They bring her back to Pina, but that night, dauntless, she returns to camp, hastily bandaged. Her teeth are chattering. In her *Journal,* Simone does not refer to the accident. We shall find her notes again from September 5, from Sitges. At Pina, she was given first aid by a barber, who functioned as a doctor; the bandage did not cover the entire wound and he ordered her to walk. She dragged herself along the road. She was picked up first by a colonel and then by Pierre Robert, a Swiss syndicalist; at length she reached Barcelona.

Her parents had, in the meantime, been able to cross the frontier, thanks to a network of solidarity between the French and the Spanish. With their rucksacks, they wandered in search of Simone in Barcelona, from one organization to the other. They left their address everywhere they went. A journalist said to them, "Are you the parents of Simone Weil? You will never see her again." At length, calmed by a card from "Aunt Louise," an anarchist, they patiently began waiting on the Ramblas, in front of the headquarters of the POUM, until late in the night, because the convoys from the front arrived at night.

But Simone arrived during the day and, all happy and serene, told her story. On seeing the condition of her leg, Dr. Bernard was worried to distraction.

At Sitges, the hospital was set up in the Terramar hotel, the finest in the city, but the doctors were hostile to Simone (since she was an anarchist,

Collinet thinks).[25] For no reason, she was put in a little room in the rear and neglected to such a point that the Weils took her away to their pensione, where her father began to care for her. If she had remained in that hospital, she would probably have been forced to have her leg amputated.

Ridel and Carpentier came to visit her. Her friend Collinet took her several times to Barcelona, where she visited some factories. Although she was pessimistic about the outcome of the revolution (either there would be a victory for Franco or Spain would be transformed into another Russia), Simone did not want to leave Spain.

Only on the promise that she would return to the front once she was cured, were her parents able to convince her to return to France. Gorkin gave them the necessary safe-conduct to cross the frontier. This happened on September 25.

Simone Weil was saved by the accident she had. The Durruti column, which subsequently became larger, was decimated at Perdiguera; the women who had joined it were all killed.

Even though she showed solidarity with the Spanish republicans in meetings, where she would appear with the red-and-black foulard of a militia-woman while she defended the anarchists of Catalonia and their achievements, Simone did not return to Spain. And it was not for medical reasons or for the love of her parents. She burst out crying in the presence of Dr. Cadenat and she would not have wanted to do that. The impossibility of returning to Spain was inside herself and did not depend on external circumstances.

She will explain her reasons to Bernanos:

> I no longer felt any inner necessity to participate in a war which was no longer, as it had first seemed to me, a war of famished peasants against landowners and their accomplices, the clergy, but a war between Russia, Germany and Italy.

Her disillusion was bitter and total. Simone turned to the author of the *Journal d'un curé de campagne* (among her favorite novels), because she felt the need of sharing with him an experience similar to that described by Bernanos in *Les grands cimetières sous la lune*.[26] Simone terms her own "shorter, less profound . . . and experienced in appearance—only in appearance—with an entirely different spirit."

And she tells her story. The same night the militia returned from

Majorca in defeat, they went out (in little Sitges) on punitive raids against real or presumed Fascists. "Among the slain, a baker of around thirty . . . His father, whose only son and support he was, went mad."

Aragon. After a skirmish, a small international group took a fifteen-year-old prisoner. Full of fright from having been present at the death of his comrades, the young man says he was conscripted by force. They beat him and find a medal of the Madonna on him, and the card of a Falangist. He is brought before Durruti, who spends an hour with him as he outlines the beauty of the anarchist ideal; he offers him two choices: death or immediate entry into the ranks of those who have captured him, "as they fought against his companions of the watch." After twenty-four hours, the young man said no, and was shot. "And yet Durruti was under certain aspects an admirable man. The death of that little hero still weighs upon my conscience."

In the rear, some anarchists seized two priests. They killed one on the spot and said to the other that he could go away; when he had gone twenty steps, they shot him down. "The man who told me this episode was surprised that he did not see me laugh."

At Barcelona, with about a million inhabitants, fifty men were killed a night. This was a much lower proportion to that of Majorca; but it is not the numbers that count but "the attitude in the face of murder."

> Right in the middle of a meal replete with comradeship, I have heard them recount with a good fraternal smile how many priests and how many "Fascists," quite an ample term, they had killed.

While Bernanos attributed the taste for slaughter to fear, Simone had discovered, in otherwise brave men, an unconscious satisfaction with killing. Neither the Spanish nor the French had shown the slightest sign of disgust or disapproval of the blood they had shed in vain.

Simone's conclusion is this: when spiritual and temporal authorities exclude a category of human beings from the company of those whose life is of value, and there is no longer any fear of punishment or blame, "there is killing, or at least there are smiles of encouragement for the man who does kill."

Any possible revulsion is smothered, for fear of "lacking manhood," and it is difficult to resist such intoxication. She has seen "dull and inoffensive" compatriots who had not been involved personally with any killing steep themselves "in that blood-drenched atmosphere with visible pleasure." It is an atmosphere that destroys "the very goal of the struggle."

> One departs willingly with ideas of sacrifice and ends up in a war which is like a war of mercenaries, with many more cruelties and much less sense of the consideration due the enemy.[27]

The war in Spain will never depart from her; it settles in her as a cautionary experience and will lead her to her concept of real *action*. As always, Simone finds in herself the signs of the danger.

Meditations on war recur in the *Cahiers*, for war is the apex of the use of force.

> Contact with force is hypnotic. It plunges one into dreaming. As far as yourself is concerned, be awake in enduring force and in managing it—but be careful: among the other aspects of the state of sleeping there is an illusion of extreme lucidity which is not being awake.[28]

Is there then any criterion we can use?

> Fear and the taste for killing. Avoid them both. How? In Spain the effort seemed one that would break my heart . . . Become such that you endure it.[29]

War acts upon the imagination and flattens the vision of reality and makes you lose consciousness of yourself and of the real and manifold data of a situation. You no longer exist, neither you nor the world.

In handling a weapon (Simone is here speaking of a sword), you persuade yourself that you are holding suspended over others "the gravity" of reality and you derive from that an "illusion of elevation," the "false exaltation associated with power, with murder, with sexual possession."[30] It is the triumph of dreaming over reality.

====

Her pacifism became more and more decidedly oriented towards a morality of international relations and found expression, in the first place, in a struggle against empty words, which are supporters of dreams.

And perhaps in March, 1936, she had already sent to *Vigilance* her immediate reply to a question of Alain.[31]

After Hitler had remilitarized the Rhineland, Alain asked, "Men who speak of honor and of dignity as the most precious goods, more precious than life itself, would they be the first to risk it, i.e., life? And what should we think of them, if they are not?"

Simone examines the two words, "dignity" and "honor," the two most deadly words in our vocabulary. In fact, the formulas "peace with dignity" and "peace with honor" were a prelude to the slaughter of the first world war.

If by dignity one understands self-esteem, "war has never been a means to avoid disdain for oneself," inasmuch as it does not put to the test either courage or will. Noncombatants do not have to confront dangers, combatants are forced to do so, and the power of beginning or ending hostilities is in the hands of those who are not fighting. "The very soul of honor is the free decision to put one's own life at risk." War, then, does not constitute for anyone the safeguard of honor; as a consequence, no peace is dishonorable.

In international relations, the term dignity is opposed to *humiliation*. If preferring death to disdain for oneself "is the basis for any morality," preferring death to humiliation "is simply the point of feudal honor." Who then is sent to die to defend this point of honor between nations? The disinherited and the weak, those who in time of peace have humiliation as their daily bread.

If the principle of rejecting humiliation as the price of life were applied within society, the entire society would be subverted. Making this principle a rule of international politics is truly "the peak of irresponsibility."

In April of 1937 another analysis of words appeared under the title "Ne recommençons pas la guerre de Troie." The article was intended for the section "Pouvoir des Mots" in one of the first issues of the review *Nouveaux Cahiers*.[32]

This fortnightly review was the result of meetings of a group created by Auguste Detoeuf in the spring of 1936. "Intended to establish very close contacts between workers and men of affairs, directors of business and intellectuals, it should express controversial ideas in absolute liberty from sympathizers of union, industrial and university provenance." So explains Guillaume de Tarde, one of its founders.[33] The association, which can be defined as "a group hostile to the spirit of a group," represented the "maturation of the need for social redress, which France had felt for a long time. The problems which at first were posed on precise questions went deeper in a more general political sense."

The subjects were topics of internal and external policy ("the action of foreigners and of foreign powers in France"), the industrial regime ("labor sabotage and owner sabotage," "the regulation of hiring and dismissal"), the reform of instruction. To this last topic an appropriate study group was devoted; both de Tarde and Simone were part of it. They often met at the Weil home, in Simone's room or in the studio on the seventh floor.[34]

"Simone Weil: a sort of vagabond. Boris Souvarine, one of our sympathizers, brought her among us. She came quite often. The meetings were held once a week, first at the Flore and then at a cafe near Saint-Sulpice. There was in her a clear will to give no importance to her apparel; so she wound up obtaining the opposite effect. That dark cape . . . and shapeless things beneath it. No makeup. Only once did I see in her smile a flash of femininity. Ordinarily there was a hardness in her expression. She would always say important and interesting things, with a voice beyond all emotion. And yet, despite all this, Simone was a friend for me. I felt that our confidence was reciprocal, a companionship in our entering into contact with reality." De Tarde thinks back on Simone's handwriting. "It was Detoeuf who showed it to me. I told myself: the girl is either a madwoman or a genius. There were, in those letters, both candor and obstinacy: the serenity and the tension where madness lurks."

Denis de Rougemont, the secretary of the group and chief editor of the *Nouveaux Cahiers,* always saw her as beyond a pane of glass; something always prevented him from approaching her personally. He remembers her "with her temple resting on the sloping board of a desk, her hands that squeezed its edges, to ease her headache."[35]

Pierre Bost, a friend of Detoeuf, took part in the *Nouveaux Cahiers* sporadically. "Detoeuf knew how to make people intelligent. Generous in mind and heart, he had many enemies. The movement of ideas in *Nouveaux Cahiers* characteristically brought together all kinds of voices, no matter where they came from. For this reason, Simone Weil was interested in it."[36]

Paid for by members of the group, without any publicity, the review was published by Gallimard between March, 1937 and 1940.

The rubric heading *"Pouvoir des Mots"* was intended to examine "the evolution of opinions and the influence that facts had upon it."[37]

At the core of Simone's article is this assertion.

We live among mutable realities, diverse and determined by the fickle play of external necessities . . . but we act, struggle, sacrifice ourselves and others in the name of crystallized, isolated abstractions, which it is impossible to arrange among themselves or with concrete things.

The abstractions are masked by words. "Nation, security, capitalism, Communism, Fascism, order, authority, property, democracy"; they are words with capital letters.

And they are "swollen with blood and tears"; if we try to squeeze only one of them, we find that it has no contents. And yet for them men commit "lethal absurdities," without ever getting anything, except the destruction of other men, who make use of "inimical words." For they go in antagonistic pairs: Fascism and Communism, dictatorship and democracy . . .

The oppositions between them are never examined in the light of the essential concepts which guide the intelligence: "limit, measure, level, proportion . . . the bond between means and ends," which we no longer have today.

It is Simone who does it, by summoning us to the use of reason, which, if used properly, can still save us from a war before which the war of Troy appears "a model of good sense." The "phantasm" of beautiful Helen, for whom this war was waged, was a "substantial reality," compared with the opposition between Fascism and Communism. The two words, in fact, conceal social and political conceptions which are almost identical. And yet Germany and Russia, the most similar of nations, are menacing each other with an "international crusade." A hatred, as obstinate as it is illogical, identifies the two words with two groups of enemies, who, inspired by this hatred, "resign themselves in advance to death, and above all to killing."

The opposition between dictatorship and democracy is, on the contrary, true in itself, but it loses its sense if the two terms are seen as two "entities" and not as references to a social structure. The latter presents the two aspects in diverse degrees. The "level of democracy" depends on the relations between the various gears of the social machine and the conditions which determine their functioning. One must examine relations and conditions. But generally one thinks of a dictatorship or a democracy incarnate in human groups, nations or parties. So the person who by temperament is inclined to order, related to dictatorship, or to liberty, associated with democracy, will be "obsessed" with the desire to smash the one or the other of these groups.

The only conflict between human groups which has any foundation is that indicated by the term (still to be made clear) of class struggle. The vital motive upon which this conflict is based is the eternal struggle between those who obey and those who command. The latter tend more or less unconsciously "to grind under foot the dignity" of the man underneath, while the former have to struggle "not to lose all the rights of a human being." The encounter between *pressure* from below and *resistance* from above, a resistance which, beyond selfish reasons, corresponds to the ideal of defending order, creates "an unstable equilibrium," which defines the fabric of a society. This encounter is a struggle but it is not necessarily a war. There is danger of it becoming one if its protagonists allow themselves to be blinded by *entities*. Capitalism becomes the incarnation of absolute evil; an ensemble of mutable phenomena is crystallized in an abstraction upon which are projected "all sufferings we have endured or seen others endure." And a man with blood in his veins dedicates his life to the destruction of capitalism, i.e., to revolution in its present, "purely negative" sense.

It is easier to kill and even to die than to ask some simple questions. How are we to define in a system the laws which regulate economic life? Up to which point are the bonds between one economic phenomenon and another necessary? What are the influences that the change of one or another economic law would have?

> To what degree are the sufferings caused by the social relations of our epoch dependent upon one or another economic law or upon these laws taken as a whole?

What are the "new sufferings, transitory or permanent" implied by the method of transformation put into effect? And which ones come from the new organization?

Studying the problem in this way would mean circumscribing capitalism as a "relative evil" and proposing a social transformation only in order to obtain a "lesser evil."

Simone appeals to the *mind* and to the *responsibility* of those who desire transformation and also of those who want to preserve too much. For, in the present world, the struggle between the adversaries and the defenders of capitalism, between innovators who do not know what to innovate and preservers who do not know what to preserve is a blind struggle among the blind . . . which for this reason runs the risk of becoming a general slaughter.

In analyzing all the formulas which, in the course of history, have stirred the "spirit of sacrifice and also cruelty," we shall find them all empty. But if the formulas are phantasms, behind the formulas are very concrete things: the Greek and the Trojan army, the various states with their various offices and customhouses, barracks, arsenals and prisons . . . "To every empty abstraction corresponds a human group," each dominated by desire for power.

All the absurdities because of which history resembles an extended delirium have their root in an essential absurdity, the nature of power.

It is necessary for a power to exist, because "order is indispensable to existence"; but the attribution of power is arbitrary, for

The very heart of power is prestige, that is to say, illusion.

A power must appear absolute and untouchable to those who exercise it, to those who obey it, to foreign powers.

If "every social situation rests on an equilibrium of forces," there is no equilibrium to stabilize prestige. For prestige does not bear limits; satisfying it means assailing someone else's prestige. For men it would seem that but one choice is offered: anarchy associated with weak powers or wars of every sort connected with desire for prestige. How can we get out of this blind alley? There is not always war, so it is not impossible to think of lasting peace. But we must set the problem "in all its real terms." And the problem of international and civil peace has never been set in that way.

How are we to see its real terms? By freeing them of the "cloud of empty entities." The *"hunt for entities"* in every field of political and social life becomes an urgent work of public health.[38]

These meditations on the possibility of conceiving of an international and civil peace were, for Simone, a later stage on the road towards real equality among men. They harmonized with the kind of political participation she had set for herself since the autumn of 1934.

In the practical field she had decided to limit herself to two actions: the struggle against preparation for passive defense and the struggle against colonial oppression. The first was a way of opposing war. "Simone believed that preparation increased the probability of war, both by accustoming people to the idea of war and by making civilians hope that in case of conflict they would be safe, unlike soldiers who would be exposed to death."[39] The second was a way of compelling the French state to become conscious of its own offenses against the colonies and to remedy the inevitable consequences in time.

The same profound desire for equality which animated her article on "entities" is confirmed. In that article Simone wanted to reveal to men their real selves, so they would be able to grasp for themselves their very real problems, beyond abstractions. In these actions she wanted to achieve real parity among men, beyond differences of role and race.

This desire, replete with a sense of justice, made her inflexible as ever in her moral judgment. Confronted with revolutionary riots in Tunisia, she commented: "Labor papers write, 'Blood in streams in Tunisia.' Perhaps it will cause them to remember the existence of workers in that land." There are millions of them and "we have all forgotten them." Why? Because they are far away. And "they all know that suffering decreases in proportion to distance." And then, "those men, black and yellow . . . are people accustomed to suffer . . . The best proof is that they do not complain . . . At bottom, they have a servile character. Otherwise they would resist." Those who resist are "agitators," probably in the pay of Franco and Hitler. Repress them: there is nothing else to do.

In the end, Simone loyally asserts, "we—I mean all whose who adhere to an organization of the Popular Union—are exactly like the bourgeoisie." Like an owner who is moved at the sight of a beggar on the street and condemns his own workers to die of hunger, we join in the struggle against misery and oppression and remain indifferent to the inhuman conditions imposed by our government on millions of men.

For this reason, when she thinks of a possible war, a certain sense of relief is blended with her distress.

A European war could serve as a signal for the great revenge of the colonial peoples to punish our irresponsibility, our indifference and our cruelty.[40]

And confronted with the proclaimed necessity of French intervention to prevent Hitler's occupation of Czechoslovakia, she finds it a "bitter irony," that France uses the defense of a people as a pretext for war when there is no lack of peoples, in Asia and in Africa, to free and to defend . . . and peacefully.

War. There are numerous letters in the first months of 1937 to ward off the horror. They are addressed to Belin, a director of the CGT.

> I assert . . . that a defeat without a war is preferable to a victorious war. Who would prevent us, every time that a diplomatic conflict, actual or latent, threatens to degenerate into a war, from granting to the adversary the confessed or secret objectives, symbolic or real, that he intends to achieve with a military victory?[41]

Furthermore, she pointed to the preparation for war as the greatest obstacle to a change in the condition of workers. Neither "reforms" nor "revolution" could have the slightest influence upon the basic conditions of workers as long as the general structure of the economy was subject to the necessities of war industry, which engendered excessive "privations and overtime," and accorded a privileged position to branches of the economy "which do not contribute either to the development of the body or to that of the mind."[42]

The last of these letters concludes with a sorrowful prophecy.

> This I predict to you, and we can fix a date: we are entering a period in which incredible madness will be a common sight in all lands, and it will seem natural. Civil life will continue to diminish. Military preoccupations will dominate all the details of existence . . . Capitalism will be destroyed, but not by the working class. It will be destroyed by the development of national defense in every land and it will be replaced by a totalitarian state. This is the revolution we shall have. Luckily, there will come a day when the world will have no more iron, copper and manganese.[43]

13

Italy, or Beauty

The letters to Belin date back to February–March, 1937. The last was written from Montana, where Simone had gone to attempt a cure for the persistent headaches, which together with the aftereffects of her burns and her anemia prevented her from teaching school for a whole year. Furthermore, Montana was on the way to Italy. And she wanted to know Italy, before the terrible events she foresaw began.

She was terribly exhausted. Let us pause for a while and look at her. There is a photograph from 1936, taken in Spain, upon her return from the front.

Her face, as though colliding with the wind, unleashes, beneath her good and brave, if somewhat wild, smile, an incurable sadness. Her bare features, casually crowned with her hair, are well-designed, pleasing and true. Her eyes, without their usual glasses and slightly closed, are darker. What strikes us most in this face is its vulnerability, which expresses a complete fusion of being and appearance.

Simone reveals herself, in her weakness and the consciousness of her own worth. She writes to a friend:

> I am not up to any task, in any field. I cannot undertake anything without forcing myself, with the inner agony of the swimmer who asks himself if he will really reach the shore . . . On the other hand, I am growing ever more clearly conscious of what I have within; and if I must be utterly honest, I am convinced that they are the seeds of great things. This contradiction makes me desperate.

She sees no way out except to push herself to the limits of the possible and, once the disproportion between her abilities and her tasks to accomplish becomes too large, "to die."

And to carry away with me all that I keep closed within myself as so many others of much greater worth have done over the centuries.

The other torment, upon which the contradiction rests to a great extent, presents itself in the long periods when her headaches become unbearable: she asks herself then if the moment for dying has not arrived. To prevent herself from being swept away and caught up in an "unreasonable" depression, she decides not to make any decisions on suicide "until six months or a year has passed." Then, when her courage "is exhausted," there appears the "terrible temptation" of using the headaches as an excuse for laziness and "all" her weaknesses. And once the pain has slackened and she has recovered, to some degree, the freedom of her mind

she hurls herself upon life with such fire and ardor that a renewed phase of illness appears every time, once proper allowances are made, like a condemnation to death for a being brimming with youth and vitality.

Finally, with all her being she declares:

"life is supremely beautiful in my eyes—but for me it is more and more inaccessible."[1]

In Simone's life, Italy represents a phase of nourishment. It is an emotional nourishment, which she receives above all through casual encounters, an aesthetic inspiration, which she draws from the painting, the sculpture, the architecture and the music, a spiritual value of her surroundings, which she derives from the cities, in particular Florence and Assisi on the first journey, Venice on the second. And she knows how to receive this nourishment. She has prepared herself with her reading (Machiavelli, the poetry of Michelangelo) and listening to music (the discovery of Monteverdi, a little earlier, by way of Simone Pétrement). Above all she has prepared herself with her desire and will to fulfill it. "When one has truly dreamt of something, one must finally do it: that is my moral." She wrote this to her parents in 1938.[2]

For the first and only time in her life, we see her in a period of healthful vacation. Her studies and her readings highlight the appearance of the terrain and the appearance of the terrain is interpreted and described with emotional abandon. Italy is for her an island of the soul, at which she lands with ardor.

Her letters to her friend Posternak, whose room in Montana was so rich in atmosphere that it became "the center of her social life there,"[3] and her letters to her parents express this joyousness. Simone does not have enough eyes to see or ears to hear. She walks tirelessly, she never complains of a headache.

She profits from everything. Her first encounter with an Italian occurs on the shore of Lago Maggiore. He is a young and pleasant wagon-driver with a load of flour; despite her limited knowledge of the language, Simone quickly grasps that he is not a Fascist. At Milan, "the kind of populous city I like," the waiter in a delicious little café on piazza Beccaria sees her writing and when Simone lifts her head, "he smiles enchantingly."[4]

She mingles with the people. She spends hours in the laborers' suburbs of Milan. "Having herself paid a very high price for it," she can read from the eyes of those who pass by their state of mind. That evening, in a neighborhood movie theater, "a ticket for a lira, a serial romance," she feels the audience as frank and enthusiastic, "applauding the unmasking of the villain."[5]

She goes from Bologna to Ravenna, seized by an "irresistible" temptation; it is market day.

The people are most attractive, especially the young peasants. A superabundance of gifts, when Providence places beautiful beings among beautiful things. Every day in this town, one is confronted, in some of the people, with a noble simplicity of figure and of manners which compels admiration.[6]

On a train to Assisi, a worker who speaks French and intends to go to Paris, after an hour of conversation, proposes marriage. "We do not know each other well enough," Simone replies.[7]

At Florence she eats in "fiaschetterie" (a name she finds "delicious"); she eats "paste al sugo for between 70 centesimi and 1 lira." In one of these, quite close to the Carmine and the frescoes of Masaccio, "young workers and little pensioners entertain themselves with improvising canzoni, both music and verses!" Simone feels sorry for those unhappy ones who have the misfortune to have money and eat at restaurants from 8 to 10 lire.[8]

Fiesole, a bus stop. A mason of the town, seeing her with some books, attempts conversation. He would so much have loved to study. Fiesole is in an awe-inspiring location and life would be beautiful, but he makes too little and lives too poorly. And he says all of this "with the most simple tone in the world and a happy smile." When Simone asks if he is married, he replies: "I love freedom too much to want to get married." Enamored of music, "every Sunday he walks the roads of the countryside with his friends and a guitar . . . How can you not be fond of such a people?"[9] Simone finds in these people the true Italians, in whom to hope, and she contrasts them with others, intoxicated with the Fascist mentality. All the same, she judges even these latter, not with partisan superficiality, but with sorrow. While on the one hand there are "men who love and think," on the other there are "those who bend heart and mind to power, disguised with the mask of ideas."[10]

The mark of the totalitarian state appears in an obsession with myths, an obsession that deforms; Simone notices this in Lucien, a young friend of Posternak, whom she meets in Rome. Their conversation is fierce. For a good while Simone had wanted to speak frankly with a young man of this sort, Fascist in his opinions but also rich in intelligence and personality, with a "character full of repressed ardors and great unconfessed ambitions," which always interest her. At the end, the young man thinks that the proper and legitimate place for Simone in society would be in the pit of a salt mine. And Simone:

> The salt mine would seem less suffocating to me than such an atmosphere as this, with its obsession with the nation, its adoration of force in its most brutal form, the collective (see the gross animal in Plato's *Republic*, 1.5), its camouflaged deification of death.[11]

In a system that presents some positive aspects, she is especially alarmed by this exaltation of war, because it "sounds false."

> The seduction of war is all too real, but it has nothing to do with these empty words. They seem even more empty in this land, among this people.[12]

Never satisfied, she spends hours before the *Last Supper* of Leonardo and the *Christ* of Mantegna, the Michelangelo of the Medici chapels and the *Concert* of Giorgione. She is struck by the room of Botticelli in the Uffizi. She experiences a "particular tenderness for the *Perseus* of Cellini;[13] the Greek statues of the Vatican Museum "intoxicate" her (at least "those of absolutely pure style" surpass even Michelangelo.)[14] In Assisi, the only thing equal to the Franciscan beauty of the place is the frescoes of Giotto.

For Giotto, too, on her second journey, there will be "the intoxication" of the Scrovegni in Padua.[15]

It was a true contemplation that allowed her to discover the compositional secret of the *Last Supper* of Leonardo, in which:

> all the straight lines that constitute the ceiling and almost all the lines from both sides joining the hands of the apostles converge at a point in the head of Christ.

From every side,

> the eye is carried to the face of Christ by a secret influence, which is not perceived but which contributes to give its serenity something of the supernatural.[16]

The art of Michelangelo transfixes her in the depths of her experience.

> I never expected to experience what I have experienced . . . How sorrowful is this Dawn! It is the awakening to a bitter life, to a day that is too burdensome, the awakening of a slave . . . Even Night is the sleep of a slave who does not manage to relax, who sleeps to suffer less.[17]

She writes to her parents:

> *The Dawn* has awakened vividly in me the memories of my awakenings as a slave in rue Lecourbe.[18]

In the area of Italian architecture the most beautiful thing seems "the divine cupola" of St. Peter's, which brings her "infinite pleasure, like the piazza that lies before it. It deserves indeed to be the universal church of Christianity."[19] Her favorite church, "the most beautiful in Florence," is San Miniato. The viale dei Colli emits perfumes "that go to the head," most of all because they merge with the vision of "those slopes thick with olives."[20]

Although she was fond of Milan, Ferrara and Ravenna, she pauses to use special words about Florence:

> It is my city. Surely I have lived among its olives in some earlier life. I had hardly seen the beautiful bridges on the Arno when I asked myself what I have been doing so far from her for so long. And certainly Florence has asked it herself, because cities love to be loved.[21]

In Florence she harvests, in a short time, "a bundle of pure joys." In the atmosphere of its sites fluctuate verses of Dante, Petrarch, and Lorenzo the Magnificent (recently discovered), vivid scenes from the *Florentine Histories* of Machiavelli (the episode of the revolt of the Ciompi she had translated in 1934) and Galileo, whose complete works she acquired. The latter is a reading that excites an aesthetic pleasure analogous to works of art, "especially here."[22]

Music, too, allows her to share in the life of the people. The Mass of Palestrina at St. Peter's for Pentecost; the chorus was composed of men and boys; "women wore handkerchiefs on their heads."[23] "There is nothing more beautiful than the texts of the Catholic liturgy."[24] It is a complete art, because the people share in it. She had begun at Milan with *Aida*. She stood for the performance, already tired from long standing in line, during which she had sought help from her "dearest friend" Stendhal.[25] The music of Verdi is "pleasant, but . . . always a little ridiculous." *The Elixir of Love* enchants her: "a very lively libretto, music of perfect grace."[26] Rossini's *Signor Bruschino* delights her. But the most powerful impression is of Monteverdi's *Incoronazione di Poppea* in the amphitheater of the Giardino di Boboli, beneath a sky full of stars: "one of those marvels whose memory lasts a lifetime." In the midst of a cold audience, "a band of brutes!," Simone enjoys the opera for everyone, since "the music is simple, serene, sweet and dancing."[27] Upon her return, she will give an emotional rendition to her friend Pétrement of the scene of Seneca's death, where his friends implore him: "Do not die, do not die, Seneca . . . This life is too sweet."[28]

She had prepared herself for Assisi by reading *I Fioretti;* she quotes in Italian for Posternak the episodes of St. Francis, who considers "a great treasure, where nothing is the product of human industry; but what there is consists of bread which has been begged, a stone table which is so beautiful and a spring which is so clear." These are for her "the pure pleasures." She will subsequently repeat this and define Francis as the image of "happiness." For the love of poverty "is not at all ascetic; it grasps and savors all joys in their fullness, all pleasures that are possible." It is part of the "poetry of true contact . . . with the universe in which we have been placed."[29]

Assisi is, for her, a homeland of the soul. Milan, Florence, Rome, everything else disappears. "The countryside is so charming, evangelical and Franciscan." Everything preceding Francis is Franciscan. "One must believe that Providence created these happy fields and these humble, stirring oratories to prepare for his appearance." The Umbrian race is beautiful, healthy, vigorous, joyous and charming."[30]

Italy is truly for her the place of personal abandon. She tells her parents the story of the woman hermit of the Quattrocento. Dressed as a man, she had climbed up to the Carceri, where she was accepted as a Franciscan and lived for twenty years; only with her death did they discover her sex. She has been beatified.

> You almost lost me forever . . . If I had known this story before climbing up there, who knows whether I would have provided a new version?[31]

And to Posternak she writes:

> Since I have been in Florence, I have been looking around, in the hope of meeting Tomasso [sic] Cavalieri, but I have not yet found him. Perhaps it is better this way; if I did meet him, they would have to drag me away with force.[32]

Venice, which she will visit in 1938 along with her mother, will remain hidden within her,[33] to reemerge, marvelous and enchanting, as the symbolic city of nourishment for a human society in *Venise sauvée*, the unfinished tragedy which Simone will work on especially during 1940.

Italy in fact reawakens in her a vocation which for various reasons had been hindered since her adolescence, the vocation of poetry.[34]

14

The Encounter

In the summer of 1937 Simone wrote to Posternak after some delay. Things had not gone well since her return from Italy. Perhaps it was the fact "that she no longer saw olives."

> The feeling with which I think of Italy I can only express with the word *Heimweh*.[1]

It is a German word; it means "nostalgia for one's native land."

She is full of ardor. She thinks of writing poetry and drama. "Why do I not have all the lives I would need to dedicate one of them to the theater?" She says she is "inhabited" by the idea of a statue, that of Justice,

> a nude figure, on her feet, her knees bent a little from weariness . . . her hands chained behind her back; she is tense but her face is serene, despite everything.[2]

She suffers from political developments. Franco's forces have seized Bilbao. The government of Léon Blum has resigned. For Simone, the Popular Front is dead. On this subject she writes her "Meditations sur un cadavre." Drawing from the short history of France between June, 1936 and June, 1937, "a beautiful dream for many, a nightmare for some," she thinks that Blum, a man of intelligence and culture, of notable moral elevation, lacked "that point of cynicism essential for clear-sightedness." So he did not know how to use the movement of popular opinion efficiently.

> The proper material of the art of politics is the double perspective, ever unstable, of the actual conditions of the social balance and of the movements of the collective imagination.[3]

The political man, who knows the art of politics, must use the collective imagination as a driving force, though not sharing in its illusions. And he must take, at the moment when he has the opportunity, "all those measures of rigor he believes necessary," as Machiavelli, "that physicist of the art of politics," teaches.

The fundamental principle of power and of every political action is that one must never project the appearance of weakness.

Force rules and determines social life. It makes itself not only feared, but "always loved a little," even by those it oppresses. Weakness, on the other hand, is not feared and is always "a little despised and loathed even by those it benefits."

There is no more bitter truth than this one, and for this reason it is generally disregarded.

The usual belief is that men are guided in their decisions by "considerations of justice of personal interest; in reality the authority of force shapes sentiments and thoughts with full sovereignty."

Such force that holds sway even in consciences is in great part imaginary.[4]

The mind is dulled by it. Almost everyone wants either to preserve or to overturn the relations of command and submission that prevail; they do not listen to the lessons of history which show that everywhere "the masses are under the yoke and only a few lift the whip." Force has hindered the study of the mechanism of society. On the other hand, a Galileo has not yet been born who is able to discover a concept of "social force," that would allow society a better way to develop according to a balance between determined laws.

The power of the minority depends principally on the fact that the few form "an aggregate, i.e., a force" and the many "a juxtaposition of individuals, i.e., a weakness." The opposite cannot happen because it is impossible to organize the masses. If at times a common yearning creates a cohesion in the crowds, ordinarily beyond realization, these moments in history are very brief and cannot last, because "they result in the suspension of daily life." The mighty have a vital interest in the greatest possible prevention of such *crystallizations of the crowd*.

Two illusions, the sense of inferiority considered natural in the one who obeys, and the sense of superiority considered just as natural in the one who commands, preserve the situation.

What are the most important *consequences for the individual*, the most important ones as far as Simone is concerned?

Even the soul most heroically endowed with firmness cannot maintain a consciousness of inward worth when such a consciousness can find no external basis of support.[5]

Such was the precise conclusion, drawn from her own experience, which she had tried to explain to M. Bernard; she had also seen this consequence in Spain (the disparity between peasants and soldiers, caused by the possession of arms) and she deduced it, in all sorrow, from the news about the colonies.

And she no longer hoped to bring men to reflection, as she had at the time of Le Puy or even at the time of the *Perspectives,* in which, even though she realized she was a heretic, she looked forward to a Fourth International.

She was now even more convinced of the truth she had written to a pupil of Le Puy in a letter of 1934.

The refractory individual is morally and materially alone—I speak of those who are truly refractory and I do not mean . . . those Communist leaders who pretend to fight against a form of oppression but then accept an even greater one . . . that of Stalin; I do not mean the Socialists, always ready to genuflect before force.

And she makes a bitter declaration of defeat. In 1934 she had written,

Only those who are truly brave, pure and generous will be able to resist.[6]

Now she affirms,

Those who wish to think, to love, and to bring into action what inspires them in their hearts and minds, in all its purity, must perish in a slaughter, abandoned even by their own, abused after their death by history, like the Gracchi.

For there is an incurable contrast between the good and social order. The good, or the pure effort of love and thought to give to every being the sense of its proper worth, is "corrosive of order."[7]

These pages of bitter reflection remained in a drawer.

She continued to operate in the orbit of the *Nouveaux Cahiers,* in the sense that there she found an outlet for her activities, of which two instances seem significant.

The first was a synthesis she was asked to write by Detoeuf as a conclusion for a series of studies on the conditions of workers in various countries, a series the review had already published. It appeared as an unsigned article entitled "Conclusions" on November 15, 1937. In it Simone underscores the great disparity in situations and the imbalance deriving therefrom.

In those countries where the condition of the workers has improved, the rhythm of work has slackened, and the countries find themselves at a disadvantage in international competition. So, to set in operation a true internationalism for workers, until now "more a matter of words than reality," we must advance to a certain leveling-off "towards the top" in the conditions of living for workers in the various countries. And yet such a leveling-off can only be conceived "as an aspect of the famous general regulation of economic problems in the world . . . which everyone recognizes as indispensable for peace and for prosperity, but which no one takes up."[8]

The second was her opposition to a proposal presented by the commission for the reform of instruction.[9] The proposal was based on the principle of establishing a selection that would guarantee "access to instructional careers to all those who are worthy." This would be achieved through the creation of more scholarships to allow the poor to pursue higher studies. Like Alain, Simone felt that the problem was not so much giving to the "apparently" more gifted the opportunity of raising themselves as offering to all a level of adequate instruction. Elevating only a few meant impoverishing the workers and peasants' classes by removing their best elements.[10]

She struggled in defense of Messali Hadj, the founder of the organization, L'Etoile nord-africaine, which united Algerian workers in France. This organization had been dissolved by the first government of the Popular Front and Messali had been threatened with arrest. Simone had met Messali many times and had argued his case before Blum; she had succeeded in preventing his incarceration. Messali himself has told this story; he says that she was a fully sympathizing interlocutor.[11] When he was arrested during the second government of the Front, Simone worked hard and got a vote of protest from the Comité de vigilance des intellectuels antifascistes (Saint-Quentin section). The protest noted "with sorrow" that North Africa remained subject to the "same regime of brutality, oppression and terror" it had experienced in previous governments, and it drew attention "to the deservedly dire consequences which could flow from the desperation of the native masses."[12]

In the spring of 1938, she described to Posternak what she saw around herself.

> France? She is today a quite sad land. The spirit of June, 1936 . . . is rotting. The most sorrowful thing is to note the continuing Communist influence upon workers. The strikes of the metal-workers who labor for the national defense are scandalous. If . . . they were inspired by a spirit of pacifism, they would have the beauty of every forceful manifestation of faith; but these workers . . . almost all of them are in favor of the armaments . . . they are suspending their construction to increase their salaries, which are already exceptionally high . . . Underneath all of this, probably, is a complicated maneuver of the Communist party, anxious to take part in government to push for war.

France is conscious of her own decadence. There would be no inconvenience, should she become a small country.

> Liberty, justice, art, thought, and every form of greatness are found equally . . . in a small country.

But the passage from being a great power to being a small one is hard for a people that "is still intoxicated with Louis XIV and Napoleon and has always thought of itself as both the terror and the love of the universe." What will happen? Since no one wants to "admit" it, such a passage brings with it an incredible amount of "lying . . . demagogy . . . vainglory mixed with panic (an awful mixture!)," briefly, "an intolerable moral atmosphere." Simone feels nations as she does people; she grasps their moral life, their illusions, blindness and sins.

Minds saturated with fear confront two possibilities: the first is a war against Germany because of Czechoslovakia. Public opinion "is not the least bit interested" in that far-off country, but it prefers war to German hegemony over central Europe. The second is an antidemocratic *coup d'état,* engineered by Daladier and the army, "accompanied by a violent explosion of anti-Semitism and savage measures against the organizations of the left." With extreme disinterest, the Jewish Simone declares: "I would prefer the latter possibility, as the less deadly for the whole of French youth."

Since she had foreseen all of this "since 1932," she feels less downcast by it; yet she finds that all joy has disappeared. And, in accord with a theory she had developed over several years, she thinks that

> Joy is an indispensable ingredient in human life for the health of the mind; thus, the complete absence of joy and madness are equivalent. If there is a little truth in all of this, the reason of the French is beginning to be threatened—not to mention the rest of Europe.[13]

After the *Anschluss* (March 13, 1938), Simone signs, along with other anti-Fascist intellectuals, a declaration, an appeal intended to halt the rush to war. In all probability it was drafted by Simone herself, since she otherwise refused to sign petitions or declarations. The appeal asks the French government "to join resolutely" with the peace-making action of Neville Chamberlain; after achieving "an international relaxation, the negotiations should tend . . . towards a fair regulation of both European and colonial conflicts, a condition and starting-point for progressive and controlled disarmament."[14]

Nothing could be worse than war.

In a letter to Gaston Bergery, the editor of the weekly *La Flèche,* Simone expresses her thought fully.

> A war in Europe would be a certain tragedy, in every case, for everyone, from every point of view. A German hegemony in Europe, as bitter as that prospect may be, can in the end turn out not to be a tragedy.

She underscores the deep reason, for her the most serious morally, why France is constrained to go to war: France cannot appear weak before her colonies.

> And this is a dishonorable hindrance, since it is no longer a question of France preserving her own independence but rather the dependence of millions of men.

If she does not want to see her empire lost, her policy of concessions abroad must be accompanied by "a rapid evolution of her colonies towards quite a vast autonomy."[15]

And yet she continued to be preoccupied with the problem of national defense, which Bergery had posed to her. They had to find "the way to make an eventual invasion difficult to the point of hindering temptation for neighboring states." To this end the political, social and economic life of France should be decentralized, as well as her eventual armed resistance; it would become "more guerrilla activity than war." But this type of war would demand a true *public spirit,* "a lively consciousness of the benefits of liberty in all Frenchmen." Such things did not exist, given the great prestige of the "dictatorships" with a vast section of the population, "beginning with the intellectuals and the workers."[16]

In the meanwhile, for the year 1937–38, Simone had begun teaching at Saint-Quentin, an industrial town quite close to Paris, a position she had desired for a time. She gave courses in philosophy and Greek to a few students.

She persisted in the method of Bourges: literary works must induce reflection upon concrete situations of life.

In a notebook of one of her students we read a quotation from *Colonel Chabert* of Balzac: "That type of humility that perverts the actions of the unfortunate man."

The unfortunate man is caught in a tangle, insofar as he senses "contempt, the immediate reaction to misfortune."

A detestation for the unlucky develops; it is very difficult to reach the level of goodness which allows one not to feel resentment towards them for their misfortunes.

It is always a matter of *seeing others,* even when they are rendered similar to objects, things crushed to the earth by their weakness. Simone added: Christian revolution has consisted in not despising the unfortunate and the weak.

The God of the unfortunate is weak.[17]

On April 10, Palm Sunday, 1938, Simone left for Solesmes with her mother. Dom Boissart,[18] the abbot of the Benedictines of rue de la Source, had made it possible for her to attend the rites of Holy Week at the abbey, famed for the beauty of its Gregorian chants. It was these Simone wished to hear.

Their hotel is across from the abbey, which on that side presents a more intimate aspect. The grand portal, crowned with green, seems to lead to a villa; one usually enters by a little side entrance, guarded by a cypress. One proceeds to the church in the ancient shadows of immense trees. Charles Bell speaks of "a great redwood tree."

When Bell met Simone Weil, she was seated in the hall of the hotel reading *Doctor Faustus* of Marlowe. It was not the woman he hailed, but the book, with a quotation from it, "Ah Faustus, 'Now hast thou but one bare hour to live.'" The young woman lifted up her face.

"A severe Jewess, thin, dressed in mannish clothes . . . Every trace of beauty that could have been hers was erased; it could be glimpsed now in the solemn depths of her eyes." He strives anxiously to find her again, to recreate her. He felt she was "far removed from himself, she had advanced to a lonelier outpost." Introduced by a common acquaintance, Simone called him the "Greek rhapsodist" and wanted him to continue reciting verses.

They had walked along together, for "a brief space," along the Sarthe, where the abbey looms like a fortress.[19]

The "girl of Solesmes," as Bell continued to call her for many years, since he had not learned her name, followed all the rites of Holy Week. Some people were dumbfounded by this. "And she is not even a Catholic!" they said to Selma.[20]

Charles Bell, an American, was termed by her "a young Englishman" and later "the devil boy." She must have found great pleasure in his inexhaustible knowledge of English texts, Chaucer, Shakespeare . . . the metaphysical poets. As for these last, who were so important to her, she does not mention them in her only letter to Bell;[21] they reached her through another young man. This was John Vernon, also "a young Englishman," but a real one, called by her *"the angel boy."*[22] She saw him every time he returned from Communion transfigured "by a light truly angelic."

Chance . . . has made him a true messenger for me.[23]

These two pages, with their title, "Prologue,"[24] were found in the middle of one of the *Cahiers*, without any relation to the themes handled there. Perhaps they were really meant to serve as a prologue to a book, the traces of whose planning are to be found in a list of motifs in the *Cahiers*[25] and in titles now and then recurring to bring together her thoughts.

What are they? An evocation, the interpretation of a state of mind, a narrative of days she had lived? What is sure is that these pages try to recover a reality and to describe it faithfully.

He entered my room and said, "Wretched one, you understand nothing and know nothing. Come with me and I shall teach you things you have not the slightest inkling of." I followed him.

He led me into a church. It was new and ugly. He brought me before the altar and told me, "Kneel down." I told him: "I am not baptized." He said, "Throw yourself on your knees before this place with love, as before the place where truth exists." I obeyed.

He made me come out and climb to a garret where, from the open window, one could see the whole city, some piles of timber, the river where boats were being unloaded. He made me sit.

We were alone. He spoke. At times someone would enter, he would join in the conversation, then he would leave.

It was no longer winter. It was not yet spring. The limbs of the trees were bare, without buds, in a cold light, full of the sun.

The light would rise, would shine and grow dim, then through the window there would enter the moon and the stars. Then again the dawn would return.

Sometimes he would be silent and take from a sideboard a loaf of bread and we would share it. That bread had the true taste of bread. I have never found that taste again. He poured wine for me and for himself, wine that had the taste of the sun and the earth from which that city rose up.

At times we would lie on the floor of the garret and the sweetness of sleep came over me.

He promised me an instruction but he taught me nothing. We would speak of things of every sort, completely at random, like old friends.

One day he said to me, "Now go away." I fell on my knees, embraced his legs and begged him not to chase me away. But he thrust me down the steps. I went down the steps without knowing how, my heart in pieces. Then I realized that I did not know where that house was located.

I have never tried to find it again. I understood that he had come for me in error. My place is not in that garret. It is anywhere else, in the cell of a prison, in one of those bourgeois salons full of knick-knacks and red plush, in the waiting room of a station. Anywhere else, but not in that garret.

Sometimes, in fear and remorse, I cannot help but repeat to myself some of the things he told me. But how am I to know that I remember them correctly? He is no longer there to tell them to me. I well know that he does not love me. How could he? And yet deep within myself something, a part of myself, cannot be kept from thinking, as it quakes in fear, that perhaps, despite everything, he does love me.[26]

15
Jaffier, or Pity

On her return from Solesmes, at the end of April, 1938, Simone went to thank Dom Boissart. "Of a very pronounced racial type, she looked weary. She told me about her experiences in a factory. She lived completely inside her soul, indifferent to everything. She had suffered much." These are the words of the Benedictine.

Since January, the headaches had begun again; they were so bad that she had to ask for an initial leave of two months. The leave was renewed for the rest of the year, then for 1938–39 and again for 1939–40. She never undertook teaching again.

There had been a period in which, following the example of Simone Pétrement, who had gone from school to the Bibliothèque Nationale, she had thought of a similar solution; she soon desisted because the technical preparation for that type of employment seemed to her a time stolen from activities she could not renounce.

Now, in September, 1938, she followed with great concern the negotiations in Munich. The *Nouveaux Cahiers* published a special edition on the subject; on the one hand, it suggested that France should avoid measures of intimidation, such as a general mobilization; on the other, it advised that the field of negotiations should be broadened, towards a comprehensive settlement of the international situation. Simone approved.

On receiving the news of the Munich pact, on September 30, she was relieved. But her forecast was very dark. She said to Simone Pétrement: "Everything indicates that war has just been delayed."[1]

She thought that, if the French government had "a thousand times" reason for yielding, the situation was "fearful" for the people in the Sudetenland opposed to Hitler's regime, "most sorrowful" for Czechoslovakia and "bitter" for the democratic states, whose "prestige, and hence security" appeared diminished. These reflections are expressed in an article devoted to the colonial problem. It is in the "clear and urgent" interest of France, Simone writes, to transform her subjects into "fellow workers." Once they have become autonomous, they will, perhaps, contribute voluntarily to the defense of a territory that has become their own. If such a policy is "necessary" from the French point of view, "from the human point of view—which, by the way, is naturally mine," it would be a "happy" policy.

The autonomy France would concede would avoid the perils involved in an emancipation seized by force, which would run the risk of making populations, until now intolerably suppressed, "leap" "into a desperate nationalism, imperialistic in its turn."[2] Simone feared in particular the development of Arab nationalism and soon Jewish nationalism as well. On November 21 she took part in a debate on the Israelite immigration to Palestine and the terrorism with which the Arabs were fighting it. "Why create a new nationality? We have already been suffering from the existence of young nations, born in the nineteenth century and inspired by an exacerbated nationalism."[3]

She is a pacificist, but she is conscious of the humiliation the French have suffered. Once again, she is free of partisanship and, as ever, eager to share the bitterness of the defeated.

> We have been humiliated much more profoundly than simply in our attachment to national prestige; everyone, at the center of his being, has suffered what is the essence of humiliation, the thought of being debased by the power of facts.[4]

What should be done then?

> Doubtless, virtue consists in not entertaining greater hate after the offense than before it nor greater confusion in the face of peril than the one experienced before it.[5]

Charles Flory, a friend from the *Nouveaux Cahiers,* saw her clearly when he said of her: "In our meetings she was not very active, but when she said anything it was quite striking. One sensed in her an interior search for truth based upon an inner life which kept on surfacing. She confronted social problems by grafting them on to it. And the whole of her person shed that inner life around her."[6]

As ever, she pursued two courses of action: a practical and attentive activity in support of individuals, and the activity of her mind.

An incident from this period illustrates the many ways she expressed her profound sense of equality. One day in 1938 she went with her friend Pétrement to meet the reader in German at the Normale, Fuchs. This young man was the subject of constant persecution on the part of his students, because he was a native of the country where Hitler ruled. Simone felt it extremely nauseating to vent upon a single, defenseless German the anger which the mere name of Hitler provoked. So she wanted to relieve, to some degree, the bitterness Fuchs must be experiencing and to provide him with the chance for some normal relationship with the French. "Politics was not broached; we spoke of contemporary German philosophy (phenomenology, the philosophy of existence . . .) and he provided us with considerable interesting information."[7]

Between 1939 and 1940 she provided the greatest assistance to the young writer Julien Blanc, a very poor man; she let him live with her family, she tried to assist him, with the help of de Tarde, in avoiding enlistment; afterward, when he became ill in the service, she succeeded in having him sent to Val-de-Grace and at great danger to herself she brought him the drugs he wanted her to get for him.[8]

She also provided great assistance, along with her family, to Edoardo Volterra. In 1923–24, André had gone to Rome to study with Edoardo's father, the mathematician Vito Volterra. The two young people had become inseparable friends; Edoardos's trips to Paris and Simone's to Italy had strengthened the friendship in time. Now, persecuted for political reasons, Volterra was living in Paris in a little boarding house; he was constantly required to renew his residence permit. Simone would accompany him to the prefecture, and each time she would become angrier at the restrictions imposed upon foreigners. When Edoardo traveled for conferences or lectures, Simone took care of his correspondence; she would read the letters addressed to him and summarize their contents. Simone's letters to Edoardo were lost in the course of searches conducted by the Italian police in Bologna in 1943. Only one has survived. In it Simone corrects her friend's French in an article on the subject of Egyptian law, "Le testament de Ptolemée"; she furthermore advises him, in those difficult times, to reread Marcus Aurelius and Epictetus, Aeschylus and Sophocles.

Is it not, perhaps, an extraordinary privilege for us to understand today the only language in which men have known how to express with nobility the relationship between man and his destiny?[9]

"We used to speak of history, philology, literature and sociology. Simone would talk in a very logical, lucid and integrative fashion. One felt that she had thought a long time about everything. She would say only what was essential. She would avoid using anybody else's ideas. She expressed only her personal ideas, developed by herself. Her culture was vast, extraordinarily rich." These are the words of Edoardo Volterra, recalling their common endeavors. "There were many of them. We would talk about them and then continue our discourse by letter. We tried to translate Tacitus into a modern language with the same number of words used by the Latin author. Which language would be best suited for the task? Italian, German (which she knew beautifully) . . . We finally discovered that the only one to use was French."
Her face? "It was very intelligent and expressive."[10]

═══════

After the declaration of war in September, 1939, her reflections were focused, on the one hand, on the real objectives to pursue so that the war, now inevitable as a demonstration of resistance and firmness, would result in the creation of an effective international balance and, on the other, on the profound reasons, rooted in Europe's past, why the present civilization had made possible the rise of Hitler.

One must free oneself of all commonplaces, ideological and racial prejudices and declarations of principle; one must then look reality in the face and adopt the strength of a lucid and responsible policy. The comprehension of the past and the careful vision of the future were the two instruments to use to confront events in a *physiological manner*.

Simone undertakes what must be defined as an examination of conscience for France and the West, which find themselves facing a war of "limitless" character, a war, that is, that involves everyone, even to the ultimate sacrifice, against the danger of "universal domination." For France and her allies the very continuation of national existence has been called into question. To defend it, to the point of obtaining an absolute guarantee of security, implies the annihilation of the nation that poses the danger, in this case Germany. Such an annihilation would mean, however, the passage of universal domination from German hands to those of others, "who would not be better," or the complete ruin of Europe, destined to become "in her turn" a colonial territory.

The only precedent for a "universal domination" is the Roman empire. Hitler aims at an analogous domination, and to achieve it he uses methods inspired by arbitrariness, brutality and absolutism, which go hand-in-hand with a strong sense of organization, of effective labor, and of the state. These last aspects, which contain some positive elements, have been viewed as positive in an absolute sense in the process of the civilization of nations. The deplorable side of the Roman system found its justification in this way. The colonizing effort of ancient Rome has become the defining characteristic of civilization, proposed as exemplary in all the manuals of history. It has served as a model for all political structures that have sought universal domination, from the Holy Roman Empire to the papacy, from the kingdom of Louis XIV to the empire of Napoleon. Clearly, the aspiration to attack and to colonize is not a fatal racial flaw of "eternal Germany." And if we wish to find an example of the state, conceived as "a blind machine . . . producing order and power . . . the adoration of which implies an explicit disdain for all morality," we shall see that the most recent true precursor of Hitler is Cardinal Richelieu.

Hitler is condemned as an example of the greatest barbarism. It is evident that he is not a barbarian. The cruelties of barbarians, which alternate with gestures of loyalty and are tempered by inconstancy, do not endanger anything vital in the peoples that survive their attack. Hitler, on the contrary, commands with a "blazing and pitiless will" a state constrained to a taut "dynamism," a "basely" civilized state, like Rome. The only difference is this: the political methods of Rome are admired as civilizing, while those of the Nazis are deprecated as barbarizing. Since there is always a tendency to attribute *barbarism* "to causes extraneous" to the circumstances in which we live, we see it incarnate "in human groups that are extraneous to us or which we declare are such." We are prone to live in the dangerous illusion that a people, a race, or a class can preserve civilization. Simone Weil proposes instead the following concept.

We should consider barbarism as a permanent and universal aspect of human nature, which develops more or less in accord with the space which circumstances allow it.

From this she derives the postulate:

> Except at the price of an effort of generosity as rare as genius, men are always barbarous to the weak.[11]

At the center of human relationships stands the notion of *force*. Rome used all the force at her disposal, she cultivated it, she exalted it. She abolished with force the various cultures of the Mediterranean basin, except for Greek culture, which she relegated to a secondary position. Upon these peoples she imposed "a culture almost completely devoted to the exigencies of propaganda and the desire for dominion" and produced around herself "that moral decomposition which brutally and definitively . . . snaps the continuity of spiritual life."

The influence of Christianity was not able to counterbalance this *force* because "unfortunately" Rome fashioned with Christianity "an alliance which contaminated it." Unfortunately, also, its place of origin has "imposed" on Christianity a heritage of texts which often express "a cruelty, an inhuman contempt for enemies who have been conquered or are destined to be, and a respect for force—all of which accord well with the spirit of Rome." For two thousand years, this double tradition, Hebrew and Roman, "has suffocated" to a great extent the divine inspiration of Christianity.

The idea of the despised and humiliated hero, common among the Greeks and the theme of the Gospels, is almost extraneous to our tradition. Despite many noble spirits who have not been enslaved to force, from Villon to Rabelais, from Montaigne to la Boétie, from Descartes to Pascal, from Théophile de Viau to Maurice Scève, the cult of "grandeur" according to the Roman model has prevailed. It has been diffused through the internal codes of our culture. Since

> Man is not made of watertight compartments,

it is impossible for him to admire methods used in other eras without undergoing their influence, even to the extent of letting them develop in him "a tendency to imitate them."

The state is coagulated force.

> Every people that becomes a nation by submitting to a centralized, bureaucratic and military state suddenly becomes and remains a scourge for its neighbors and the world.

This phenomenon is inherent, "not in the blood of the Germans," but in the structure of the modern state. France imperiled the peace and liberty of Europe in 1815; this was the peak of a situation which had been developing for two centuries, since she had become a unified and centralized state. Germany has followed the same course of aggressiveness. Some small European states have been exempt from it, "since they were formed with respect for local liberties." So, too, to a certain extent, is a great nation, England, which does not have all the characteristics of the modern state.

We are witnessing a phenomenon of the spread of the state's authority, whereby all the changes of the last three centuries have brought men closer to a situation in which the state will be the sole and uncontrollable "source of obedience." Not only peace and liberty, but "all human values without exception" are in great danger.

The power of the state is absolute and without legal limits. In foreign affairs, the only limit consists of the force of other sovereign nations and is expressed in war or the threat of war; "it is a *de facto,* and not a *de jure,* limit." In internal affairs, only democratic states find a limit to their authority in the *rights of the individual.* Even here, if ambitious men seize the propitious moment, they can use the very mechanism of democracy to suppress these rights.

To resist this absurd spread and to reach an international balance, we must establish "a certain federalism, not only between nations but within every great nation." This is the only road to the solution of postwar problems, if the allies triumph. The other solution, the annihilation of Germany, apart from its theoretical character ("fortunately, it is impossible to exterminate the entire German people"), involves the risk of a very serious imbalance.

> If crushing the conquered is always unjust, it also is always harmful to everyone—those who are conquered, those who conquer and those who merely observe.

In fact, it must be maintained by force, with the tension of a system similar to Hitler's.

As far as the dismemberment of Germany, we must proceed in a way that need not be maintained by force. This will be possible only if the conquerors (granted that the allies are destined to that role) "accept for themselves the transformations they would have imposed on the conquered."

Men must create among themselves *bonds* that are *different* from those that pass through the state, and help the trend of Nature. In fact, the process of centralization we have been seeing for several centuries will reach its limit and will be followed by a transformation in the opposite sense. Simone recalls two types of "dispersed organizations": cities and feudal bonds. Although they, too, are subject to tyranny and to war, they are more favorable to better forms of human life. Man can return to one of these, fuse them together in a new form, or discover a third. Unfortunately, in their death throes, states drag off with themselves to death "so many precious things, so many lives." The amount of this irreparable destruction can be lessened if responsible men in sufficient numbers commit themselves to prepare and to favor "methodically" the physiological transformation of human vicissitudes.[12]

These articles and fragments, produced with the urgency characteristic of her attitude to contemporary events, were nourished by the wide reading she was able to undertake with greater ease once she had stopped teaching.

Between 1938 and 1940 Simone read or reread a very large number of ancient historians (Herodotus, Thucydides, Plutarch, Appian, Caesar, Livy, Tacitus, etc.), narratives, chronicles, memoirs and documents relative to the Middle Ages and modern history, from the *Chanson de la Croisade* to the *Histoire de Charles VI* of the anonymous monk of Saint-Denis, the *Memoirs* of Richelieu, the letters of Elizabeth Charlotte of the Palatinate, the sister-in-law of Louis XIV, known as the Palatine Princess, the *Diary* of Pepys . . . She read and reread poets, such as Ovid and Juvenal, Plautus and Terence, Maurice Scève, Agrippa d'Aubigné, Théophile de Viau. She started the *Iliad* all over again; it will be the subject of her great essay. (Towards the end of 1939 she translated several passages to bring out from the text "the human tenderness and pity," which had never been given prominence.)[13] She also translated the tragedies of Aeschylus and Sophocles.

A great part of this reading was devoted to the history of religions. Simone Pétrement remembers her at the Bibliothèque Nationale: she was consulting the *Book of the Dead* and other Egyptian religious texts.

She read, too, for the first time, the Old Testament in its entirety; she was quite indignant at the complacent repetition of massacres and slaughters. The massacres and slaughters did not dumbfound her in themselves; there is not a people that has not bragged about them in the course of its history. What made her indignant was the fact that "the order for the slaughter was presented in the Bible as a command of God" and that "neither the author of the story nor the majority of his readers, including Christians, have ever experienced any repugnance at admitting that such a command came from God."[14] There were still things in the Bible she admired: some of the psalms, the Canticle of Canticles, Isaiah, Daniel, and Job above all.

She then wanted to read the *Manichean Homilies,* recently discovered. She was impressed with the humanity of the great masters of this religion. They never had, in the presence of death, an attitude of defiance or disdain. "Maintaining firmness in the eyes of men, they manifest sadness and express laments to God in their prayers." These were her words to Simone Pétrement, when she returned the book.[15] Love for life, which flees from blind fanaticism: this for her was true courage.

In the spring of 1940 she read the *Bhagavad Gita* (which she will reread, this time in Sanskrit, in 1941). The poem responded to her questions exactly. Arjuna, the man full of pity for others, the man who has a horror for war, is forced to it anyway. It was the same with her, tormented by the same pity and the same constraint. Arjuna must overcome himself, must act, but only in such a way that he will not be prevented from remaining pure.[16]

From that moment, in speaking of religion with her friend Pétrement and then, later, in her letters to her parents, instead of naming God or Christ, she will always say Krishna, "with a sort of reserve."[17]

═══

The German offensive began in the west on May 10, 1940. In a few days they overcame the resistance of the Dutch and the Belgians; they then penetrated France.

Simone followed the events feverishly. She wished fervently that the government would succeed in "galvanizing" the population and she thought that all should contribute to this effort. When the command was given to Weygand, she said to the other Simone: "Do you know in whose place I would like to be at this moment? Weygand's."[18]

From the windows of rue Auguste Comte, the Weils would see and hear, both day and night, the stream of vehicles and people who flowed south along boulevard Saint-Michel. They were Belgians and Frenchmen from the north who were crossing Paris in search of a refuge in the south.

Although she was tortured by the anxiety of her parents, especially of her father, Simone had decided not to leave. "I do not want to flee," she would repeat. She hoped that the city would be defended.

She was amazed at the easy resignation of the masses to German domination, but she did not feel any hatred for the German people and above all she felt pity for the fanatical young soldiers.

One evening at supper, she asked her parents what they would do if a German paratrooper were to land on the terrace of their house. Dr. Bernard replied that, if possible, he would have him turned over to the police. Simone declared that it was impossible for her to share the table with someone who had intentions of that sort. And she did not touch any food until her father promised her that no, he would never have done such a thing.

On June 13, when they had gone out shopping, Simone and her parents (André was at Cherbourg in the infantry) saw some placards that announced: "Paris an open city." Simone finally yielded to the wishes of her parents; without even returning to get luggage, they went directly to the Gare de Lyon. Only one train had not yet left; a great throng was waiting there in vain to board it. Selma Weil had the idea of saying that her husband was the physician on duty for that train. Dr. Bernard was allowed on board and set as his conditions that he bring his wife and daughter, too. The Germans entered Paris the next day, June 14.

Simone quickly regretted leaving and wanted to get off at the next station. Her parents convinced her to travel at least to the Loire, where the new defensive line would most likely be set up. She agreed to get off at Nevers. The Germans arrived there during the night.

> Problem: the defeat, not experienced as suffering in certain moments (a fine day, fine surroundings).
> A man in greyish-green uniform is not the cause of suffering (e.g., before hostilities, there were the military attachés).
> After the defeat, when a German soldier appears in the surroundings, and the suffering begins.[19]

No newspapers could be found and it was forbidden to listen to the radio. Rumor had it that all of France was occupied. They decided to return to Paris, on foot. Along the road they encountered an ex-student of Simone. Simone convinced her to overcome her fear and to listen to the transmission of news. So they learned that there was a free zone.

They bought some baskets so that they would look like peasants and they started walking towards the south; after a few kilometers, Simone had one leg rubbed raw by her skirt. A garbage-owner offered to take them as far as Vichy, as long as they would pay for the gas; luckily they had some money.

At Vichy, where they would remain for two months, the government of Marshal Pétain began. Simone there encountered some old friends and comrades, all of them pacifists, who approved of the armistice and hoped for the creation of a good republican government. She opposed their ideas violently. "She appeared beside herself with anger."[20] And she was; she thought that France should have stayed in the war. She felt a sorrow and a sense of rebellion that made her violent and made anyone she spoke with uneasy. She was shunned.

With her injured leg not responding to treatment, she spent her days on a sleeping bag in the kitchen of a little rented apartment and wrote a tragedy, *Venise sauvée*.

All her papers had remained in Paris and so, rather than writing the tragedy, she set about rewriting what she had already written and added to it. For months she had been reading and annotating the *Conjuration des Espagnols contre Venise* of the abbot of Saint-Réal (1674), a work of historical fiction based on an episode of 1618. The reality of the conspiracy, always denied by historians, especially Spanish historians, is confirmed by the following facts: the Marquess of Bedmar, the Spanish ambassador to Venice, who had arranged the conspiracy while remaining in the shadows, "had to leave the city, and several hundred men died, condemned by the Council of Ten."[21]

Simone was inspired for the political interpretation of the events by the Machiavellism of Saint-Réal, and for the title by the theatrical version by the Englishman, Otway, *Venice Preserved* (1682).[22] She created a tragedy on the seizure of power by mercenaries.

She looks at the enterprise from the inside, from the vantage point of the conspirators. They project upon their action their anguish at being "uprooted," their humiliation at not having a homeland, their hatred for the man who has one, their desire for revenge. For these reasons they wish in their turn to humiliate, destroy and dominate.

Renaud, their head, an elderly French nobleman, "a spirit of remarkable acumen, an inexhaustible treasure of deep political wisdom,"[23] illustrates

the necessity for the sack, "the sole pleasure" for his troops, an indispensable means for "shattering, in one blow, the courage of the Venetians" and
for making them "blindly" obey the man who will reestablish order and
security after the terror.[24]

"Renaud-Trotzky, a poor man, esteems virtue more than riches, but
glory more than virtue." This implicit psychological understanding, in a
note to the first draft,[25] is transposed into an exalted theory:

> Men of action and adventure are dreamers; they prefer their dreams
> to reality. But with their arms they compel others to dream their
> dreams. The conqueror lives his own dream, the conquered lives
> another's.[26]

It is Jaffier, a Provençal and captain of a ship, who provokes the impassioned and lucid oration, when he asks Renaud what measures to take to
limit the damages of the sack. Assigned to military command in place of
his great friend Pierre, Jaffier loves Venice and is already "pale" with concern for her, in the fullness of the euphoria of conquest that dominates the
whole of Act One.

He lingers on the means because he has never been attached to the end.
His *detachment* will continue to grow until it crests when he sees Venice
from the top of the campanile:

> The city, so quiet and unaware, is in my hand;
> but before long, before long she will know she belongs to me,
> because the harsh moment is coming when in an instant
> I will close my hand to crush her.
> She has no defense. She is weak and lies without weapons
> at my feet. What now could stop us?[27]

In that question there is a plea for help. The quiet of the "unaware" city is
for him a call which catches his *attention*. For Renaud it is rather the instrument to achieve devastation and dominion.

> These Venetians . . . believe that they exist. And from now on, they
> no longer exist, they are shadows.
>
> It must be that tomorrow they will not know where they are, they
> will not recognize anything around them, they will not even recog-
> nize themselves.
>
> It must be that all their life will be changed, the life of every day.[28]

For Jaffier it is this "quotidianity" that counts: the life of each day that circulates in a "human orbit which one is not even conscious of, like the air one breathes" but which all the same is like the indispensable air in its nourishment.

Venice is more beautiful than ever. She is preparing to celebrate Pentecost. And instead:

> The city I have before me will disappear.
>
> A few more hours and the city is dead:
> stones, a desert, scattered lifeless bodies,
> and the survivors, even they are corpses.
> Wordless and stupefied, they will know only how to obey.
> With all their dear ones defiled and butchered,
> each will hasten to bow before what he detests.
>
> This evening the splendid city is still happy.
>
> This last sun covers her with its rays and if it knew, it would surely stop its course out of pity. But the sun has no pity for her, alas, nor have I.[29]

The action freezes. "What happens in the soul of Jaffier remains mysterious." He reveals the plot and makes the Council of Ten swear that his comrades will not lose their lives. The Ten do not honor their oath.

Jaffier passes through all the phases of "destitution—revolt, threats, supplications, delirium, languor—he even approaches the flat world of dreams."[30] He is reduced to the state of a *thing*, as the city would have been. The agony of Venice, which he has not willed, becomes his own.

The conspirators in chains are still possessed of their "furious" initial "impulse," curbed by the imminence of torture and death. Renaud, who has not slaked, even for a day, his hunger for power, although lost ("I am nothing"), does not understand that they "have robbed him of his destiny."[31]

Jaffier, who has never participated in the "furious impulse," has never been darkened by the "mendacious values" which shroud the value of things in themselves: so he has "seen" Venice in her "vulnerability."

> The vulnerability of precious things is beautiful because it is a sign of existence.[32]

But:

> Believing in the reality of the external world and loving it are one and the same thing.

To love it truly means to respect its frailty and to safeguard it. It means *to preserve*. Destruction is the thirst for possession, the imposition of force.

Renaud wanted to enslave time to his commands, to destroy the present of Venice, to erase her past. Jaffier "stops time" by refraining from using it. "His withdrawal is supernatural," it is the gesture of detachment which implies "suffering," and it is a manifestation of "mercy."

> Mercy implies an infinite distance. One has no compassion for what is nearby.[33]

Or for what we cling to with eagerness.

Venice sauvée presents in a poetic microcosm the ideas and the intuitions which Simone had been expressing in her political essays.

At the center of the microcosm she places pure, supernatural action, the good which in this world is "something abnormal but possible" and which is, beyond question, "the good."[34] Jaffier, "the perfect hero" according to the tradition of Greek tragedy, or the humbled hero, achieves this action; it is a "passion," suffering, redemptive of evil.

In Saint-Réal, Jaffier's "pity" for Venice, even though it is given as his reason for denouncing his comrades, was interpreted "solely as an act of cowardice, the weakening of resolution in the imminence of execution."[35] Successive authors, beginning with Otway, considered this motive mysterious and absurd, so they omitted it and found other justifications for Jaffier's weakness (in Otway, his love of the Venetian patrician, Belvidera).

Simone thought, however, that this motive gave the story an *exemplary splendor* and felt that she was "the first to take notice of it."[36]

The gesture of Jaffier, *an attentive man*, "communicates something." He forces one to turn around and to contemplate.

> Action is like language. Like works of art, etc.[37]

It is a mad gesture, outside the norm, that "falls" upon the scene of the world. The scene of Venice in 1618 is the scene of Europe in 1940. The poetic transfiguration, which finds expression in a "timeless diction,"[38] remains connected with the circumstances of the moment and is nurtured by their urgency.

The motivations of the mercenaries are the motivations of the Nazis. The thrilling power of Spanish totalitarianism ("Tomorrow the sun will rise upon a simple possession of the king of Spain and we will have done this great deed. We, a band of exiles.")[39] is the sense of force that Germany draws from her centralization ("Such power is due to the union between adolescents shaped by the regime and *men*—in all responsible positions— shaped by the regime of Weimar and Wilhelm II.").[40] Venice, "the city" which represents the roots, the "contact with nature, the past and tradition," is Europe. Over both there looms the menace of *moral decomposition*. "The uprooting of conquered peoples has always been and will always be the policy of conquerors."[41]

Jaffier, who symbolizes the opposition of the principle of *weakness* to the dictation of *force* which has always dominated history, prefigures with his *madness* a project that Simone was bringing to maturity, of equal opposition. She is Jaffier.

16

The Truce

She was thinking of going to Morocco, and then to England. To this end she had asked for a teaching assignment in North Africa. She wanted to know a world different from Europe, the French of the colonies, and above all the Arabs, because of the strong attraction she always felt for "what remains of eastern cultures."[1] She was looking for a refuge, not for a "refuge from events, but a defense against her imagination." As always, she wanted to come ashore on the land of the most meager reality. Full of "pity, remorse and shame" at the thought of misfortunes and perils she was not sharing, she was looking, not for relaxation, but for "a tension of a different sort."[2]

This tension, this refuge, she was not able to obtain. She was named to the girls' lycée in Constantine with an appointment from the first of October, 1940, but she never received the letter. She had to remain in Marseilles and to live there *her own* truce. In fact, she wrote:

Every activity should have at its center moments of truce.[3]

In Marseilles, all of her previous experiences, from her life in the factory to her meditations on politics and history, from her readings in religion to her study of the Greeks, from her trade-union commitment to her juridical reflections, will merge in a series of practical and theoretical expressions, finding their reason for being in an ever-clearer inner orientation.

===

When Camille Marcoux met her again in a room dazzling with sunlight, in her apartment high above the sea, he sensed that she was different: luminous, more at peace. "Not at all," his wife interrupts, "it was not the sun;

there was electric light, I remember it very well." A little embarrassed, Camille insists all the same; for him the memory is truly suffused with light and cancels the bitterness of the old and sudden rupture over Proudhon.[4]

Whom did Simone visit in Marseilles? Where did she direct her steps, rapid, restless, always guided by a precise idea, which was secretly connected with other ideas, all leading to one center?

We must picture her in our mind as she visited the camp of the Vietnamese, to whom she gave a large part of her food coupons and for whom she was so insistent in her letters to the government in Vichy that she succeeded in having a tyrannical director replaced by a more humane man. The Vietnamese, on their free day, waited for her from the early morning, as they sat in a line above the parapet of the front. We have to follow her in her long periods of waiting at the American consulate, from which she would at times "return in tears" after exhausting discussions intended to obtain a visa for an Austrian interned in the camp at Vernet. And we have to see her as she writes her letters to another internee, the Spaniard, Antonio. She is "happy" to know him, because he feels joy at seeing mountains; this shows that "he has known how to preserve within himself his best side."[5]

The greatest result of this personal action of hers will be the "Note on the punishment of internment inflicted upon foreigners," intended for the Bishop of Marseilles. After reflecting upon this "inhuman" punishment in the first months of 1940, she would like to obtain two things from Marshal Pétain: the abolition of internment as a punishment for infractions of residence-regulations and pardon for all foreigners already sentenced to internment.

====

She would regularly visit *Cahiers du Sud,* in its lofty editorial offices perched in an attic, with a secret door for escape in case of raids. "The editor receives visitors on Wednesdays, from six to eight in the evening." The review of Jean Ballard was, like his home, a welcome port for poets, artists and writers who for political or racial reasons sought a refuge in Marseilles or made it the last stop before leaving France for Algeria or America.

The review represented a center of life. Simone Weil was brought there by Jean Lambert, who had known her, through mutual friends, at the time of the Normale. It was Lambert who supported (at the request of Simone, who had entrusted the text to him) the publication of the important Weil essay, "L'Iliade, ou le poème de la force," which was already in galleys at Gallimard; "it was no longer wanted by the NRF, because it was unpublishable in the period of the German invasion."[6]

Jean Ballard was enthusiastic about it. The essay appeared in the *Cahiers* in December, 1940 and in January, 1941, with a pseudonym required by circumstances, Emile Novis, an anagram for a name which was too Jewish.[7]

"Simone Weil: very messianic; a great intellectual. She would linger over her words; her inspiration was rich with revolt. She was so slovenly in appearance; my wife Marcelle, who adored her, would have liked so much to see her tidier. On those Wednesdays of ours, at first they smiled at her, but soon enough they smiled no longer; she had her own public. A complete indifference to money." This is the description by Jean Ballard.[8]

To Jean Tortel, the poet, she seemed a person whose physical presence was both fascinating and repulsive, "unbearable." She had a hungry look. She would cling to you, imploring you, and at the same time she would repel you, with harsh disdain. "Look: when we spoke of idle matters, just to find some relief, I felt her disdain. She was, frankly, quite ugly; but when she leaned towards you, behind her thick glasses, her glance was extraordinary."

She would ordinarily sit in a chair of leatherette and wood, 1920 style, or in the corner of a shell-shaped sofa, loaded with books. The room, which looks the same today, was "more livable" then. The large stove rumbled hospitably. Tortel recalls that Simone almost always kept her hands in her pockets and looked beyond the others; she seemed not to be listening and then she would intervene with perfect pertinence or she would take up a point which had been left up in the air an hour earlier.

"A cone of black wool, a being completely without a body, with a huge cape, large shoes and hair which looked like twigs; her mouth was large, sinuous and always moist; she looked at you with her mouth. If she had been attractive, she would have had an overwhelming fascination, sensual and sexual," Tortel lingers over the memory. "Yes, indeed, because Simone Weil was an impossible being, but not unreal."

She would always carry with her *Pyramus and Thisbe,* by Théophile de

Viau, like a Bible. "One day I made the mistake of saying, 'Theophile was profoundly atheistic.' I heard her swift retort, 'How can you think that the only true man, the only conscience of his time, did not have the faith?'"

She sought everyone's relation with God and the true essence of everyone. "She did not put up with life, with mediocrity. She lived on the outside. She wanted to involve us in the dimension of the absolute and she demanded total satisfaction. Otherwise, she knew how to tell you pitiless things with a tone of voice that was always even, moist, and muffled."

Tortel never saw her eat; he knows that she used to go to small Arab restaurants, where the poorest people eat. "Smoking, yes; once, on the mattress in her bright room, I saw her writhing, tormented by a desire to smoke. And no cigarettes could be found. It was the only time she appeared human to me."

Otherwise, she was not. Exhausted by the rarefied air that surrounded her and by her need *to exist* constantly and to the utmost, Tortel says that "he *cannot* call himself her friend." The same is true of Jean Lambert; although "he was very friendly with her, sometimes he fled from her."[9]

Lambert recalls her directly with this impression:

"I had just arrived in Marseilles and in the library I went up to a lady and asked her: 'Excuse me, but are you Simone Weil?' 'No,' replied the lady, 'I am Simone's mother; she's down there. Don't you see her?'" In his memory of Simone Weil, she had no age.

He used to go up to meet her in the morning, after a swim and a sunbath on the little beach of the Catalans, which faced the building where the Weils lived. Simone's room was full of papers and books. Everything had been sent to her on a chance, in great boxes, by Adèle Dubreuil. From the wall, "the ambiguous looks" of the musicians of Giorgione followed the visitor everywhere.[10]

"She showed me her notebooks and read passages from them. I remember her face very well, a face in which intelligence was a palpable thing. I discerned in her an intense and constant thought process. Simone Weil made a great impression on me; I was a little afraid of her. At that time she seemed ugly to me; now I hesitate to say that of her." Lambert pursues another image; it is both harsh and nostalgic towards his comrade of years past. "I never felt that she was at ease in life. And yet she always wanted to launch unsuitable enterprises, mulishly. Her parents made me pity them, they were always so busy in tidying her up. Even with regard to her work in the factory. She could allow herself to be fired. But she never doubted herself and she wanted to go to the very end of everything, without considering how much it cost others. I find fault with her on this."[11]

=====

She loved babies. "Leaning over the crib of my little Françoise, she spoke to her in Greek," says Marcelle Ballard.

She loved love. In Marcelle's album of memories she wrote an inscription to Françoise. Among the many famous names (from Valéry to Saint-John Perse to Léger, from Adamov to Breton) there stands, for the child, a passage from the *Antigone* of Sophocles, in Greek and in Simone's translation. "Love invincible . . . which hurls yourself on homes. . . The man who has you is mad." The inscription says: "So that Françoise may read the text and the translation—but above all the text—when she is sixteen, and so that her parents may preserve a trace of the passage of someone who, thanks to them, felt at home in Marseilles, at a time when so many thought they were in exile."[12]

Tortel remembers her fascinated by Maurice Scève and intent upon quoting strophe 367 of the *Délie,* rich in sensuality: "In my body, you, my Soul have returned, / to feel her hands, celestially white, with their arms mortally divine / the one crowning my neck, the other my flanks." These verses expressed perhaps her most essential inquiry, "the inquiry into the union between the soul and the flesh."[13]

She loved lovers: she had always surrounded them with her approval. There was a girl, ten years younger than she, full of life and of joy and in love with a boy. At the same time, she was a sincere Christian. "How beautiful you are," she said to them. "I would have liked so much to have had a love, too, a happy life; but that has not been possible." In the *Cahiers,* we find:

Vocation [of a thinker, etc.] or a happy life? Which has greater value? We do not know. Incompatible vocations (at least from a certain level of greatness).

. . . Everything is paid for, but reciprocally, everything has its compensations. But one thing and another at a level that is inferior, equal or superior. And what do we know about it?[14]

=====

During this time in Marseilles, she lived in an ambience warm with interchanges. She had more space. Her days were rich with diverse facets.

She succeeded in communicating better; she was received to the degree that she allowed herself to be received. And she was better apprehended in the vast range of her perspectives.

Friendship is a nourishment and an inspiration. For these reasons, Marseilles is the period in which she wrote frequently in her *Cahiers*.[15] There she deposited the gradual interiorization of the universe which here finds precision and expression in the unification of all aspects of her thought, her feelings and her actions in a supernatural orientation. What happened? A definite change has taken place; it has brought together, in the *encounter,* the city without a name, a whole journey, which had begun with her desire for truth in her adolescence, had been pursued with her reflections on the good and on purity of action in her essays for Alain, and had found practical realization when those reflections were embodied in her "com-passionate" participation in the sufferings of exiles, of those rejected by every party (see the situation in Germany and its consequences), of workers (see her experience as a factory worker), and of revolutionaries (see the war in Spain).

The *encounter* is also a new beginning: that of a relationship with the mystery by which God, a God *thought of* as ethical inspiration, becomes a God who is *lived by,* an incarnate God. We recall that at the time of Henri IV, Simone discovered, through the good, the possibility of breaking away from ourselves "as individuals, as animals, to affirm ourselves as men, that is sharers of God," which was just as much the possibility of making God Himself exist, because "action is the affirmation of God."[16] We recall, also, that then it was a matter "simply of words" and that she was "always alone, either with this God or without Him."[17] Now, instead, the unknown friend is a reality; we recall the substance and the beauty of those hours in the garret, the shared bread and wine, the simplicity of eating and sleeping.[18] And now, "deep within myself, something, a part of myself, cannot be kept from thinking, as it quakes with fear, that, perhaps, despite everything, he does love me."[19] The impersonal God has become a person. From the external description of the essays of Henri IV we have come to an evocation from within: two pages that have the incandescence of poetic vision and that testify to the passage from one conception of the divine to the other. Simone Weil has forever crossed a threshold: in those two pages, she synthesizes and relives "the experience of the transcendent," an expression that "seems contradictory" and yet is the only right one, because "the transcendent can only be known through contact . . . our faculties cannot fabricate it."[20] What happened in her was the junction of the *ego-and-the-universe;* its source had been the encounter, in which we sense an experience of profound life or a mystical experience (I use that adjective to signify contact with a mystery). The multiple and at the same time unified woman who is Simone Weil will orient all the aspects of her thought and of her action, without leaving out anything, in the direction of this contact. She will set forth the relative in the luminous reality of the absolute and we shall see this in her language as a woman author: all of her themes (social justice, labor, art, beauty, friendship, love, reality, imagination) will acquire a greater depth and a multiplication of resonances. The supernatural will be legible in the natural; and we shall have fresh evidence of the fusion of the two planes in the limpid concreteness with which she will describe the vicissitudes of the soul. Here I believe that, in a unique way in our century, we can find in her *the nature of the supernatural.*

Thus the city without a name, suspended between two seasons, can be localized as the goal of our inner space and as an age measurable in a way beyond our earthly measurements.

As she has always done, so now Simone commits herself to the race, with respect, with awful urgency, with an unslaked thirst for knowledge, with a painful impossibility of complete abandon. And yet, and we shall glimpse this, against a new background of certainty ("perhaps . . . he does love me"). This time there are extant documents of the inquiry, documents which are richer and, I would say, more personal even in their distanced clarity: the letters and the essays which will form *Attente de Dieu* and the *Cahiers.* What lie behind them are the greater possibilities Simone found for interchanges in Marseilles and her greater readiness, during this time, to nurture her inner silence, her *attente,* her waiting, not only with attention and readings but also with dialogues. There will be two principal dialogues: one with a Dominican, the other with nature.

On June 7, 1941, Simone Weil presented herself to Fr. Joseph-Marie Perrin.[21] He was expecting her and already knew what Simone wanted to ask him for: employment as an agricultural worker in the area. She had taken her friend, Hélène Honnorat, a fervent Catholic, into her confidence. The latter had thought at once of Perrin, a most active priest, despite his almost complete blindness, who helped anyone in Marseilles who needed assistance, a passport, or a refuge. In the short letter which set up their meeting, the priest wrote: "Your friend will perhaps already have told you of the love I bear for Israel, whose present sufferings cannot but increase my desire to render service to Israel." He spoke "with great gentleness" and inspired her immediately with "confidence."[22] Because of the desire which Simone expressed at once, of sharing the lot of the agricultural proletariat, Perrin thought of Gustave Thibon, an old friend and a vine dresser in Ardèche. Then, without any delay, they entered the heart of their conversation on the search for truth. Simone will lodge its motifs and fruits in letters and essays, destined not only for her priest friend but also for others, "that they may have the opportunity of entering into our dialogue."[23]

"Who was I for her? A priest, the only one she knew . . .

"Who was she for me? A soul, that I had the dreadful responsibility of serving and that showed me the poignant confidence of speaking to me of her life with God."[24]

The meetings took place as often as possible, "in accord with her, and most of all my, availability . . . With her extreme courtesy, she would remain waiting impassively in the hall; she would allow two or three people to go ahead of her; we would then talk in the time that remained. On rare occasions she would ask me to meet her at a friend's place, to have greater ease and freedom of spirit."[25]

The friendship between Perrin and Simone always possessed a very personal character, "to the degree that nothing can have a more complete intimacy than a communion based on a common search for God," and very impersonal, inasmuch as Simone never spoke of herself apart from that search.

In it she summed up her whole life, and since "a human influence implies errors and illusions on divine matters,"[26] Simone avoided the excessive personalization of a friendship in which she believed. Friendship will be pure only if it is free from the slightest trace of the "desire for pleasing or the inverse desire." For this reason, together with affection, this friendship will be marked by something like "complete indifference."[27]

Perrin always sensed "in his heart" and with a certain amount of pain this fear of Simone with regard to the powers of suggestion of friendship, the utmost fear in the setting of her "decided longing for independence."[28] But at the same time she always desired to offer to Perrin with scrupulous clarity the history of her own inner experience and to receive from him the nourishment that comes from the "friends of God": the possibility of maintaining one's "gaze, ever more intensely fixed"[29] upon God.

With Perrin, Simone relived her secret of Solesmes: "a real contact, person-to-person, here below" with God, through Christ.[30] It was something completely unexpected, in the midst of her arguments on the "insolubility" of the problem of God: the encounter that occurred at Solesmes in Holy Week of 1938.

Unexpected in its concreteness, but prepared by other moments of truth in her being, and comprehensible in the context of her life. She lists them: they are "three contacts with Catholicism that really counted." The first happened in a little village on the sea in Portugal, on a night of a "full moon." She is alone, after her year in the factory, "her body and soul in pieces, in a certain way," from absorbing "the misfortune of others," social misfortune, and "receiving . . . the mark of slavery." She sees and hears the wives of the fishermen; in a procession for the feast of their patron saint, they are carrying candles around the ships and singing hymns, "very ancient and piercing in their sadness." She compared them with the choir of the Volga boatmen. And suddenly she is seized by the certainty that "Christianity is the religion of slaves, that slaves cannot help belonging to it, and so I myself must be among them." Then there were those "two glorious days in Assisi" in 1937. In the Romanesque chapel of Santa Maria degli Angeli, "an incomparable marvel of purity," something more powerful than herself "forced her to kneel down, for the first time in her life." Lastly, in 1938, ten days at Solesmes. The Passion of Christ "entered" her forever, through "the pure and perfect joy," deriving from the beauty of the Gregorian chant and its words, a joy achieved "with an extreme effort of attention," which allowed her to let her wretched flesh, tormented by a migraine, "squat in a corner and suffer by itself."

Beauty and suffering blended together to make her understand "by analogy, the possibility of loving divine love through affliction,"[31] which is then the possibility of loving in a broad sense. The young Englishman, by chance designated God's "messenger," made her aware of the metaphysical poets. Simone began reciting, at the peak of her headaches, "Love," by George Herbert;[32] "she would cling with all her soul to the tenderness enclosed in it." That recitation, "unbeknownst to her," had "the power of a prayer." For this reason it had the force of establishing the bond between her and Christ.[33] It is a personal feeling.

I have only felt through suffering the presence of a love similar to the one you read in the smile of a beloved face.[34]

"I noticed with intensity, and from the very first moment, this bond of hers with Christ," Perrin explains. "It was a certainty with which she *lived* and assisted at Mass. But without complete abandon. She did not dare to pray."[35]

The certainty existed and Simone clung to it because "neither the senses nor the imagination" had had any part in the manifestation of that presence. Before then she had "never read the mystics" and in the *Fioretti,* the stories of apparitions "more than anything else vexed her, like the miracles in the Gospels."

After that encounter, Simone sensed the mystic in Plato; she felt that the whole of the *Iliad* was "bathed in Christian light." With "redoubled" love, without ever asking herself if Jesus was really an incarnation of God, she was now "unable to think of Him without thinking of a God." Reading the *Bhagavad Gita* ("marvelous words with such a Christian sound") had thrust her towards a more tangible inner reality.

I felt strongly that we should accord to religious truth quite a different adherence than we do to a lovely poem, a more categorical kind of adherence.

Her intelligence alone remained perplexed, "in pure preoccupation with the truth."[36] And *she did not dare to pray.*

"She did not dare," she was embarrassed by this impossibility of hers and she never managed to speak about it clearly with Perrin, who had early spoken to her of *prayer* in this fashion: "Imploring, praising God are in the very logic of any religious formation. Praying means searching for the Father, searching for a person; at first, prayer is hypothetical, but then it becomes more conscious." But she feared the *suggestion* that can be hidden in prayer, the very suggestion for which Pascal recommends prayer. For two months, before Simone left for work in the fields, the subject caused discomfort between the two of them.

Even her questions on baptism derived from this need for a deeper adherence. She had never thought of it as a practical problem, inasmuch as her feelings about non-Christian religions and hostility towards Israel had always seemed absolute obstacles to her. It was her conversations with Perrin that brought her to think of baptism. Here was located "the greatest debt she owed to any human being," a debt that stands at the center of their friendship. He had made her turn "the fullness of her attention" to faith, to the dogmas, to all the sacraments, as things towards which there are "duties to discern and to perform."[38]

These words, among the first she heard from Perrin, continued to echo in her: "Beware that you do not pass by something great without seeing it." These words made her notice a new aspect of the "duty of intellectual honesty." First, in the name of this duty, she had never linked her spontaneous loyalty to the *Christian inspiration* as a way of life with adherence to dogma. Now she began to ask herself if there did not exist in her, all unbeknownst to her, "impure obstacles to faith, prejudices, habits."

She feels that, after having told herself for so many years, "Perhaps all of this is not true," what she *should* now do was not stop repeating that but alternate it with its opposite, "Perhaps all of this is true."[39]

In an effort "to give objective testimony of her spiritual evolution," Fr. Perrin speaks of the two directions followed by this evolution from the middle of October, 1941, to the middle of May, 1942.

"The first is represented by the diffusion of the reality of God in her soul, in an ever simpler way, up to her certainty of the real presence in the Eucharist. This is the most important one. From this, now, her prayer before the Blessed Sacrament naturally flowed. With docility and with perfect straightforwardness she begged God for illumination. The other consists in the many questions she asked me about the church, the sacraments, Israel. At the center of her preoccupations were the doctrine of the Church on the necessity of baptism and the question of her own baptism.

"We often spoke of implicit and explicit faith according to Saint Thomas. And of Israel: 'I do not know what it means to be Jewish,' she repeated. She asserted that she had been brought up an agnostic and had received none of the spiritual riches of Judaism. She blamed the Catholic Church for two things: being loyal to the Old Testament and being Roman. She even asserted that God was present in all religious traditions, except for the Hebrew and the Roman. This theme upset her in a recurrent manner. With reference to these points, there was in her a will to be sincere, which ended in a kind of meticulous obstinacy. Here Simone Weil showed her shadowy character, her allergy to every enlightening thought which came from other sources; also evident were lacunae, superficial interpretations and combinations in her reading of texts. She always tended to return to the arguments already examined. She wanted to preserve complete independence even with reference to what she had already learned. She was afraid of being chained to her own certainties. Hers was a very complex attitude: baptism did not remain an isolated problem, separated from all the truths revealed by the Lord. She was reliving faith in its entirety.

"Through her ever-more-personal discovery of the Gospel and in a growing adherence to Jesus, she came to see Christ as the mediator of everyone, the mediator with whom the encounter could take place through all forms of religion. This was her most profound idea and it was at the center of a project that we dreamt of realizing together: bringing together all mystical texts, of Catholicism and of other religions."[40]

Assigned to Montpellier after Easter of 1942, Perrin would return periodically to Marseilles to study these texts with Simone. Greek sources were prevalent (Aeschylus, Plato, an "outline of the history of Greek science") and constituted the theme of the talks Simone held in the crypt of the convent of the Dominicans, before a small audience, but one that followed her with friendship.

Simone maintained all of her hesitations in the face of baptism. On January 19, 1942, she wrote:

> It seems to me that now my entry into the Church is not the will of God . . . the inhibition that holds me back is felt with equal strength in moments of attention, of love, and of prayer.[41]

As we go through the reasons that kept her from receiving baptism, we see that, on the one hand, they are connected with her personal fabric and with her vocation, on the other, they are dictated by her relation to the world, which comes into her very vocation.

If the intellectual obstacles were already removed in January, inasmuch as the priest "did not refuse to accept her as she was," others remained.

She does not love the Church. She loves God, Christ and the Catholic faith, to the degree that a being so "miserably inadequate" can love them. She loves the saints "through their writings and the narratives of their lives," except for some she cannot consider saints. She loves the "six or seven Catholics of authentic spirituality," whom luck has allowed her to meet. She loves the liturgy, the chants, the architecture. But not the Church, except in reference to all these things she does love. And love cannot be forced; she can only desire that this love "will one day be accorded to her," as long as it is a condition of "spiritual progress" and "inherent in her vocation."[42]

She fears the Church as a "social thing." "I have in myself a strong inclination to be gregarious." (We recall her with her red flag at the head of the miners of Saint-Étienne.) She would only have to hear a chorus of young Nazis and part of her soul would become "immediately Nazi." And it is no use fighting these natural weaknesses; you have to be violent with yourself and act as though they were not there, in the imperious drive of a duty. In the course of your life all you can do is take account of them and try to turn them to "good use."

The patriotism which exists in Catholic circles towards the Church, considered as an "earthly homeland," frightens her. Not that the Church is unworthy of inspiring such sentiments, but Simone wants to avoid them for herself; they are too strong, too entangling. Even some saints, through their attachment to the Church as an earthly homeland, came to approve the Crusades, the Inquisition . . .

> If . . . it did them harm, how much more harm would it do to me, particularly vulnerable to social issues and infinitely weaker than they were?[43]

It is inevitable that the Church, as an organ of the conservation and transmission of the truth, should be a social thing. But associated with this is her desire for power and for glory, a desire connected with all the kingdoms of this world. Hence, behind the veil of the same words, what is supremely pure is joined in "an almost indissoluble mixture" with what is supremely corruptive.

How are we to discern the truth without being caught in the trap of the "we"? The "we" of a party, the "we" of a class, the "we" of a race, the "we" of a nation, the "we" of a point of view. All her life she has fought against them. Now she asserts: "I do not want" to be adopted by the Catholic circles that exist and are ready, even eager to welcome her with warmth. Her words express her attitude poorly because "all of that is delicious," but for her it is not allowed.

> I feel that for myself it is necessary . . . prescribed, that I be alone, a stranger and an exile with reference to every human ambience without exception.

Why? It seems paradoxical but only in this way can she best approach others, in her identification with them as though by *osmosis*. For this reason, the thought "of the act" that would bring her across the threshold of the Church causes her suffering. It is the suffering of being separated from the "immense and unfortunate mass of unbelievers."

> I have the essential need, and I believe I can call it the vocation, of passing through men and through human ambiences as I blend myself with them . . . so that they can show themselves . . . without disguises because of me. I desire to know them in order to love them, such as they are. For, if I do not love them in this way . . . my love is not true.[44]

And confronted with a youth forced to reply with a closed fist to the salute of a militiaman, she noted in her *Journal d'Espagne,* "cruel coercion."

And there are so many things that she loves and that God loves, too, because otherwise they would not exist. All of them outside Christianity, at least as far as the Church lives it.

> The immense expanse of past centuries, with the exception of the last twenty; all the lands inhabited by races of color; the entire profane life of the countries of the white race; in the history of these lands, all traditions accused of heresy, like the Manichean and Albigensian tradition; everything to do with the Renaissance, too often deteriorated, but still not without some value.[45]

She does not wish to abandon them; rather, "she stays at their side," because she cannot accept the way in which the Church has excluded them in time, as she made a totalitarian use of those two little words: *anathema sit.* Instead:

> Christianity should contain within itself all vocations, because it is catholic. Consequently, so should the Church.[46]

Today, Christianity appears catholic *de jure* but not *de facto.* So she, too, not only can but *should,* except for the certainty of a contrary command on the part of God, consider herself catholic *de jure* but not *de facto.*

> Making visible to all the possibility of a Christianity truly incarnate[47]

is the urgent and rigorous duty she must obey during the next two or three years. Failing at that would amount to treason, because "never in any other epoch have souls been in such great peril as they find themselves today across the whole surface of the earth."

Between the Church and individuals there should occur a fruitful encounter, based on the "harmonious solution" of relations between the individual and the collectivity.

> The situation of the intelligence is the touchstone of such a harmony.[48]

The Church, the collective guardian of dogma, has often smothered expressions that "faith, love, and intelligence, three strictly individual faculties," have dictated to man in his contemplation of the dogma itself. In this she has exceeded her indispensable conservative function and has committed an "abuse of power," by imposing upon faith, love and intelligence the requirement of using "her language." There are two languages: that of the intimacy of a man with God and that of the assembly.

> The language of the square is not the language of the nuptial chamber.[49]

The Comforter, the Spirit of truth whom Christ sends us, speaks now one, now the other language. When an authentic friend of God, "like Meister Eckart," repeats the words he has heard in the silence of the union of love, and these are "discordant with the teaching of the Church," this is due to the difference between the two languages.

None of the promises made by Christ to the Church has the force of this phrase, "Your Father who sees in secret." The word of God is a secret word. A man who has not heard it, even if he adheres to all the dogmas taught by the Church, "is not in contact with the truth."[50]

This is true for everyone's journey.

> The man who desires the truth, if an error appears . . . and he perseveres, he will see it as an error. If he does not desire the truth, he is mistaken, even when he recites the Creed.[51]

The Church should not behave with totalitarian orthodoxy towards errors.

> How can one know whether the error is not a necessary stage on that determined journey?[52]

This is true for every religion, "which is an original combination of explicit truths and implicit truths." And only "one who knows the secret of hearts knows the secret of the various forms of faith." Nurturing the "comparative knowledge of religions," today almost nonexistent in Europe and perhaps in the world, would help in discerning "some hidden equivalences" under visible diversities.

Since every religion provides its nourishment like a precise "food," we know it only from the inside, and the comparison of religions can only be achieved thanks to the "miraculous virtue of sympathy." Just as, for us to know other men, we have to transfer at least some of our own soul, full of "sympathy," into them, so, too, we must transfer to the center of the religion we are studying all our "faith, attention, and love." But in general, men do not have any faith; or they have faith only in their own religion and give to the others the sort of attention that one "gives to shells of a strange shape"; or they have a form of "vague religiosity," which, indifferently, they turn this way and that.

Instead, just as we must be capable of friendship to interest ourselves with all our heart in the lot of someone we do not know, so for us to think of another religion "with the most elevated level of faith, attention, and love," which become it, we must already have accorded quite fully "our faith, attention, and love to a particular religion." A real love given to a particular object would become universal by *analogy*. Mathematics, science and philosophy prepare us for analogy, which thus comes to have "a direct relation with love."[53]

And the Church should assist this inner construction, this expansion of the soul in an intelligent love.

> To be everywhere present, as it should, religion should not only refuse to be authoritarian, it should limit itself rigorously to the plane of supernatural love, which alone becomes it.[54]

Inspired not by a desire for domination, but by love, the Church should sustain men in their *opening* to truth.

In today's world, the Church defends the cause of the rights of the individual against collective oppression, the freedom of thought against tyranny. But ordinarily these causes are defended by those who find themselves provisionally in a position of inferiority with respect to those who are stronger.

For the present attitude of the Church to be effective and to penetrate everywhere, like a wedge, in social existence, she would have to say openly that she has changed and that she wants to change.[55]

Otherwise, how could we forget the Inquisition?

Simone halts in front of the sacraments. She feels capable of a "presentiment" of contact. As symbols and ceremonies, in their human and social value, she cannot accept them.

Social sentiment resembles religious sentiment as a false diamond does a true.[56]

For all those who have always lived them in that way, the sacraments are an excellent and salutary thing as a stage of transition. But participation in the sacraments as such is something else; it implies a given contact with God, mysterious but real. Such a form of participation is possible only for those who find themselves above a certain level of spirituality.

Simone "does not feel that she is worthy of them." Why? On the one hand, she is conscious of having committed precise, serious, and repeated sins "in the order of action and of relations with human beings." On the other, she experiences "a general sense of insufficiency."

I do not say this out of humility.[57]

She found herself, in fact, in a state she would call "wrongful humiliation."

Wrongful humiliation leads you to believe that you are nothing insofar as you are yourself, insofar as you are a particular human being.
Humility is the knowledge that you are nothing insofar as you are a human being, and more generally as a creature.
Intelligence has a great part in it. You must conceive the universal.[58]

There are moments when she has the temptation of surrendering herself completely to Fr. Perrin, of asking him to decide for her. But: "I do not have the right."

She has to accept the obstacles, not pretend to jump over them, to act as though they were no longer there. There is the danger of the "phenomena of compensation."

One must look at them directly, as long as necessary, until, if they are
the result of the powers of illusion, they disappear.[59]

Above all else, she feels the horror of one thought: the thought of experiencing afterward, once she had been baptized with a disposition of mind
different from what it should be, "even for just an instant, a single twinge
of regret."

It is a risk she does not want to run, even if baptism is "the absolute
condition" of her salvation. Only the conviction that she is acting in obedience could make her decide to accept baptism.

Only obedience is invulnerable to time.[60]

On the other hand it could happen that, after remaining "for weeks,
months, years without thinking about the problem of her adherence to the
Church, one day she would suddenly feel "the impulse of requesting
baptism."

And I will run to request it. For the road of grace in our hearts is
silent and secret.[61]

———

Around the crypt of the Dominicans, also, the ambience was warm, rich
with meetings between intellectuals and scholars who were outside their
profession and without any restriction on their time.

Simone had the opportunity to meet the Catholic writer, Stanislas
Fumet, who remembers her this way:

"A very Jewish soul. There was something of the Talmud in her. Very
stringent in her logic. She reminded me of Péguy, both in her purity and
her severity with herself. I saw in her a person intent upon concealing her
own value behind those run-down clothes and those big shoes."[62]

Even for Suzy Allemand, a twenty-year-old Jewish woman, Simone
was very Jewish, "in her sense of the absolute, in her sense of justice, in her
need for the truth. A Jewish feature she had not was respect for life. I
remember we had prepared a feast in the crypt, we had baked cakes. She
did not understand these things; she did not accept happiness. She was
magnificent in speaking. She knew how to adapt herself to any audience. I
remember very well her discussions in the crypt, those brilliant comments
that followed her reading of Plato. Then, when she spoke to you indi-

vidually, it was with complete attention, as though you were, for her, the only person in the world. We read the Old and the New Testament together. The gospels became more luminous."[63]

Suzy introduced Simone to Berthe Ergas. Berthe was from a very observant Jewish family ("God was the principal personage in our house"); she was preparing herself to become a Christian. She was baptized at the end of 1941, with Stanislas Fumet as her godfather.

"When Simone asked me what Christ was for me, I replied: 'He is the opposite of space: He is the opening.'"

Berthe had a deep knowledge of her own religion; in her childhood she had suffered much from the climate of anti-Semitism which was everywhere at school and took aim at her surname, which is Spanish, rather than Jewish. She did not want to "dishonor" herself by repudiating her origins and her family, which were part of herself, but at the same time she had to follow her personal faith in Christ, which had matured since her earliest childhood. She was greatly assisted by her parents, who did not take away any of their love for her; she decided to be baptized also because baptism did not represent an escape from racial persecution. In fact, according to the Nazi racial laws, adopted by Vichy, the presence of three Jewish ancestors established that a person was an Israelite and remained such even with baptism.

This authenticity of Berthe was made to order to please Simone. Together with it they possessed in common two other ideal coincidences: the fervent desire for social justice and the choice of Christ.

"We are sheep of the same wool." This phrase from Claudel's *Joan of Arc* they heard together one evening at the theater and Simone repeated it to her. Their friendship had a spontaneous constancy and full confidence. They saw each other often. Simone would go to meet Berthe when she got off work—eight to ten hours in a clothing store, where she helped her parents. They chattered incessantly, seated on garden benches, walking, in Simone's room. Berthe translated into Spanish Simone's letters to Antonio; Simone spoke to her about the war in Spain. "I am an *anar*," she would repeat, and she would speak of some articles she was publishing in the journal, *Le libertaire*. She would then read her some of her poetry and showed her pages of Sanskrit. "How much I have gotten from Buddhism, the *Upanishad*."

"She read me the 'Prologue,' which I have never seen printed. She read very well. When she began to speak, the whole world disappeared; only her extraordinary presence remained. Look, this is what she was: a marvelously alive person, who knew how to bring others to life, too."

Very curious and spontaneous, she interested herself in everything human; so there were no social barriers for her. She did not want them to exist. "If you put yourself in the last place and take as your measure the small, the least, then you can understand the rest. There are no longer any screens between you and things." She said this to Berthe; she would say the same thing to Thibon.

"When I went to meet her for the first time and asked her where the bed was, she showed me the bare pavement in red hexagonal tiles, the *tomettes* of Marseilles.

"Her love of poverty struck me. On the other hand, I can see that from the social point of view, and above all as a young woman, she could be shocking. She was awkward as we Jews are, displaying defects and hiding qualities. Mme. Weil was distraught. "My daughter is mad; she cannot keep going about like this." And even my fiancé, who had to share me with her (they both complained, alternately, that they did not see me enough) told me: "Why does she have to look like a Hindu pilgrim?"

Berthe married a fervent Christian in February, 1942. Simone told her, "You have found the best and only way to solve the Jewish problem: mixed marriage."[64]

Even with Malou David, like Berthe twenty years old and seen alone, friendship was "a reality." Fr. Perrin introduced them, so they could work together on the distribution of the clandestine review, *Témoignage Chrétien*.

"My first reaction was bourgeois," recalls Malou. "I thought: 'I would not like to be seen with her on the street.' A beret pressed down on her frizzled hair, she was wearing maroon sandals without heels, with oval openings, the kind that children wear. It was December, and without socks, her legs were violet with the cold. Soon thereafter I sensed her great intelligence and I was ready to put her in charge. 'Don't even mention it,' she replied and she asked me to put her in the group of secret operatives, most of whom were responsible union members from Lyon. I was struck by this retreat to a secondary position, and even more so when I got to know her and realized how proud she was."

From December, 1941, to a day in May, 1942 ("it was Ascension Day"), the date of Simone's departure, the two young women saw each other every day. Simone served as a "letter box" for Malou and distributed three hundred copies of the review. It was Selma Weil who explained to Malou how painful it was for her migraine to carry those heavy packets up and down the stairs.

"She had an extraordinary potential for love, a rare sensibility. She would defend the truth with passion, without thinking of the circumstances for an instant. One evening, at a meeting of the editorial committee, the Tortels and the poet Toursky[65] were there; she spoke of the communion of saints. When we left together, she asked me why I had not supported her. 'But they do not have Christian ideas,' I remarked. 'The truth is the truth for everyone,' she replied."

Malou, a Catholic, represented for Simone "serene faith, without problems." "She spoke to me of philosophy, of the Greeks (her voice would then grow dim with emotion). She had a rare power of persuasion. At a lecture given by a priest against Nazism, she summarized the points under discussion with such precision that the priest thanked her and said, "I had not seen so far." But our friendship was not on the level of thoughts; we lived it in the solidarity of our action."

Malou lingers on a tender memory: a snack of slices of bread, covered with butter and sugar, and white wine.

"I knew well the absurd rations of the time and I did not want to taste it. But Simone insisted. She said, 'The restrictions have no power over the duties of friendship.'"

But she never stood in line for food and she had convinced her parents, too, not to do so. She could not conceive of the black market. Her refusal to think of food became intensified. She was perhaps the only woman in France really to live on ration coupons.

"I loved her very much, and I sensed a genius in her. The label of eccentricity that many have stuck on her irritates me. There was nothing artificial, nothing histrionic about her."

Malou's emotion is evident; she feels as though Simone is still alive. She has read only the *Journal d'usine*. "For me she is more alive if I do not read her."[66]

━━━━━━━

When he saw her arrive, with those incredible clothes and even more incredible pieces of luggage, Thibon experienced "sentiments which were indeed quite different from antipathy, but were all the same painful."

"I had the impression of finding myself before a being radically different from all my modes of feeling and thinking, from everything that expresses the sense and the flavor of life. She was, in a word, the revelation of my own antipodes: I found myself displaced, in a new land and under new stars."

Why had he agreed to satisfy Perrin, who had written him of "a militant of the extreme left, a Jew, excluded from the university because of the new laws," desirous of a guided experience in agricultural labor? After his first negative reflex of diffidence with regard to philosophers and the extreme left and a reluctance to admit a stranger into his own life ("it is always an adventure"), curiosity, the state of persecution in which the Jews were involved and which gave them the right to supplementary love, and the desire not to say no to a friend had prevailed.

"We began at once to discuss her arrangements. The room we had prepared for her seemed too nice and she crucified us until we found her a crumbling hovel, which she called 'my house of the fairies.' She lived there by herself, very happy; she left it when she wanted to face real agricultural work.

"On concrete issues, we were fated never to be in agreement. On the essential, however, I have never found the same profound harmony with any other human being. My great conversations with her are among the most important events of my life."

What were their days like? Every morning, Simone would climb from her hovel, sunk in the valley of the Rhône, to the Thibon house, set higher on a hill. Thibon would introduce her to work in the fields, in which "her inexperience vied with her good will, which finally triumphed." They would speak, "interminably." Every evening they would sit on a stone bench near the fountain and Simone would read him long passages from Plato.

"Her pedagogical gifts were prodigious; if she tended to overvalue the possibilities of culture for men in general, she knew how to put herself on the level of anyone to teach him anything. She would teach the rule of three to a slow-witted little peasant or introduce me to the mysteries of Platonic philosophy, but she always gave to and demanded of her student that quality of extreme attention which in her doctrine is identified with prayer."

In those days, she was reading the Greek fathers and the Rhenish mystics. Thibon gave her a small popular Spanish edition of Saint John of the Cross. "If we think of the three orders of Pascal, the body, the mind, and grace, her dimension was located in grace. I sensed that at once, quite soon after her arrival, when I found her seated on the trunk of a tree and immersed in the contemplation of the Rhône. Her glance, a stupendous relic of her ruined beauty, slowly reemerged from her vision to return to sight; it was so intense and pure. I thought, 'Look, she is contemplating, at the same time, the horizon and interior abysses.'"

A craggy character, she was above all rigid in obeying her vocation of self-annihilation. "Her pursuit of discomfort in small things and affliction in large made her overlook the reactions to such discomfort and affliction which others could experience. Perhaps, there was this, too: she thought, in her humility, that she was not worthy of being loved and so she believed that she would not make anyone else suffer. Once, after asking me to intervene with Vichy for a Spaniard [Antonio] who had been deported to Algeria, she made me swear that I would do nothing for her, if she were imprisoned. I, who had a day earlier promised exactly the opposite to her parents, protested and concluded with telling her, 'Let's reverse roles: would you be pleased if you were free and I were in prison?' She lifted her head a little, her glance dimmed, and said, 'I would not bear it.' Those are, I believe, the most affectionate words she ever said to me."

She was not open to the flow of practical reality; she did not have that "sense of life, that spontaneous sense of the relative which allows one to place everything in its place and to achieve a universal comprehension and benevolence. She always wanted to rebuild the world on the data of her own experience and she brusquely rejected every truth which she had not elaborated or verified from within herself. For this reason they have accused her of pride." Thibon never saw any external signs of this pride. If she was tough, "hard as an unripe fruit," "locked" in her own opinions, she was never touchy or injured in her self-love. "And I often contradicted her brutally, in epic discussions, or just as brutally I said to her, 'Enough, I am sleepy.'"

She had a funny side, one that was very pleasant. She looked upon her own life with humor. "One time she told me, 'I am a failure; I went to be a worker and I got sick; to war, and I returned with burns. All I have left is walking the streets.' 'I would not want to take away your last illusions,' I replied, 'but in this you have even less of a chance to be a success.' 'Not at all, you are wrong,' she shot back, with pride. 'Someone made a pass at me. Listen. I was unemployed and a worker asked me, "Are you coming?"'

"No." "I'll pay you, understand?" "No." "Why?" "Because it says nothing to me."' Her tone, without the shadow of moralism, must have been such that the worker stopped at once, confused and discouraged."

Another time she was doing the dishes; a total failure. "She held the dishes like a ciborium. And she said: 'In heaven we shall have all perfections.' 'Surely,' I observed. 'My wife will be intelligent and you will know how to clean dishes.' I got a box on the ear for that."

She had a sense of the authenticity of the spirit, of duty, of justice and of heroism, above all the Stoic. Marcus Aurelius (the Greek text which belonged to her is there on the long table and has notes at the end in pencil) was at the center of our discussions of Roman spirituality. Simone considered him Greek, because he had written in that language. And Job, the *Canticle of Canticles,* the things she loved in the Old Testament had to be of Egyptian or Persian inspiration. She was unmovable; good faith incarnate, in discussing those topics she gave the impression of bad faith.

And yet her failure to convert to Christianity, which had very complex reasons, depended among other things on her "desire not to abandon the Jews."

"She wanted to choose; for us who are born in the Christian religion, the Church is like our parents, whom we do not choose. For her it was like marriage. She wrote me: 'If you speak to me of the divinity of Christ, only my unworthiness keeps me from the Church but not if you ask me to accept all the formulas of the Council of Trent.'"

They promised each other to learn the Our Father in Greek. It was then that Simone began to pray. She recited it every day before picking grapes.[67]

> Since then I have made this my only exercise, reciting it once every morning with absolute attention. If during my recitation my attention wanders, even in the slightest way, I begin again, so that I achieve, one time, an absolutely pure attention.[68]

In September, she was finally employed in a "school" of women grape-pickers with a great landowner at Saint-Julien de Peyrolas, near Thibon.

At last, in submitting "time and the course of her thoughts" to the labors of those who all their life do not have any part in the privilege of

culture, she would *understand* that privilege and "the terrible responsibilities" that come with it.[69]

To Gilbert Kahn,[70] who had come to see her in Marseilles, she had
written on August 6:

> I anticipate being present at the extinction of my intelligence because
> of my labor . . . Why should I attribute a great value to this part [of
> me] which anyone, using a whip and chains . . . or a piece of paper
> filled with particular signs, can take from me? If this part is all there is,
> then I am entirely a thing of the least value, and why should I spare
> myself? If there is something which is imperishable, that is what has
> infinite value. I shall see if that is so.[71]

On October 3, she wrote to her great friend Pierre Honnorat:

> See me transformed into a grape-picker, a harsh task which I love all
> the same . . . I feel more and more strongly that this is what I should
> do . . . Why that is so, I could not explain . . . What one feels one
> should do, poetry or grape-picking, one must do that; that's all.[72]

She worked every day for eight hours, except for the days it rained,
which were frequent enough that she could have a "certain intellectual
activity."[73] The owner and his family, fine people who boarded her, had
had an "impression which was not happy." "We thought that she would
not endure the strain; her will and her courage made us admit our
mistake."[74]

She did not accept a room; after many discussions she allowed them to
put a thin mattress under her sleeping bag in the dining room. "But she
must not have slept much, with all those letters to write." They always had
to force her to eat, or she would have limited herself to onions and toma-
toes . . . insufficient food. When her parents came to meet her, she did not
want to waste an hour of picking to be with them. They knew from a letter
she had sent that she was proud of some "magnificent" clogs she had
bought for fifty francs. Those magnificent wooden shoes soon were hurting her ankles with their straps but she continued wearing them throughout the picking.[75]

> Exhaustion sometimes crushes me but I am finding in it a kind of
> purification. In the very depths of my weariness I find joys nothing

else could get for me, joys which forbid me to regret the inevitable decrease of intellectual lucidity.[76]

She wrote this to Gilbert Kahn on October 5.

It was the answer to the desires she had spoken of to Thibon in her first letter.

Perhaps I shall receive in addition, at least for short moments, the compensation connected uniquely with working the land, the sense that the earth, the sun, the countryside exist in reality and not merely as scenery.[77]

Here we reach the center of her dialogue with nature. This dialogue strives to achieve an osmosis between a human being and the world around through labor.

Associating the rhythm of the life of the body (breathing which provides a measurement of time) and that of the world (the rotation of the stars), feeling constantly that association . . . and sensing also the perpetual exchange of matter through which man is immersed in the world.[78]

In manual labor, *time enters the body*. Man submits to time in the same way as matter, he becomes matter himself, "as Christ does in the Eucharist."

Labor is like a death.[79]

Laboring means experiencing in oneself both time and space. "Thought is forced to pass from one instant to the next."[80] That can be done by assimilating *habit* which coincides with grace, understood in the physical sense of the word. Simone thinks here of Mlle. Agnes, the perfect picker, who was able to "cut the clusters more rapidly than the others, without leaving . . . a single grape on the ground."[81]

Quite often, labor without any incentives depresses a man; and such is labor in the fields when it is a matter of *preserving* one's life. It is not accepted; the peasant rebels against it. He sees it as "intolerable," that he has spent his energy for all that which is to be found back again where it had begun.

A field in autumn and the following autumn; everything is the same; the man weighs the same, his house is as it was, the provision of grain in the barns is the same . . . The only thing is that he is a little older.[82]

Simone recalls Lecarpentier, who hardly found the energy to begin again each time and "always dreamt of getting away."

For the imagination, preservation is empty, destruction is unlimited.[83]

But our only adherence to reality consists in our expansion in the universe, to love it and to recognize it as our homeland. We achieve this only through labor: so it should be "regular and relentless. But varied, like the days and the seasons."

Acting, with a renunciation of the fruits of action.[84]

We should live our action without hope, in *obedience to our toil,* which is the acceptance of law. Then, there should be joys which parallel our pain.

Sensible joys. Eating, resting. The pleasures of Sunday (of the past).
But not money.
Nor the unlimited possession of more land.[85]

Labor will become an *active contemplation,* experienced daily. Man will be able to achieve this perception:

The beautiful in nature: the union of the sensible impression and the feeling of necessity. It *must* be so (in the first place) and it is precisely so.[86]

He will draw close to things and they will speak to him.

Stars and trees in blossom. The complete permanence and the extreme frailty of things will equally provide the sense of eternity.[87]

One of the forms of the *implicit* or indirect *love* of God is love for *the beauty of the world.* Physical labor can establish a contact with this beauty, "a fullness which has no equal." If the artist, the scientist, the thinker *must* "really admire the universe beyond the film of unreality which veils it," they are often not in position to do so.

One whose members are broken with fatigue after a day in which he has been subject to matter bears within his flesh the reality of the universe like a thorn. The difficulty for him is to behold and to love; if he reaches that point, he loves the real.[88]

This privilege, which God has reserved for his poor, they do not know; it is not told them. Perhaps they knew it once upon a time, when there was a popular culture, of which we today gather crumbs in the form of *folklore*. Today they are thwarted by "their excessive exhaustion, their urgent preoccupation with money and the absence of a true culture."[89]

How should we define the beauty of the universe?

> The universe is beautiful as a perfect work of art would be, if something deserving that name could exist. So it does not contain . . . any finality, except universal beauty itself.[90]

It is an all-encompassing beauty, to which everything contributes because of its *inexplicable appropriateness,* in the same way every word of an almost perfect poem contributes to the beauty of the entire piece of poetry.

> The appropriateness of things, of beings, of events, consists only in this: they exist, and we should not desire that they not exist or that they be different from what they are. Such a desire is an impiety with regard to our universal homeland, a failure in our Stoic love of the universe.[91]

And we are made in such a way that this love can exist. For what we experience of this beauty "has been destined for our human sensibility." For this reason the universe is our homeland, our only homeland here below.

> Let us love it. It is real; it resists our love. It is what God has given us to love. He has willed that loving it would be both difficult and possible at the same time.[92]

Imitating the beauty of the world, coinciding with the absence of "finality, intention, discrimination" means stripping ourselves of ends and renouncing our own will.

> The image of God in man . . . is the faculty of renouncing our personality. It is obedience.[93]

In the man who elevates himself, in art, in thought, in sanctity, to such a level of excellence that he becomes, by participation, a divine being, there appears *the impersonal*.

> His voice is enveloped in silence.[94]

In this sense it is true that we must conceive of God as impersonal and love the perfection of our heavenly Father in the "impartial diffusion of the light of the sun."[95]

This leads to our respect for others. As God has created our autonomy so that we may be able to renounce it out of love, for the same reason we should will the preservation of this autonomy in our fellow creatures.

Stripping ourselves means renouncing our being, in our imagination, the center of the universe, and seeing all the other points of the universe as having as much right to be the center. It means consenting to the kingdom of mechanical *necessity* in matter and of free choice at the center of every being. Here is the place of Weil's fundamental concept of *reading,* which is at the basis of every action, of every impartial comprehension of reality.

The only things we can experience are *sensations* but we cannot think them. "We read through them." This reading, which is imposed upon us by the actual circumstances of our lives, depends on us to the degree that we have trained for it.

> The world is a text of many meanings and we pass from one to an-other with work. A work in which the body always has a part, as when we learn the alphabet of a foreign language. This alphabet must enter into the hand by the effort we make of tracing the letters. Beyond this, every change in this way of thinking is illusory.[96]

Loving our neighbor as ourselves essentially means

> having with respect to everyone the same relationship as one way of thinking of the universe has with respect to another way of thinking of the universe.[97]

Not seeing the other as part of the universe but as the starting point of a *perspective*. This is the foundation of true tolerance.

———

Simone asked questions of priests and monks, with whom Hélène put her in contact. "She made the circuit of all the canons I knew in Marseilles and in Catholic circles (where Simone showed a sort of shyness) I gave her her cue, like one of those modest confidantes of classic tragedy."[98]

The most important of these conversations was with the Benedictine Dom Clément Jacob, of Jewish background.[99] Simone gave the priest a questionnaire in which she listed five of her conceptions and asked if they could be considered more or less worthy of anathema on the part of the Church: the impossibility for her of accepting the Christian conception of history; her adherence to some of the ideas of Marcion, especially his concept of the superiority of the "so-called" pagan peoples to Israel; the admission as possible, even probable that there were incarnations of the Word before Christ, that the ancient religion of the Mysteries had flowed from such a revelation and that, as a consequence, the Catholic Church was their legitimate heir; the conviction that God was not the source of the command by which Israel destroyed cities and massacred peoples; the further belief that the attribution of such a command to God is an error much worse than the lowest forms of idolatry; the thought that until the exile, Israel had not had any knowledge of the true God, a knowledge present in the elite of other contemporary peoples; the thought that it was very doubtful and probably false that the true knowledge of God was spread more widely among the Christians of today than in antiquity or, presently, in non-Christian lands such as India.

She ended in this fashion:

Is it honest, with such thoughts, to wish to enter the Church? Is it not better perhaps to endure the deprivation of the sacraments?[100]

Dom Clément replied to these questions in conformity with the thought of the Church.[101] He thought he discerned in Simone "respect, confidence, a certain sense—albeit unconscious—of superiority (the certainty of being right, touchiness, a sense of deception)"; on his side, disconcerted by the physical appearance of the woman (the intentional absence of femininity), he experienced a certain irritation, a resentment provoked by fear of being dominated and a maladroit desire to convince her. He later wrote: "The rigor of her moral and intellectual requirements did not admit any evasions . . . Now that I understand her better, I think she found what she was looking for." And again: "There has been a lot of talk about her exceptional intellectual gifts; I believe that what most struck me in her were her nobility, her straightforwardness, the purity of her soul."[102]

Dom Clément, a composer, has set the thoughts of Simone to music.

According to Hélène and Pierre, the meeting with Dom Clément was a turning point for Simone; until then, despite her objections, she believed that she was headed towards the Church.

Next to the Benedictine abbey for men, En-Calcat, there is the abbey for women, Sainte Scholastique. Still led by Hélène, Simone went there to get to know Sister Colombe, a former student of medicine, "a serene woman of good sense."[103] What Sister Colombe remembers most of all about her was "the silence, the quality of attention," which she later found in her writings. "She had the poverty of those who are searching."[104]

Simone followed all the services of Holy Week, 1942. "I saw her enter the Church all by herself. She had a very Catholic attitude, a respect . . . as though she had been baptized. Since I had responsibility for visitors, I was the one to receive her." The very elderly Mlle. Thérèse de la Marguette, ninety-two years old, recalls an encounter she had anticipated and looked forward to, but then suffered a little from. "She did not want to try the dessert, she did not show that she liked anything. And I was doing my best so that the guests would be comfortable. I find that she lacked *savoir vivre*. She was disordered in a heavenly manner. But what did she expect? A miracle. She intimidated me, she upset me. On the one hand, I admire her courage in not thinking about the impression she could make on others. On the other, I would not have wanted to live with her."[105]

========

The *Cahiers du Sud* were the crucible for a special number: *Le Génie d'Oc et l'Homme Méditerranéen*.

Jean Ballard had been developing the project for years, in the "spiritual climate" of the room of the great invalid-poet-*genius loci* Joë Bousquet at Carcassonne. To Bousquet, to Déodat Roché, the greatest representative of Catharism, to René Nelli, a Provençal scholar of the troubadours, he had directed his request to find their true spirit, which coincided with a fallen civilization. It was the Provençal civilization, which had cultivated "the life of man to subject it to the secret demands of the soul," considering existence as "a ladder towards the spirit." Although it had failed on the practical plane when Provence had been brutally annexed to France, there still remained in it a buried seed of "poetic salvation," from which "the conscience of modern man could still possibly pour forth."[106]

As soon as she heard of it, Simone "caught fire" for the project.[107] She read the work of Roché on Catharism and his essay "L'Amour spirituel chez les Cathares," intended for the special issue.

On January 23, 1941, she wrote Roché a letter. In it she declared herself "strongly attracted" by the Cathars, principally because of their criticism of the Old Testament. With Roché, she thought that adoration of power had caused the Hebrews to err in their ideas of right and wrong. She held that Catharism was in Europe "the last living expression of pre-Roman antiquity," that epoch in which the same thoughts breathed under diverse forms "in the mysteries and the initiation sects of Egypt, Thrace, Greece and Persia." Of these thoughts Plato has left us the most perfect expression. From them has flowed Christianity, but "the Gnostics, the Manicheans, the Cathars seem the only ones to have remained truly faithful to them." Indeed, some of the "splendid conceptions" peculiar to the Cathars, "the divinity that descends among men" and "the spirit torn and dispersed in matter," are new aspects of Manicheism.

The thing that makes her most happy is having read in Roché that Catharism can be considered a sort of Christian Platonism.

We must "reawaken some such way of thinking," because never before have so many felt, in a confused but vibrant way, that the so-called Enlightenment of the eighteenth century is, science included, "an insufficient spiritual nutriment." For this reason she hopes that Roché will expand his studies on Catharism, but above all "publish a collection of original texts."[108] For people to look, read, contemplate, and discover the treasures of the spirit in time: this always returns as her most cherished desire.

If, in her spiritual thirst and in the multiplicity of openings of her soul, she felt an affinity for Catharism, Simone did not want to be enclosed within its confines or to exhume it as a religion.

> We cannot . . . be partisans of something that does not exist . . . whether it be the restoration of the Carolingian dynasty in France, the Cathar religion or the Order of Templars.[109]

(Roché still repeats: "Her letter defines her as a Cathar.")[110]

Engrafted here is the particular function Simone Weil attributes to the past. She believed in the "germs of eternity," enclosed in the past, and in the vitalizing influence that we can still draw from the moments and the ambiences in which those germs had the opportunity to develop.

One of these ambiences was the "Provençal land," which under different aspects was the center of Romanesque civilization.

Simone recalls its climate in two essays: "L'Agonie d'une civilisation à travers un poème épique"[111] and "En quoi consiste l'inspiration occitanienne." Both of them, even if the first is restricted in a mostly historical fashion to the events described in the poem and the second traces the inner story of a civilization from its beginnings to its death, amply consider the relationship between the past and the present.

In the twelfth century, in that land, ideas did not collide; "they circulated in an ambience which was in a certain sense continuous . . . Catholics and Cathars, far from forming distinct groups, were so well mixed together that even the shock of an unheard-of violence did not manage to separate them."

The atmosphere was suited to intelligence. The Greek spirit had been reborn under a Christian form, which is its truth.

> The supernatural did not mingle with the profane, it did not crush it, it did not seek to suppress it. It left it intact and just for this reason, it remained pure. This was its origin and its destination.

Romanesque architecture, even if it was borrowed from Rome, is not preoccupied with power and force but "solely aims at balance."

> A Romanesque church stands suspended like a balance around its point of equilibrium. This point rests upon the void and is felt, although there is no indication of its position. It has to be so to encircle that cross which was the balance upon which the body of Christ became the counterweight of the world.

Medieval Gothic, which appeared after the destruction of the Provençal homeland, was an attempt at totalitarian spirituality; the profane as such had no right of citizenship in it.

> In the surge of the Gothic spires and in the height of the pointed arches there is some contamination of force and of pride.

The disposition to combine diverse backgrounds and traditions in an organic equilibrium was valuable not only in nurturing thought; it also made the society fruitful in bearing a true order composed of "liberty and union between the classes." There was that spirit of "voluntary fidelity," which makes the slave equal to the master and allows him to obey without humbling his own pride. On this land was being prepared "a civilization of the city, without the dire seed of disputes which would desolate Italy."

The "chivalric spirit" provided the coherence. It was the "common sentiment" which spontaneously united these districts against Simon de Montfort; it still led the free city of Avignon to submit voluntarily to the Count of Toulouse after his defeat, when he was stripped of his lands and almost a beggar. They called their homeland, "the language."

The spirit of the conquerors was quite different. In their civic life, a struggle separated the feudal spirit from the spirit of the cities, "a moral barrier" divided the nobility and the common people. Once the power of the nobles was exhausted, a class prevailed which did not know the values of chivalry, a regime in which obedience became "something bought and sold." Order, on the contrary, can only hold sway where "the sense of a legitimate authority allows one to obey without debasing himself."

They began the annihilation of a civilization, which the poem reveals to us as happy, with the massacre of Béziers, a blow struck against the people to spread panic and decisive despondency.

> Those men, accustomed to obey out of duty and with nobility, were forced to obey in fear and humiliation.

The essence of Provençal inspiration, like the inspiration of the Greeks, consists in the "knowledge of force." To achieve this knowledge there must be "supernatural courage" present. Knowing force means seeing in it the "almost absolute sovereign of this world" and "rejecting it with disgust and contempt."

> This contempt is the other side of the compassion for all that is exposed to the blows of force.

The rejection of force finds its fullness in love, not in natural love, which is slavery and leads to constraint, but in supernatural love, which in its truth is always directed towards God, either directly or indirectly. Courtly love is nothing other than an expectation intended to provoke the *consent* of the beloved. In its fullness, this love "is the love of God through the beloved." In Provence, as in Greece, human love was one of the "bridges" between man and God.

Greece was a *builder of bridges* (philosophy, art, science); we have inherited her vocation, except that now we believe that we can inhabit them. We do not know any longer that these bridges are here only to cross and reach "the other side."

From the Renaissance to our days, all investigations have more and more been stripped of the supernatural. Today, that loss which the *Bhagavad Gita* would term the *loss of opposites* incites us to find the opposite of humanism. Some look for it in the *adoration of force*, of the social Beast, others in a return to medieval Gothic.

> The first is possible, and even easy, but it is bad; the second, even if desirable, is chimerical, because we cannot help it that we have been

shaped in an almost completely profane ambience. Salvation would be going to where the opposites are one.

What is the inspiration we are to find in this civilization which has disappeared, although we still, "all of us every day," feel the effects of its defeat? The social destiny of Europe would have been different if the nobility had disappeared without dragging down in its own ruin the spirit of chivalry, which is what happened with the ascendancy of a civilization in which the classes were already divided. The same is true of the religious destiny of Europe, if the Church, in its anxiety for orthodoxy (a sign of little faith), had not supported and incited foreign armies to destroy a spiritual liberty which Europe has never found again in that degree.

We must adopt the *value of pity* in our approach to homelands which are dead. For:

> There is nothing crueler towards the past than the commonplace according to which force is powerless to destroy spiritual values; by virtue of this opinion we deny that civilizations obliterated by the violence of arms ever existed . . . So we slay a second time what has perished, and we associate ourselves with the cruelty of arms.

Pity, on the contrary, insists that we carefully and lovingly review even the slightest traces of civilizations which have been destroyed to attempt "to grasp their spirit." And the spirit of the civilization of Provence seems to contain an answer to certain *aspirations* that we still carry within ourselves, unsatisfied, and that "we should not allow to vanish." They have to do with "our destiny as men."[112]

———

Joë Bousquet was the soul of the *Cahiers du Sud.* In his baroque bedroom, suffused with perfume, populated with paintings of the surrealists (Tanguy, Magritte), among whom was his great friend Max Ernst, full of objects in a disorder worthy of an antiquarian, he would receive visitors at night, a moment of truce from his spinal sufferings.[113] Books invaded his bed. His visitors were numerous, from Gide to Valéry to Eluard, known and less known; constant, like the poet Louis Esteve, in passing, like Aragon. Young people often found there the road to a poetic vocation. Jean Ballard had found there from the very beginning a fascination which he was to preserve in its secrecy, like "the perfume of an unknown city where one arrives in the evening."[114] Jean Tortel could not remain there. "I was suffocating."

Simone Weil wanted to meet him; Jean Ballard brought her there "at two in the morning." After a long "passionate conversation," Simone stretched out on the mat of the next room, before leaving for Dourgne, the site of the abbeys. A correspondence ensued between them during April and May, 1942. They never saw each other again.[115]

Bousquet was deeply struck by this "different" sort of woman, even if at the beginning he was put off by her offer ("I shall sleep at your door like a dog").[116]

"Bousquet was quite ill, quite drugged," says Lanza del Vasto.[117] The opium with which he had for long years fought against pain had separated him from reality. Since he possessed the natural magic of language, he had reached the point of translating the world of the *imagination,* with all of its presentiments and intimations.

Simone gave him her unfinished tragedy and some of her poems, including "Nécessité."

"Very much in control of herself; with her abstract tone of a philosopher, she could convince philosophers, but not men," René Nelli says of her. And of Bousquet he adds: "He was pretty much an atheist. He did not believe in death or in an incarnate God. He spoke coldly of the previous lives he had led, but he was not a philosopher."

In reality, the meeting between Simone and Bousquet, very brief as it was, reached great depths. Through her Bousquet reflects upon the point he has reached; he glimpses and depicts the particular *poetic creativity* which was hers, one that coincides with spiritual creativity. Simone feels that she is like her friend and actually becomes like him; she identifies with him through a penetrating "sympathy" and grasps his key point: the will to overcome pain, which on the one hand turns in flight, and on the other creates a desperate courage. For this reason, she expresses to him alone, for the first time, her ideas on the bond between the *acceptance of affliction* and the *consent* of the soul to *the good.*

"All that you have told me has inspired passionate reflections," writes Bousquet. "More than anyone else, you could aid me in eradicating everything that remains in me of the involuntary, the inherited."

He sees in Simone a moral loftiness, which he has not been able to reach. "I envied you because you have the intuition of the good and the sense of the bad . . . Perhaps all I am searching for is happiness and the forgetfulness of death." He tended to escape into dreams, "towards a happiness that creates for us a boundless vision of all that we were."

He places himself at the center of *being* as an *ego.* "We are not ourselves except in our own hearts. We love only what can take refuge in our hearts. We are only happy to the degree that we are our own hosts."

He well understood the *self-spoliation* of Simone: "You are paying a high price for your moral qualities: you do not have enough confidence in yourself; to be created by God certainly means embodying the essence of our own being . . . If this should make us tremble . . . it should not make us doubt the capacity for revelation that is found in each of us."

He has a profound appreciation for her writing; he finds her a poet at the root of her self. "I would say that the rhythm of verses is for you that of conscience." But there is something deeper to which she could give voice: "the poetry of faith." "I do not fear for you those feminine contentments which all your aspirations belie. Just because you could not be weak without doing yourself violence, I expect much from a mystical abandon to which you would give a very difficult consent. Consider this: the most exploited and debased themes are waiting for some being, chosen without his or her knowledge, to reveal true greatness. You would write very beautiful things about divine love."

For Simone, her friend has "the privilege" of living, through his own body, the *reality* of the present state of the world. For twenty years, through his thought, he has rebuilt "a destiny," which has seized him forever. He is very close to *thinking* it truly. When he achieves that, he will break the shell and emerge from the darkness of the egg. A most ancient image.

> The egg is this visible world. The chick is Love, the Love that is God Himself and lives in the depths of every man, at first as an invisible seed.

When the creature emerges, it still finds itself in the world, but:

> Space is open and torn. Leaving its miserable body, the spirit is transported to a point outside space . . . from where this visible world is seen as real, without perspectives . . . The moment is motionless. The whole of space is filled . . . with a complete silence . . . more positive than a sound, since it is the secret word, the word of that Love which from the start carries us in His arms.

Then her friend will know *the reality of war,* the reality of something that is also *unreality itself.* This knowledge coincides with Pythagorean harmony, the unity of opposites.

The comrades who fell around him that day have not had the time "to focus upon their lot the frivolousness of their wandering thoughts." Those who returned intact have "killed the past with forgetfulness." War is affliction, and directing our thoughts voluntarily towards affliction is difficult in the same way as "convincing an untrained dog to enter a fire."

> To think of affliction, one must carry it in one's flesh, fixed in it like a nail, and for a long period, so that thought may have the time to become strong enough to look at it.

Body and soul remain motionless, transfixed, in anticipation. And it is in this anticipation, as the Gospel says, that the soul grows and bears fruit.

Those who bear in their own flesh the affliction of their age have "the opportunity and the function" of contemplating it with love, that is to say, of *redeeming* it. They are the redeemers. During the Roman empire, affliction was represented by slavery, at the end of which was crucifixion.

Unhappy are those who do not fulfill this function. How can they fail in it? By escaping it through dreams. *Dreaming* is "the only consolation, the only wealth of the unfortunate, the only support to carry the awful weight of time." It is innocent and indispensable, but it is not real.

> Renouncing dreams out of love for the truth means truly abandoning all of one's goods in the folly of love and following Him who is the Truth . . . and carrying one's own cross. The cross is time.

This acceptance of reality coincides with the *consent of the soul to the good,* a consent which the soul fears because it is an eternal commitment, in which the soul loses its virginity. But if it does not say yes at the moment determined for its consent since all eternity, it will be seized by evil.

> A man may yield to evil at any moment of his life, because we yield to evil unconsciously, without knowing that we are introducing into ourselves an external authority; before abandoning her virginity to it, the soul drinks a narcotic.

The narcotic is dreaming; it is found at the "root of evil," because it is unreal. It is unreal in all of its forms, from the most childish and apparently harmless, to the more serious and apparently respectable, because of their relations with art, with love, with friendship, even with religion. A dream is an untruth and we should never forget that.

Dreaming excludes love. Love is real.

When her friend says that he does not sense the distinction between good and evil, it is "another man who speaks in him, the evil in him." With a careful examination we can succeed in distinguishing the other man and what nourishes him in our thoughts, our words, and our acts at our expense, as we are nourished on him at his expense. This means that her friend has not yet agreed to recognize the distinction between himself and the other as "the distinction between good and evil."

And yet he is very close to that point.

I would never dare to speak to you like this if these thoughts were an elaboration of my mind . . . Despite me, I have the sense that God, out of His love for you, is directing these thoughts to you through me. In the same way, it is unimportant that the consecrated host is made of flour of inferior quality, even if it is three quarters mouldy.[118]

This letter, which accompanied some books (her beloved T. H. Lawrence, the Gospels in Greek, the Grail, Swinburne), was dated May 12, 1942.

Simone was about to leave France. André Weil, in the United States since March, 1941 with his wife Eveline,[119] had found a way to bring his parents and sister there, a solution that had become indispensable.

As far as Simone was concerned, the idea of departure had been tormenting her for a long time. It looked like flight to her. She knew well that the idea of being far from Europe would make her suffer "to the point of making her lose all of her moral equilibrium."[120]

She saw Thibon for the last time at the end of April. "I had the impression that I was in the presence of a being of complete transparency, one ready to return to its original abode of light. I still hear her voice in the night, along the deserted streets of Marseilles, on the way to my hotel. She was commenting on the Gospel: her mouth was speaking as a tree gives its fruit." These are Thibon's words.[121]

At the station, the next morning, Simone handed him a packet containing her *Cahiers;* she was entrusting them to her friend. He should do whatever he wished with them.[122]

The definite departure was decided upon at the last moment. Malou remembers that it was a Thursday. Simone had to give up a concert by Pablo Casals for the Red Cross (the Gestapo had granted special permission). "I always have to give up what I love," she said. Hélène and Pierre Honnorat accompanied her to the ship. This is how they said good-bye. "Till we see each other again, Simone, in this world or the next." She replied, "No, there's no seeing each other again in the next world."[123]

17

Supernatural Knowledge

Aboard the ship and at the refugee camp in Casablanca she does nothing but write letters.

To Thibon:

> We love this distance woven completely of friendship; those who do not love one another are not separated.[1]

To Antonio:

> I charge the stars, the moon, the sun, the blue of the sky, the wind, the birds, the light, the boundlessness of space, I charge all that is forever near you, with my thoughts for you and with the joy that I desire for you and that you so richly deserve.

To Simone Pétrement:

> I am fervently hopeful . . . that you will bring forth from yourself, for the good of all, what you bear within yourself. And that you be as happy as you may in the light of your destiny and your vocation. You know that I am always thinking of you.[2]

At the Ain-Seba camp there were not many chairs; Simone monopolized one from morning to night. When she had to leave it, her parents occupied it for her in turn; because of this chair they were the first to get up and the last to go to bed.

Simone wanted to maintain her contacts with her world in Marseilles; the need to continue a conversation which had nurtured her was intertwined in her with the necessity of making lucidly objective her own spiritual condition. These two reasons struck roots in the only area of feeling where she had been allowed to stop and which she had still not left. After her departure from Paris, this is the second great separation of her life.

In connection with Perrin, she feels like

> a mendicant who, reduced by his impoverishment to the state of always being hungry, presents himself now and then in the course of a year in a rich house in search of bread and for the first time in his life does not experience humiliation.[3]

Not even if she had "one life for each piece of bread and were to give them all in return," could she repay the debt.

And yet she will not give him any indication of gratitude; she will only tell him things that she "does not dare to keep silent" because she has thought them. God, who may like to choose for his intermediaries "the vilest objects," has chosen her this time.

Her intention in tracing for the priest her own "spiritual autobiography"[4] was that of offering him a "concrete and certain" example (she does not lie, and the priest knows that) of "implicit faith." Educated by her parents and her brother in *complete agnosticism,* she has never made the slightest effort to leave it and to adhere to a precise creed. And yet "from the very day of her birth" she had perceived the existence of a perfect truth in which to believe and the words "vocation, obedience, spirit of poverty, purity, acceptance, love of neighbor" have always had a rigorously Christian meaning. Then, and ever increasingly, the love of things outside the Church has contributed in the same measure as the love of things visibly Christian, to "making her a prisoner of Christ"; and they are the same things that keep her outside the Church. A "spiritual destiny" perhaps incomprehensible to the priest, it will have the wholesome effect of bringing him to reflection.

It is good to reflect on what makes us come out of ourselves.

But the priest, despite the exceptional probity of her ideas, does not accept with complete openness the possibility of implicit faith. Here he shows a "grave imperfection," which is not proper to him, any more than "a false note" is proper to a beautiful song. What is the source of this imperfection? It is due to his human and inevitable *attachment* to the Church as his earthly homeland. But the children of God should not have any other homeland here below than the universe, with the totality of the rational creatures it has contained, contains, and will contain.

We should love it with a love that does not love beings and things in God, but from God's perspective.

The age in which we live, unlike all others, requires an *explicit univer-sality*, which should saturate our language and all entire manner of being.

There is need for "a new sanctity." It is a "spring," a "discovery." It corresponds to "a new revelation of the universe and of human destiny."

The world needs saints rich in genius as a city convulsed with the plague needs doctors. Where there is a need, there is a duty. And the friends of God should ask this genius of the Father in the name of Christ, with an insistent prayer every day, every hour, "as a hungry child asks for bread."

As far as she herself is concerned, she can make no use of such ideas, because she has vilely allowed too much imperfection to remain in herself and because she is a "corroded instrument."

I never read without trembling the story of the barren fig. I think that it is my portrait. Even its nature was fruitless, and yet it was not excused. Christ cursed it.

So she entrusts these thoughts to the priest because he, since he has for her "a little friendship, and that true," is the only one who may use them.

For the others, in a certain sense, I do not exist. I am to them the color of dead leaves, like certain insects.[5]

They embarked on a Portuguese ship, June 7, 1941. The crossing lasted a month. Simone had wanted to travel fourth class. It was so bad there that she ended up sleeping on the bridge. She had christened the ship "the floating bordello," since the passengers were so eager to amuse themselves. She became a friend, above all, with a Boy Scout, Jacques Kaplan, who took care of the poorest refugee children. "She was very civil, very protective, very sarcastic. She could not stand the first-class passengers."[6] She also made friends with a half-witted young man. She maintained contact with both of them.

From the Weil apartment in New York, on Riverside Drive, one could look across the Hudson to New Jersey on the other side and see the majestic arch of the George Washington bridge.

Within the apartment, the rooms opened into one another. The only room with a door became Simone's.

≡≡≡

She had always been ready for an extreme project, she had begun to present it in 1939 and had gradually brought it to completion. She had agreed to come to America on André's advice, only if that journey "would permit its realization." She had asked her brother to obtain for her *formal* promise of an authorization from the proper officials.[7]

She had hardly arrived when she was confronted with precise information from André: the departure for England, indispensable for that realization, was very difficult, if not impossible.

She received the news like a death-blow. For about two-and-a-half months she could not write. She threw all of her energy into letters, visits and appeals.

She began with a letter to Maritain, with the request that he establish contact for her with the authorities, all the way to Roosevelt. She then wrote to Admiral Leahy, the head of the president's staff, and to an English captain who had spoken warmly of France on July 14. The captain invited her to dinner at his hotel; Simone misunderstood and arrived at lunch time and waited until seven. The captain most likely could not do much. Maritain found the idea noble and exalted but did not know if it could be realized; he would do what he could to help her. Leahy replied directly that the plan had been submitted to competent authorities.

At the same time she decided to appeal to her old student comrades who were in London in the Free French Forces.

Two letters to Maurice Schumann are fundamental,[8] one sent by mail and the other through Captain Mendès-France. She enclosed with the first her "Project for the formation of nurses of the front line."

The project, which had found favor with the French Ministry of War in 1940, proposed to enroll small groups of volunteer nurses for first aid in the most dangerous zones of the front. The necessary preparation could be quickly obtained; the indispensable moral qualities ("of a type that is not acquired") would be brought to light at the first examination.

Simone supported the following points.

Apparently "impractical because novel," the project is really easy to put in operation. It is sufficient to begin with a small nucleus of volunteers; if the first experience yields good results, increasing the number would create the organization. Failure would be due only to the failure of the volunteers to fulfill their mission. There are only two things to fear: that the courage of these women would fail them in battle and that their presence among the soldiers would have a harmful effect upon their morals. But we would have neither of these two things if the volunteers were of a quality corresponding to their decision; they would have the *manly coolness* to go beyond every consideration of self in certain circumstances and the *maternal tenderness* necessary for comforting the suffering and dying.

Ready to run all the risks of soldiers in the front line, they would have to face them "without being sustained by an offensive spirit." This was the *meaning* of the project. Beyond the unquestionable practical advantages (prompt medical attention and psychological comfort), there were moral advantages of a much greater range in relation to the general conduct of the war. As Hitler has been the first to understand, the fundamental requirement is "to strike the imagination of everyone." To this end, Hitler has forged some instruments: special units, the SS, composed of men ready to die, because they are inspired by a kind of religious faith. And Nazism is without doubt "a substitute for religion." The SS create *propaganda* for it, as they display a *heroism* that draws its energy from an *extreme brutality:* they are indifferent to death, not only their own, but that of the rest of humanity.

If Hitler's methods cannot and should not be copied, we must recognize their effectiveness; we must offer *equivalents,* which would demonstrate a *moral vitality.* It is a question of creating an analogous propaganda, but one that would draw its origin from a different inspiration, not idolatrous but *religious,* in a sense much more difficult to define than simply belonging to a particular church. By way of acts that show our purity and authenticity of inspiration, we should and we can

demonstrate a courage of a different quality, much more rare and difficult.

It is the courage to sustain for a long period the vision of suffering and death. The persistence of *gestures of humanity* at the very center of the battle, at the apex of barbarism, would be a "dazzling challenge" to that *barbarism,* which the enemy has chosen and wishes to impose upon us.

A body of this type on one side and the SS on the other would create by contrast a picture preferable to any slogan. And it would be the clearest representation of the two directions between which mankind today must choose.[9]

In the *Cahiers* we find:

There are two ways of changing in others their way of reading sensations, their relation with the universe: force (of which war is the extreme form) and instruction. They constitute two actions upon the imagination. We cannot associate ourselves with the first (we can only react), while we do associate ourselves with the second . . . With the use of force we can cast others down or prevent them from being cast down; we can lift them up only with instruction.
    There is a third way, beauty (example).[10]

And she asks herself this precise question,

Does a life exist—in the world, not in solitude—that is as pure, beautiful and complete as a Greek statue? Or is it only a single action that can be such?[11]

Thereafter, confronted with the project, DeGaulle will comment: "But she's mad!"[12] and will reject it without appeal. And on the external plane of human circumstances, he will be right.

━━━━━

If the creation of the nurse corps was not realized, she requested that she be sent to France on "a secret mission, preferably dangerous."

The *greatest* danger would be welcome, if only I could do something really useful. As long as Paris, my native city, is under German control, my life will have no value for me. And I find it bitter that it will be liberated only at the cost of someone else's blood.[13]

She thought of some sabotage operation or the possibility of serving as a courier. She knew the founder of the review *Témoignage Chrétien* very well. She begged, "Don't let me waste away in sorrow here below."[14] She also wrote to Mme. Rosin, a great friend of the Weils in Montana and Paris; she was now living in Paris and might get her the desired approval.

The newspapers had provided accounts of a patriotic demonstration at Marseilles on July 14: police repression, two dead, some casualties. For two days she could not touch any food. "Luckily you are here!" they told her, and irritated her in the extreme.

"I cannot continue living like this. I shall end up going south to live among the blacks; at least I shall die in their terribly hard way of life," she confided to her mother.

"If I needed the help of the Nazis to leave, I would use it!" she told Souvarine, who had been in New York for a time.

In the meantime, she decided to take a course in nursing in Harlem. She went to the lessons with another Frenchwoman she had known in Marseilles; she, too, was eager to leave for England. They were the only white students.

In Harlem, every Sunday, she attended services at a Baptist church. She was stirred by the atmosphere "of authentic faith," which she thought she perceived in the shouting, the dancing, the Charlestons of the faithful. She wrote this to Bercher,[15] who was convinced that if she had remained in America, "she would have become a black." Nothing would have been easier: her association with the blacks would have made her as much one of them as if she had been born black, in the minds of the whites.

═══════

Her constant research in the library concentrated upon folklore. She had written: "*A study to be conducted in a wholly new manner.*" She brought this idea to the science of religions, which is the *science of the supernatural* in its diverse manifestations across the different human societies.

> One can study the supernatural either in itself or as a phenomenon . . . To study it in itself, one must first of all be able to discern it. Faith, in the true sense of the word, is required.

For, on the plane of the intelligence, the supernatural is at the same time "what is obscure and the fount of light."[16]

On the other hand,

> the object of my research is not the supernatural but this world; the supernatural is the light. We should not dare to make it an object, otherwise we debase it.[17]

So the route of this knowledge is the universe; the reading of its super-natural meaning depends upon our ability to leave the cave and *accept the light*, which is so dazzling at first that it hurts us.

How do we arrive at the point of feeding on this light? We should begin by imitating things, obedient things.

> The manner in which things receive light at dawn—time—patient waiting for the light, docility.[18]

And yet this obedience is not passivity.

Matter, nature, contains in itself something that permits the super-natural to exist: it is a principle of purity, of light (the *sattva* of the *Upanishad*): it is *energy*. Plants absorb it and transform it into chlorophyll, "man eats the sun" and transforms it into animal, mechanical energy.

What should be done so that in certain instances a man can transform "the decomposition of his organic syntheses" into *radiant energy*? There is someone who possessed this type of energy, as much a source of force as muscular energy: Saint Francis.[19]

> Strive to become capable of nonviolence . . . Strive to substitute *ever increasingly* in the world *effective* nonviolence for violence.[20]

How can we make this happen? By using our power of *attention* based on detachment, for a reading of the world that allows us to see the *ātman* (the individual "self") in everything. This reading is a contemplation that wells up from your entire nature, not from your mind alone, which is subject to fatigue. Fatigue debases you and contains in itself the seeds of laziness and discouragement. You should listen to what is "motionless" in you, the soul, and gather through it the balances that are found in the universe. There are no imbalances in the "natural phenomena" of the physical world. Nor are there in the body, in reality, except in relation to its effects upon the soul. There are imbalances in the desires and the relations among human beings. We should become able to see ever more clearly the bal-ances that arise from the accord among various readings achieved by oth-ers and in ourselves.

> That *my* world may be in balance.[21]

Contemplation, which establishes contact with the good present in the universe, is translated into action. This action does not "allow delay," be-cause it is associated with natural duty, with the will. The body must serve as a "balance" among the various motives that urge you to action, so that you weigh clearly the problem that confronts you and

Do only what you cannot help doing.[22]

How shall we make the balance ever more just? By creating within ourselves a moment of suspension, which coincides with our reception of the supernatural. This suspension is a detachment from the fruits of action and engenders the capacity for "superimposed readings."

Read the necessity behind the sensation, read the order behind the necessity, read God behind the order.[23]

This capacity is the capacity of creating links. God wills it in His saints. Of a saint, "He wills suffering and at the same time progress, and He wills the link between the two—and an infinity of other links as well."[24] It is as though the saints had to find all the threads of the tapestry of the good and restore it.

How are we to become saints and perfect, since "perfection is the moral vocation of each of us"?[25] By acquiring a greater "capacity for feeding on light." For sin is nothing but the absence of such a capacity. We should understand that the source of moral energy is like that of physical energy: it is outside ourselves. We believe, instead, that the principle of conserving this energy is within ourselves; and when we sense ourselves deprived of it, we believe we can acquire it by throwing ourselves avidly upon anything edible. For we are hungry, hungry for an unknown but all the same foreseen good, of which all the other goods are only images on the earth. And our hunger is not stilled. We should understand that it cannot be stilled and that the good things, all of them, are there to serve us as a way to the good. And these things contain light but we must become able to perform a chlorophyll synthesis of the light they contain.

To achieve this, we should imitate Him who "emptied Himself of His divinity" (she cites Philippians 2, 6–7) or we "should empty ourselves of the world," of appearances, of cupidity. We should reduce ourselves to the "point we occupy in time and in space. To nothing."[26] In obedience, founded upon humility, there occurs the only passage "from time to eternity." In an indifference to good and evil, which is an "impartial projection" of the light of attention, the good prevails automatically.

This is the essential grace. And at the same time the definition, the criterion of the good.[27]

By directing, even in an imperfect way, our power of attention to the proper *reading* and imploring light from on high for this reading, we progressively climb a little higher, and this happens with every action we achieve with this attention.

Nothing good is ever lost.[28]

This engenders *hope* in us, which is

fearlessness in spiritual matters.[29]

It is the knowledge that the evil we bear within ourselves is finite and that the slightest orientation, even the most infinitesimal, towards the good destroys a little of it. Discouragement in the face of our repeated failings is a "perversion associated with an absence of hope." This perversion is a temptation to laziness, connected with discouragement, born of the loss of energy. For this reason, we should *forgive our debts*.

> Not only to men, but to things. We should not ascribe to things or to beings the energy we have spent for them (including the energy that allows us to endure suffering).[30]

Thus we shall ask that our own debts be forgiven to us, that we have restored to us "the energy we have squandered," since we expect to receive this energy only from the "Father" ("Father, save me from this hour." John 12, 27). And this is *faith,* which is "detachment from the past," or pardon and acceptance of all that has taken place, considered as the past.

Charity, which conceives the totality of time as the present, asks light for the life we are leading. While *hope* projects into the future (that the kingdom may come), in an expectation "composed of fear and confidence," charity experiences a desire as strong as hunger that the order of the world be "consecrated" to God, *now.*[31]

It is a question of living in the dimension of the transcendental ego, as we humbly feed ourselves on faith and hope. Faith means believing in the source of light and hope knows that this light will increase in us. And so it happens.

> With time, the light produces an accommodation to the light that allows us to receive ever more light. Grace advances exponentially.[32]

For the desire for light is always present in man. This is how the Eskimos express it:

During the time when the eternal night covered the earth, the fox took advantage of the darkness to steal pieces of meat from the hiding places of men. But the raven, which could not find food in the eternal night, desired the light, and the earth was illumined.[33]

———

If within herself she had traversed, from room to room, the inner spaces, where our "contrary potentialities" are stored and had sought to arrange them all within herself, although it cost sorrow, until she reached "*the middle room, where God awaits us from all eternity,*"[34] there was still an area in which she remained tied to the approval of the world. There were mingled, in her desire for approval, her pride and her restlessness, her need for total coherence and her desire to make her intuitions of truth, of which she was certain, penetrate the world, so that they would appear on the plane of an incarnate religion. There was also her taste for provocative discussions and her impatient intransigence when confronted with others' arguments, which always seemed to her slow-witted and satisfied either with convictions reached once and for all or with systems already established.

So she went from priest to priest in New York as she repeated her questions.

She spent a whole afternoon in conversation with Fr. Oesterreicher. He saw in Simone "a tormented and unhappy soul, of absolute sincerity, whose thoughts showed traces of internal conflict."[35] A Jesuit, after an hour of conversation, excused himself, desolate that he could not spend any more time with her or see her again, since he was traveling so much. Perhaps he believed that he had soothed her when he said that, after "sufficient efforts of comprehension," she would succeed in reading the stories of the massacres in the Old Testament "with a proper attitude . . . since he himself found no difficulty in them." He gave her the address of another Jesuit. "I wonder if this one will not refer me to a third, and so forth, until exhaustion. I am sorry for them." These are her words to her parents, who had gone to visit André in Pennsylvania.[36]

Her conclusion is that, even in the mind of priests, "Catholicism has no fixed boundaries. It is both rigid and imprecise."

Personally I have not yet been able to discover whether a priest who baptized me would be committing a sacrilege or not.[37]

But it was with solicitous tenderness that she advised the baptism of the child expected by Eveline and André. She had nicknamed him Patapon and thought that, "when he has reached the age of manhood (or of womanhood)" he would in no way be able "to regret" something that "could only benefit him (especially socially) and not harm him at all."

Once the child was born, on September 12, and it was a girl, Sylvie, she immediately wrote to her brother: "If I had a child, I would not hesitate a second in having him baptized." As advantages, she points to the future happiness of Sylvie if she falls in love with a "practising Christian" and the social ease of being a baptized half-Jew without having to be guilty of "cowardice" as an adult in the face of other Jews. As far as disadvantages, she saw none.[39]

We note that she insists upon the practical aspects of the question; it is a diplomatic pleading. In the very urgency of her advice appears her deep desire to give Sylvie spiritual nourishment from the very beginning, the milk of grace that would aid her in secret.

"How beautiful you are in your angel's robe!" she said to the baby, as she held her ever so tenderly on her knees. And she was eager to give her her bottle.[40]

It was the middle of September.

To Alain, ten years of age, the son of Eveline's first marriage, she told stories. "Quite seriously, the way you tell things that have really happened. She spoke to children as though they were adults. They always felt they were being treated as equals and at the same time protected."[41] For the boy, too, she was equally anxious that he receive a religious education. She told André to see Fr. Couturier, a Dominican of great intelligence and openness, whom Maritain had recommended but she had scarcely met. In the meantime she studied a *manual of piety*, which had "weighed" heavily over the childhood of Pierre Honnorat. From it she concluded that the two most bothersome practices for children were confession and daily prayer.

For confession, it was necessary "to persuade Alain that there was no need to torment himself with the fear of forgetfulness nor should he go into particulars . . . he should rather follow general lines and not confess too often."[42]

As far as prayer is concerned, the Pater once a day, "with the greatest attention possible," was the maximum of appropriate prayer for a child and perhaps also for an adult. She found the various "acts of faith," as they are presented in manuals of piety, "horrible." In Rome she had sought in vain for a missal; she had found only "horrible booklets crammed with the most banal texts in Italian."[43]

With regard to herself, Simone writes the questions that she will later ask Fr. Couturier aloud when she has an opportunity to speak to him calmly. She asks for an answer, "precise and certain, whether a priest can or cannot grant baptism legitimately" to someone who holds her opinions and does not wish to abandon them.

All of this is very far from being a game with me. From early childhood I have felt attracted to the Catholic faith.

But with the passage of time the thoughts that keep her away from the Church gather strength, the same strength as the thoughts that bind her to the Church.

It follows, it seems to me, that my hope of sharing in the sacraments is very slight or nonexistent, at least until the Church modifies the conditions with which I do not agree. I hope fervently that she will do so some day, since I believe that this is for her a question of life or death; but I do not reckon that it will happen during my life.[44]

A letter from Maurice Schumann gives her the hope of at least getting a job in London. André Philip, Commissioner of the Interior and of Labor in the National Committee of Free France, anticipated this, even if her project for nurses was declared absolutely impracticable.

She felt relieved and began to look around herself. For the first time she saw what was beautiful and interesting in New York. She wrote to Schumann:

The misfortune spread over the face of the earth obsesses me and depresses me to the point that my faculties are annihilated; I can recover them and free myself from this obsession only when I have a large part in the danger and suffering . . . I am disposed to accept any position in any office . . . but only provisionally. Otherwise, the same sorrow that consumes me in New York will consume me in London . . . This is not simply a question of character, I am sure, but of vocation.[45]

It is probably in this period that we can locate the following episode. André is speaking: "I brought her a newspaper to look at. There was a huge ad by the department store, Macy's; it took up the whole page. They were selling, for sixteen thousand dollars, a Spanish cloister of the twelfth century. The stones of the building were in the store's warehouses and were numbered accurately, one after another. I believed that this would amuse her; she had the capacity for black humor. Instead, this news threw her into a violent bout of fever. She experienced a kind of horror I had not expected. She was no longer herself; with time, her sensibility had gone beyond the limits of the normal."[46]

Simone was living the "dark night" of the world in her own body.

═══════

For Simone, too, it was the "dark night," a passage of the soul as Saint John of the Cross has defined it and as Simone in particular lives it. "Fervent with a love full of anxiety," she pursued her inward road "in darkness and in certainty . . . without any other light or guide except for that burning in her heart."[47] She was in complete isolation from the point of view of human interchanges ("I lived, as it were, in a desert," she would later say) and at the same time she found herself sheltered from the immediacy of danger and this, as always, filled her with anxiety. A news item like that of the "Spanish cloister" was a cry for help which the world directed to her, an indication of the *malheur*, the affliction of her era; thence derived her pathological fever, to burn that *malheur*. Inherent in the vegetative world of force, of *pesanteur*, of weight and shadow, of injustice, *malheur* darkens and desiccates the senses, the mind, and the soul; it is the test to which the creature is compelled. If the creature does not succeed in overcoming the *malheur* by saying yes to the light, it is withered forever in its capacity for loving and being loved, for giving life and being vivified. This happens on all the planes of what Simone defines as the *implicit love* of God: the love of neighbor, the love of the order of the world, which is at the root of artistic creation, and friendship.

Where does she now find herself? From the eager liveliness of multiple action ("Remember that you have the whole world . . . before you."),[48] from the thirst for a creativity which wanted to stamp its seal in the field of art and thought (envy of Bach, Leonardo)[49] or of wise command (such as T. E. Lawrence),[50] she has reached the point of needing not to misrepresent her own powers of action to herself.

If she was conscious from the very beginning of the limits inherent in her circumstances and in the requirements of her own moral norms and thus encouraged herself *not to teach* but to *hide* herself, she still continued to trust enormously in the force of knowledge and of intelligence. And she did not want to depend on anyone.

> Mathematics: an abstract universe in which I depend on myself alone. The kingdom of justice, because every good will there finds its proper recompense.[51]

Having then descended into the heart of human toil, she had received full in the chest the blows of affliction. Pierced and yet preserved in the very marrow of her being, she had learned what one should seek, desire and request. The three movements coincide, towards one and the same thing. She had come to recognize her own hunger as a creature.

First of all, *desire,* an ambiguous term, had to be suppressed and replaced with *will.* One must work, and what is not repayment for work, one must receive as grace. And yet even grace ("the most beautiful of words")[52] remained an ambiguous word. Then, her vocation changed aspect. Ever so gradually she was stripping herself of her active self, her personal self, and trusting in an *amor fati* that made her indifferent to every consideration of her own destiny as a value. "I have never disturbed, and I never shall disturb, the order of the world. What significance then does my destiny have?"[53] But . . . in this indifference there lurked the seed of estrangement and estrangement does disturb the order of the world. With it comes withering and then death. The *necessity* of things must be loved, to become beauty in our eyes. Only in this way do we encounter God. God traverses the thickness of the world to come towards us. This is "Grace."[54]

In her *Cahiers d'Amérique,*[55] begun after about two-and-a-half months of being unable to write, is the diary of her journey. Between the dialectical inquiry carried on with priests and the contact she found so attractive with the instinctively religious character of the services in Harlem, there is here evident her poetic individuality as a creature. While in the earlier *Cahiers* the landscape had been that of the earth, valleys, cultivated fields, trees in flower, and the prevailing light that of dawn, in the *Cahiers d'Amérique* one breathes in a horizon of the sea at night; one seems to be on the shore of a dark and glimmering body of water, upon which stars appear.

Stories and legends of every land bubble up; the notes she had made in the library for her new, eagerly pursued study of folklore are interwoven with conclusions she had already reached. And with the parables from the Gospels.

The first step is the *amor fati,* which requires the princess of the story to say, "It is delicious" when presented the most horrible beverage.[56]

This means the acceptance of sorrow. For we are prisoners amidst opposing powers, held under lock by an apparent, temporary harmony. And

sorrow turns the key.[57]

We must leave this harmony and move until we reach the center from which the powers flow: the center of the soul. It is another harmony that we seek, the point of equilibrium between knowledge and love, *humility.* Humility is the true knowledge of ourselves. We are exposed in the bareness of *being.* Appearance and possession disappear.

> The being of man is located behind the curtains, beside the supernatural . . . *The ego* is hidden for me (and for others); it is beside God . . . it is in God . . . it is God (ātman).[58]

The knowledge of self is the consciousness of our own misery as creatures, of the desire for a fullness that will satisfy us. We must cultivate this desire, since God Himself gives it to our souls; He, too, thirsts for our love. ("I thirst," Jesus said on the cross.) The parable of those invited to the wedding feast expresses this love of God. Those invited were precisely the ones to refuse, each alleging a reason he believed just; but each reason was a pretext, the pretext of the *mediocre part of the soul* that flees the light. We must instead cling to the light with the same force and steadiness of desire we find in children.

> A child stretches his hands and his whole body towards whatever shines, even if it is the moon.[59]

In this sense we must be like children. It does no good to rationalize the desire, nor to use the will to try to satisfy it. The discursive intelligence and the will are faculties of adults which have no function here. We simply must run through them until they are exhausted. The discursive intelligence will be "destroyed" with the contemplation of clear and unavoidable contradictions: the *koan* for the Buddhists and the mysteries for the Christians. The will will be consumed through the performance of impossible tasks, like the ordeals of the fairy tales, ordeals which, in general, it is the foolish son, the one who has no sense of the things of this world, who succeeds in overcoming. Even sweeping one's room is an impossible task, "if it is too much for us." Beyond the will there is *obedience.* And, if obedience requires it, we shall achieve with it what other men achieve with the will and the discursive intellect.[60]

The primary contradiction is this:

Truth is exclusively universal and reality, exclusively particular, and yet they are all the same inseparable, in fact they are one and the same thing.[61]

If a contradiction cannot be gotten around except by a lie, then the contradiction is a door. At this door we must knock, tireless and humble at the same time.

Humility has made us accept death, which alone teaches us that we only exist as one "thing among many other things."[62] It is the first step; when we have grasped that we are nothing in ourselves, we can ask to grasp where we have been placed in the universe to realize the life God has thought for us.

Creation is a tissue of the particular thoughts of God. We are a cluster of these thoughts . . . All of our thoughts, or all the relationships of our soul with things of the past, present, and future which are related to us in any kind of rapport must . . . every one of our thoughts must coincide with a particular thought of God.[63]

Why is this so? Because if God, in creating us, has abandoned us in "all our being, flesh and blood, sensibility, intelligence, and love to the pitiless necessity of matter and the cruelty of the devil"[64] (this is one of the few times that Simone speaks of the devil), the eternal and supernatural part of the soul remains under His protection. This is what longs for His Kingdom, the kingdom of power that is uniquely spiritual. There is lodged "the mustard seed, the pearl, the leaven, the salt,"[65] the pledge of love between the soul and God, between the soul and the good. This uncreated part of every creature is "the Life, the Light, the Word. It is the presence of the only Son of God here below."[66]

There is a similarity between this part of the soul and God. They are always looking for each other and wish to meet.

God stands like a mendicant, waiting, motionless and silent in front of someone who may give him a piece of bread. Time is that waiting.[67]

God expects that I will finally "agree" to love Him. The stars, the mountains, the sea drenched with time, express the prayer of God.

> God and mankind are like two lovers who have mistaken the place of rendezvous. They have both come early, but each to a different place, and they wait, they wait, they wait. The lover is standing, motionless, nailed to the spot for the everlasting course of the ages. She is inattentive and impatient. Woe unto her if she grows tired and leaves! For the two points are only one point in the fourth dimension.[68]

The image of such permanence, such perfect attention of God, is the crucifixion of Christ. In Christ, God has emptied Himself of His divinity and taken on the "essence of a slave";[69] the good is the opposite of power. The good and humility coincide in Christ. In our quest we should take on a like essence, to achieve the *nuptial union* with God. Of this the old stories are always speaking; they contain a treasure of spirituality even older than mythology.

They are the stories of the soul and of its journey, composed of sacrifices and of patience, hampered by folly and rashness. The soul can find help or harm in things, in animals, in human beings, at times messengers of love and good counselors, at other times deceitful servants.

A cobbler wants to marry a princess. At the inn, the place of their rendezvous, he tells everything to his hostess, who gives him a sleeping potion. The princess arrives at the inn and calls him in vain. She leaves word with a shepherd lad that she "would wait for him for seven years at her father's." To reach her castle, he has to cross a forest. A sage advised the cobbler: "Seven times seven years will not be enough time. But cross it." In the forest there are no paths. The cobbler gets an axe and begins cutting his way but the trees leaf again and they grow ever more dense. To escape a lion, he climbs up a tree and gets an idea; he will go from one treetop to another. After seven years, he arrives at a castle illuminated for a festival. The princess is going to be married. The cobbler presents himself, covered with rags, unrecognizable. He marries the princess.

> We should not tell the lower part of our soul that we have such a rendezvous. It must be kept secret . . . above all to ourselves . . . The devil does not enter into the secret. The heavenly Father dwells there.[70]

For this reason it is better that the supernatural virtues be implicit rather than explicit, "except for the stringent duty of offering witness to them."[71]

The forest symbolizes the evil that is in us and that hides the absolute Good from us. It is useless to want to uproot it, to commit ourselves to an unequal struggle.

> We must have our thought directed with desire, across the evil, to the infinitely far away good.[72]

The eternal part of the soul will be progressively penetrated by love because it will trust the intuitions of good, those "supernatural mysteries" at the heart of necessity, which are beauty, the working of pure intelligence, whether in contemplation of the world or in the practical incarnation of theories, and "the lamps" of justice, compassion and gratitude among men. It will believe ever more firmly that "reality is love, and see it exactly as it is."[73]

It will be a question of loving what is intolerable, and not through masochism. "Masochists are excited by the sham of cruelty because they do not know what cruelty is." It is not cruelty that we should embrace, but "blind indifference and impassivity."

> It is only in this way that love becomes impersonal.[74]

Impersonal love, which is compassion, is the only feeling of love that is legitimate insasmuch as it allows us to communicate with others without doing them evil, without eating them, without destroying them.

We owe compassion to every creature, insofar as it is vulnerable, "infinitely distant from the Good,"[75] and famished for this Good. We even owe this love of compassion, which implies detachment, to ourselves in our "indestructible attribute" of being *creatures*.

In general our love is that "of cannibals," anthropophagous. We love others as nourishment. Their presence, their words, their letters . . . "have upon us the same effect as a good meal after an exhausting day of work." Equally anthropophagous are "our hatreds and our indifferences."[76]

Loving our neighbor with an unconditioned love means the renunciation of eating him and the wish no longer to "be nourished by anything but God." From the very beginning, "the substance of God" nurtures a point of the soul that is so much at the center of ourselves that "we do not know of its existence." The rest of the soul, in its famished condition, would gladly eat man. Here, only those will find salvation who are "constrained to stop" before their beloved. Their appreciation of the beautiful has awakened contemplation in them.

> Make the perishable part of the soul die while the body is still alive. It is in this way that a body of flesh passes directly to the service of God.[77]

Only the body can transform into actions the movements of the soul. Indeed, with the will, "I can push the body in good behavior further than the soul's progress; it is up to the body to drag the soul along."

> On the plane of duties, this operation is continually occurring; any other kind of procedure is imaginary.[78]

For "only by their fruits shall you know them."

The proof of the nuptial union of the soul with God consists in the appearance of supernatural virtues in the "face it turns towards creatures in its conduct." The *faith* of a judge "does not appear in his attitude in church, but in his attitude on the bench." You cannot sense the presence of God in a man but only "the reflection of His light" in the way in which the man conceives of earthly life, in his original actions and thoughts.[79] In this way, *faith,* "a certainty in a kingdom different from this inextricable tangle of good and bad that constitutes the world,"[80] unites with *charity,* which is *mercy* towards the created, temporal part of every creature, without exception.

The greatest realization of this comes in those in whom the love of God lives: those generated twice, creatures and at the same time "sons of God." "God is absent from the world, except for their existence."

These have passed through the death and the resurrection of Christ. Christ has said:

> You were hungry and you ate me.
>   It is true that you must eat him.[81]

Even in connection with them, the love for others as food is legitimate; it coincides with the love for Christ. In them, in fact, "the desire and the satisfaction and the nourishment furnished to others are one and the same thing." And then, too, we shall not diminish them even in eating them, because our love for them cannot be the love of owners. As a man who has bought a Greek statue, even though he has bought it, cannot (unless he is a brute) consider himself its owner. Pure good escapes any particular relationship.[82]

It was to them that Christ said, "Love one another."

They succeed in interpreting the thoughts of God in the world, in reading the "great metaphor" of the universe, "the key" to which is Christ.[83]

Pantheism is not true except for the saints who have reached the state of perfection.[84]

Lower states do not contain the truth. For this reason, evil has no truth, except in the form of a perfect being who suffers, the Redeemer. He, perfectly pure, experiences it to the very depths and halts it.

Like Christ we are all put on the earth to witness to the truth; some desire to witness to it and some demonstrate it as if by a misunderstanding (Cain, Judas):

In spite of its being the opposite of good, evil is constrained to include its image. For everything witnesses to the good.[85]

Once this is understood, there can no longer be any fear of disobeying God. From this *joy* is born. If our soul will not consent to obey Him, the flesh will obey, in accord with the laws of mechanics. And:

He who consents to obey God, the spirit in him obeys, that is, it is subject to the laws of spiritual phenomena; the rest of his being, by a mechanism we do not know, conforms to the spirit inasmuch as is needed so that the laws be fulfilled.[86]

For this reason, the saints are convinced that they are performing the orders of God in their every action. They travel serenely in a vertical direction, since they have learned to do so. Saint Francis believed that he had been ordered to carry stones for the reconstruction of San Damiano and, as long as he lived with this illusion, God truly willed the reconstruction.

Supernatural actions naturally flow one after the other.

The good begins beyond the will, just as the truth begins beyond the intelligence.[87]

How is that? When we have truly come out of ourselves, there is no longer any pride, and "we fly." Bound up with pride and associated with the ego is the *sense of guilt,* a great obstacle to the loss of personality.

The sense of guilt we battle only with the practice of virtue.[88]

This *gratuitous action* of the saints, which has everything in common with a work of art, inasmuch as it is dependent upon inspiration and upon the "inexpressible reality" towards which their action is directed, derives from their humility. This humility is *perfect joy* insofar as it is complete adherence to the image of you willed by God, an identification with the Son as a slave of love in obedience.

This knowledge is supernatural.[89]

The saints have erased their sense of guilt and forgiven God His debts. In every sin, there is a grudge against God.

If we pardon God, we cut the root of sin within ourselves.[90]

This wrath and grudge against God derive from the suffering we experience as finite creatures, powerless in affliction.

Innocent affliction, the greatest good to whom the greatest evil has been done, is Christ. And yet He continued to love the Father and to accept His will, even in all of His suffering, experienced to the very depths ("My God, my God, why have You abandoned me?").

Evil is judged in a complete vulnerability to suffering. When this vulnerability becomes an *identification* with the suffering of another and is linked with a supernatural *serenity,* you have compassion. Only this serenity can communicate the certainty that the good exists and can instill in a person stricken by affliction the gentleness of gratitude.

Giving with a pure heart implies the readiness to receive. Mercy implies gratitude.

As long as pride hinders our reception, we have no right to give.[91]

We must pray to be freed, to be enlarged within. Supplication is "sacred," as is prayer. How should we pray?

We should cry like a newborn child whose mother has forgotten to give him milk, "without interruption, indefatigably"; or we should pray with our actions, with all the laborious efforts of the will straining to fulfill its tasks. This is "mute prayer."

> An ant climbs up a slippery vertical surface, it makes a few centimeters and falls, it climbs again and falls . . . A child watching this is entertained for ten minutes or so and then can no longer bear it; he puts the ant on a straw and lifts it above the vertical surface.[92]

This prayer of the ant is even humbler than a prayer in words or inward crying, or along a "silent direction of desire."[93]

Prayer is the concrete manifestation of faith. And faith is only this, "believing that the desire for good is always answered.[94]

> If we believe that we shall obtain, the very fact of asking is an act. Such words then are acts. For this reason it is difficult to pronounce them.[95]

So prayer has great power on the soul. It will be directed towards God, only if it is "*unconditioned,*"[96] or in the name of Christ.

Thy will be done—whatever it may be.

This becomes in action:

> May my soul be to my body and to God just what this pen is to my hand and to the paper—an intermediary.[97]

Simone wanted to be a bridge, a route, a *metaxu*[98] of mercy, the only real action.

She was walking away from the cave, in the dark night, in the depths of which the soul will be completely assimilated with God, annihilated in pure good.

> Everyone will be destroyed by contact with God, but the person who has died in spirit for love will be rendered perfect by this destruction.[97]

There is a *terrible prayer* that she utters at one point of this journey. In the name of Christ, she asks that she be deprived of movement like a paralytic, deprived of sensations like someone who is blind, deaf, and without the other three senses. She prays that she not be able to put together two of the simplest thoughts, like an idiot who could never learn even to speak. She begs that she be rendered insensible to every sort of joy and pain and incapable of love even for herself, like an old man destroyed by arteriosclerosis. Why? So that all the aspects of her being, brought to perfection on the other side by agility, keenness, intelligence, and sensibility, may be "devoured by God, transformed into the substance of Christ, and given to the unhappy whose body and soul are without any sort of nourishment, so that they may eat."

She asks that the transformation take place now, in the name of Christ. Even though she is making the request in imperfect faith, she begs that it be heard as though it were prompted by perfect faith.

"These are things that one does not voluntarily ask for." This she told herself.

> It comes despite ourselves. Despite ourselves and yet with our consent . . . Not with abandon. We consent with a violence done to the whole soul by the entire soul. But the consent is entire and without reserves, given with all our being.[100]

Then, between parentheses, there follows a quiet self-analysis, according to which "all these spiritual phenomena" are beyond her competence.

> I do not know anything about them. They are reserved for beings who, just for a start, have the basic moral virtues. I am speaking of them at random. And I am not even able to say sincerely that I am speaking of them at random.[101]

This was *bad self-abasement*[102] in her feeling herself unworthy, *anguish* that insinuated itself in her fear of disobeying God, of not knowing how to answer His call.

> Man is like a castaway clinging to a board, wallowing in the waves. He is in no way able to alter the movement the sea forces upon him. From the heights of heaven God throws him a rope. The man grabs it or not . . . His hands grow bloody with the strain . . . The sea sometimes gets so wild that he lets loose of the rope; then he grabs it again.
> But if he voluntarily rejects it, God draws it back.[103]

This was *the climbing of the ant,* the dark night of the spirit which with its alternation of the sense of damnation and the sense of salvation, "lasts the longer, the farther the soul is destined to travel on the road of perfection." These are the words of Saint John of the Cross.[104]

André Philip, a commissioner of the Comité national de la France libre, came to New York in October. He had a conversation with Simone; he would take her on as one of his assistants.

Her departure was now decided upon. Simone often embraced her parents, with greater tenderness. They were drawing up plans. But Simone made them promise that they would not put any of them into action until she had departed.

She wrote three important letters. On November 4, she wrote her brother and entrusted her parents to him. "Their youthful appearance does not prevent their being old and tired and most in need of attention . . . Unfortunately my departure will be a great sorrow for them."[105]

A few days later she wrote to Fr. Couturier and to Jean Wahl. In her letter to the priest, she extends to thirty-five the subjects of her conversation with Dom Clément at Dourgne. Couturier never replied, probably because he was not a theologian. "An artist, the coordinator of all the work at the Matisse chapel in Vence; a very handsome man, he used to give the finest sermons for the nuns of a little convent in New York. He said, 'I feel at home with them,' who were simpler women than my sister. It would have been as though someone had asked me for very precise explanations in physics." These are André's words, as clear as usual.[106]

What is the most important subject of her letter to Jean Wahl? In answer to Wahl,[107] who had written that there were rumors that Simone sympathized with Vichy, she said, "As far as this is concerned, you can deny it." She tells him the story of her participation in the war: her fervent desire not to leave Paris, her consternation at seeing it declared an open city, her stay at Nevers in the hope of a front along the Loire; with the coming of the armistice, her immediate decision to leave for England and her abandonment of France only to realize this project; in the meantime, her contribution to the circulation of the illegal press; almost as soon as she had arrived in New York, her ubiquitous requests to be sent to Great Britain, where André Philip ("a very smart man") will employ her in his office.

From the day when, after a hard inner struggle, I decided within myself, despite my pacifist inclinations, that my first responsibility was to pursue the destruction of Hitler with or without any hope of success, from that day I have never varied; it was the moment of Hitler's entrance into Prague . . . Perhaps I arrived at this attitude too late. I think that is so, and I regret it very much.

Perhaps what has given room for these rumors has been (as always) the fact that she does not much like "listening to people who are quite comfortable here, treating as cowards and traitors those who are doing their best in France in a terrible situation . . . Baseness and treachery are collective states; they constitute the armistice. As far as I am concerned, the armistice has appalled me from the very beginning; and yet, despite this, I think that every Frenchman, myself included, bears responsibility for it like Pétain, since, at the time . . . the nation as a whole received the news with relief . . . On the other side, since then Pétain has done almost everything that the general situation and his physical and mental state of health have allowed him to do to limit the damages."

The only person who should be considered a traitor is the man who desires the victory of Germany and does what he can to achieve that goal. And when we know this certainly. As far as the others are concerned, those who have agreed to work for Vichy and even for the Germans, "they can have honorable motives that correspond to particular situations." Still others may be the object of pressures such that "they could not resist them without heroism."[108]

As ever, she was capable of an *impartial reading* of the situation.

Around November 10, she embarked on a Swedish cargo ship, the Vaalaren. Her parents were not allowed to come on board. They said goodby in a sort of shed. As she left them, Simone said, "If I had more than one life, I would dedicate one to you, but I have only this one."[109]

18

The History of Her Social Thought

During the crossing, she told stories and invited the small group of her companions (ten passengers in all) to do the same. On one clear moonlit night, feared by the others because it was favorable to torpedoing, she brought them to the bridge to entertain them.

One of her fellow travelers, a Mr. Kirby, who was an official among the fire fighters, told her that she did not eat enough; she replied that she felt she did not have the right to eat more than the comrades she had left in France. She seemed obsessed by the desire to return there, to fulfill some mission.

Arriving in Liverpool around November 25, she was kept in a detention center on the outskirts of London. For eighteen-and-a-half days she was absolutely forbidden to telegraph, write, or telephone. "The usual stay here lasts from six to ten days. I have not had any luck (always Antigone!)" she will write to her parents.[1] This may have been due to her activity as a committed pacifist in the prewar period or to the suspicion that she was a Communist, the kind of suspicion that hovered around every veteran of the war in Spain.

Maurice Schumann intervened to free her. On December 14, she was in London, provisionally "camped"[2] in the barracks of the French Women Volunteers.

She presented herself to Louis Closon, of André Philip's office.

"It was difficult to distinguish her from her beggar's clothing. Everything was confused in a single blur. She was wearing a long skirt of faded maroon and a sweater knitted by her mother, as I learned later from André and Eveline Weil; but I still see her dressed in a sack, shapeless, her frail body slightly bent. Weary in her appearance, in her attitude, and in her voice, which had a lingering, inward tone."

But those beggar's garments were not an external wrap; Simone had made the misery of the world her own.

And yet her glance "expressed energy, will, along with the refusals and exigencies of her constant meditation. At times she would visibly stiffen; then, without rising, the tone of her voice would change suddenly, to collapse into greater weariness.

"Infrequent ironic sallies, quickly spent," were all that was left of the Normale student who loved *canular* (practical jokes).[3]

In the first two meetings, which Philip also attended, the two men felt ill at ease. "That frail creature had a dimension that did not correspond to ours. Despite our every effort, communication with her remained difficult. Philip requested me to deal with the question of how and where to occupy her." Work in the office, even if concerned with action in occupied France, "did not suit her; the first task was to leave her free to write what she needed to."[4]

From her perspective, Simone wrote to her parents:

Everyone has been most courteous to me. The task I have been assigned is purely intellectual, entirely personal and I control it as I please. All in all, I should be very happy, if I did not have, as you well know, a very particular idea of happiness.

She fell in love with London, England and the English people. She confirmed "in the little scenes of daily life" and in "quite diverse circumstances" the recurrence of two typical traits of the English character noted by T. E. Lawrence: "a sense of humor and courtesy." This courtesy was all the more admirable because "their nerves are stretched tight but they conduct themselves with self-respect and show a real kindliness towards others. There are none of the reciprocal outbursts of anger we know from the continent."[5]

A Potato Fair, an exposition intended to encourage the consumption of potatoes, enchants her: "It is a distillation of the pure English spirit." Conceived as something for children, it presents nonsense stories on the subject, distorting mirrors that showed what happens to someone who does not eat potatoes, etc. What strikes her in this people is "their good humor, neither spontaneous nor artificial, springing from their sense of comradeship, both tender and fraternal, in a trial common to all."[6]

She proudly writes that "without any help" she has found a room with a Mrs. Francis, 31 Portland Road, Notting Hill. She was the widow of an elementary school teacher, who had died ten years earlier, leaving her with a boy of four and a newborn baby. She had no resources but her small house. This made Simone feel that she was in an atmosphere of "pure Dickens." "The sentimental side of his stories, in the modest levels of English society, is the most true."[7] She would help David and John with their homework. As they remember her today, "Miss Simone is a legendary figure, a being endowed with special powers, who knew how to go from the everyday world to that of dreams."[8]

On Sunday, she spent "hours" in Hyde Park, watching the people thronging around the speakers. She thought that this was the last vestige, "perhaps in the world," of the conversations in the agora of Athens, in which Socrates took part.[9] She associated the scenes in the inn from *Twelfth Night* with the life of London pubs, where people are happy, especially where they stand to talk, a great mug of beer in their hand.

She reassures her parents: she is eating well, sleeping well, her headaches have just about ceased. They have nothing to worry about. A mutual friend who returned to New York could tell them that "he had found her comfortably installed at the back of an office, in good health and perfect tranquility." For this reason, she regretted more and more "the decision taken in May," which to her eyes took on, with growing bitterness, the aspect of flight.[10]

> I work very much . . . as far as time is concerned . . . as to the intensity and the results, I have no means of control, since they have assigned me a labor that is purely intellectual.[11]

André Philip had charged her with subjecting to critical analysis all documents that arrived from France which were the work of committees established, principally in the free zone, to prepare for the postwar period and to "organize the peace."[12]

What should be the character of the new constitution? What should the laws be? Everything had to be begun anew. There had to be a reform of the administration and of education. They had to establish a new statute for labor. De Gaulle, on December 2, 1941, had established four national commissions to find solutions for French and international problems dealing with economy and finance, society, law and culture, and foreign affairs.

We shall see how Simone will work out solutions, both practical immediate programs like the establishment of the Supreme Council of the Revolt and broadly conceived projects based on a *social doctrine* whose intuitions will be distilled in her book, *L'Enracinement*. The central point upon which every initiative will be based will be *man*.

This had always been true of her thought, since the time of *Réflexions sur les causes de la liberté et de l'oppression sociale,* begun as an article and developed into a full and powerful essay, of the dimensions of a small book. The essay, which had so pleased Alain, takes up and projects on a much broader theoretical level all her previous and contemporaneous articles.

She had begun writing it in the spring of 1934, after "Perspectives," in the spirit of her translations of Machiavelli's *History of Florence* on the insurrection of the Ciompi; she worked on it with unflinching intensity and was profoundly absorbed in it during the summer and fall. The essay gradually grew to such an extent that she began to call it, jokingly but not completely, her *Grand oeuvre* or her "Testament." She loved it; in 1940 she entrusted it to a friend, who would keep it for the whole duration of the war.[13]

> It will be *impossible* for me to rest until I have finished it. At this time I am like a woman in labor whose baby's head has already emerged but for some reason he has stopped . . . It is painful to bring forth at once everything that one has in one's belly . . . And yet, what satisfaction it is to feel something still in one's belly. The time when I wrote the article for the *R.P.* ["Perspectives"] seems an idyllic age when I wrote without effort . . . And at the same time a far distant infancy when I did not understand anything about anything.[14]

She never published it, because she considered it imperfect. The criticisms of a friend influenced this decision. She later much regretted not having done so.

The essay includes at its end this phrase of Spinoza: "In what has to do with human affairs, do not laugh, do not weep, do not grow indignant, but understand."

She wanted in fact *to understand* the motives for the oppression in which man lives and at the same time the motives for his unconstrainable aspiration for liberty.

She wanted to understand, because she was striving to formulate, at least as a "purely theoretical concept," a society in which collective life would be subordinate to men considered as individuals.

Who is an individual? He who has the possibility of using his reason and has always dreamed of liberty.

The most recent form of this dream is the Communist revolution. But like all dreams, it has remained vain until now.

What do we ask of it? The abolition of social oppression. To know to what degree this would be possible, it is necessary "to grasp concretely the conditions of a liberating organization" and to analyze the mechanism of oppression, while we are careful to distinguish between oppression and the subordination of individual whims to social order.

Society has to limit the life of individuals and to impose its rules upon them; such an unavoidable constraint deserves the name of oppression to the degree that it separates those who exercise it from those who endure it. This division is linked with the system of production, a system that has become ever more complex as time passes, in association with the struggle against nature.

It is a question of knowing whether it is possible to conceive of an organization of production which, although unable to eliminate natural necessities and the social constraint that results from them, "at least allows them to hold sway without crushing minds and bodies under oppression."

The cause of oppression, as Marx was the first to understand, resides in *objective conditions,* or the material conditions of social organization. Questions arise all the same, which Marx did not know how to answer. Why does the division of labor generate oppression? Why is oppression invincible as long as it is useful, or why do those who have power and privilege turn them into instruments of organization (time after time, ritual secrets, arms, technological secrets, money)? Why have the oppressed, in their revolts, never succeeded in establishing a nonoppressive society, whether on the basis of the productive forces of their age or even at the price of an economic regression which could not but help worsen their plight? In conclusion, the general principles of the mechanism by which one specific form of oppression has been replaced by another have remained completely unknown.

The Marxists have not even posed the problem, since they limit themselves to asserting that "social oppression corresponds to a function of the struggle against nature." They have ended with applying unconsciously to social phenomena Lamarck's principle, "Function creates the organ." But biology became a science the day when Darwin substituted for this principle the notion of *conditions of existence*. Function is no longer the myste-riously determined cause of an organ, but the effect of the organ, which evolves and adapts itself in a given sense in relationship to the ambience, in part inert, in part living, that surrounds it, and above all in relationship with similar organisms which compete with it.

Since then, adaptation has been conceived in relationship with living beings as an external necessity, no longer an internal one.

Even the causes of social evolution should only be sought "in the daily efforts of men considered as individuals." These efforts depend on many factors (temperament, education, habits, prejudices, natural needs and gains, circumstances, etc.) beyond *human nature,* a term difficult to define, but probably not without sense. The conditions of existence, with their obstacles, limit and direct necessarily the form of social organization born of this assemblage of efforts. These conditions are mostly unknown by those who are subject to them and who proceed by trial and error. These conditions are determined by the *natural ambience,* by the competition of other social groups, and by a third separate factor, the *organization of the natural ambience by the work of man,* which implies the construction of means and methods, exerts an action upon the form of social organization, and undergoes, in its turn, a reaction.

Until today, social transformations have never been accompanied by a clear consciousness of their "real import," because they have not been at-tributed to the actions and reactions of men. Progress, associated with a "mythologizing" of productive forces, contemporaneous with the devel-opment of industrial society, has been connected, with illusory security, to an unlimited development of production or of things.

The only possible principle of social progress must be "the enlightened good will of men who act as individuals."

It is a question of seeing clearly if this good will has the power of ad-dressing social necessities and intervening in them, or if they escape it, like the necessities that rule the stars. In this last case, we could only resign ourselves to watching the development of history as we do the succession of the seasons, as we defend ourselves, as far as possible, from the "calam-ity of being an instrument or a victim of oppression." But if this is not so, our first task would be to define as "an ideal limit" the *objective conditions* that would yield a society without oppression, and thereafter to attempt to transform present conditions in such a way as to approach this ideal.

Only in this way could political action become something like a labor, instead of being, as it has until now, "either a game or a branch of magic."

> The ideal is unrealizable in the same way as a dream, but with the difference that it is related to reality; it allows, as a hypothetical limit, the establishment of real or realizable situations that range from the least to the greatest value.

Only in this way can we begin to "grasp" liberty. It is necessary to present, even in vague terms, the civilization that we hope humanity will reach. The *utopia* serves this purpose; it can give men of good will the goal which "the purely negative conception of the weakening of social oppression" cannot give them. Simone emphasizes the importance of the *motive,* insofar as the right motive can stimulate men and enroll their *thought.* Well-used thought furthers liberty. The heroic conception of liberty, which is that of common sense, is the liberty of action as we put into operation, from beginning to end, the projects of action we have conceived in our minds. Even this is an ideal, useful to keep before us if we can discern at the same time what separates us from this ideal and what circumstances bring us closer or push us further away.

What are the obstacles to liberty, and so the factors of slavery and oppression to which man is subject?

The first is *the extension and the complexity of the world.* We shall never be able to foresee all the consequences of our actions. What must happen at all costs is "to take away from chance all our actions, so as to subordinate them to the direction of thought." To that end it is necessary for us to construct a method of work that will allow us to confront the unexpected, by relating means and instruments suitable to achieving action with the *relative stability* reached by the *human organism.* And yet our body remains an unending source of mystery and "an impenetrable shadow will always engulf the immediate relationship that binds our thoughts to our movements."

The second obstacle for each person is *the existence of other men;* on careful consideration, this is the unique factor of slavery. Matter can belie our forethought and ruin our efforts, but it remains inert, made to be conceived and managed from the outside.

Human thought can never be penetrated and managed from the outside.

When the lot of a man depends on others, it escapes not only his hands but also his intelligence. Judgment and resolution serve no purpose. We stoop to begging and menacing, in a feverish alternation of fear and desire. Nature can break, but not humble you.

> There are no limits to the satisfactions and the suffering that a man can be exposed to by other men.

But it would still be a small matter to depend on beings that, even if they are extraneous, are real, visible, and comprehensible by analogy with yourself. In all oppressive societies, everyone depends not only on those above and below him, but on the *workings of collective life,* which alone determines social hierarchies. Collectivity is a thing "absolutely abstract, absolutely mysterious and inaccessible to the senses and to thought."

But man, as he is not made to be "the plaything of blind nature, is not made to be the plaything of blind collectivities that he forms with his fellows."

In one field alone does the individual overcome the collectivity, in the field of thought. A man thinks when he is alone with himself.

> Collectivities do not think at all.

In our desire to formulate, on the basis of pure theory, the conception of a society in which the collective life would be subject to men considered as individuals, we must imagine a form of material life in which only "efforts exclusively directed by clear thought" would play a role.

> The less negative society is the one in which the majority of men are obliged as often as possible to act with thought; it has the best chance of control over collective life, and it possesses the greatest degree of independence.

The "most fully human" civilization would be the one having at its center *manual labor,* in which manual labor would become the supreme value, not with reference to what is produced but *with reference to the man* who performs it. It does not have to be the object of honors and rewards but it must constitute for every human being "what he essentially needs so that life may assume for him a sense and a value."

It would have to be a labor transformed in such a way as to exercise fully all our faculties and it would have to be found at the center of culture. Culture, which once was judged by many people an end in itself, has become today a means to escape real life. Its true value, instead, would consist in *preparing men for real life.*

Nothing could be more opposed to the ideal cherished by Simone than the present state of civilization.

> Never has the individual been more completely abandoned to the mercy of a blind collectivity and never have men been less able, not only to submit their actions to their thoughts, but even to think.

The very terms, oppressors and oppressed, are very close to losing all meaning in face of the anguish and impotence of everyone caught in the social machine, which has become a "machine that breaks hearts, shatters minds, creates unconsciousness, stupidity, corruption, cowardice and, above all, dizziness."

What are we to do? Imagining that we can "change history in a different direction by transforming the regime by blows of reform or revolution . . . means daydreaming."

A regime that is so utterly inhuman, far from forging beings able to build a human society, shapes everyone in its own image, all its subjects, oppressed and oppressors alike.

Mental confusion and *passivity* give free rein to the *imagination.* Everywhere we encounter an obsessive representation of social life that, although different in each ambience, still is composed of "mysteries, occult qualities, myths, idols, and monsters." In the circles of the working movement, dreams are filled with mythological monsters that have the names of Finance, Industry, Exchange and Bank; the bourgeoisie are obsessed with monsters they call demagogues, agitators, popular leaders; politicians regard capitalists as "supernatural beings" who have the key to the situation, and vice versa; every people looks at its neighbors as "collective monsters," animated by diabolical perversity. In a situation of this sort, any board becomes king and any myth is believed. Where thinking is absent, force can do anything. We should not be surprised at the appearance of "totalitarian" regimes without precedent.

> Today, every attempt to brutalize human beings finds powerful means at its disposal. In compensation, one thing is impossible, even if one possessed the best platform: the wide broadcast of clear ideas, sound arguments and reasonable observations. Without factories, without armaments, without mass media, nothing can be done against those

who possess them; if the powerful means are oppressive, the weak means are worthless.

The only possibility of salvation would consist in the methodical cooperation of the weak and the powerful towards a progressive decentralization of social life. But that is an absurd idea.

What then can those men do who insist, "against everything and everyone," on respecting human dignity in themselves and in others? Nothing, save obstructing, wherever possible, the gears of the machine, save "reawakening thought" and favoring everything in politics, economy and technology that is susceptible of leaving any freedom to the individual.

It is something, but not much.

Altogether, we are in the state of utterly inexperienced travelers who find themselves riding in an automobile racing at top speed without a driver across uneven terrain.

What will perish and what will survive of contemporary civilization? We do not know. We know only that "life will be less inhuman to the degree that man will be able to think and act." If contemporary civilization contains what can crush man, it also carries, at least in germ, what can free him. Despite the obscurity of the new learning, science offers areas of luminosity, stages of bright methodology for the mind. Even technology has germs of liberation from labor: the machine-instrument. Perhaps an industry scattered in innumerable small enterprises could develop an evolution of the machine-instrument in a sense opposite to the progressive automation of today.

Methodically preparing the new civilization is a task that exceeds the restricted limits of one human life; directing oneself in this sense means "condemning oneself to moral solitude, to incomprehension and to the hostility of the enemies and servants of the existing order." And yet it would be madness to complain about the present situation and to give up doing one thing, when it is clear that there is "only one thing to do."

In our present civilization, it would be a question of:

Separating what by right belongs to man considered as an individual and what by nature is fit to furnish arms against him to the collectivity, in our quest to develop the former elements to the detriment of the latter.

Simone thinks that, even if a series of reflections directed in this sense would not have any effect upon the further evolution of the social organization, it would not lose its value for this reason. It is here and now that we must try to make life happier.

Only fanatics can find a value for their existence solely in how much it serves a collective cause.

Reacting against the subordination of the individual to the collectivity implies that we begin with refusing to subordinate our own destiny to the course of history.[15]

=====

On March 1, 1943, she will write her parents:

Since my being here, my own personal and wretched ideas and my small understanding of the world have continued in a certain way to present characters of cancerous proliferation. My work does not disturb this process, rather to the contrary, because there are interconnections; and the solitude in which I live favors this considerably.[16]

She rethought the whole history of France and of Europe; she had foreseen it and had suffered it point by point but now she was reaching the dramatic apex of a first conclusion: the end of the war. Everything had to begin again on new indispensable bases, foundations that had to be laid *presently*, given the urgency of a reorganization of daily life, and *well*, of course as starting lines, given the proven perniciousness of the principles so far followed. Presently and well were closely connected.

What did *presently* mean? Making it possible for France to contribute to her own liberation directly and in cooperation with the other enslaved peoples of Europe. Above all, in view of the urgent problems of the postwar period, it was necessary to proceed to the utilization of the potential for revolt against oppression through a "fraternity of arms between England and the continent." This task would be performed by a Supreme Council of Revolt, proposed by the Free French, presided over by England and formed of representatives of all the territories occupied by Germany (to which it was "desirable" to add the Italians, Spanish and Germans "sincerely scornful of Nazism"). Taking military advantage of such a source of energy and placing it in the front ranks of the general strategy of the war meant restoring more than liberty to Europe; it meant restoring honor and lost confidence, its moral identity. By trusting only in the "military power of the dollar" there was the danger of losing that identity.[17]

What did *well* mean? General De Gaulle, who had proclaimed himself the "guardian" of the legitimacy he had saved for France, could continue to exercise that role for a certain period after the liberation. What urged this was the necessity of making immediate decisions on the economy, with regard to the colonies, and on the life and death of many Frenchmen suspected of collaborating with the enemy. What required this was the situation of the whole of French civilization: a country that had experienced "a kind of death" needed to find the inspiration to "invent a new life." How could she be helped? The general should lay immediately the foundations of a *practice of thought* destined to involve the whole French people, to form a constituent assembly composed of members chosen for being "distinguished" in this activity, not because they were parading with the support of "degrading publicity." To this end, there was another basic duty to perform: offering the country guarantees of the absolute respect for justice. How? By declaring himself ready, along with his principal associates, to submit all of the actions of his provisional authority to a tribunal set up by the Assembly from outside its own members and by pledging not to create in the country any type of organized group of his own supporters.

Legitimacy must be based on justice, which demands in the first place "a balance between power and responsibility." The exercise of *provisional power* in such "terrible" conditions demands a "purity" which does not fit well with the preoccupations of a further political career.

To put such a suggestion into practice one had to inspire in the people a confidence in a pledge made in good faith. It was not easy.

A question of preparation, of atmosphere, of emphasis.[18]

A *new life* had to be invented, or new political institutions. Simone Weil studies the "project for a new constitution," issued by the government in London and, first of all, dismantles its empty formulas, derived from the past. In the first place, this one: *Sovereignty resides in the nation.*

She proposes instead:

Legitimacy is constituted by the free consent of the people taken as a whole to the authorities to which it is subject.[19]

Taking form here was her ideal of a balance between the individual and the collectivity, between revolutionary impulse and the conservatism necessary for social stability. The new constitution should refer to a people of individuals, not as a piece of deception or a maneuver, but as guidance through laws, to which the people could give their "free consent" because, in the first place, they are respected by the authorities. Laws are clear ideas, appropriate to translate the needs, the aspirations and the latent thoughts of the people.

It is the task of a constitution to establish the meaning, the field of action, the means of designation and control and the coordination of the three powers: judiciary, legislative and executive (this is their true hierarchy). This is the theme of her "Idées essentielles pour une nouvelle constitution."[20] There are two essential ideas:

1) More significant than the way in which the head of government is named is the way in which his power is limited, the way in which he is controlled in his exercise of it and the way in which he will be punished, if he has to be. This holds good for every power: political, administrative, judicial, military, economic, etc.

2) The legislative activity consists of thinking of the concepts essential for the life of the country. The people, which has "aspirations" but does not have the possibility of transforming them into "clear ideas," must name men who will think for them, not who will "represent" them (something that means nothing). Men are required, and not parties, which think "*less*" than the people.

Laws (rigorously separated from decrees, which are measures of daily administration), in the care of legislators and magistrates, are texts of quite a general character, destined to serve as a guide, both for the government in its daily administration and for judges. They should always and only be the projection of the fundamental declaration in the field of concrete facts.

Upon what was the fundamental declaration based? Simone calls it a "declaration of duties towards the human creature."

The individual of *Oppression et Liberté* has become a creature. The *ideal* of a society without oppression, to be set as a goal to approach, has become the *certainty* of the possibility of a new civilization we should strive to realize, with the acknowledgment of the *transcendent as a given fact*. This given fact is found at the center of every man under the form of the *aspiration for the good* and corresponds to a reality situated "beyond every orbit accessible to human faculties." Still, between this reality, which is "the sole foundation of the good," and that "need for an absolute good that does not find any object in the world," there exists a bond of desire so powerful that it becomes for every man the route of internal and practical regeneration. For himself and for others. By this desire everyone can be made an intermediary between the world and that other reality. But for this to happen and for "the good to be able to descend in the midst of men," the desire must be transformed into attention and love. From an unconscious restlessness, always projected in vain onto false values, it must change into *consent,* given to the real hunger after the true good.

Despite all the *de facto* inequalities, this need for the good makes all men identical. The only motive which can bring us to a *universal respect* for all human beings lies in the recognition in us of such a need, which coincides with the recognition of the other reality.

> Our attention, when it is in fact directed beyond the world, alone may have contact with the essential structure of human nature. Only it possesses a faculty, always of an identical sort, to shed light upon a human being of whatever kind.[21]

Here below, this respect, saturated with light, finds only an indirect expression. It is rendered to a *creature situated in the reality of the world* and its expression is made possible by "the terrestrial needs of the soul and of the body."

This expression must be based on the consciousness of the bond between the *aspiration for the good* and the *sensibility,* a bond which is lodged in human nature. When, by way of the acts or omissions of other men, the life of a man is destroyed or ruined by a wound or a privation of the soul or the body, not only his sensibility, but his aspiration for the good "suffers."

> A sacrilege has then been committed against what is sacred within a man.[22]

The possibility of an indirect expression of respect for the human creature is the *foundation of duties towards it.*

The "profession of faith," which we have just cited in its essential nucleus, was supposed to serve as the basis for a "doctrine," destined for practical use in France on the part of study groups, whose projects Simone was charged with examining.

She well knew that "conceiving, understanding and adopting the best doctrine is easy":

The fundamental truths are simple.[23]

What is difficult is their *application,* which has to ripen like a fruit by the complete *assimilation* of the doctrine.

The primary difficulty consisted in the *language.* The translation of the fundamental truths into a language suitable for the men of France and Europe, smitten by affliction, is the theme of *L'Enracinement,* which she considered "her second [*grand oeuvre*]."[24]

L'Enracinement, or "Prelude to a declaration of duties towards the human creature," fully expresses what had been the desire of her entire life: the regeneration of society. Here that desire is animated by a hope that is the culmination of her inner attainment. It is hope based on Christian certainty.

Simone has come forth from the cave, she has exposed herself to the light of the sun, has succeeded in looking at it as she always desired, and now gives her discoveries to men with humility. She is a "foundress of the city," according to Plato.

In both *Oppression et Liberté* and *L'Enracinement,* her starting point is the concept of *conditions of existence* or factual data at the basis of an evolution within the ambience. In *L'Enracinement* she inserts a new set of data, *the needs of the soul.* Not having taken them into consideration has led to the illness of Europe. If, in *Oppression et Liberté,* she had perceived the symptoms, here she is sure of the causes, makes a precise diagnosis after presenting the clinical history and then sets forth the therapy.

The cure must be thought of in relation to the structural reality of man. It is long and difficult but indispensable. Long, because we are paltry and little given to the labor of thought; difficult, because we prefer to lie to ourselves, not to listen to our profound discomforts, and to accept false solutions to our problems or to accept false problems; indispensable, because curing Europe means attempting the possibility of a maturation in a positive sense for mankind upon earth.

What is this illness?

Simone uses for the first time the term *uprootedness,* total estrangement of a man from himself. Completing here her reflections on all the internal and external vicissitudes of her life, she analyzes the forms of uprootedness which have slowly fragmented and impoverished contemporary man. Historically, she directs her gaze from the visual angle of France but what she says of him, the human creature, extends in time and space to the world of today. Uprootedness derives from the nongratification of the needs connected with our moral life or the needs of our soul.

In the first place, they have never been studied or defined. The absence of such a study forces governments, even when they have good intentions, "to bustle about at random." Simone is the first person to define them; she then places them at the basis of her project for a constitution, here nurtured from within.

The *needs of the soul* are in immediate relationship with the *duties towards the human creature*. In the same way as the needs connected with the life of the body, they are expressed on the earth and require gratification here below. If they are not gratified like all *vital needs*,

> man falls into a state more or less like death, more or less akin to purely vegetative life.

The *fundamental duty* towards the human creature is *respect*.

This respect must be demonstrated in a real and not fictitious manner.

The fundamental need is *hunger*, which is the first of the physical needs. Not allowing a human being to suffer hunger when one can help him is the most obvious duty, always recognized as such by the "human conscience." In this way, it will serve as a model to extend "the list of eternal duties" towards every creature.

It is easy to enumerate the *physical needs;* they have to do with protection against violence, housing, clothing, warmth, health, healing in case of illness.

The *moral needs* are more difficult to define, and yet we recognize that they exist. Everyone realizes that there are cruelties of such a kind that they impair a man even if they leave his body intact. And as there are some duties towards "human things" which provide a man with physical nourishment (a field of wheat), so there are duties in this sense towards the collectivities which provide him with moral nourishment (country, family, whatever other collectivity). What does respect mean in this case? The duty of respect should bind together among themselves

> all human beings who compose, serve, command, or represent a collectivity, whether in that part of their life bound to such a collectivity, or in that which is independent.

For *"man does not have power but a responsibility."*[25]

Therefore, the first study to be made regards the needs which are for the soul the equivalent of the needs for food, sleep and heat for the life of the body. We must not confuse them with whims, fantasies and vices. We must distinguish the essential from the accidental and recognize "diverse but equivalent satisfactions." Finally, with great care, we must distinguish nourishment from the poisons that can give the illusion of substituting for it.

Simone gives some "indications." These vital needs can, for the most part, be evaluated in pairs of opposites that "balance and complete each other." They are: equality and hierarchy, obedience and liberty, truth and free expression, private and collective property, punishment and honor, security and risk. At the basis of all these needs is the *need for order*. They all flow into another fundamental need, perhaps the most important and least understood: the *need for roots*.

The need for *order* coincides with the aspiration for the good and with the desire for that "wisdom," which we would want to possess to realize that aspiration, by fitting it into "a true human order." The hope of realizing this order, even at the cost of our life, is the sole orientation for man, "a voyager who travels in the night without a guide."

> Order . . . is a fabric of social relations such that no one should be constrained to violate some rigorous duties to fulfill others.

Today, the level of incompatibility among duties is extremely high. There is no method to diminish the incompatibility and there can only be good will to follow the orientation. *Respect* for this fundamental need demands that, in formulating the declaration, "anyone who exercises or wishes to exercise a power,"[26] should take the declaration itself as a practical guide and create institutions which will favor *the health of society* or the individual balance of creatures that compose it and the balance in their relations.

The two principal actions which are inspired by the respect due in equal measure to all creatures insofar as they are such are *the tangible demonstration of equality* and *the elimination of falsehood*.

The public and effective recognition that "an equal degree of attention is due to the needs of all human beings" demands that a balance be established between equality and diversity. This balance can make use of a proportion between power and risks, based on *responsibility*. This implies a definite organization of risks and, in penal law, a conception of punishment in which *social status* would have the role of an *aggravating circum-stance* in determining the penalty; and this would be even more reasonable on the level of high public office. Other factors of balance: removing as far as possible from the equation every "quantitative character" (money, which we have made both "judge and executioner," is the agent of a "shift-ing, fluid inequality," which stirs up in every life obsessive desires) and considering the various human situations not as superior and inferior to one another but as simply *different*.

Hierarchy is the scale of responsibilities. Given that attention is more inclined to "linger at the top," we need special dispositions to make equal-ity and hierarchy actually compatible. Hierarchy should be true, i.e., every-one should fulfill his own responsibilities; only then will it have the effect of inducing each person "to put himself morally in the role which he occupies."

Obedience in the context of hierarchy presupposes consent to pre-established rule or to human beings recognized as leaders. It implies the consciousness of three things: "the mainspring of obedience is consent" (in particular, those in charge should understand this); "those in com-mand know, on their part, how to obey"; "every hierarchy is directed towards a goal whose value, and even grandeur, is felt by all."

Preestablished rules are necessary to limit the area of choices of *liberty*. They must be "quite" reasonable and simple in such a way that the connec-tion with their usefulness and with the necessities they have imposed should appear with clarity. And not too numerous, but fixed and general, so that "thought can take them in all at once and not bump up against them in every decision we take."

The *need for truth* is the most sacred. Never, in the field of thought, should a "material or moral pressure that proceeds from a preoccupation different from the preoccupation with truth be exercised." This implies the absolute banning of every type of propaganda and demands the protection of the public against error and untruth. To this point:

> Everyone knows that when journalism is confused with the organiza-tion of untruth this is a crime. But this is considered a crime destined to escape punishment . . . Whence comes this strange idea of crimes that cannot be punished? This is one of the most monstrous deforma-tions of the juridical spirit.

The need for truth is an aspect of the *need for liberty of expression* (or of opinion). This latter is an absolute need of the intelligence. And

when the intelligence is uncomfortable, the entire soul is ill.

There has to be a field, separate and open to all, where intellectual inquiry can be conducted in "absolute liberty." But when this inquiry has its own ends and tends to influence the so-called opinion, in reality the conduct of life, publications become real actions and should be subject "to the same restrictions as all other actions." This is the field of the daily press and the weeklies, of the reviews that defend the boundaries of a single nucleus of thought, of literature whose authors aspire to the "responsibility of directors of conscience."[27]

Liberty of opinion cannot be claimed by any group; in general it is associated instead with *liberty of association,* which is not a need but an expedient of practical life. If, as an expedient, it can be admitted with certain restrictions (for example, for *interest-groups*), it should not, in any case, be granted to those groups which pretend to impose upon their members a uniformity of thought. Here the individual eventually is excluded "for the crime of opinion." This is the way in which totalitarian parties are formed; they in turn, as we have seen, generate totalitarian states.

The immediate practical solution is the abolition of political parties.

Justice demands that *private property* (or personal) should be "as inalienable as liberty," when it is conceived as the appropriation of concrete objects, such as a house, a field, furniture, tools of labor, "which the soul considers as an extension of itself and the body."

Collective property, which cannot be defined juridically, is a "state of mind" by which a human association considers certain material objects (in a city: monuments, gardens, the magnificence of ceremonies) as "an extension and crystallization of itself." Every collectivity should provide this satisfaction. When the real and direct bond with the things of personal or collective life loses its meaning (land cultivated by farm workers at the orders of a supervisor but owned by city-dwellers; a modern factory which does not really belong to any of its component elements), we have "the waste of material and moral nourishment." Then, the methods of exchange and acquisition which are the causes of such a waste "must be transformed."

Punishment satisfies the moral need for justice and for pardon.

Every human being who has placed himself outside of the good has the need of being reintegrated in the good by means of pain.

For punishment to be perceived as an honor and "as a supplementary education in devotion to the public good," it must be conducted in a fashion that communicates the sacred sense of respect for justice in form and in substance. In the first place, the severity of the punishment should correspond to the character of the duties violated and not to the interests of the security of society. In both misdemeanors and felonies, "exemption from punishment should increase, not when one goes up, but when one comes down the social scale." Further:

> Every innocent human being, or one who has paid his debt, needs his honor to be recognized as equal to that of all the others.[28]

Instead, in France this happens: former convicts, along with policemen, prostitutes and the sub-proletariat of immigrants and colonial natives form social categories which are totally deprived of consideration. They experience the extreme level of deprivation of *honor,* a need of the soul associated with a human being not only in himself but as part of a social group. The collectivity in which a person lives should offer him a share in a tradition contained in its past and recognized publicly. This fullness of tradition should vivify every profession and every population.

Fear of violence, of hunger and of any other sort of extreme evil is a *disease of the soul,* which, to be protected from it, has need of security. Even *boredom* is a sickness of the soul, for which, in all aspects of social life, a certain dose of risk is necessary to involve the resources of the soul and to put courage to the test.

> Situations that involve widespread anguish without risks transmit both diseases at the same time.

(Kafka describes them very well.) The need for security and the need for risks balance each other in the *need for responsibility,* in which the necessity for making decisions is linked with the desire to be useful, even indispensable. Complete privation in this sense is experienced by the unemployed, even if they are helped in the way of food, lodging and clothing.[29]

But above all else, "the human soul needs to be rooted in diverse natural ambiences and to communicate through them with the universe." Some examples of natural ambiences are one's country, ambiences characterized by language, by culture, by a common historical past, by profession, by locality.

> Everything that has as an effect the uprooting of a human being or the thwarting of his sending forth roots is criminal.[30]

Simone then turns to the analysis of the three principal forms of uprootedness in our time: the uprootedness of workers, the uprootedness of peasants and the uprootedness that may be termed "geographical" and concerns collective groups and their rapport with territories.

These instances of uprootedness are the sum of the *"moral diseases of destitution,"*[31] caused by the nonsatisfaction of the vital needs of the human creature.

What is the criterion we may use to recognize them?

> The criterion that allows us to recognize that in some area the needs of human beings are satisfied is the flowering of fellowship, of joy, of beauty, of happiness. Where there exists a collapse upon oneself, sadness, meanness, there are privations to heal.[32]

What does it mean for a human being to have roots? It means to share in a way that is "real, active, and natural in the existence of a collectivity that preserves certain treasures of the past and certain presentiments of the future." Exchanges of influence among diverse ambiences are no less indispensable.

Rootedness and the multiplication of contacts are complementary.

A determined ambience should not receive an external influence passively, as an addition, but should experience it as a stimulus to make its own life more intense.

The imposition of a foreign influence causes uprootedness, an immediate consequence of military conquest, which is almost always an evil. The least degree of uprootedness occurs during the invasion of migratory peoples.

Even without military conquest, *economic domination* can produce uprootedness. Today, in our countries, one of the principal poisons that spreads this disease is *money*.

> Money destroys roots wherever it penetrates by substituting the desire for profit for all other motives.

Its victory is easy because it is the easiest motive to understand.

The most acute form of the disease is found in the *condition of workers*, inasmuch as "they are totally and perpetually dependent on money." The worker is not at home anywhere, not in the factory, not where he lives, not in the parties and unions which say that they are "made for him," and not in intellectual culture.

In the factory he is alienated from his work. There is a sharp distinction between his life at work and his life in his family. He does not own his own house. Parties and unions have always supported his interests in money without being concerned for his true disease and "without defending justice," the ideal that expresses the sound inspiration of the working movement (they have never thought about the most miserable part of the population that works: adolescents, women, foreign and colonial immigrants). Culture, elaborated in an ambience that is "closed, spoiled . . . deprived of contact with this universe and of any opening to the other world," has been given to them like "seed for the birds" under the form of *popularization*. Marxism itself, now "reduced by Marx's paltry epigones to a medley of confused and more or less false ideas," has become for the workers a contribution they cannot assimilate.

In the *condition of peasants* the disease is less advanced but is even more scandalous: it is "unnatural" for the land to be cultivated by uprooted beings. In comparison with workers, peasants suffer from an *inferiority complex* which dates back to a long-distant division between the classes. In today's world, the workers have the tendency, "which should not be encouraged," of believing that they are the people; even the intellectuals of a populist bent are convinced of this. From this derives among the peasants a hatred for what is called the left in politics. Tortured by the idea that "everything happens in the city," they make the city into a mirage. This, along with the sense that the situation of the workers is privileged, produces the *depopulation of the countryside*, a phenomenon which ultimately leads to *social death*.

Another factor of serious uprootedness is *the barracks*, which corrupt our forces, insofar as they are an artificial preparation for war at the time of peace. They do not create a real rapprochement between workers and peasants since they do not create a climate of common action and they are found in the city in conjunction with prostitution. The condition of the "professional prostitute" constitutes the lowest level of uprootedness and has a great potential for propagation.

With regard to the life of the intellect, peasants have been "brutally" uprooted by the modern world. The present system consists in presenting every form of instruction to them as the exclusive property of the city, and of this instruction they are given "a small part," because they are incapable of "grasping a large part." This is the colonial mentality, even if it is in a less acute form.

> In every political, juridical, or technological innovation which would have social repercussions, it is necessary to have, first of all, an arrangement that will allow human beings to form new roots.

For this purpose it is necessary to base this arrangement on the correct interpretation of symptoms and to link them with *sensibility*.

> The affliction of workers and the remedy for their sufferings are not located on the juridical plane.

Their claims, which are the product of their affliction, generate only dreams of compensation and should be understood as a sign of their sufferings. A list should be made of them, a list which only could provide us with the matters we must modify.

They all converge in one central need: "the transformation of the very idea of technological research." Until now *machines* have been built with only two purposes in mind, the benefit of the enterprise ordering the research and the interests of the consumer. They should now be planned in relationship with the *moral welfare of the workers*. This is the effort of attention that must be undertaken to inspire a whole series of changes on the level of organization, syndical action and culture. There should be constant contacts between conscientious unions and the research offices of enterprises; the state should assist these contacts with subventions and workers' organizations should assist them with prizes. In schools of engineering, an atmosphere should be created that is favorable to workers. The construction of machines in relationship to the necessities of those who use them should become the object of substantial instruction in all technical schools.

To further the *physiological development* of the worker it is essential that the first contact of an adolescent apprentice with work should not be a shock. Factories, therefore, should not be barracks; a worker could show his wife where he works and teach his little son, after a school with appropriate hours, the first elements of his trade. Familiarity with work would begin at a time in life when work is still "the most enthralling game."

The discipline that prevails in the factories of today will lose its reason for existence when the following possibilities are realized: workers, most of whom will be highly qualified, responsible for their production and for their machine, will be able to work either at home or in small cooperatives, with a number of orders to fill in a time structured by themselves.

The *full development* of young workers, especially in France, involves their participation in an intellectual culture.

True culture is found "above" all social classes. At the present time it is the culture of "intellectual functionaries" and difficult to transmit to the people, not because it is exalted but because it is "too mean." An effort of *translation* is needed. This does not mean taking the truths of an already impoverished culture and diluting them even more, but it means expressing them in their fullness in a language that makes them *sensible to the heart,* according to the idea of Pascal.

This would give birth to a new form of instruction, in which *study associated with the factory* would provide a simple way for introducing the necessity of geometrical laws in a professional school. In the orbit of *letters,* the object of which is the human condition, the people, who have a more direct experience of it, would be quite ready to appreciate *works of the first rank.*

A prerequisite for workers' culture is the union of those "who are called intellectuals" and the workers. Such a union, difficult to achieve, is today favored by the situation of forced labor into which many young intellectuals have been plunged (factories and concentration camps in Germany). It is necessary to further this process by involving the prisoners in rethinking their own experiences in view of the new orientation of culture.

The system of this social life would be neither "capitalist nor socialist." Its direction would be no longer the interests of the consumer (which cannot be other than coarsely materialistic), but *the dignity of man at work,* which is a spiritual value.

Postwar reconstruction would have to begin by following this clear rule: "the dispersion of industrial labor."

Given the suspicious and edgy *sensibility* of the peasants, who think that they are always forgotten,

> no sign of attention should be given to the workers without a similar one for the peasants.

Simone recalls here "the great ability" of the Nazi party prior to 1933: it was able to present itself as a worker to the workers, a peasant to the peasants, a petit bourgeois to the petite bourgeoisie, with promises for everyone, easy to give because they were untrue. Now, "something difficult but not impossible," we must do the same, but *without lying to anyone.*

The peasant must rediscover his roots in the land and the joy of working it. Satisfying his *thirst,* sound and natural, for *property* is the first thing we must do. The land, owned in small portions or for technological reasons cultivated in common in a cooperative fashion, must be considered a means of labor, and not riches to be divided among one's heirs. The same should happen with the threefold property of the laborer (his house, land and machinery).

Even too much stability, all the same, generates by contrast uprootedness. If, for the fourteen-year-old peasant who begins to plow the earth, labor in the fields is "poetry, elation," in time it becomes repetitive and insufficient to involve all the wealth of his energy. For this reason, his first contact with labor should be celebrated with a *solemn feast.* Then, three or four years later, his "thirst for new experiences" should be satisfied with free but not compulsory trips that would be linked with education, in France and abroad, not in cities, but in the countryside. Simone looks forward to similar trips for workers.

Just as capitalism cannot be left master of the professional formation of youth, the army cannot be left master of its military formation. *Civil authorities* should take part in the organization of a military service, intended for the *moral welfare of the soldiers.* For young peasants, barracks would be established in the country, to avoid the scandal of houses of prostitution.

So that culture would no longer be extraneous to peasants, new methods must be invented. To begin with *science,* founded upon the marvelous phenomenon of chlorophyll photosynthesis, all instruction in the villages should have as its object the beauty of the world. The transmission of this culture should come by way of a new figure: *the rural teacher.* By birth a peasant, he should receive an education completely different from that of teachers destined for cities. He would devote a wide study to *folklore* with all of its philosophical values and dedicate himself to the reading of peasant works, from Hesiod to the few authentic contemporary works in this field.[33] Later, he would be sent for a year to serve as an apprentice on a farm, anonymously, in another department. This experience should be prepared morally, because it would be liable to elicit reactions of disdain and aversion rather than to foster those of "compassion and love."

Even the condition of the *curate or village pastor* should be prepared by the church in a particular manner. It is scandalous to see how religion is absent from the daily life of a Catholic village, when there are so many parables based on country life in the Gospels.

If, on the contrary, on the one hand "the whole life of the soul" and on the other "scientific knowledge" of the material universe are oriented towards "the act of work,"

> work has its just place in the thought of a man . . . It is a contact between this world and the other.

Simone uses here a very beautiful and very feminine comparison,

> A happy young woman, pregnant for the first time, is sewing a little shirt; she intends to sew well, but she does not forget for an instant the baby she is carrying within herself; at the same time, in the workroom of a prison, a convicted woman is also sewing. She, too, intends to sew well because she is afraid that she will be punished. One could think that the two women are doing the same work at the same time and that their attention is fixed on the same type of technical difficulty. And yet between the one labor and the other there is a vast gulf of difference. Our entire social problem consists in making workers pass from the latter to the former of these two situations.

We must create between this world and the other such a rapport that, in their *double beauty,* they are both "present and associated with the act of labor, as the baby that will be born is with every stitch of the little shirt."

The unhappy peoples of Europe have more need of greatness than of bread. There are only two types of greatness: "the old lie of the greatness of the world" and "authentic greatness," which is of the spiritual order.

> The contemporary form of authentic greatness is a civilization made of the spirituality of labor.[34]

The disease of uprootedness with respect to territory has as a symptom the "profound moral incoherence" in which the French live. This incoherence is caused by two fundamental contrasts: the one between *reason* and *patriotism,* the other between *laical morality* and *national morality.* On the one hand, the French have always felt the vocation of using reason for their intellectual and institutional expansion (from the Paris of the thirteenth century, "the heart of Christendom," to the France of the Revolution, the inspiration of modern constitutions). On the other, patriotism has always served them in practice as an instrument of subjugation, first in the conquest of the internal territories and then in colonial expansion. Laical morality, based on the concepts of "justice and respect for one's neighbor," is taught in the schools and is felt vaguely and instinctively by everybody. National morality, connected with the reigning idea of history, understood in the name of patriotism to exalt injustice and the crudest form of haughtiness, in reality implies a nonmorality. The two contrasts, which are really just one, even more carefully hidden by Christians from themselves, engender in them an extreme discomfort, inasmuch as pagan patriotism acts as a "solvent" upon the soul.

France is never wrong, France has a divine right to victory, the growth of France is always a good under all apsects and it does not matter what means are employed.

In reality, this is *blind nationalism* and hinders the French from establishing a true rapport with France, their homeland. But what is a homeland? It is a concept that must be thought through for the first time, to know the kind of love we should give to our homeland and why.

A homeland is a *vital ambience*.

There is in everyone a zone of the soul, there are modes of action which circulate from some men to others and exist only in the national ambience and disappear when a country is destroyed.

Until now, the homeland has been set up as "an absolute" to worship idolatrously, but it is a "fact." As a "purveyor of life" it is a good towards which we have duties; it should be nurtured in turn, respected in its development and in its health. We must conceive of the reality corresponding to the name of France in such a way that "it can be loved just as it is, in its truth." For this reason, we must overcome our sense of shame before the moral disintegration of the country, to surmount the instinctive rejection of a deserved affliction and to clarify the reasons for the disintegration. Simone now writes a history of France which is the psychoanalysis of a personality.

There have been fundamental errors connected with the idolatry of power. The *nation* has engulfed smaller territories and treated them as conquered lands, with the degradation of ancient allegiance by the imposition of taxes. Power crystallized in the state, "the thing that it is impossible to love." The state "morally killed" what was smaller than it. In the apparently peaceful years before the war, the *boredom* of provincial cities was "as real a cruelty as the most visible atrocities" (crimes caused by that boredom; we think of Gide's *La séquestrée de Poitiers*):[35] in a country whose members were already cold, only the heart was still beating, and that heart was Paris. There were no exchanges among the regions, separated as they were by "prison walls," all the way to the extreme isolation of lands which had never been integrated and had been relegated to the depths of society, such as Brittany (Bretons constitute a majority of prostitutes and illiterate soldiers) and Corsica (the colonized Corsicans have spread through the colonies the brutality they had endured by way of policemen and inspectors recruited prevalently from among them).

In place of a love for the past as *tradition,* as the history and expression of diverse civilizations, has been imposed the imitation of a mirage of greatness, a mirage perpetuated in time by conquerors. The past has been slain, in absurd opposition to the future, which gives us nothing. We must give it everything, to constitute it. And we must have something for us to give anything. All that we have been allowed to have are "the treasures inherited from the past." So today "protecting, loving, and preserving" the little that remains "should become an *idée fixe.*" It would be the demonstration of respect for the frustrated aspirations and the scattered traces of the vanquished. It would be the retrieval of the characteristics that express the *identities of the several ambiences* and at the same time the preparation of a homeland (composed of many small homelands) as a terrain in which to take root.

"Assuring a bond between the past and the future" is the mission of the collectivity.

We must *regret the evils done by France,* without, however, applying useless surgical remedies through lopping off rapports created through time, but rather by encouraging *the development of regional cultures.* By making all the diverse ambiences participate in public life through special missions entrusted to individuals, we would succeed in emphasizing "fellowship" in the relations between Frenchmen, now mixed together only by the force of circumstances. It is a matter of respecting equality in diversity, by encouraging exchanges with other analogous cultures, even outside France. Would it not be natural that "in a given field, Brittany, Wales, Cornwall and Ireland would feel themselves part of the same ambience"?

Considering our homeland as *one vital ambience among many others* means eliminating the contradictions and the lies which make patriotism unhealthy, and asserting that our homeland is something imperfect but does exist and should be preserved as "a treasure for the good it contains." Feeling that one's homeland is a *source of life* creates *loyalty* towards it. If it is threatened with the peril of disappearance, the obligation of military service to defend it expresses this loyalty. It is a real obligation, even for conscientious objectors, for whom some equivalent for armed service will be found. Thus, there could also be changes in the way in which war is considered. First of all, *the distinction between soldiers and civilians* should be abolished;[36] in that way the sufferings and perils would be shared between "young and old, men and women, healthy and infirm." It is a game of honor for everyone; but since compulsion is most contrary to honor, one not wishing to fulfill this obligation of defending his homeland would be exonerated. And his failure would be punished with exile, the loss of his homeland (not with the absurdity of the loss of liberty or life).

It is clear that this concept of the homeland is incompatible with the present conception of the history of France as a nation. Just as clear is this:

France must choose . . . between a soul and the Roman, Corneille-endorsed conception of greatness.

Simone involves in the responsibility for bringing France to the proper choice all those who "are in the position to speak and to hold a pen in the hand." Bringing her to the wrong choice would be a "crime." In order not to commit it, we must make sure that there is in our thought of the homeland "not the least trace of a lie."

There is but one legitimate love for one's homeland, *compassion,* the same compassion that Jesus felt for Jerusalem and Judaea. It is a love that coincides with *charity.*

It is a love with eyes open to the cruelties and lies of the country, a love made all the more sorrowful by this: "it disposes us to discern the good" in its object and so it would not pass over "the authentic greatness" of France in the past, in the present and in its aspirations. Not only an unhappy country is worthy of this love. Happiness, an earthly matter, "incomplete, fragile and fleeting," deserves equal compassion. Pity does not drain energy; it gives another type of energy, "pure" and rich in "heart-rending tenderness." Furthermore,

Pride does not become the unfortunate.

Evoking the historic greatness of France in these circumstances can seem derisive or risk being a poison for the soul, as it was for Germany.

The search for compensation in affliction is an evil.

Compassion for France

is not a compensation but a spiritualization of the sufferings she has endured.

Again, while pride in national greatness is exclusive, compassion is "universal by nature." It can cross boundaries and spread to all peoples without exception.

This new conception of the homeland is essential for the reconstruction of the country.

National pride is far removed from daily life.

Serious disturbances derive from this situation (the crisis of the Romantics followed the Napoleonic period). These disturbances endanger social stability, which is indispensable to the new life we must invent.[37]

What should the state do? Taking its inspiration from the ideals of justice of the French Revolution (an element of greatness in the past) and from compassion for the homeland, it should strive to put those ideals into practice by establishing institutions which would make the country a reality, to safeguard in order and in peace. Otherwise, the state, which in its administrative function is "the steward of the homeland's goods," will lose all its authority and no one will feel any duty of obedience, which is more difficult to accept anyway, after years of total turmoil.

The conception of politics must change. It is clearly impossible to start over again with the same kind of parliamentary life and party strife. The first provision to take is the recasting of the police. So that its members may acquire standing in the eyes of the people, we must liquidate the staff in charge and recruit their replacements in a new way, through public competition; they should receive a higher level of education and of compensation. At the same time juridical categories of prostitutes and convicted felons, categories that supply the police with victims and accomplices, with resulting double contamination and mutual dishonor, should not exist.

On the other hand,

It is necessary that the crime of dishonesty of public officials towards the state be really punished more severely than armed robbery.

The first task is the creation of a fabric of responsibilities by which "everyone exercising or wanting to exercise power" would pledge to follow the *declaration of duties towards the human creature* as the practical guide of his conduct, and the people would adopt it consciously as the practical inspiration of the life of the country.[38]

From now on, the provisional government in London would have to act in this fashion. Its present moral posture is favorable, since it has been able to demonstrate loyalty to France as its homeland and it has not been contaminated by power. It must now find the *language* for both witnessing and true communication, to make the French *feel* that "it recognizes the duties corresponding to the essential aspirations of the people." Otherwise, there are three alternatives: disorder, Fascism or Communism.

Refashioning the soul of the country is a problem which is both *urgent* and *practical*.[39]

For centuries, we have grown accustomed to regarding politics as "the technique of acquiring and preserving power." In reality, *power*, in its essence, nature and definition is only a means, which stands in relation to politics "as a piano does to a musical composition."

Political action, as Simone foresees it, implies, at the basis of every decision, the simultaneous contemplation of various considerations of diverse sorts. So it demands an *attention* of the same order as that necessary for creative work in art and science. Politics determines the destiny of peoples and has as its object justice. Why should it require less attention than art or science, which have as their objects the beautiful and the true?

The poet draws the level of attention indispensable for *composition on multiple levels* from inspiration, the tension of the soul's faculties. If he is not competent, he will still receive this attention as a gift, so long as he has an unswerving and violent desire for it, together with a humble perseverance in his work. On the plane of political responsibility, "whoever has a hunger and thirst for justice," should yearn for such attention and he will "infallibly" receive it.

As far as the language of men is distant from divine beauty, and as far as their senses and their intellect are distant from the truth, just so far are the necessities of social life distant from justice. It follows that political life has, like an art or science, an equal need for *laborious creative invention*.

To excite an inspiration in a people, a proven *method* does not exist (except in Plato, the problem has never been posed) and history is of little assistance to us, since our situation has no precedents. Only the practical circumstances exist to show us the way to follow.

As, when one confronts a broken machine, one begins to look at it carefully, but looking at it does no good unless one has clearly in mind the *idea of the mechanical relationships,* so, when one confronts the daily aspects of the shifting situation in France, one must begin looking at them with the clear *idea* in mind *of public action as a mode for the country's education.*

To whomever one turns, education consists in *exciting motives* to furnish the energy necessary for the execution of what is beneficial, what is obligatory, what is good.

> Wishing to bring human creatures—ourselves or others—towards the good by merely showing the direction, without having made certain of the presence of corresponding motives, is like wishing an automobile, which has run out of gas, to go forward by pushing down on the accelerator.

To avoid (at last) this error, condemned by a "very famous" text, which has been read and reread for more than two thousand years, we can think of three means of education in public activity, overlooked until now: *official expression,* or officially authorized expression of some thoughts that are already in the heart of the masses or of certain active elements of the nation; *example; the very modalities for action and organization* forged for action.

> Men have such need for words that a thought not expressed in words cannot for this reason be translated into actions.[40]

Words are food that supplies energy. In private life this food is gotten from "friends and natural guides," who clarify and strengthen our inner thoughts. In circumstances where the public drama prevails, such thoughts can "insensibly affect" a whole people. Expressing them means awakening the deep resources of every soul and evoking the possibilities of an action which is not collective but remains personal in its "essence."

There is a need for words that will introduce the good; they must come from a source in whom men have put their confidence and they must be weighed and pronounced in such a way that they nourish this confidence. They must then form an appropriate language, which can derive its authority only from a *loftiness of thought,* "commensurate with our present tragedy."

We need constant cooperation between a "receiving organization" of observers in France and the government in London, which should make the *choice of words*. Indispensable qualities for the observers are: a passionate interest in human beings and in their souls; the ability to put themselves in others' shoes and to pay attention to the mute signs of their thoughts; a certain intuition for history as it occurs; the ability to express in writing delicate shadings and complex relations. Rare qualities, a very broad task. The choice of words remains by far the most important and the most feasible matter.

Two criteria for choice are conceivable: *the good*, in the spiritual sense of the word, and *the useful*, in relationship with the war and with the national interests of France.

For the first criterion: we should carefully examine this postulate and then either reject it or adopt it for good.

What is spiritually good is good with regard to everything, in every relationship, in every time and place, in every circumstance.

("A Christian must adopt it.") Our use of this thought must be extremely rigorous; it is a thought based on faith in God, on the certainty of *another reality*, "above this earthly realm . . . an inexplicable medley of good and evil." There on high, "the good is only good" and "produces only the good."

Every pure good that derives from on high has similar properties. We must seize the echoes of the good and transmit them "untiringly" by way of the barest and simplest words, without examining anything but their authenticity. And in these terms we should reject everything that is solely evil, hatred and baseness. So much for fundamental motives.

For middle-range motives, the effects must be foreseen on each occasion with great care, under all possible aspects, and with respect to various clusters of circumstances in time and in space. Composing a list of the circumstances in their various complexity would mean finding the key for solving the most essential problems of the war and the peace.

The reality of motives is put to the test in *actions*.

So that the very modalities of the action may be a means of education, they should be indicated in the fullest measure and with the greatest precision, in the constant consciousness of the direct virtue and the indirect virtue of the action.

It is the directions, the *orders* that elicit the direct virtue of the action, inasmuch as they make it real. They must answer to their immediate end, *strategic usefulness*. If this usefulness is the first consideration for an action to be real, there are other considerations much more important for the indirect virtue of the action.

We must hinder the exhaustion of the initial motives (through weariness or discouragement) and encourage the propitious evolution of successive motives (a taste for action in itself). For this reason the greatest problem lies in the choice of actions and the mode of ordering them. The principal means of transmission: the radio.

What should our criterion of choice be? Although the study of how a motive is transformed into an act is still to be undertaken, and it is impossible for us to bring ourselves and others always to link desirable actions with desirable motives, there still do exist actions which are good or bad in themselves and from which good or bad may result in our motives and in our sentiments. Simone offers two very clear examples:

> If, to serve France, you kill German soldiers, and at the end of a certain period of time the killing of human creatures becomes a pleasure, it is clear that this is an evil.
>
> If, to serve France, you help workers to escape from convoys headed for Germany, and at the end of a certain period of time assisting the unfortunate becomes a pleasure, it is clear that it is a good.

In a general sense,

> we must always choose the modes of action that contain the inception of an apprenticeship in the good.

This is necessary not only for the good, but for the useful. For although it is rare, when the pure good becomes an active motive in a soul, "it remains there as a source of an impulse that never varies or dries up."

> Faith is more realistic than realistic politics. A man who does not have certainty of this does not have faith.

Example, one of the three means for the education of the public unites all three.

The choice of actions should not be left to the technicians of a conspiracy; they would act through their separate actions and give priority to the means over the ends. It is the government which should clearly and precisely subordinate every technique to particular ends, subordinate to the two fundamental criteria. Only in that way will the mode in which orders are transmitted demonstrate consciousness. The tone of the transmission should be nourished by a "warm, real" friendship between the French and the English. For

> personal feelings have in the great events of the world a role that has never been understood in its full expansiveness. The fact that a friendship exists or does not exist between two men, between two ambiences, can be decisive in certain cases for the destiny of the human race.

Furthermore,

> the circulation of truths among men is dependent, on the whole, on the state of feelings; this is true for all types of truth.

The organization which coordinates the actions has a reality superior to the action itself. To study the organizations[41] which have sprung up spontaneously in France in the midst of daily necessities, to contemplate them on the spot, and then through the French authorities in London "to shape" them with patience and discretion, according to a clear vision of a good, would mean using them as means of education.

A *method of education* is not a great thing if it does not inspire men to the conception of a certain human perfection. When it is a question of the "education of a people," the conception has to be that of an entire civilization.

The orientation is provided by the relation between the soul and the other reality. We recall that in Marseilles Simone had meditated in this fashion:

> Apply to the supernatural (in the soul or in history) the concept of the *conditions of existence*. Conditions of existence of the Christian religion in the year . . .[42]

Now she turns to describing them. They are the circumstances we must keep present in mind to rediscover the orientation, which is eternally traced in the soul through its aspiration for the good.

There are four principal obstacles that separate us from a form of civilization of real value: *the false conception of greatness, the degradation of the sense of justice, the idolatry of money* and *the absence of religious inspiration.*

Our *greatest flaw* is *our conception of greatness*. It is the same conception that inspired the whole life of Hitler. He desired it with all the desperation of an uprooted man and had the courage to realize it. We confine ourselves to yielding our mind to it with baseness, and, though we continue to imbibe it in history and pass it on in teaching, scandalized, we condemn it in our enemies and, cowards, we abstain from it in action.

We are subject to force, which alone forces us to admire in time Napoleon, Caesar, Alexander . . . We accept history as objective, when all that it really does is subordinate thought to the only kind of documents that, given the nature of things, can remain: the evidence of the conquerors.

There is talk of punishing Hitler. No punishment will be able to hinder this idolater of history from thinking that he is "grandiose," since he is forever there in history. And above all, it will not hinder, within twenty or a hundred years, a young solitary dreamer, whether German or not, from aspiring to imitate that grandiosity. The only way to punish Hitler and to prevent, in the future, young men with a thirst for greatness from following his example is *such a complete transformation of the sense of greatness* that Hitler would be excluded from it. We must begin to achieve this in ourselves.

Is admiration possible without love? And if admiration is a love, how do we dare to love anything other than the good?

It would be "simple" to make a pact with ourselves to admire only the actions and the lives "through which there shines the spirit of truth, of justice, and of love."

This spirit is eternal; the only distance that separates thoughts and actions from it is evil. Once we have taken account of the "circumstances," the "meanings" which change according to actions and to words, the "symbolic language" of a definite ambience, what we can recognize as *cruelty* (whether of the tenth or the nineteenth century) must engender *horror*. Instead,

The dogma of progress dishonors the good by making it a question of fashion.

The *good is scorned* also in all the study materials set before children, and when they become adults they find in the food offered them only reasons to be hardened in such a scorn. Among both children and adults there runs a truth that has become a commonplace: talent has nothing to do with morality. And only talent has been proposed for them to admire. They see this talent, in all its manifestations, flaunting its lack of the virtues they have been encouraged to practice. What can they conclude except that virtue is the portion of mediocrity? This attitude has become so current that the word virtue has become ridiculous, like the words "honesty" and "goodness."

In the atmosphere of false greatness, it is useless to want to rediscover true greatness. We must scorn false greatness first.

And then discern true greatness.

In history, the study of which, "linked with life experience," is the only process by which we can come to know "the human heart," we must be certain not only that the facts are exact as far as we can check, but that they are shown in their true relationship with good and evil. We should search out "indirect evidence" of the scanty and largely hidden "purity" which shines forth now and then from a "fabric of meanness and cruelty."

For literature and the arts, which are also subject to the transmission of false greatness, we must be conscious that talent does not have bonds with morality because it does not have greatness, but that on the plane of true greatness, among perfect beauty, perfect truth, and perfect justice

there is a mysterious unity, because the good is one.

Thus, in Giotto one cannot distinguish the genius of the painter from the Franciscan spirit; in Zen paintings and poetry from China one cannot distinguish the genius of the painter and the poet from the state of mystical illumination. A tragedy like *King Lear* is the fruit of the pure spirit of love; Monteverdi, Bach and Mozart were pure in their lives and in their works.

The *degradation of the sense of justice* is connected with the idolatry of force and derives from the *modern conception of science*, which is responsible, along with those of history and of art, for contemporary monstrosities.

"Man should never yield to the error of believing himself lord and master of nature . . . In a world in which planets and suns follow circular orbits . . . in which force rules everywhere and alone is mistress of weakness . . . man cannot avail himself of special laws." This passage from *Mein*

Kampf, cited by Simone, expresses in an "irreproachable" manner the only conclusion that can "reasonably" be drawn from the conception of the world contained in our science.

For two or three centuries we have believed that we can live with a contradiction that tears us apart. On the one hand, basing our view on the modern science founded by Galileo, Descartes, etc., and pursued in the eighteenth century especially by Newton, now in the twentieth century we see force as the absolute mistress of nature. On the other side, basing our view on the humanism that arose in the Renaissance, triumphed in the Revolution, and inspired, in a degraded form, the Third Republic, we believe that men can and should found their relations upon justice acknowledged by reason.

In reality, we are not alive; we are walking forward blindly, without the courage to look this contradiction in the face. "Dishonesty of the intelligence" is always punished by error. All the confused attempts to solve this contradiction have degenerated into error.

Utilitarianism (with its manifestation, economic liberalism) supposes the existence of a "small marvellous mechanism" by which force immediately produces justice; the only condition is that force is under the guise of *money*. *Marxism* believes in a similar mechanism. Force is christened history and expresses itself in *class warfare;* justice is relegated to a future, before which there must occur an apocalyptic catastrophe. Even Hitler, after his moment of intellectual courage, yielded to a belief in the little mechanism; he selected the notion of the *chosen race,* destined to subdue everything, then to establish among its slaves "the type of justice that is appropriate to slavery."

All these ideas, in appearance quite different and in reality quite similar, have just one problem: they are lies. The victory of Hitler was the victory of a coherent untruth over our incoherent lie. For this reason the spirit, too, has surrendered together with arms.

> There is but one choice. Either we discern in the universe a principle at work in addition to force, different from it, or we must recognize force as the sole mistress and sovereign, even in human relations.

Force, a blind mechanism, cannot produce justice. So, if force is absolutely sovereign, justice is absolutely unreal. But this is not so. We know this from our experience.

Justice is real in the depths of the human heart. The structure of the human heart is a reality in the midst of the realities of this universe, no more and no less than the trajectory of a star.

Therefore, science is wrong. We must show its error and change it, if we wish to start hoping for a better civilization.

This is a matter of the greatest importance, given the immense prestige of science and of scientists; in nontotalitarian countries it is the dominant prestige. Together with technology, which is its application, it constitutes our "sole claim to self-esteem, inasmuch as we are western, modern, and of the white race."

There is in everyone, believer and unbeliever alike, an enslavement to science, an enslavement which coincides, on the one hand, with our *idolatry of force,* symbolized today by money, and, on the other, with *the absence of religious inspiration.*

Since, throughout the week, the spirit of science is sovereign in Christians, religion has become "an affair of Sunday morning." If unbelievers submit to it every day, they are wrong to have a triumphal sense of interior unity (their morality is as much in contrast with science as the religion of the believers), Christians experience a dull, unconfessed discomfort, which makes inner cohesion difficult.

Common people of the cities, in more constant and "carnal" contact with the applications of science, have been more disturbed by it in their devotion and have abandoned the churches; common people of the countryside, although to a lesser degree, have imitated them; the *bourgeoisie* have continued to attend them. This has been due, on the one hand, to the absence of that contact and, on the other, to the absence of faith. With only a few exceptions, religious faith has become for the bourgeoisie "a question of convenience." This has accentuated the separation between the classes, and religion has automatically become a "thing of the right." Except for a few centers of light, *Christianity* reveals itself as a "convenience relative to those who exploit the people." We should not then be surprised if it has such a poor record in the struggle against contemporary forms of evil.

In actuality, it is *irreligious,* even in the hearts and the ambiences of religious life of the most sincere and intense sort. At its center there is an *insufficient spirit of truth;* it is experienced confusedly as a sentimental need, and it is subject to the superstition of progress.

It is in the face of science that in reality "there are no unbelievers." This assigns to the scientists the same responsibility the priests had in the thirteenth century. Both the former and the latter are human beings nurtured by society so that they may have the time to seek after, to find, and to communicate the truth. Then as now, "it is a matter of bread being thrown away or worse."

Science does not deserve the fine name of truth; it is a mere list of known facts to add onto, without motive. Increasing the quantity of known facts is not a motive sufficient to awaken the desire for truth. *Truth* would be desired if it were considered *a good*. This has not been possible since the time when the very conception of science became that of "a study whose object is placed beyond good and evil, and above all beyond good."

To this insufficient central motivation are added shabby intellectual motives: an impulse similar to that found in hunting, sport and play, and the sense of prestige that scientific technique confers on science through its applications. Slaves of false greatness, scientists feel elated at being part of *something great*. Even meaner are social motives. The sense of professional duty is not enough. They want chairs, honors, foreign receptions, recompense in money. The habits of scientists across time prove such shabbiness. In the fifteenth and sixteenth centuries, they would fling out challenges to one another, conceal the phases of their research, and scramble the sequence of their computations to guarantee themselves priority in their discovery. Today, because of the ease of communications, scientists of the entire world form a planetary village subject to gossip and fashions. Not even the larger public fails to realize that, since science is the product of collective opinion, it is subject to its dictates and whims. And yet it is not scandalized by this.

We are too brutalized to be aware of a scandal.

We are suffering the disease of idolatry, so profound that it takes away from Christians "their ability to testify to the truth."

The spirit of truth, absent from the motives of science, cannot be found in science itself. If the spirit of truth is not there, neither can the good be there.

Every sort of knowledge incompatible with truly pure motives is itself stained with error.

This is the first article of faith, because

Faith is the certainty that the good is one.

But . . . What does science study? Facts as such. Mathematical relations are considered facts of the mind. Force, matter, facts isolated in them-selves: *here there is nothing for human thought to love.* But at the base of knowledge, there has to be love. One loves "something which exists, of which one thinks"; a truth is always "the truth of something."

> Desiring the truth is desiring a direct contact with reality. Desiring a contact with reality means loving it. One desires the truth to love in the truth.

While every other sort of love desires in the first place some gratification, and for this reason is the source of error and of untruth, "real and pure love desires always first of all to dwell entirely in the truth."

> Real and pure love is of itself the spirit of truth.

In antiquity, fiery breath expressed the concept that today science indicates with the word *energy.* Pure love is this *active force.*

Today, the spirit of truth is just about absent from religion, from sci-ence, from all thought. What should we do for it to come down again among us?

In the first place, we should bring about a reconciliation between re-ligion and science.

The spirit of truth can dwell in science, on condition that *the motive of the scientist* is *love* for the object of his study: the universe in which we live. How can this object excite love? By way of its *beauty.*

> Science is the study of the beauty of the world.

Force, matter, these escape thought in reality. Thought is made to grasp "the impalpable and unalterable net of order and of harmony," in which force and matter are immersed.

> The scientist has as an end the union of his spirit with the mysterious wisdom eternally written in the universe.

Once this is granted, how can there be "opposition or even separation" between the spirit of science and that of religion? Scientific investigation is nothing but a form of religious contemplation.

So it was in Greece. The Romans killed Archimedes and then they killed

Greece. The memory of Greek science, transmitted by the Middle Ages through so-called gnostic thought, in initiatory circles, remained only in a conservative form and did not serve as a creative spark. Revived at the beginning of the sixteenth century in Italy and in France, after about two millennia of lethargy, this science had become materialistic. What had produced this transformation? Not the earliest Christianity, which, as we find it in the Gospels, was perfectly capable of being the inspiration of a rigorous science, but Christianity in its developed form as the Roman state religion. God had become a "copy of the emperor" and dominant Christian thought allowed no other notion of divine Providence than that of a *personal Providence*. The notion of orthodoxy, indispensable to the Church for the purposes of its temporal domination, rigorously separated the domain relative to the "good of souls," in which thrives an "unconditional submission of thought to an external authority," and the domain relative to things called "profane," in which "the intelligence is free."

If the notion of personal Providence occurs in the Gospels since God is called Father, it is, alongside the other, that of an *impersonal Providence,* in a certain sense analogous to a mechanism. "That you may become sons of your Father . . . who makes the sun to rise upon the bad and the good . . . Be perfect then, as your Father is perfect" (Matthew 5:45–48).

The conception of Providence as the "personal intervention" of God for particular goals is an arbitrary judgment. The specific ends attributed to God are so many "clippings" that we make in the more-than-infinite complexity of the chains of causality. In reality we cannot do so; furthermore, to judge them as intentions of God for the benefit of a Christian is a narrow idolatry. So this kind of conception has covered the faith with ridicule in the eyes of the unbelievers and is incompatible with true faith. The forced separation of the soul from the intelligence

> makes impossible that mutual penetration of the religious and the profane which would be the essence of a Christian civilization.

Both the intelligence and the soul run a course, traverse a "duration" of contemplation, of patience, of humility: the intelligence in relationship with the beauty of the world, the soul in relationship with the pure good.

"Natural mechanisms" are the conditions for producing events as such, without any reference to value. The forces here below are under the sovereign sway of necessity. Necessity is formed of relations which are *thoughts,* the thoughts of "eternal, unique Wisdom." Divine Providence is this Wisdom.

> The brute force of matter, which seems sovereign to us, is nothing else than perfect obedience.

This is the guarantee granted to man, the visible and palpable promise, the stay of hope. This is "the truth that stings our heart every time we are sensible to the beauty of the world," the truth that "explodes with incomparable tones of joy" in the beautiful and pure pages of the Old Testament, in the Pythagoreans, in Lao-tzu, in the sacred scriptures of India, in countless myths and stories.

> Force, which is sovereign here below, is under the sovereign sway of thought. Man is a thinking creature; he is on the side of what commands force.

He is surely not the lord and master of nature, and if he believes he is, he errs. He is the son of Him who commands nature, he is "the child of the house." Science is the proof of this. When he sits on his father's knees "and identifies with Him in love, he shares in His authority."

The most complete identification in love occurs in *sanctity,* the achievement of that perfection set before us in the Gospels, in which we find "a supernatural physics of the human soul." The laws of "supernatural mechanics" are the conditions for the production of "pure good" as such. Even here, an impersonal Providence is evident. *Grace* descends from God upon all beings, but its fruitfulness depends upon what they are and requires a period of time marked by successive stages, in a manner analogous to a mechanism. We see this in all the parables of the sowing. Even all that has to do with petition calls up something like a mechanism.

> Every real desire for a pure good, from a certain degree of intensity onward, makes the corresponding good descend.

Supernatural mechanics, a precise study of which, for example, we find in Saint John of the Cross, are at least "as rigorous as the laws of gravity." The practical experience of the saints assures us that "the good does descend upon the earth," but only to the degree that "certain conditions upon the earth are actually realized." From this derives the only "supernatural fact" here below, the only miracle: the love of God, which becomes in those who love Him an "active force, a driving energy."

Truly Christian inspiration has been preserved by mysticism, which has still been unable to abolish, within the tradition of the Catholic Church, the Roman conception of God. But this abolition is one of the principal "purifications" which the soul must go through.

To find the road which has been lost between modern thought and ancient wisdom, science must make an effort of *true attention*. As long as a man has his soul thronged with personal thoughts, he is completely subject "to the constriction of needs and the mechanical play of forces." The man who empties his own soul allows the thoughts of eternal wisdom to penetrate him. Then he understands that indeed necessity is obedience to God. He has proof of this in the relations among things, expressed in the symbols of geometry, which will appear to him like a *double language*. It both gives information on the forces at work in matter and, at the same time, speaks of the supernatural relations between God and creatures. The same will happen with mathematical relations, which science detects, in its various branches, in all phenomena. Every phenomenon is a modification of the distribution of energy and is consequently determined by the laws of energy. But *several types of energy* exist, arranged in a *hierarchic order*, from mechanical force or *gravity*, which constantly makes us feel its constraint, to impalpable and weightless *light*, which despite gravity causes trees and stalks of grain to grow. Psychic phenomena, too, like physical phenomena, are "modifications of the distribution and the quality of energy" and are subject to the laws of energy. Thus, even the study of the soul can become a science and so, too, the study of society, which should "describe in minute detail the anatomy, the physiology, the natural and conditional reflexes, the possibilities of the training" of the collectivity, with Plato's notion of the "great animal" as our basis. Psychology and sociology must accept "the notion of the supernatural" and after defining it scientifically they should handle it "with extreme precision." For

> If the sciences of man were founded in this way upon methods of a mathematical rigor and at the same time were maintained in their rapport with the faith, if in the sciences of nature and in mathematics symbolic interpretation took once again the place it once had, the unity of the order established in the universe would appear in all of its sovereign clarity.

This return to the truth would among other matters make the *truth of physical labor* stand forth. Already, in *Oppression et Liberté*, labor had been the point of encounter between thought and action, the nexus we must contemplate to find the key to necessity. Here it becomes the *spiritual center* of society, inasmuch as it represents the nexus between the passivity of matter and the beauty of the world in its concrete manifestation of *perfect obedience to God.*[43]

In *La Connaissance Surnaturelle* she had written:

The goal of human life is constructing an architecture of the soul.[44]

In *L'Enracinement* she looks forward to an architecture of society, which would proceed in an analogous fashion. The keystone would be Christianity. She was not heard.[45]

She wrote to Schumann:

Praises for me that are completely out of place . . . The fact that they can use words like superiority or inferiority with reference to thinking shows to what extent we are breathing a contaminated atmosphere . . .

A meal is not confronted, it is eaten. In this way words, written or spoken, are eaten, to the degree that they are edible, that is to the degree they contain some truth. They have no other destination.[46]

Increasingly irritated by the tone of haughtiness, by the edginess, and by the "absurdities" (she was beginning to hear a little too much about "being on the side of victory")[47] of the French milieu in London, she grew ever more isolated. On July 26th, she wrote Closon to send in her resignation. At the moment of liberation, she did not want to have anything to do either with the Free French forces or with the structure of government. This was "essential" for her.

I shall not squander myself in an activity more or less political; I know that the amount of energy necessary in politics for the minimum effectiveness is as much beyond my capacity as that necessary for the explorers of Everest.[48]

They found her unconscious on the floor of her room.

19

The Meaning of a Woman's Life

Schumann returned from Algiers around the beginning of August and went to see her in the hospital. They had dreadful, violent conversations. "One day or another, I shall make him ill," she had written her parents.[1]

De Gaulle had claimed for his movement alone the right to represent France; for Schumann, this was necessary for sound negotiations with the allies. Simone, however, saw in the disputes between De Gaulle and Giraud only "personal rivalry." Gaullism seemed to her a kind of party and she feared that this party might become Fascist. She thought that the movement of the Free French was "worn out."

She scolded her friend for his radio broadcasts. She reminded him of a phrase that might cause animosity against the whole German people. "She was the only one who could have told me something like that," recalls Schumann, and he thanked her. She also did not like the way he had spoken of the Russians. One should not hide the truth about an ally, just because he is an ally. Finally, she wanted to know why he had not been able to have her dropped by parachute into France.

He had not really been a friend to let her die of sorrow like this, in England. She was deeply moved by revolt against him and Gaullism, since they had not allowed her "to realize her vocation." She told Schumann that she would not speak with him again. In their last meeting, her friend brought her *The Silence of the Sea,* by Vercors; in silence, Simone returned it to him, "without even glancing at it."[2]

What did she want of me in those last months of her earthly life? Even now, after thirty years have gone by, I would not ask this question of myself aloud, if it were only the pricking of personal anguish. But I believe that the answer has reference to those millions of human beings who owe or will owe to Simone their ability to recognize the quality of their soul. The answer has to shed light upon the agonizing mystery of her end."[3]

This mystery is also the mystery of her life. If it is impossible to present it clearly in all of its aspects (as would be true in the case of every human life), it is possible for me, as well as precious, "to transport myself to her center" with all the *attention* I can muster and to strive to understand her with *sympathy*.

Her life, as rarely happens, was shaped into a coherent design, guided by a precise inspiration; at the same time, within the scope of this design, she has been able to preserve all the complexity of her contradictions; she has respected them as something precious. She is a person who unites the most scrupulous commitment with the greatest openness, who synthesizes in her practice the manifold contributions of her watchful, subtle, and analytic sensibility. Her writings remain a clear and incandescent image of her being.

"Her life and her work underline yet again how difficult it is for a genius, and even more for a woman, to be heard and understood, during her life or after her death." These are the words of Suzy Allemand.[4]

She was both a genius and a woman. Her being the latter is for the most part responsible for her self-laceration and for the reactions of others to her, especially if they were negative. She bore these wounds within herself and she lived with them; in large measure they were responsible for her exhaustion.

She wanted to have an impact upon the world. Her volcanic impulse to nonconformist action was especially frustrated by being a woman. This was reflected in the first place by her way of looking at herself, feeling inferior to her brother, brooding upon her own "mediocrity."

Hers was a mad naïveté. For this reason she tended to mythologize persons and thus to place too much confidence in them. This naïveté was always associated with an inner infantilism; on the one hand there was an extreme purity and, on the other, an inability to accept the life of a grown woman on a daily basis. In this infantilism she remained tied to her family, especially to her mother. Her mother's love embraced her so strongly that it led to some anguish. She wrote to her in 1934:

Dear Mime . . . I had a strange dream this morning. I dreamt that you told me: I love you too much, I cannot love anyone else. It was dreadfully sad.[5]

André says: "In some ways my mother had a possessive character and, except for those times when she felt the necessity of an essential duty, my sister always did her best to maintain in my mother the illusion that she belonged to her as one of her possessions. This certainly produced a tension for her; along with her many other tensions, it finally led to her death."[6]

The contrast between her desire to reach the truth by way of a will directed by thought and her aspiration for earthly happiness (should she choose her "vocation" or a "happy life"?)[7] was evident in the clear "hostile relationship" Simone had with her own body. At a particular point she began not to inhabit it any longer (we should recall, on the other hand, those photographs from Baden-Baden), to consider it unfit for communication with others and unacceptable to them. So she erased herself from her friends' sight and did not want to impose upon them. She could enter in real contact with them only rarely; her wavelength was too strong.

She writes to Thibon from Casablanca:

I am not a person with whom it would be good to link one's own destiny. Human beings have always more or less realized this.[8]

At the same time, she reached out passionately to others. She most often failed in this reaching out because of her excessive need and her failure to appreciate the relative and the ordinary; it also collided with her *fear of devouring*, a fear that is to a great degree at the root of her lasting anorexia. This fear coincided with her fear of being devoured, of losing her own integrity. Her "proper pride" of this integrity was often misunderstood as haughtiness.

Schumann poses the question, "Lost, or better put, wandering on the height of the mountain, did she perhaps try to be Christ rather than to find Christ? Is this perhaps the secret that makes it impossible to distinguish her pride from her humility?"[9]

She did not want to be either a determinist or someone determined; so she always defended her integrity as a creature before an official religion, tied to its own orthodoxy, as she had refused, as an individual thinker, to "subordinate herself to the course of history."

The most important thing is "to pardon oneself." She had said this to her friend Pétrement in 1931, and she was echoing Alain. Simone was essentially successful in this, at the center of herself: she accepted herself as a creature in relation to God. It illuminated her life from within and coincides with her *intuition of joy*, "which is not the opposite of sorrow." It is the joy of Easter,

the joy which soars above sorrow and completes it.[10]

She did not succeed in living her faith as she understood it, for she was consumed by a compassion which could not become impersonal, by a sense of her unworthiness and by a fear of devouring God, of deriving too much satisfaction and comfort from it.

For in her manner of accepting the supernatural, all the aspects of her nature fit together.

To begin with her initial orientation, there was a gradual transmutation. The will to control herself became the progressive "capacity of feeding on the light." The Christian virtues, which she had always naturally desired,"[11] flowed together in the complete assent of the *amour inconditionné* (unconditional love).[12] Violent, insubordinate, and powerful in intelligence and acumen as she was, she pointed to the weakness one accepts and the obedience one agrees to as the sole salvation of the soul. May the kingdom of weakness begin: a prelude to it was her own "project," an instance of a fundamental choice of the good. The war, a moment of truth, imposed the choice upon the world. Simone had achieved the passage from action to inaction, or to true action, radiant with beauty.

Her naïveté matured in an ever-more-penetrating purity of heart. Her interpretation of the evils of the world would not have been so acute, nor her remedies so true, without her *confidence in man*, which she expressed in her respect for the human creature.

<hr>

How do others see her life and her religious sensibility?

"A Simone forever dissatisfied," in the relentless rigor with which she conducted discussions. This is how many militants of Le Puy remember her.

For Albertine Thévenon, she carried with herself "a breath of liberty." Her "freedom from conformity was fascinating." And, surely, she owes her extraordinary power of attention, her ability "to discover within the dust of daily life the grain of purity that is there" to all the "unnecessary sufferings" she had ("and which I would have gladly avoided for her"). Her great merit was having united "in total harmony her need for perfection and her life, and she did this before any religious experience." Despite her passage from unbelief to profound religious sensibility, Simone's life thus appears to possess a *"perfect coherence."*

And yet it is much easier to admire her now, in the solitude of one's study, as one reads one of her books, now that "nothing hides her thought," which was then hidden behind the awkward and strange displays of her being exceptional.[13]

Duperray remembers, "After the march of miners, at Saint-Étienne, she had an idea for one of those jokes she thought 'popular.' At a stall she bought wooden caricature pipes for the comrades. They cooperated and put the pipes in their mouths, bowl forward; then they quickly put them in their pockets. Simone never realized that this joke did not please them at all. For those men, smoking was a consecration of their manhood and the pipe a sacred object to be respected by others."[14]

At Carcassonne, in 1942, she paid a visit to her old friends, the Roubauds. She was dressed in sackcloth and her feet were bare in their sandals. Stripped of all bodily concerns, she seemed a medieval saint. "She had aged considerably and carried a child's notebook under her arm. At first she expressed political judgments. She had never declared herself a Jew, she said, because she felt it was her duty. With a sort of childish pride she related tales of her experiences as a grape-picker. Everyone gathered that she had mystical preoccupations." She left an impression of uneasiness.[15]

Her ascetic behavior irritated some people.

Jean Lambert says: "It may very well be that she slept on the floor, even though I do not remember whether there was a bed in her room. She was so hard on herself." L. O., a girl from Marseilles, declares on the other hand: "Yes, she slept on the floor; I remember her room. What was she like? She never gave me the impression of a humble person. For this reason I think that her attitude with regard to baptism was derived from her pride. I found her above all an eccentric. But she had her own truth. I think it is good to know one's own truth and to live it. Those who manage to do so always serve as an example for someone else and for the masses."[16]

Here appears her ability to awaken others.

Lanza del Vasto sees in her "a fervent soul." "After ten minutes with her, and she was the most unattractive girl I have ever known, you no longer saw her appearance but only *her,* that soul. She had the ideal of love as charity; always unquiet, troubled by the ills of others, she died of compassion. I do not know if she was unhappy. She was dramatic, but so full of fervor. She had the strongest intellectual and spiritual satisfactions, she had friendship. She was not attractive and she was not loved the way women like to be, but she did not seem much bothered by the absence of such things. She seemed neither depressed nor desperate to me."[17]

"I used to dread her visits," says Fr. Jacques Loew, then the editorial secretary of the review, *Économie et humanisme,* for which Simone had written an article in 1941 on her experiences as a factory worker. "I dreaded her because I sensed in her a compassion for the unhappy pushed almost beyond the limit of the bearable. I experienced the dogma of the communion of saints. Those visits were a moment of truth for me. In comparison with her, I felt myself miserable. My presence with the stevedores did not have Simone's human and spiritual quality. At the root of the gratitude I feel towards her is the vision of the disparity between what she lived and what I was."[18]

Anne Reynaud, a pupil of hers at Roanne, is also grateful to Simone, who had called her "my beauty." What does Simone represent for Anne?

"Her influence upon me as an adolescent was very much that of *a rationalist.* Then, little by little, this impression was softened or rather transformed across the years and my own human experiences. As I have read her writings, I could see that the personality of my teacher, too, had undergone a profound evolution (if not a revolution), but without any disavowal.

"What have I learned from her? Essentially these things: the Holy Spirit breathes where He wants, Christ can reach the personality apparently most rebellious in structure, and no one should ever be *categorized,* frozen in an attitude or way of thinking. This, too: what may seem a failure can be more important than deceptive brilliance. And finally: the infinitely difficult accord between one's life and thought is attainable, since we find it incarnate in her."

Simone Weil seems to Anne "the antidote to the most grievous ills of our society." In an age when the majority lives in pursuit of money, social success, immediate achievement and power, Simone was indifferent to money, no title made any impression on her, because no title corresponded to the truth, she did not bother in the least about achievement, not even for the success of her students in examinations (although at Roanne in 1934 it was 100 percent). As far as power is concerned, "the anonymous worker she wanted to be, the teacher who was *influential without being overbearing,* the author who wrote for herself without publication, did not have any power in the world other than her radiation, the radiation of her life, her thought, her soul."[19]

Here there is the problem of the modes of her *communication*. Her awkwardness, her harshness, her different wavelength, and the confusion engendered by her being a woman/nonwoman according to the norm interfered with these modes.

Pierre Dantu, who was enthusiastic from their first encounter, "from the strength and clarity of her mind, her simplicity and obvious generosity," described her to a friend. "But you are in love with her," the friend said. It was not at all like that. "My relations with Simone Weil (and this must have been true for other men, too) were on the plane of comradeship and friendship, without the shadow of sentimentalism or amorous friendship, even less of flirtation. It was not that she was ugly or without attraction, but one sensed clearly in her a refusal of such things, as in a nun. Her way of dressing (no working woman of that time would have agreed to go around dressed like that) made one think of a lay religious, determined to align herself with the most wretched." Perhaps it was this way of being together, lively, sincere but after all detached, that influenced Dantu's failure to listen to her. "She had advised me to direct my engineering activity towards research on perfecting machines in relation to the creative freedom of the worker; I should have made contact with her friend Auguste Detoeuf. I did not follow this advice and I much regret it."[20]

For Jacques Redon (Jacquot) there was the problem of language. "For me it was difficult to read *L'Enracinement:* I kept the dictionary always at my side. Further, in the factory, her language was always so *peculiar.*"[21] The motif that speaks most strikingly to him is the abnegation with which Simone lived her convictions.

Abnegation and *coherence* are the two religious traits, in the wide sense, that strike many. As we have seen, one of these is Albertine. Then, Marcelle Ballard: "Her death was in strict rapport with her intransigence, her honesty, the beauty of her soul; it may be said that her death was its most simple and natural expression."[22] De Tarde says: "She never changed. When, at the moment of publication of *Attente de Dieu (Waiting for God)*, Fr. Perrin held a conference in Paris, I was astounded to realize that everyone considered Simone Weil *a Catholic without knowing it. La Pesanteur et la Grace* had been read breathlessly; it corresponded to a mystical and spiritual need of the moment and satisfied it. But Simone was neither a Catholic nor a Cathar. She was attracted by Perrin, a man of considerable fascination and devoid of intransigence. As for God, she already had Him. Her definition of "waiting" was that of the Greek: motionless, without the hope of anything in particular and without anguish at not obtaining it."[23] Simone Pétrement affirms: "The first test of her mystical experience is her life."[24] For Alida de Jager, of the International Workers Movement, the need is to make men aware of Simone without distorting her. There is a danger of that, if she is not considered of the left. "She understood everything; when we were together we were always talking of changing the world. It was after the failure of the Popular Front that she naturally passed or rather, fell naturally into Christianity."[25]

Pierre Honnorat, who proclaimed himself "an official unbeliever" and who had suffered much from loneliness and silence in his relations with his father, found a source of nourishment in Simone. "She alone has given me words of life."[26]

For Marie-Magdeleine Davy, Simone Weil has the stature of a prophet. Because she has *seen*. "She lived in a dimension of such profundity that few beings can reach it. When one lives in such a dimension, time no longer exists; in its place, there is a tapestry, upon which everything can be read, the past, current events and what will happen. She simply knew. *It was the end of wandering*. When I speak of wandering, I mean Adam and Eve, full of fear and condemned to wander without any direction. She understood that Christianity was to be lived internally, that the external does not count. All values can then be attained, even those involving one's country and the world."[27]

According to Perrin, "everything in her has a relationship with Christianity." She reproposes truths "heard from the beginning," she repeats them with her genius, and she lives them with her profundity and force. At the center, perhaps, is her "doctrine of attention, whether one turns to facts, to ideas or to persons." Very important is her conception of the duty of sanctity. It is an appeal launched to "all Christians": to scholars, especially those studying the history of religion; to statesmen, called to construct the new world; to technicians, who must find in this sanctity the meaning of man and of their responsibilities in regard to the civilization they must preserve and promote . . . "Sanctity for *everyone*, to which nothing human or divine is foreign, so as to communicate a well-being, an ease, which makes one feel at ease with God."[28]

For Gustave Thibon, it is important to grasp the real range of the criticism Simone Weil leveled at the "miseries of the Church," in her aspect as a "proud and aggressive clan"; the Church which had been "betrayed by the mirage of the temporal" and "menaced by shipwreck in the social area." It is true that the Church not only "is made of men but is made also *for* men" and that Simone, instead of making level the paths of God, turns them into unscalable ascents, "unmanageable" by human weakness. But we must "elevate the debate" and consider Simone Weil no longer from the sole perspective of her relations with Catholicism and her failed conversion but "in the timeless clime where dwells her supreme inspiration." The "philosophical cleansing of the Catholic religion," which Simone looked forward to (or "psychological and moral," as Thibon would define it), began when Jesus expelled the merchants from the temple. "In forms more or less subtle we are all merchants of the temple," we all bargain with heaven. The whip of Simone recalls us to order or to our nothingness, and to the unconditioned love of God. This is "the most positive part of her message, that which invites us to the exalted regions where there no longer are heresies, because there, eternal love is wed to eternal silence."[29]

What is it that removed Simone from our "common threshold"? This is Schumann's question. He gives two answers, or rather "two elements of an answer," insofar as he takes them from Simone herself. The first is biographical, the second is derived from her thought.

Simone could not "accept the God of Saul and David (too much involved in the world and in power). She felt unable to condemn one genocide without repudiating them all, including that of the Amalekites. She looked in vain for a Catholic priest who would disavow this exterminating God. So, strangely but logically, this God was interposed between her and baptism, for the same reasons as those pyres set afire by the too frequent use of the *anathema sit*. Only with the passion of partisanship would one dare to call anti-Semitism in Simone Weil what she considers her right: "the right to utter rebellion against an inferno invented by man." And yet, once it is "understood that the God of Simone is not in the first place He who created the world but He whom the world crucified, we are forced to follow her along a path whose end we may never see."

Shortly before her death, she wrote (or said) to a friend: "You, too, like me, are a piece badly cut off of God; but I shall soon be united and reattached." This is the kernel of the "great disagreement" that rends the soul of the believer. Is man an "emanation of God" or a "detached creature of God," capable of free choice even against Him? Simone chooses a third way, already pursued by others, but not to the same conclusion. She creates "a sublime and subversive myth." So that men would be free to love Him and themselves, God did not create beings outside Himself but made Himself part of them, as He "emptied Himself of His divinity." So, on our part, "the renunciation" of being, "the decreation" is the only way of refinding our union with God.[30]

Angelo Giuseppi Roncalli, then apostolic nuncio in Paris, was a friend of Maurice Schumann. Schumann says: "I spent many hours in his library; we would look for books together. With that familiarity that is common to Italians, he soon asked me about Simone. 'Tell me about her! Tell me about her!'" He read *La Pesanteur et la Grace* as soon as it appeared in 1947, then *L'Enracinement* and *Attente de Dieu*, and *La Connaissance Surnaturelle*. The "Prologue," which reminded him of *The Dark Night* of St. John of the Cross, made a great impression on him. He read it aloud and exclaimed, "O yes, I love this soul!"[31]

=====

There are not two facts; there is only one. Simone Weil is a *genius-woman*. She is a moral genius in the orbit of ethics, a genius of immense revolutionary range. By reviving the inward quest of man in history, she has discovered the key to a wisdom which can be applied to the daily life of every man on both the individual and the social plane.

She is a woman inasmuch as she has all the feminine characteristics of spiritual fruitfulness: the importance of nurturing, of tending, of protecting in accord with the physiological exigencies of beings, vicissitudes and things; attention to preservation, healing and use; the prevalence of weakness over force; the importance of words, of language that communicates; the significance of participation and warmth in relation to sensibility, in the way one lives, works, studies and teaches; the emphasis placed upon the practical application of wisdom for the greatest possible happiness of man on earth.

These two basic characteristics of her personality find expressive unity in her work. Her contradictions are there reconciled in an equilibrium above the biographical plane of her existence.

From the point of view of the diffusion of her thought and then of her resonance and effectiveness, her being a woman brought her few chances of fulfillment, a very limited audience and unfocused criticism. All of this is due to the limitation of practical circumstances (to which she was always most opposed), to her relation with herself as a woman (inferiority complex), with her mother (which has engendered, together with her indispensable love, a constant tension), with others (difficult rapport), with life (which life to choose?), and to the unconscious attitude of others to her. Especially in the criticisms of her pessimism and her abstractedness, criticisms which have always been directed at her, one must discern in the background a discomfort in the presence of an intelligence they consider unclassifiable because it is secretly associated with their preconceived idea of woman.[32]

On the other hand, had she been a man, she would have communicated better and been more authoritative, but she would have encountered greater hostility and been fought more bitterly. If she had been more necessarily involved in a practical role, Simone would have had to accept compromises or she would have died in the war. On the whole, she would have been less intact and less free. She would not have reached that complete humility, that absolute disinterestedness, that shuffling off of every role by which she succeeded in saying "the pure and simple truth," like the *fools* of Shakespeare.

It is in her way of seeing a woman that she makes you think of a man, a young transparent man, full of energy. Her mythical figure of woman is Violetta of *Venise Sauvée*.

Happy innocence . . . precarious happiness, bound to chance.[33]

She is like apple blossoms. Violetta is happy and young; she awaits the festival and foresees love; she "drinks" her sleep with serenity: she has to be saved, saved by the action of true innocence. True innocence is the purity that stops evil, endures it and redeems it. It is conscious action, it is Jaffier. It is Simone, as she expresses herself in the equilibrium of her work.

At the center of that equilibrium is her *intuition of perfect joy*, which is a comprehension of the meaning of life. In ways more or less conscious, we all search after this comprehension. Restlessness, boredom, cruelty flow from a misguided line of the quest. The meaning of life which Simone communicates to us, which the saints have discovered, is this: knowing that we are nothing and accepting that. As a consequence, saying yes to the good. Our proper orientation is directing ourselves to the good, being sustained by our *attention*.

The authentic and pure values of the true, the beautiful, and the good
in the activity of a human being are produced by way of a single act, a
concentration upon an object in the fullness of one's attention.

Teaching should have no other goal than that of preparing such an
act with the exercise of the faculty of attention.[34]

So to bring to an ever greater life that share of "active truth"[35] that is in
us. Attention expresses an impersonal love towards ourselves and towards
others. It is the principle of equality.

But how are we to leave the impression of the impersonal upon the
collectivity, so that all men may really be respected one by one, soul, mind,
and body? This is the question that echoes throughout *L'Enracinement*.
Simone replies:

On the one hand, love everything without distinction. On the other,
love only the good. A mystery.[36]

This is the inspiration to the response. The response is the key to the
wisdom Simone has left us. Every fact that depends on the will of men is
bound together on the basis of reciprocal duties that men have towards
one another. To be happy in the realm of the human, we cannot deny our
duties, because they correspond to some of the needs of our reality.

Nor can we erase the contradictions, in the first place the opposition
between good and evil. In time, men have used two methods: the "irreligious," which denies the reality of the opposition, and the "idolatrous," in
which the two opposites, good and evil, have no "right of access." Within
this enclosed perimeter, this fortress, are those who are conscious of being
part of the system; they feel unbound by any ethical consideration. This
can happen to a scientist, an artist, a soldier, a priest, a nation, a church, a
party. Our century has tried both methods. The first, based on the principle that "one thing is the same as another," deprived men of their orientation for thought and action, and has caused Europe to fall into *boredom*
since the First World War. If, in periods of prosperity, one escapes
boredom by play, in misfortune the void becomes unbearable and the
whole system is rejected in horror. One then turns to the other, which
gives the sense of illusory power based on a substitute for religion, in
reality "the adoration of social reality under the names of diverse di-
vinities." Being relieved of the choice between good and evil is such a
privilege that many men and women, "having chosen forever" to shut

themselves within the fortress, remain "inflexible before love, friendship, physical suffering and death." Cruelty is the fruit of their inner state. Both methods have brought Europe to tragedy, the first by generating decomposition, the second, totalitarian destruction. Both methods produce *madness,* in the medical sense of the term.

The third method, difficult but not impossible, is mysticism.

> Mysticism is the passage beyond the sphere where good and evil are opposed, and this by way of the union of the soul with the absolute good.[37]

The seed of such a union is found in every soul, which, in its aspiration for the good, is in contact with *the other reality* beyond the sphere.[38]

In fact,

> The true good is beyond conflict—and yet it takes part; the supreme mystery.[39]

Mysticism is contained in the Gospel, which expresses "a conception of life, not a theology."[40] Simone Weil desires with her whole self to offer us a transposition of it that would be suitable to the individual and social life of our own time, in a language of one person to another. She affirms, "Unite all behind Christian aspirations." And she wants to define them "in terms that even an atheist could accept in their entirety. And so that the one who professes Christianity could "break down the watertight compartments, not only among men, but in his own soul."[41]

We should recall:

> I am experiencing, increasingly, a sort of inner certainty that there exists in me a deposit of pure gold to pass on.

She adds:

> Experience and the observation of my contemporaries are forever persuading me more surely that there is no one ready to receive it.[42]

But what about us today? Our only hope is that since the disease is further advanced, it is clearer in showing the road to recovery and the symptoms of its worsening state. Good and evil are engaged with more obvious violence. The thought that recovery is necessary becomes ever more pressing.

Perhaps the moment has come when we can read her, listen to her as she wanted to be listened to, and feed on her. Reading her, furthermore, is like eating good bread when one is really hungry and drinking good water when one is really thirsty. She not only provides knowledge, she provides understanding; she can help us *live*.[43]

No longer determinists and fatalists and subject obscurely to history for what concerns our own actions: this could be one way of beginning *to make history*.

Because

Something mysterious in this universe is an accomplice of those who love only the good.[44]

Awakening such complicities would mean making history increasingly the attempt to put into practice, in all the laws of individual and social life, *the aspiration for the good;* in so doing, we would be following such an aspiration humbly as our guide.

20

Her Testimony

On the admission form to the Grosvenor, the place reserved for *religion* remains blank, at the wish of the patient. She would have said to Dr. Broderick, "I am a philosopher and am interested in humanity." And then she would have told one of the two doctors in charge of the sanatorium, but we are not sure which one, "I am Jewish; but I want to become a Catholic, although there is still a point not settled."[1]

Philosopher, in its proper sense of "a lover of wisdom": perhaps this is the only definition that we can hazard for a woman we cannot define or categorize in her private or public life. Confronting her, we possess no point of reference to a role, a color or an idea. And at the same time, her clearest heritage for every one of us is the task of loyal devotion to everyone's personal calling.

Lonely, she was a tissue of force and vulnerability; the force is that of life, of the sap that both torments and nourishes *The Pear in Flower* of van Gogh. She had decidedly started from the conscious use of the will to arrive at the true; she wished to touch the very nub of reality, to reach the *essential,* because that alone satisfied her. She always had a natural solidarity with the *other reality,* with the place where contraries are one. For this reason, she has listened to the word that echoes in the depths. The pages of the "Prologue" are a chronicle of these conversations: the air was "cold and full of sun."

Simone has set out along the narrow path, towards the Light. She has brought nothing with her. She has never wanted to lean on anything during her life, much less would she want to in the journey of her spirit.

The abbot De Naurois, chaplain of the Free French forces, visited her three times between May and June in Middlesex Hospital.

From the very first visit, Simone Weil appeared "terribly thin, feverish, exhausted."

"She wanted to talk . . . We dealt always with the faith, the Church and Christ, the salvation that is offered even 'to the unbelievers' . . . Her method, if I can call it that since I have underscored the haphazard character of her discourse, exasperated me (even if I am sure that I never let it show). Yet she always remained *in a climate of truth*. The mainspring of her thought was always the passionate Love of living Truth . . . I found her so *humble*, so far from anything that could seem to be intellectual pride, and at the same time so absolutely loyal!"[2]

She knew her own soul, with its shadows and its needs; she respected the uniqueness of her own soul, fashioned for an embodiment and expression which could not be repeated, like the soul of every one of us. For this reason, she did not receive baptism. There remained a point that was not settled. The point related to her two given realities: the requirements of her calling and her compassion for human beings.

> My calling requires me to remain outside the church . . . And this because of the service of God and of the Christian faith in the field of the mind. The level of intellectual honesty required of me, because of my particular calling, demands that my thought be indifferent to all ideas, including, for instance, materialism and atheism.[3]

This duty coincided with her duty towards her own *intellectual creativity*. And the conditions of "intellectual and artistic creativity," which are one and the same, as are those of *moral creation*, "are so intimate and secret a matter that no one can reach them from the outside."[4]

Making these conditions mature in herself meant coming ever closer to bringing reality to light, to expressing "that mute thing" which must be expressed. This is precisely what writing and translating meant for her. Respecting her own creativity was living in obedience to her own calling. The souls which God enters should give *testimony* of His coming through "sensible signs (language, works of art, actions)." Their responsibility is immense.

> The role assigned to them is to testify as do apple trees, as do the stars.[5]

As for *compassion,* she knew well that her vision was dimmed by it. Her contact with the misfortune of others, even those she hardly knew or knew not at all ("perhaps even more so in their case"), even those who had lived long ago, "so shreds my soul that the love of God becomes almost impossible." She wrote this to Perrin in May, 1942. And she added, "I hope that Christ will pardon compassion."[6] She could not reach the level of serene compassion, which coincides with the comprehension of joy.

> I experience a torment that increases remorselessly, both in my mind and in the depths of my heart, because of my inability to consider together, in truth, the misfortune of mankind, the perfection of God and the bond between them.[7]

How could she separate herself from mankind? If she were to feed upon the sacraments as she wished, according to her faith in them as nourishment, she would have separated herself from other men, or even insulted them.

> Given the general and permanent plight of humanity in this world, eating until one is full is an abuse.[8]

And she adds in parentheses "(I have been guilty many times)." Perhaps she was recalling her intellectual repasts, the joys of beauty, the capacity and time for writing as "terrible privileges."

Real communication with other men could only come by way of personal impoverishment. The most necessary virtue to radiate around oneself was spiritual poverty. It had to be embodied in chosen beings who could instill such an inspiration in the masses that they would become "creators of civility." Here her faith in man and her trust in the good (which coincide), were expressed in creative action on the plane of society.

There is no need for sackcloth or convents, signs of separation. These chosen ones should be in the masses and touch them, without any intervening barriers. They should not "allow themselves any compensation" for the misery of their every day, they should sincerely experience their relations with the masses, so as to identify with everyone, to soothe humiliation, to soften harshness, to bind up separation.[9] All of this to reach the unification of mankind in love. "That they may be one."

The church had to change. To increase unity and to save herself along with the whole of mankind.

The church must become like a mother.

The child who, under the eyes of his mother, rebels, disobeys, and acts rashly because he believes that the presence of his mother will protect him from all bad consequences, if he is away from his mother, fears his own freedom.

So, too, the faithful who receive all that they ask for in the spiritual realm would start to fear and to seek refuge in God.[10]

Simone was not baptized. She never asked a priest formally for baptism. Neither baptism nor extreme unction occurred, as one might conclude from her burial in the Catholic section of the New Cemetery. Father Gilligan, the chaplain of the Grosvenor along with Father Miller at the time of Simone Weil's stay, has written that neither baptism nor extreme unction was administered or there would have been a record of this in the registers of the Church of Saint Theresa of the Child Jesus, "as Father Miller was meticulous about such things."[11]

This is what Simone wanted, since she considered it her "duty." *Her nonbaptism was her testimony to the Christian faith.* She explains this in the pages that follow with clarity to herself and loyalty to the Catholic Church.

I believe in God, in the Trinity, in the incarnation, in the redemption, in the Eucharist, in the teachings of the Gospel.

I have said that I believe in these truths, not that I subscribe to them insofar as the Church affirms them, with an affirmation like that made with reference to the data of experience or the theorems of geometry. I adhere to them thanks to my love for truth, perfect, ungraspable, and contained in those mysteries. I try to open my soul to this truth so that I may allow the light to shine in me.

I do not grant the Church any right to limit the operations of the mind or the illuminations of love in the realm of thought.

I grant her instead the mission, as the possessor of the sacraments and the guardian of the sacred texts, of formulating decisions on essential points, but only for the information of the faithful.

I do not grant her the right to impose her comments on the mysteries of faith as being the truth. Even less do I grant her the right to use threats and force, by exercising the power of depriving the faithful of the sacraments, to impose that truth.

For me, in my effort to understand, an apparent or real disagreement with the teaching of the Church is only a reason for the suspension of thought over a good period of time, an invitation to push one's examination, attention and care to the furthest point possible, before affirming anything. But it is everything.

After saying this, I reflect upon every problem concerned with the comparative study of religions, their history, the truth contained in each of them, the connections between religion and the secular forms of research into truth and the whole complex of secular life, the mysterious meaning of the texts and the traditions of Christianity. I reflect upon all of this without any ambition of agreeing or disagreeing with the dogmatic teaching of the Church.

I am aware that I am fallible and that I have been indolent in allowing a mass of evil to live in my soul, where it surely produces a proportional amount of lies and error. So, to a degree, I even doubt the truths that seem obvious and certain.

But this same doubt I apply in equal measure to all my thoughts, to those in agreement as well as in disagreement with the teachings of the Church.

My belief and firm intention is to maintain this attitude until my death.

I am sure that this language does not hide any sin. If I were to think differently, I would commit a sin against my calling, which demands an absolute intellectual honesty.

I cannot discern any human or diabolical cause for this attitude, which can produce only pain, moral discomfort, and isolation.

Above all, pride cannot be its cause, because pride cannot flatter itself in a situation where one seems a pathological case to unbelievers in accepting absurd dogmas without the excuse of social influence; on the other hand, Catholics react with a protective, somewhat disdainful kindness, like the greeting accorded to a newcomer by those who have already reached the goal.

So I do not see any reason why I should reject the belief I have, i.e., that I remain in this attitude in obedience to God, and that if I were to change, I would offend God, I would offend Christ, who has said, "I am the truth."

On the other hand, I have, for a long time now, experienced an intense and ever-mounting desire for Communion.

If the sacraments are considered a good and if I so consider them, too, if I desire them and if they are refused to me for no fault of my own, there has to be a grave injustice in all of this.

If I were granted baptism, even though it were known that I persisted in the above-mentioned attitude, a routine of almost seventeen centuries would be broken.

If this rupture is just and desirable, if, especially today, it appears urgent and vital for the salvation of Christianity (and it does so appear to me), then it should happen in a clear and largely visible way, for the welfare of both the Church and the world; it should not be the isolated initiative of a single priest administering baptism in a secret or unknown way.

For this and similar reasons, I have never addressed a formal request for baptism to any priest.

I do not intend to do so even now.

And yet I feel the need, not abstract, but practical, real, and pressing, to know if it would be given me or not, should I request it.

[The Church would have an easy means for achieving salvation for herself and for mankind.

She should recognize that the definitions of councils have no meaning except in relation to their historical circumstances.

These circumstances can be known only by specialists and often not even by them, because of the lack of documents.

So all those *anathema sit* are a part of history and have no present validity.

In fact, they are so considered, because no adult must read the *Manual of the Decisions and Creeds of the Councils* before his baptism. A catechism is not its equivalent, because it does not contain everything that is "of strict faith" and does contain matters that are not.

It is, on the other hand, impossible to discover from asking priests what is and what is not "of strict faith."

It would be sufficient, then, to explain what is more or less put into practice, by proclaiming officially that an acceptance in one's heart of the mysteries of the Trinity, the incarnation, the redemption, the Eucharist, and the revealed character of the New Testament is the only condition for access to the sacraments.

In this case, the Christian faith, without any danger of a tyranny exercised by the Church over men's spirits, could be placed at the center of secular life and of all actions that form it; the faith could then fill everything, absolutely everything, with its light.

Such is the sole path of salvation for the wretched humanity of today.][12]

For the last time, Simone demonstrates her consistency. For the last time, she weds thought with action. This time it occurs in the light of a higher unifying equilibrium: faith.

She must have died between ten and ten-thirty, in her sleep. She appeared very serene.[13]

Notes

Abbreviations

Works of Simone Weil

AdD	Attente de Dieu
CI, CII, CIII	Cahiers, 1, 2, 3
CO	La Condition ouvrière
CS	La connaissance surnaturelle
E	L'Enracinement
EdL	Écrits de Londres et dernières lettres
EHP	Écrits Historiques et Politiques
GtG	Gateway to God
OeL	Oppression et Liberté

Works of Other Authors

Cabaud *Exp*	J. Cabaud, *L'expérience veçue de Simone Weil*
Cabaud *SW*	J. Cabaud, *Simone Weil à New York et à Londres*
Pétrement	S. Pétrement, *La vie de Simone Weil*, 2 vols.
Alain, "Actes"	*Alain, philosophe de la culture et théoricien de la démocratie,* proceedings of the conference, "Vigueur d'Alain, Rigueur de Simone Weil," Cerisy-la-Salle, 21 July–1 August 1974

1 The News

1. From my conversation with Iris Woods, in her house at Ashford, in August, 1975.
2. The newspaper was in error; the lung specialist at the Middlesex Hospital was really named Bennett. Dr. Roberts was the director of the Grosvenor Sanatorium in Ashford.
3. From an account of the coroner's inquest, published in the *Tuesday Express,* Ashford, August 31, 1943, on the first page. Cabaud, *SW,* pp. 90–91.
4. Cabaud, *SW,* p. 89.

5. From my conversation with Mr. Andrews, the superintendent of the cemetery, in August, 1975, at Ashford.

6. The remark appeared in two papers, the *Kent Messenger* of Thursday, September 3, and the *South Eastern Gazette,* Sunday, September 12. Cabaud, *SW,* p. 92.

7. From a conversation between Dr. Broderick and May Mesnet in 1954. Pétrement, 2:516.

8. Dr. Roberts or Dr. Broderick. Pétrement, 2:517.

9. From my conversation with Mr. Frank in August, 1975, at Ashford. He lives on the long avenue that leads to the Grosvenor. The old sanatorium has become a training center for the police.

10. From the conversation between Broderick and Mesnet. Pétrement, 2:516.

11. Cabaud, *SW,* p. 86.

12. Ibid. and Pétrement, 2:516.

13. Letter of Thérèse Closon to Eveline Weil, Simone's sister-in-law, August 27, 1943, Pétrement, 2:516.

14. Ibid.

15. Letter of Simone Weil to her parents, March 1, [1943], *EdL,* p. 231.

16. Letter of Simone Weil to her parents, August 16, 1943, *EdL,* p. 257.

17. Pétrement, 2:519.

2 Loneliness in London

1. Cabaud, *SW,* p. 92.

2. Today, a simple stone of white marble, streaked with grey and slightly raised in the middle, bears the inscription "Simone Weil (1909–1943)". It supports a rectangular plaque of dark green marble, with these verses engraved in Italian: " . . . la mia solitudine/l'altrui dolore ghermiva fino alla morte . . ." (" . . . my solitude/up to death was strangled by the aching of others' sorrow . . .") by an unknown "C. M." Her grave is surrounded with fuchsias, little blue lobelias, and two rose bushes, one of which was ablaze with red roses. An old man of sweet disposition and neat appearance helped me find it; he explained that many visitors come from quite a distance to find the "brave French lady." The woman who cares for the grave is employed by the town government.

3. Pétrement, 2:519.

4. Cabaud, *SW,* p. 39.

5. Pétrement, 2:492.

6. Ibid., 493.

7. Ibid., 452.

8. Testimony recorded by English papers, Cabaud, *SW,* p. 91.

9. From my conversation with Mr. Frank in August, 1975.

10. Pétrement, 2:501.

11. Ibid., 520.

12. From my conversation with Iris Woods in 1975.

13. Pétrement, 2:499.

14. Ibid., 502.

15. Ibid.

16. For Déodat Roché, see chap. 16, n. 110.

17. René Nelli, *Les Cathares* (Paris, 1972), p. 210. Clémence Ramnoux (see chap. 5, n. 4) also interprets her death as an instance of "endura."

18. From my conversation in the summer of 1971 with Madeleine Marcault, a friend of long standing, who died in 1976. She taught Italian in Montpellier. Born a Protestant, she converted to Catholicism. She had the opportunity to know Simone Weil between 1941 and 1942.

19. From my conversation with Albertine Thévenon in September, 1973. See chap. 7, n. 43.

20. From my conversation with Camille Marcoux in September, 1973. See chap. 5, n. 2.

21. From a letter to her parents, July 18, 1943, *EdL*, p. 250.

22. Letter of Simone Weil to Louis Closon, July 26, 1943, cited in Pétrement, 2:507–508.

23. *EdL*, p. 74.

24. *CI*, p. 166.

25. *EdL*, p. 213.

26. *AdD*, p. 37.

27. *EdL*, p. 213.

28. *CI*, p. 202. Italics mine.

29. Letter to her parents, June 15 [1943], *EdL*, p. 244.

30. Letter to her parents, August 4, 1943, beginning, "Darlings," as did all the letters she wrote them from London, *EdL*, p. 255.

31. EdL, p. 256. The italics are the author's.

32. Giovanni Vannucci, *Libertà dello Spirito* (Centro di Studi Ecumenici Giovanni XXIII, Sotto il Monte, 1967), chap. 2, "Le Beatitudini."

3 Infancy and Childhood

1. In the apartment of her parents at 19 boulevard de Strasbourg. The house was destroyed in 1912 for the construction of rue de Metz. Pétrement, 1:20.

2. From my conversation in the summer of 1976 with Raymonde Nathan, a cousin of Simone Weil; she has many vivid memories of Simone until she was fourteen. Raymonde Nathan is presently a psychologist; she teaches at the École des Psychologues Practiciens and practices psychotherapy in the neuropsychiatry section of the Necker Hospital in Paris. Hers is a "cure eleuthérienne" (from the Greek word for freedom); it strives to "develop autonomy and to strengthen the free will" of the individual. It is a new method, which Nathan explains in a sprightly and clear book, *La cure eleuthérienne* (Paris, 1979).

3. Pétrement, 1:16.

4. Interview of Malcolm Muggeridge with André Weil, *GtG*, pp. 152–53.

5. From my interview with Raymonde Nathan.

6. *GtG*, p. 152.

7. From my interview with Raymonde Nathan.

8. From my conversation with Elisa de Jager (Geneva, July, 1977), the daughter of Alida de Jager. Both were close friends of the Weils; on Elisa, see below, chap. 19, n. 25.

9. Pétrement, 1:19.
10. Ibid., 21.
11. *EdL,* p. 248.
12. Pétrement, 1:22.
13. Undated letter (presumably from October, 1913) from Selma Weil, Paris, 37 boulevard Saint-Michel, where the Weils would live until 1929, Pétrement, 1:25.
14. From my first conversation with André Weil, in his house in Paris, September, 1973.
15. Pétrement, 1:24–25.
16. Ibid., 49.
17. Ibid., 41.
18. Ibid.
19. Ebba Olsen, a Dane, had been Raymonde's governess for several years; she stayed for two years in the Weil house; she spent her evenings reading French books with Grandmother Reinherz. She would accompany Simone to school. Pétrement, 1:49.
20. Letter of Selma Weil to Mlle. Chaintreuil, Mayenne, June 26, 1915. Cited in Pétrement, 1:31.
21. Ibid., 24.
22. This is how Mme. Letourneux tells the story.
23. Pétrement, 1:45.
24. "Kisses are dirty," she used to say, according to Mme. Letourneux, the director of the high school at Mayenne, which, transformed into a war hospital, had Dr. Bernard Weil as its medical officer. "It was then that I knew the Weils; Simone was six, André around nine. I gave English lessons to André. I would see them two or three times a week." See also chap. 5, n. 11.
25. Interview of Malcolm Muggeridge with André Weil, *GtG,* p. 148.
26. This is also from Mme. Letourneux.
27. Undated letter of Selma Weil. Pétrement, 1:31.
28. Letter from Selma Weil, November 24, 1917, from Laval, where they had moved from Chartres to be with Dr. Bernard. Pétrement, 1:41.
29. *GtG,* p. 148.
30. Pétrement, 1:38.
31. Ibid., 46.
32. This is Raymonde Nathan's description.
33. Pétrement, 1:53.
34. *AdD,* pp. 38–39.

4 The Birth of a Thinker and a Style

1. It was a stranger who stopped them. "Her parents indignantly rejected the request." Pétrement, 1:52.
2. Interview of Malcolm Muggeridge with André Weil, *GtG,* p. 152.
3. This is Mme. Selma's description of him. Pétrement, 1:56.
4. Ibid.
5. This is how Elisa de Jager describes her.

6. Letter of Selma Weil to Gabrielle Chantreuil, June 21, 1914, Pétrement, 1:67. Mlle. Chantreuil had taught Andre for a year.

7. Letter of Selma Weil to Gabrielle Chaintreuil, June 8, 1916. Pétrement, 1:33.

8. Muggeridge-Weil interview, *GtG*, p. 151.

9. Pétrement, 1:48.

10. Testimony of Mme. Naudet di Tarbes in the review *Liens,* cahiers mensuels des lettres et des arts, Club francais du livre, June 14, 1954, p. 2.

11. Testimony of Anne Reynaud-Guérithault. Cf. chap. 19, n. 19.

12. *GtG,* pp. 149–50.

13. From my conversation with Colette Audry, Paris, 1974. *See* chap. 11, n. 53.

14. Pétrement, 1:50.

15. Ibid., 49.

16. From my conversation with Adèle Dubreuil in Paris in September, 1973. She had been in service with the family of Dr. Bernard since 1930, in the house on rue Auguste Comte, behind the Luxembourg, where the Weils lived after May 1929. Her first memory of Simone comes from 1920, however. She remembers her, at eleven years of age, "banging her fists on the table" with vehemence, to defend her ideas during a family meal at her uncle Isidore's (a step-brother of the doctor). Isidore had been in America "to make his fortune," and supported his niece in the discussion. For Adèle, Simone had "a unique sensibility; with Simone, everything was a matter of enjoyment, both happy things and sad. In the afternoon she would come humming down the hall and into the kitchen, she would talk to me of history and now and then nibble a crust of bread or a lump of sugar. She liked sweets, but she did not like to eat. The only one who succeeded in nourishing her was Mme. Selma, a fine cook. Most of all, she hated meat. When she had to pass in front of a butcher's, she would hold her head down, to keep from seeing." Adèle is tied to the Weils by a bond of affection full of admiration. "You don't find families like that anymore." She showed me a letter from Dr. Bernard, of January 19, 1945, which told her how Simone had died, far away from them and without letting them know of her illness. "I do not know what we shall do in the future; we do not have the heart for any project." And in another letter, undated, Mme. Selma says, "I do not know when we shall be able to see one another. I would like to, but at the same time I am afraid, as I am of the idea of seeing rue Auguste Comte again, where we used to be happy."

17. This is what Camille Marcoux said in our conversation in September, 1973.

18. Pétrement, 1:66–67.

19. Ibid.

20. He got this idea from reading Scandinavian stories; so André Weil wrote me in a letter of September 2, 1976.

21. Marie-Magdeleine Davy, *Simone Weil* (Paris, Editions Universitaire, 1961), p. 13.

22. Cabaud, *Exp.,* p. 33.

23. Pétrement, 1:70.

24. Alain, *Journal* (unpublished), quoted by Pétrement, 1:65; with regard to the nickname, Pétrement adds, "I do not know if Simone was ever aware of it."

25. Alain was the pseudonym of Emile Auguste Chartier (Mortagne, 1868–Paris, 1951). A

student of his, Annette Baslaw, says: "He could have been many things: an engineer, a musician, a painter, a novelist, a poet. He chose to become a professor and devoted his entire life to instruction." He began teaching philosophy at Pontivy, Lorient, Rouen; then, beginning in 1901, with an interruption of four years due to the war, he was in Paris, at the lycée Henri IV and the Collège Sévigné (at first only for women). In 1933, he stopped teaching. He started his career as a publicist with brief articles appearing in the *Dépêche de Rouen*: the "Propos d'un Normand." In fifty lines, he would express his reflections on daily life in an incisive fashion. The propos would become his principal literary genre. This is Simone Pétrement's description (1:115–16) of him as a political figure: "Alain alone, perhaps, represented a radicalism which it is not absurd to call so, inasmuch as a radical like him was truly more violent and caused more scandal than a socialist. Certainly, his liveliest passions were aroused by political developments, from the Dreyfus affair, in which he sided with Dreyfus, to the war of 1914, the great sorrow of his life, in which he enlisted as a volunteer, even though he loathed it. (To share in the common misfortune, and judging that he had to pay that price to continue to think freely.)" The works of Alain, with a preface by André Maurois, are collected under three titles: *Propos 1*, 1956, and *2*, 1970, edited by Maurice Savin, who can be considered his "spiritual son"; *Les Arts et les Dieux*, 1958; and *Les Passions et la Sagesse*, 1960, edited by Georges Bénézé, who was also a student of Alain; (all Bibliothèque de la Pléiade, Gallimard, Paris).

26. From a letter of Edi Copeau to Simone in January, 1926. Pétrement, 1:78.
27. Testimony of Edmée Hatinguais, a former student, in "Alain et l'Enseignement" by Annette Baslaw, quoted in Alain, *Actes,* p. 42.
28. Testimony of André Amar, ibid.
29. From my conversation with Louis Goubert, Paris, July, 1976. Goubert is an impassioned student of Italian art and civilization. He has taught at the lycée Chauteaubriand in Rome and has been the president of the Union des professeurs français d'Italie. A student of Alain, he remained close to him until his death.
30. Pétrement, 1:78.
31. Alain, "Propos du 24 avril 1921," *Actes,* p. 43.
32. Testimony of Samuel de Sacy, *Actes,* p. 41.
33. Alain, *Histoire de mes pensées* (Paris, Gallimard, 1936). See also *Actes,* p. 44.
34. Alain, Propos 77, "Amitié," December 27, 1907, *Propos sur la bonheur* (Paris, Gallimard, 1966), p. 193.
35. Propos 36, "De la vie privée," September 10, 1913, Ibid., p. 96.
36. Propos 37, "Le couple," December 14, 1912, Ibid., pp. 97–99.
37. H. Mondor, *Alain* (Paris, Gallimard, 1953), p. 251. Rather than a true and proper biography, this is a collection of "memories, observations and entertaining notes of the encounter between Alain and Valéry." Gilbert Kahn wrote me this on January 6, 1981.
38. Alain, Propos 36, "De la vie privée," September 10, 1913, *Propos sur la bonheur,* p. 96.
39. Alain, *Morceaux choisis* (Paris, Gallimard, 1960), p. 278. See also *Actes,* p. 34.
40. Alain, "Propos, mai 1934," in *Bulletin of the Association des Amis d'Alain,* no. 13, pp. 38–39. See also *Actes,* p. 37.
41. Pétrement, 1:75.
42. Alain, *Vigiles de l'Esprit* (Paris, Gallimard, 1942), p. 151. See also *Actes,* p. 37.

43. Alain, *Vigiles de l'Esprit*, pp. 35–36. See also *Actes*, p. 45.
44. From the text of Alain, *Les Dieux*, quoted in the contribution of Jeanne Alexandre, "Rencontre de Simone Weil et d'Alain," *Actes*, p. 187. Jeanne and Michel Alexandre had founded, after the First World War, the review *Libres Propos*, so that Alain "could there freely express his opinions on the course of events" (Pétrement, 1:116). The first number of the review appeared at Nîmes on April 9, 1921, from the presses of the Imprimerie-Coopérative "La Laborieuse." At the suggestion of Alain, "free right of reproduction and translation in all countries was granted." In Paris the principal source of distribution was the Picart bookstore, rue Saint-Michel. Its last number was that of September, 1936. The vicissitudes of the review may be read in "Esquisse d'une histoire des Libres Propos," by Jeanne and Michel Alexandre, in *Bulletin of the Association des Amis d'Alain*, no. 25.
45. Alain, *Dialectique des Sentiments* (Paris, 1971), p. 67. See also *Actes*, p. 187.
46. Alain, "Propos du 7 juin 1928," *Actes*, p. 188.
47. Alain, "Propos du 21 juin 1932," *Actes*, p. 188.
48. Alain, *Les Dieux*, quoted in *Actes*, p. 188.
49. Alexandre, "Rencontre," *Actes*, p. 184.
50. Testimony of André Amar, in Annette Baslaw, "Alain et l'Enseignement," *Actes*, p. 44.
51. Pétrement, 1:83.
52. These judgments of Alain on Simone are found in a register preserved at the lycée Henri IV. For the third trimester of the year 1927–28, Alain formulated this judgment: "Excellent student, uncommon intellectual force, wide culture. She will succeed brilliantly, if she does not take dark paths. In any case, she will make herself known." Pétrement, 1:96–97 and 97, n. 1.
53. This and the preceding quotations are in Pétrement, 1:80–82.
54. Ibid., 103.
55. This is the name by which the students of Emile Chartier, alias Alain, were known.
56. Pétrement, 1:104.
57. Ibid., 70.
58. From my conversation with Marie-Magdeleine Davy.
59. Pétrement, 1:141.
60. *See* chapter 18.
61. From the introduction to *Oppression et Liberté* (Paris, Gallimard, 1955), p. 8.

5 The Youth of a Different Kind of Woman

1. Pétrement, 1:65.
2. From my conversation with Camille Marcoux in September, 1973, at Poitiers. Camille Marcoux (1906) came from the humble *cagne* of Poitiers, where he had studied philosophy with a disciple of Alain, the Kantian Georges Bénézé. "I already knew Alain through the *Nouvelle Revue Française*. I was attracted to the atmosphere of the lycée Henri IV, so much more lively than Louis Le Grand, which was quite flat and conformist. But every day I would try to compose a *propos*, to free myself from the excessive fascination of Alain, who would to a degree turn his students into machines. Or one had to be like Bénézé or Simone Weil." He met Simone in 1927 at the competi-

tion for admission to the Normale. He was 21, she 18. That year she was not admitted, but Clémence Ramnoux, who came from the lycée Condorcet, and Simone Pétrement were admitted. "Simone Weil had a key made for me so that I could easily let myself into their *turne*, which was both a dormitory and study, but which the girls seldom used. Thereafter, with some companions, I volunteered to be a guinea pig for some courses in modern mathematics organized by André Weil and his group, the *bourbaki*." Marcoux is not a philosopher but a Hellenist, teaching at a lycée. In the course of time he has had many students who prepared for their competition for the Normale by studying the Greek classics on the basis of the translations made by Simone. (*See* chaps. 12 and 15.)

3. Pétrement, 1:104.

4. From my conversation with Clémence Ramnoux, in the summer of 1976. Clémence Ramnoux was admitted to the Normale in 1927, the same year as Simone Pétrement. Of Simone Weil she says, "I began to discover her in 1931; on the basis of little things, I saw that she wanted to get close to me. For example, one time she came to look me up to congratulate me on how I had conducted a lesson. Then, our careers took different routes." Until 1952, Clémence Ramnoux taught philosophy in the last year of the lycée; then, at the University of Nanterre, she taught courses in the history of religion and on the pre-Socratics, a topic on which she is a specialist. "Presently I am writing; I have written *Heraclitus*." She speaks with both rapidity and self-absorption, in a low voice.

5. Simone de Beauvoir, *Memoires d'une jeune fille rangée,* (Paris, Gallimard, 1973), p. 336.

6. The *première de modes* is a dressmaker to whom is entrusted the direction of a workshop in a designer's establishment. Louis Goubert's mother had also been the top modiste of Caroline Reboux, after the First World War.

7. From my conversations with Marie-Magdeleine Davy and from the book of Marianne Monestier, *Elles étaient cent et mille-femmes dans la resistance* (Paris, Fayard 1972), pp. 202–203.

8. De Beauvoir, p. 336.

9. *CIII,* p. 19.

10. Pétrement, 1:105.

11. I had a conversation with Mme. Letourneux, an elegant and lively nonagenarian, in her well-kept home in Aix-en-Provence, in 1974. Of this period she says, "Simone had become a different person. As a child she had been happy, very gracious, all black ringlets. Now, in her angular face, only her eyes remained very beautiful. She dressed badly, always in the same masculine suit; her pockets were stuffed with tobacco. And she never wanted to have it cleaned. Material life did not exist for her."

12. Pétrement, 1:119–20.

13. Ibid., 105.

14. Ibid., 163.

15. Gavroche is the adolescent urchin of *Les Misérables* of Victor Hugo; he has become the symbol of the rebellious spirit of Paris.

16. Pétrement, 1:162.

17. Alain, "Pensées d'avenir," in *Revue des vivants,* September, 1928; then in *Libres Propos,* n. s., January 20, 1929. This new series of *Libres Propos* was also desired by Jeanne and

Michel Alexandre, in March, 1927 (*see* chap. 4, n. 44). The Alexandres were "deeply devoted to Alain and disposed to fight with ardor for peace. Many *cagneux* or *ex-cagneux* of Henri IV, including Chateau and Ganuchaud, collaborated with this journal. Simone Weil began to write in it a little later, but from the very beginning she wanted to support it with all her powers and formulated the project to collaborate with it." Pétrement, 1:116.

18. Jacques Ganuchaud, "Réflexions sur la pétition des normaliens," in *La Volonté de Paix,* then in *Libres Propos,* n. s., February 20, 1929, p. 90. *See also* Pétrement, 1:130.

19. Bouglé was the assistant director of the Normale. Pétrement, 1:131.

20. Ibid., 132.

21. An interview with Jean-Paul Sartre, in Madelein Chapsal, *Les écrivains en personne,* Paris, Union Generale d'Editions, 1973, pp. 271–72. *Thala* or *tala* means a student who practiced his or her religion, went to Mass; a word of student slang.

22. Pétrement, 1:126.

23. Ibid., 134.

24. Ibid.

25. "She loved the Seine's waterfront with its quais more than any other place." This love had been born in her during the year 1920–21, when, without going to school, she had studied, privately, literature with Mlle. Sapy and mathematics with Mlle. Cotton. Mlle. Sapy lived on the Île Saint-Louis, at the angle of a quai which Simone rebaptized the "quai Sapy." Pétrement, 1:51.

6 The Growth of a Vocation

1. In November, 1920, a small group of men and women of six nations went to a village near Verdun, devastated by the war, and worked hard for five years on its reconstruction. This was the first nucleus of the International Civilian Service, founded by a pacifist Swiss engineer, Pierre Ceresole, with the intention of offering "a fraternal, disinterested labor . . . to affirm that we are men and that no sorrow of a human being is extraneous to us" and to offer "to the young people of the nations that have obligatory military conscription a practical model, that works, of alternative, voluntary service for conscientious objectors." Since then, the organized fields of labor, even those organized by Italians, in the International Civilian Service, have been hundreds and hundreds. Aldo Capitini, *Le tecniche della nonviolenza,* Milan, Feltrinelli, 1967), by permission of the Fondazione Centro Studi Aldo Capitini, Perugia.

2. Pétrement, 1:126.

3. Ibid., 109.

4. Simone Pétrement (1:111) quotes an interview of Jacques Cabaud with Michel Letellier, in 1958.

5. Pétrement, 1:109–110.

6. Letter of Simone to her parents. Pétrement, 1:149.

7. *AdD,* p. 45.

8. *Libres Propos,* n. s., 3rd year, no. 5, Nîmes, May 20, 1929.

9. Pétrement, 1:145.

10. Ibid., 146.

11. *CI*, p. 19.
12. Pétrement, 1:48.
13. Simone Weil will write in this way to Georges Bernanos.
14. From the interview of Malcolm Muggeridge with André Weil, *GtG*, p. 153.
15. Pétrement, 1:115.
16. The draft of Simone's text on the duties of a representative of the people, on white paper, without title, is written in a calligraphy similar to that of her years at the Normale. Pétrement, 1:148.
17. Second letter to Albertine Thévenon, *CO*, p. 23.
18. Jacques Copeau (Paris, 1879–Pernaud-Vergelesse, Bourgogne, 1949). He studied at the lycée Condorcet, where his first comedy was presented, *Brouillard du matin*. He married a Dane and lived for a year in Denmark, where he taught French; on his return he joined André Gide and Jacques Rivière to found the *Nouvelle Revue Francaise*. But his interest always returned to the theater, and in 1913 he wrote an article-manifesto, "Essai de rénovation dramatique: le Théatre du Vieux Colombier," in which he announced that he was taking over the direction of this theater. There he showed in practice the stern principles of his directing in his *Twelfth Night*. Reacting to the general depreciation of the theater, he rigorously reestablished a scale of values; he revived masterpieces of the theater which had been overlooked (Shakespeare, Gogol, Mérimée, Musset . . .). He sought, above all, to bring to light the meaning of a work by means of simplifying the staging, the gestures, and the diction of the actors. After nine years of successes, he left the Vieux Colombier and the school he had founded there to retire in solitude to Bourgogne. He returned regularly to Paris for his sessions of readings (Simone Weil attended them enthusiastically with her mother) and was for a short time associated with the direction of the Comédie Française. He had great influence over the French theater, in the formation of actors like Dullin and Jouvet and in his vision of a national and popular theater, which would be realized later by Jean Vilar. In Italy, he contributed to the prestige of the Maggio Musicale Fiorentino with three important presentations: *The Representation of Saint Uliva* (Cloister of Santa Croce, First Maggio Musicale Fiorentino, 1933—from a text of the sixteenth century, music by Ildebrando Pizzetti, composed and directed on the precise instructions of Copeau, to provide both commentary and atmosphere; *Savonarola* (Piazza della Signoria, 1935, by Rino Alessi); *As You Like It* (Boboli Garden, 1938, by Shakespeare). These presentations were the basis of his feeling that the *plein air* was the only creative space adequate for that *univers théatral* that he looked forward to, "a frank, total and self-sufficient convention." ("La mise en scène", in *Encyclopédie Française*, vol. 17, 1935.)
19. From my conversation with Mother François Copeau (Edi), in the convent of Vanves (1974). Mother François Copeau, sent to Madagascar in April, 1934 with three other religious women for the foundation of the first Benedictine monastery, was mistress of novices for twenty-nine years. "From time to time, Simone wrote me down there, three or four letters. I did not save them." She says it with melancholy. Since 1963 she has been prioress general at Vanves. The convent is not attractive; on the inside it is dark, and it looks like a factory on the outside. In the garden, many large trees have been cut down to their stumps.
20. From an essay written during her time at Henri IV. Pétrement, 1:92–93.

21. Ibid., 93.
22. Ibid., 174.
23. Ibid., 94.
24. *AdD*, p. 36.
25. Free dissertation (topo) on "Le beau et le bon." Pétrement, 1:95.
26. Ibid.
27. Another essay from her time at Henri IV "which clearly shows the sense and the limits of her belief in God." Ibid.
28. Pétrement, 1:173.
29. Ibid., 178.
30. From a letter that Simone Weil wrote to Simone Pétrement (1:179).
31. A letter of Simone Weil to the minister of public instruction, August 10, 1931; dossier of Simone Weil in the Ministry of National Education. Cabaud, *Exp.*, p. 39.
32. Pétrement, 1:179.

7 The Beginning of a Quest

1. Marcel and Yvonne Lecarpentier were the keepers of the lighthouse of Réville from 1936 to 1970. For a long time Mme. Yvonne substituted for her husband, who was busy on the sea. "When we began, there was not even a road to get up here. Only reeds and puddles." The solitude was great. Its consequences are widely visible in the obvious alcoholism of their region.
2. These songs were included in *CI*, new ed., rev. and augmented, 1970, pp. 44–60.
3. All of this conversation comes from two talks I had with Marcel Lecarpentier in September, 1973.
4. Letter of Simone to her parents (they should have received it around the fourth or fifty of November, 1931), Pétrement, 1:198.
5. Article dated January 12, in *Le Memorial*, Le Puy, January 13, 1931. Pétrement, 1:225.
6. *Le Nouvelliste de Lyon*, January 14, 1932. Pétrement, 1:227.
7. *Le Charivari* (a Parisian weekly), January 23, 1932. Pétrement, 1:241.
8. Pétrement, 1:241.
9. An article by Villard in *La Tribune républicaine*, Le Puy, January 14, 1932. Pétrement, 1:228.
10. In the meeting of the council of the Syndicat national des instituteurs of January 14, 1932. Pétrement, 1:230.
11. The article was published in *Le Populaire*, February 8, 1932. Pétrement, 1:232.
12. Letter of Alain to Villard of January 15, 1932. He said: "to begin with, I shall defend her as best I can . . . since it is evident that I will be considered responsible for such gestures of generosity; at least I hope so, and in a certain sense I deserve it, even though more than once since the war, I have yielded to the temptation to stay by the fire and avoid trouble . . . Pass on to her my affectionate thoughts and congratulate that courageous child and ask her to continue laughing at the administration, which is nothing but an old lady." Pétrement, 1:232.
13. The letter appeared in *La Tribune* of January 22, 1932. Pétrement, 1:240.
14. CGTU stands for Confédération Générale du Travail Unitaire.

15. From the article, "Après la mort du Comité des 22" (the twenty-two syndicalists who, in a meeting of November 9, 1930, had published an appeal for syndical unity), in *L'Effort* of January 2, 1932. Pétrement, 1:184.

16. Report by Simone Weil on the intersyndical meeting of November 11, 1931, at Le Puy, published in *L'Effort* of November 21. *L'Effort* was the paper of the Cartel autonome du Bâtiment, at Lyon, which Thévenon had told her of; in her report, Simone said that "the initiative for the meeting had been that of confederated and autonomous militants; she passed over her own role in silence." Pétrement, 1:199–200.

17. Article dated January 12, 1932 in *Le Mémorial*, Le Puy, January 13. Pétrement, 1:224.

18. Pétrement, 1:192.

19. From my conversation with Adèle Dubreuil in Paris, September, 1973.

20. Pétrement, 1:190.

21. Letter of Simone to her family, perhaps datable to October 20, 1931; it bears the greeting, "Chf," i.e., "Chère famille." Pétrement, 1:194.

22. Pétrement, 1:192.

23. Claire Claveyrolas, who was a student of Simone Weil at the girls' lycée of Le Puy, gave this description of her in a testimonial to the BBC, intended for the film, *The Life and Death of Simone Weil, Pilgrim of the Absolute*. Coordinated by Malcolm Muggeridge and directed by Vernon Sproxton, the film was presented on April 20, 1973, a Good Friday.

24. From the testimonials of four students, C. Claveyrolas, S. Faure, Y. Argaud, M. Dérieu, "Simone Weil professeur," published in *Foi et education*, May, 1951, pp. 170–73 and quoted in Pétrement, 1:186.

25. Idem, Pétrement, 1:219.

26. Idem, Pétrement, 1:187.

27. Dossier of Simone Weil at the Ministry of National Education. Cabaud, *Exp.*, p. 80.

28. Marie-Magdeleine Davy, *Simone Weil* (Paris, Editions Universitaires, 1961), p. 14.

29. Preface by Albertine Thévenon, *CO*, p. 8.

30. Letter of Simone to her family, the end of October, 1931, Pétrement, 1:197.

31. Pétrement, 1:188.

32. "La vie syndicale: en marge du Comité d'études," *L'Effort*, December 19, 1931. Pétrement, 1:201–202.

33. Article on the visit to the mine published in *L'Effort* of March 19, 1932. Pétrement, 1:258–59.

34. Pétrement, 1:260.

35. Article of January 30, 1932, in *L'Effort*, with the title "Les modes d'exploitation," which bore at its end the notation, "to be continued." No article with the same title followed. Probably, "the continuation is found in *Le capital et l'ouvrier*, and one can also link with it the article on her visit to the mine." Pétrement, 1:260.

36. Cabaud, *Exp.*, p. 95. The italics are Simone's.

37. Ibid., p. 48.

38. Simone Weil, *Sur la science* (Paris, Gallimard, 1966), pp. 103–104; a letter of the summer of 1932, in which Simone responded to the inquiry of a scientific journal on the usefulness of the historical approach to teaching science.

39. This happened during the course of the Groupe d'éducation sociale, of rue Falguière.

For the conference on feminism, Simone asked Jeanne Alexandre to hold it. Pétrement, 1:118.

40. From "L'enseignement des mathematiques," in Simone Weil, *Sur la science*, p. 109. The text, presumably written in the summer of 1932, was intended for some comrades; in it she refers again to her experiences in Le Puy.

41. Letter of Selma Weil to her husband, March 4, 1932. Pétrement, 1:257.

42. Cabaud, *Exp.*, p. 65.

43. From my conversation with Albertine Thévenon at Saint-Étienne in September 1973. After that first encounter-invasion, a deep relationship developed between Simone and the Thévenons. Albertine recalls: "Simone and Urbain would talk for nights on end. I, who had been married before I was twenty and already had two small children, a teacher and the wife of a militant (and that was enough!), did not have the physical resilience to join them. Then, too, with her there were no evasions; you had to pay absolute attention. But if with my husband there was a joint militancy in projects and discussions, between her and me there was an equal way of understanding things on the level of sensibility, from which there grew, without effort, a communion that I have shared with no one else."

44. Jean Duperray, "Quand Simone Weil passa chez nous," cited as unpublished in Cabaud, *Exp.*, p. 48. *See* notes 46 and 47.

45. *CIII*, p. 67.

46. Jean Duperray, "Quand Simone Weil passa chez nous," *Les Lettres nouvelles* [pt. 2], June-July-August, 1964, pp. 125–26.

47. Jean Duperray, "Quand Simone Weil passa chez nous," in *Les Lettres nouvelles* [pt. 1], April-May, 1964, pp. 96–98.

8 The First Test: The Situation in Germany

1. *CI*, p. 14.

2. Pétrement, 1:277.

3. Letter to the Thévenons, "definitely" from the second half of July, 1932. Pétrement, 1:277.

4. Letters to her parents from Berlin, where she lived with a working-class family. Pétrement, 1:279–81.

5. We find a startling confirmation of this Weilian interpretation of the German reality in the film of Leni Riefensthal, *The Triumph of the Will*, a documentary on the National Socialist Congress at Nuremberg, September 5, 1934. The circumstances are related in all their particulars in a strictly chronological sequence. Their continual transformation by images intended to sublimate them (the shadow of Hitler's airplane, protectively hovering over the old city; the hand of the Fuehrer, which seems to glide in saluting the crowds; the references to the sky, the clouds, the semidivine youths who, in a halo of light and elation, appear in the foreground to pronounce their names and their places of origin, Hans, Peter, Wolfgang . . . Swabia, Prussia, Saxony: the Fuehrer grasps their hands along with the border of the flag) makes their meaning precise and allows us to understand the thirst for myth that animated the Germans and how this thirst was employed and assuaged by Hitler.

6. This and the preceding quotations are taken from "L'Allemagne en attente" (1932) and "La situation en Allemagne" (1932–33), *Écrits historiques et politiques*, pp. 126–42 and pp. 144–94. The first essay was published in *La Révolution Proletarienne*, no. 138, October 1932 and in *Libres Propos*, n. s., nos. 10 and 11, October 25 and November 25, 1932. The second essay appeared as ten articles in *L'École émancipée*, between December 4, 1932 and March 5, 1933 (23rd year, nos. 10, 12, 15, 16, 18–23); their order of appearance has been preserved in *EHP*.

7. Letter of Simone to the Thévenons, written after her arrival in Auxerre, in September, 1932, quoted in an article by Urbain Thévenon, "Une étape dans la vie de Simone Weil," which appeared in *La Révolution Proletarienne*, no. 362, n. s. no. 61, May, 1952, pp. 16–160.

8. This is Albertine Thévenon's assertion on a program dedicated to Simone Weil by French television, April 18, 1969.

9. Duperray, "Quand Simone Weil passa chez nous," pt. 1, pp. 88–91. Albertine Thévenon remarks, "We formed a small united group, the two of us, Jean Duperray, Gustave Claveyrolas which was very well disposed to Simone . . . The syndicalist movement was a fraternal movement; at first, in her view, camaraderie prevailed, then they were all fascinated by the vastness of her extraordinary intelligence."

10. MOR stands for Minorité oppositionnelle révolutionnaire; within the Fédération unitaire de l'Enseignement, MOR was composed of those who belonged to the Communist party, or at least those who in fact subordinated their syndicalist action to the directives of the Communist party.

11. *See* n. 7. The italics are in Simone's letter.

12. Pétrement, 1:306.

13. Ibid., 316–17.

14. Ibid., 318.

15. Simone Weil, "Quelques remarques sur la réponse de la MOR," *L'École émancipée*, May 7, 1933. *See EHP*, pp. 197–202.

16. A fragment of a letter to someone who remains unknown, which can be dated at the end of January, 1933. Pétrement, 1:307.

9 The Heretic

1. Letter from Simone to the Thévenons, shortly after her arrival in Auxerre in September, 1932, quoted in Thévenon, "Une étape," pp. 13–18.

2. Ibid.; italics hers.

3. Ibid.; italics hers.

4. Pétrement, 1:321.

5. Unpublished article by J. Rabaut, "Simone Weil et la IVème Internationale," quoted by Pétrement, 1:322.

6. Ibid., 323.

7. Fédération unitaire d'Enseignement.

8. "Réflexions concernant la technocratie, le national-socialisme, l'URSS et quelques autres points," in *OeL*, pp. 39–43.

9. From the report of Ferdinand Charbit on the Congress, *La Révolution Prolétarienne,* October 10, 1933. See also Pétrement, 1:357.

10. "Réflexions," p. 40.

11. This and all the preceding quotations are drawn from "Perspectives. Allons-nous vers la révolution prolétarienne?" *OeL,* pp. 11–38.

12. From an article by Jean Rabaut, *L'Âge nouveau,* no. 61, May, 1951, p. 20. Pétrement, 1:353. Boris Souvarine began his life as a militant socialist at a very young age during the First World War. Afterwards, he was a Leninist and a champion of the International. He broke with the USSR around 1925, shortly after the death of Lenin, and thereafter with the Trotskyites, too. How did he meet Simone? He was struck by an article of hers on Germany and sought to meet her to get her to collaborate with him on his review, *La Critique Sociale.* Colette Audry says: "In 1933, Simone Weil was very closely associated with Souvarine and his group; for Souvarine she had an intellectual passion." Simone followed with interest the biography of Stalin which Souvarine was writing between 1930 and 1935. It was published for the first time in 1940 and reprinted in 1977. It gives an extraordinarily complete picture, for that time, of the Russian regime, and anticipates many of the explicit declarations we would later receive in the writings of Solzhenitsyn and Medvedev as well as the report of Khrushchev.

13. Letter of Roger Hagnauer, *La Révolution Prolétarienne,* September 25, 1933. *See also* Pétrement, 1:354.

14. *CO,* p. 170.

15. *CI,* p. 143.

16. A little work of October 13, 1933, "La Quatrième Internationale et l'URSS," Pétrement, 1:355.

17. A. Patri, "La personne et la pensée de Simone Weil," *La table ronde,* February, 1948, pp. 312–21. A teacher of philosophy, since 1929 a disciple of Jean Wahl, Aimé Patri knew Simone Weil, especially between 1930 and 1933. "She was madly altruistic," he says of her.

18. *Leçons de philosophie de Simone Weil* (Roanne, 1933–34), (Paris, Plon, 1959), p. 250.

19. Jacques de Kadt, "Chez Simone Weil: rupture avec Trotski," *Le Contrat Social* (Institut d'Histoire Sociale, Paris) 11 (May–June, 1967): 141–45. The article, dated June, 1964, has an introduction by Boris Souvarine.

20. Information on the monthly review, *Libération,* can be found in Aldo Capitini, *Le tecniche.* Presently *Libération* is printed in New York.

21. Among the Weils, Trotsky had the nickname of "Papa."

22. A letter of Simone to her mother of October, 1933. Pétrement, 1:383.

23. De Kadt, p. 141n.

24. Natalia Ivanovna Sedova says: "The papers announced the discovery of a clandestine revolutionary cell in Barbizon; they even spoke of a clandestine press! Gone was our tranquility. For a few days we would hide in Paris (this was at the end of 1933)." Quoted in Victor Serge, *Vie et mort de Leon Trotski* (Paris, Maspero, 1973), 2:49.

25. Pétrement, 1:384. This observation is confirmed by other friends of Simone, including Edoardo Volterra.

26. Ibid. This is Boris Souvarine's description of the scene: "Natalia Sedova and Mme. Weil were in the parlor, but they still heard the sounds of a lively argument coming from Simone's room. They were discussing Kronstadt . . . Natalia said to Mme. Weil, "How that girl is not cowed by Trotsky!" On leaving her room, Trotsky delivered the final blow, "You belong to the Salvation Army!" Simone, unperturbed, was not the sort of "man" to be dismayed by something like that." (de Kadt, p. 140.)

27. Letter of Simone to her parents, Pétrement, 1:199.

28. Ibid., 268.

29. From my conversation with André Weil, September, 1973, Paris.

30. The SAP (Sozialistische Arbeiter Partei) was a dissident splinter group of the Social-Democratic Party, to its left.

31. Pétrement, 1:397.

32. Cabaud, *Exp.*, p. 94.

33. Souvarine writes: Simone Weil belonged "to the small Cercle communiste démocratique which published irregularly a *Bulletin communiste* and then *La Critique Sociale* . . . in 1932, when the men for whom she felt admiration and with whom she felt solidarity were all outside the tamed "party," which had betrayed its own origins and denied its own reason for being (de Kadt, p. 139).

34. Pétrement, 1:422. Simone Pétrement does not specify the period in which Simone Weil showed her disagreement with the Cercle communiste démocratique, with which "she had never explicitly associated herself. At any rate it was before the disappearance of *La Critique Sociale*."

35. Bataille's review of Malraux's *La Condition Humaine* (which won the Prix Goncourt in 1933) appeared in *La Critique Sociale,* November, 1933. Bataille emphasized "the unusual negative aspect" which the revolution assumed in the book and emphasized that for revolutionaries "the value of the revolution is associated with the value of catastrophe and death." Pétrement, 1:425.

36. The article by Simone Weil, which criticized both Malraux and Bataille, was not published in *La Critique Sociale.* "It was perhaps the time when the review ceased publication." Pétrement, 1:425.

37. Ibid., 401.

10 The Completion of the Design

1. Pétrement, 1:412. "Marcel Martinet was a poet; although he had no political roles, he was known as a man of the left." Simone Pétrement wrote these words in a letter to me, September 12, 1978.

2. Simone Weil had confided this personally to her friend Pétrement, who says, "It was a confidence to inspire terror, knowing her almost inhuman energy and the absence of mercy on herself." Pétrement, 1:413.

3. Ibid.

4. Adèle Dubreuil recalls, "There was a meal in honor of a patron, Detoeuf; Simone Weil had put on a white blouse which suited her very well." Between Auguste Detoeuf, who called himself "a philosopher of the countryside," and Simone, a great

friendship developed. There was "a fundamental affinity" between them, despite their often violent discussions; Simone was "very absolute in her affirmations." This is how Detoeuf's son, Jean-François, then an adolescent, remembers the relationship. Simone gave him lessons in Greek. In one of her letters Simone speaks of Detoeuf as "a free spirit and a man of rare goodness." And she adds, "I like him very much." ("Cinque lettere a un studente e una lettera a Bernanos," *Nuovi Argomenti*, Rome, no. 2 [May–June, 1953], p. 98.)

5. From my conversation with Jacques Redon in August, 1976.

6. Albertine Thévenon, Preface, *CO*, p. 12.

7. From my conversation with Albertine Thévenon, September, 1973.

8. From my conversation with Jacques Redon, August, 1976.

9. Third letter to Albertine, *CO*, p. 26.

10. Ibid., pp. 26–27.

11. Letter from Simone to the Thévenons, at the beginning of her life in the factory, late 1934, quoted in Thévenon, "Une étape," pp. 13–18.

12. First letter to Albertine, *CO*, p. 21.

13. Third letter to Albertine, *CO*, p. 27.

14. Ibid., pp. 28–29. For her, "human brotherhood could only exist in misfortune, otherwise the relationship lost its meaning." These are the words of Aimé Patri, and he still is suffering from it. The break between them came in 1934, after her experience in the factory.

15. Except where there are separate indications, this and all the quotations which precede it are taken from *CO*, pp. 45–168 (*Journal d'usine* and *Fragments*, pages written in the period of her life in the factory and the following year). The period of her work in the factory occurs between the following dates: between December 4, 1934, and March 6, 1935, she was employed as a hand at the presses at Alsthom (created by the combination of Alsacienne and Thomson); from April 11 to May 7, 1935 she was a packer at J.-J. Carnaud et Forges de Basse-Indre, in Boulogne-Billancourt; from June 6 to August 23, 1935, she was a skilled worker at Renault. (Cabaud, *Exp.*, pp. 106–113.) Simone Pétrement believes, however, on the basis of information that shows some free time available for Simone, that "perhaps her last day at work was August 9, 1935." All the same, the certificate at the Renault plant was signed on August 23 and bears the above-mentioned dates. Pétrement, 2:49–50.

16. *Journal d'usine*, in *CO*, p. 116.

17. Ibid., p. 119. Mme. Forestier, who worked with her and "sometimes on leaving would walk part of the way with her," would find her literally "crushed" by her exhaustion. From *Cahiers Simone Weil*, Association pour l'étude de la pensée de Simone Weil, vol. 1, no. 3, (December 1978):41.

18. This and all the quotations which precede it, unless otherwise noted, are taken from *CI*, pp. 13–90. The italics are in the text. Simone Pétrement, who was responsible for both the first and the last edition of the *Cahiers*, describes the notebook on p. 9. "This notebook is not numbered. The label which should have borne no. 1 has been partially torn out and on the fragment which remains, Simone Weil wrote this phrase, "This doesn't count."

11 Love

1. *CI*, p. 27. Italics hers.
2. "Lettre à une elève," 1934, *CO*, p. 34.
3. Quoted in Pétrement, 1:55–56.
4. Cabaud, *Exp.*, p. 74.
5. Ibid., p. 121.
6. Pétrement, 1:393.
7. Ibid., p. 68.
8. From my conversation with Camille Marcoux in 1973.
9. From my conversation with Guillaume de Tarde in 1974.
10. From my conversation with Camille Marcoux in 1973.
11. Letter of Jacques Ganuchaud to Simone Pétrement, March 26, 1960, Pétrement, 1:70.
12. Ibid., p. 58.
13. *CI*, p. 70.
14. Ibid., p. 62. The italics between the quotation marks are in the text.
15. Ibid., p. 13.
16. Ibid., p. 41. Italics hers.
17. Ibid., p. 35.
18. This is an unpublished text in which Simone reflects upon her own character; quoted in Pétrement, 2:13. In *CI*, p. 21, we find, "And insofar as X . . . endure it to the limit for his welfare, not for his sake."
19. *CI*, p. 20.
20. *CI*, p. 81. The italics are in Simone's text.
21. Pétrement, 2:12–14. *See* n. 18.
22. Ibid.
23. Ibid.
24. Ibid., pp. 24–25.
25. Duperray, "Quand Simone Weil passa chez nous," pt. 2, p. 136.
26. Second letter of Simone to Albertine, *CO*, p. 23.
27. Georges Bataille, *L'azzurro del cielo (Le bleu du ciel)*, Italian edition, trans. Oreste del Buono (Turin, Einaudi, 1969), pp. 51–52.
28. Ibid., p. 66.
29. Ibid., p. 52.
30. Ibid., p. 83.
31. Pétrement, 1:351.
32. Bataille, p. 124.
33. Ibid., p. 106.
34. Pétrement, 1:351.
35. Bataille, p. 123.
36. Ibid., p. 133.
37. Ibid., p. 63.
38. Pétrement, 1:349. The mechanism of human vicissitudes greatly interested Simone Weil; I think that it is to this interest that we should attribute her passion for detective

fiction. Mme. Denise-Aimé Azam (cf. chap. 19, n. 31) told me that Simone owned a whole collection of English detective stories (Green Penguins).

39. *CI*, p. 116. As happens frequently, in the *Cahiers* the source of the story is not given. This is also true of other texts which Simone now and then cites as a commentary upon, a confirmation of, or an inspiration of her thought. Where she has been able to, Simone Pétrement has supplied the source in her notes.

40. Pétrement, 2:13, 14. *See* n. 18.

41. *CI*, p. 18. The italics are in Simone's text.

42. Ibid., p. 78.

43. Pétrement, 2:11. *See* n. 18.

44. *CI*, p. 68. Italics hers.

45. Ibid., p. 78.

46. Ibid., p. 73.

47. Pétrement, 1:391.

48. Duperray, "Quand Simone Weil passa chez nous," pt. 2, pp. 130–131.

49. Ibid., p. 128.

50. Jacques Brezolles, *Cet ardent sanglot . . . Pages de mon journal*, Lettre-Préface de Gabriel Marcel (Paris, Beauchesne, 1970), pp. 206–207.

51. From an unpublished text of Simone Weil, "Quelques remarques au sujet du Code pénal français," quoted in Pétrement, 2:266.

52. Pétrement, 2:14. *See* n. 18.

53. Again from the conversation in 1974 with Colette Audry: "I met Simone Weil in 1933; we were together in the Fédération unitaire de l'Enseignement. What most united militants like her and me in that period was the criticism of Stalinism in the context of the struggle for an authentic socialism."

Born in Orange, in the south of France, a teacher of literature and a friend of Jean-Paul Sartre and Simone de Beauvoir, Colette Audry became a member of the Socialist party in 1969 and is currently working as a general delegate in the training of activists. Among her works: *On joue perdant* (Gallimard, 1946, coll. Espoir); *Aux yeux du souvenir 1947, Sartre et la réalité humaine*, Seghers, 1966; *Léon Blum ou la politique du Juste*, Juillard, 1955; *Les militants et leurs morales*, Flammarion, 1976. She has collaborated with *Temps moderns*; since 1964 she has edited the collection Femme, of Denoël, and currently is the editor of the political bulletin, *Synthèse-flash*. She is the author of *Derrière la baignoire* (Paris, Gallimard, 1962).

54. *CO*, p. 112.

55. Ibid., p. 115.

56. Duperray, "Quand Simone Weil passa chez nous," pt. 1, pp. 98–101.

57. Ibid., pt. 2, pp. 135–36.

58. *CI*, p. 67.

59. Ibid., p. 21.

60. Jean Anouilh, *La sauvage, suivi de L'invitation au château* (Paris, coll. Folio, 1976) Act III, pp. 181–82. The remark is by Hartman, who ends the comedy.

61. *CI*, p. 16.

12 The Second Test: The War in Spain

1. *CO*, pp. 92, 102.
2. Cabaud, *Exp.*, p. 123.
3. Ibid., p. 122.
4. From the outline of a disquisition, "On right and force," Pétrement, 2:61.
5. Ibid.
6. From the dossier of Simone Weil at the Ministry of Public Instruction. Cabaud, *Exp.*, p. 130.
7. Cabaud, *Exp.*, p. 130.
8. A letter from Bourges, March 16, 1936, *CO*, p. 215.
9. Ibid.
10. A letter dated Wednesday (June 10, 1936), *CO*, p. 213.
11. From "La vie et la grève des ouvrières métallos (sur le tas)," *CO*, pp. 219–37. The article appeared in the *Cahiers de Terre Libre*, July 15, 1936, as well as *La Révolution Prolétarienne*, June 10, 1936, with the same pseudonym, Simone Galois.
12. *CO*, pp. 267–87.
13. From "Remarques sur les enseignements à tirer des conflits du Nord," *CO*, p. 277. We cite, to confirm her observations, "the anti-strike revolt," which in August, 1977 involved around 1,500 British Leyland workers against their union, with the slogan, "We want to work." This strike "confirms an elementary truth, which has been known for a time to specialists in the psychology of collective labor. Discontent in offices and factories does not derive solely from economic reasons. At least to the same degree, it depends on the frustration of the workers, who see themselves reduced to the plane of robots, forced to obey the distant decisions of the apparatus, whether of the company or the union." (Report of Renzo Cianfanelli, *Corriere della Sera*, August 28, 1977.)
14. Simone told this to her parents. Pétrement, 2:120.
15. Letter to Georges Bernanos, "Cinque lettere," p. 104.
16. From "Non-intervention géneralisée, *EHP*, pp. 252–53. The article, perhaps not immediately published, may date back to the first months of 1937. Pétrement, 2:114.
17. From "Non-intervention," *EHP*, p. 255.
18. From "Réflexions sur la guerre," in *EHP*, pp. 229–39. The article was published in *La Critique Sociale*, the review of Boris Souvarine, no. 10, November, 1933.
19. *CI*, p. 19.
20. Quoted in Pétrement, 2:94–95.
21. POUM stands for Partido obrero de unificación marxista. Colette Audry comments: "In 1936 I was working in Barcelona, in the POUM. I had gotten down there through the anarchists of Perpignan. We went in a group to see Durruti on the front at Aragon, near the Ebro. Simone Weil was there."
22. CNT stands for Confederación nacional del Trabajo.
23. Buenaventura Durruti (Léon, 1896–Madrid, 1936). A metal worker from a very large family (seven brothers and a sister), the son of a railway worker, Durruti had been an active revolutionary since his adolescence; he was persecuted, imprisoned, exiled, deported, the leader of the liberation of Barcelona on July 19, 1936, and finally, the commander of the legendary anarchist column on the front at Aragon. Of him, Hans

Magnus Enzensberger writes, in *The Short Summer of Anarchy* trans. Renato Pedio (Milan, Feltrinelli, 1973): "The story of Durruti is to be understood . . . not as a biography that collects the facts and even less as a scientific project. Its narrative scope exceeds the depiction of a single individual . . . He defines himself through the very struggle he has waged; this is what determines his social climate, which in turn colors everything he has done, expressed, or undertaken." He died in Madrid in November, 1936, in circumstances that have never been clear. "His grave is on the outskirts of Barcelona, in the shadow of a factory. On a bare stone there are always some flowers . . . Only if you look closely can you read what some unknown person has scratched, with a pocket-knife, in awkward letters: the name Durruti on the stone." One last testimonial: "It was unbelievable, but he owned nothing, nothing, absolutely nothing. Everything he had belonged to everyone. When he died, I tried to find a suit to bury him in. At length we found an old leather jacket, completely worn out, a pair of khaki slacks, and a pair of perforated shoes . . . he was a man who gave away everything . . . In Durruti's bag, the following effects were found: a change of underwear, two pistols, a pair of binoculars, and a pair of sunglasses. That was the whole inventory." Enzensberger, pp. 12–13, 253, 270–71.

24. *EHP*, pp. 209–16.

25. Pétrement, 2:105.

26. We are in 1938. Hardly had the book been published by Plon when it provoked violent polemics. A Catholic, monarchist, and initially a sympathizer with those supporting Franco, Georges Bernanos, in *Les grands cimetières sous la lune*, condemned the murderous madness associated with the regime of terror established by the Fascists on Majorca. Living on the island since 1936 (it was there that he wrote his *Journal d'un curé de campagne*) he expressed himself with passion, as both a witness and a judge.

27. Letter to George Bernanos," "Cinque lettere," pp. 104–109. Also *EHP*, pp. 20–224. With reference to this letter, Ignazio Silone wrote, "It would be difficult to cite a testimony more pure and disinterested and a situation more exemplary" (*Uscita di Sicurezza* [Milan, Longanesi, 1971], p. 147).

28. *CI*, p. 141.

29. Ibid.

30. Ibid., p. 189.

31. The question was the last of ten in a "Questionnaire à propos des récents événements internationaux," published on March 20, 1936 by Alain in *Vigilance*, the bulletin of the Comité de vigilance of the anti-fascist intellectuals, no. 34. Simone Pétrement (2:82) holds that "perhaps" Simone sent *Vigilance* her reply, later published with the title "Réponse a une question d'Alain," in *EHP*, pp. 244–47 and, in a variant form, pp. 394–97.

32. From *Nouveaux Cahiers*, 1, nos. 2–3, April 1–15, 1937. In *EHP*, pp. 256–72.

33. From my first conversation in Paris, in 1974, with Guillaume de Tarde. A very tall man, with a fine noble head, this Gascon gentleman is, incredibly, over ninety. Of a legal and literary background, he was part of the Conseil d'État. He directed the project for forming the *Nouveaux Cahiers;* the group had already been in existence for a number of years and periodically met for meals with a manager, Ernest Mercier. The lively interest shown by Auguste Detoeuf for that group gave form to the initiative.

34. On the commission for the reform of instruction, see chap. 14.

35. From my conversation in France in 1974 with Denis de Rougemont (Neuchatel, 1906). A Swiss writer of the French language, he founded in 1951 the Centre Européen de la culture, which he directed in Geneva until his death. In 1938, immersed in the climate of the *Nouveaux Cahiers,* he wrote, "in three months," *L'amour et l'occident,* which has since then known mounting success. Committed to the "defense of the whole man against everything that tends to mechanize him, to disqualify him, to strip him of all spiritual and creative energy," (*Journal d'une époque 1926–1946,* [Paris, 1968], p. 94), de Rougemont affirms that it is his ambition "to aid the reader to deepen what is alive, to assume responsibility, to get control of himself" (from an interview with Liana Milella, *Euro,* 2, no. 2, February 1979).

    In collaboration with the Cadmos Group (composed of thirty members from nine West European countries, philosophers, economists, ecologists, political scientists, sociologists), de Rougemont was the author of the *Report to the European people on the state of the union of Europe,* published simultaneously in 1979 in five languages.

36. From my conversation with Pierre Bost in 1974, in Paris. A man of letters and of the stage, learned and sensible, he preferred, among his nine brothers and sisters, the youngest, Jacques-Laurent Bost; increasingly over time he shared his interests and his milieu (that of Sartre and Simone de Beauvoir). He died in 1975.

37. This was the explanation of Guillaume de Tarde, in 1974.

38. From "Ne recommençons pas la guerre de Troie," *EHP,* pp. 256–72.

39. This is the explanation given by Simone Pétrement in a letter to me, January 12, 1978.

40. From "Le sang coulé en Tunisie," *EHP,* pp. 336–38. The article appeared for the first time in *Feuilles Libres,* March, 1937.

41. Several drafts or copies of these letters, "surely intended" for Belin, have been found. Belin was, with Jouhaux, the leader of the CGT. This quotation comes from the longest and most carefully written one ("at least five drafts,") where Simone Weil confutes Belin's opinions on foreign policy and national defense. Pétrement, 2:133.

42. Ibid., p. 134.

43. This is the conclusion of the last of the five drafts of the letter to Belin (*see* n. 41).

13 Italy, or Beauty

1. Pétrement, 2:80–82.

2. Simone was referring to her parents' desire to go to Madonna di Campiglio. Pétrement, 2:199.

3. "Cinque lettere," pp. 80–103. Simone had met Jean Posternak, then a medical student, at the Moubra clinic, where he, too, was a patient. Posternak had a phonograph and some records, among which were the Brandenburg concerti, directed by Busch. Simone would write him later, "listening together—really listening—to the andante of the fourth Brandenburg creates a bond powerful enough to resist time and silence." Posternak knew Italy quite well and gave her much useful information, advice on the Maggio Musicale, and the address of a young Roman, the son of a high Fascist functionary. The letters to Posternak from Italy are without any date. They bear only the name of the city.

4. "Cinque lettere," p. 81 (Milan).

5. Ibid., p. 85 (Florence).

6. Ibid., p. 86 (Florence).

7. This refers, presumably, to a letter to her parents. Pétrement, 2:151.

8. "Cinque lettere," p. 90 (Florence).

9. Ibid., p. 93 (Florence).

10. Ibid., p. 98 (Paris, 1937).

11. Ibid., p. 91 (Florence).

12. Ibid., p. 93 (Florence).

13. Ibid., p. 86 (Florence). She adds, "above all the figures of the base (the nude Virgin, the wingless genius that flies aloft)."

14. Ibid., p. 94 (Florence).

15. Letter to her parents (presumably before June 15, 1938), Pétrement, 2:199. While her first trip in Italy took place between April 23 and June 16, 1937, her second trip occurred between May 22 and July 31, 1938. Simone had hardly arrived in Padua when she went to visit the Chapel of the Scrovegni and wrote to her parents that same evening.

16. "Cinque lettere," p. 84 (Florence). She adds: "after an hour or two of contemplation . . . (In those moments it seemed that there could not exist a rational motive for not spending one's whole life in that refectory.)"

17. Ibid., pp. 82–83 (Florence).

18. Pétrement, 2:146.

19. Ibid., p. 148. She is referring especially to her mother, since she remembers that Mme. Selma did not like St. Peter's.

20. "Cinque lettere," p. 86.

21. Ibid. In another letter (p. 89), she says: "Florence has a beauty that D'Annunzio would not succeed in describing, or at least I think so. I am saying this in praise of Florence, for I am far from sharing your fondness for his *Fuoco,* which you recommended that I read in a letter; that manner of understanding art and life makes me shiver."

22. Ibid., pp. 89–90 (Florence).

23. It was the Mass of May 16, 1937, the day after her arrival in Rome. Letter to her parents, in Pétrement, 2:148.

24. "Cinque lettere," p. 94 (Florence).

25. Ibid., p. 81 (Milan).

26. Letter to her parents from Milan, towards the end of April, 1937. Pétrement, 2:143.

27. "Cinque lettere," p. 89 (Florence). She probably attended the opera on June 3, 1937. Pétrement, 2:154.

28. Pétrement, 2:163. André Weil has shown me the "death of Seneca," transcribed by Simone.

29. *EdL,* p. 181.

30. "Cinque lettere," pp. 91–92 (Florence).

31. Letter to her parents, Pétrement, 2:151. To Posternak she wrote: "I almost decided to spend my life—if they admitted women—in the little convent of the Carceri." "Cinque lettere," p. 92.

32. "Cinque lettere," p. 87 (Florence). She attaches to this letter two sonnets to Tommaso

Cavalieri by Michelangelo. "I entertained myself by copying them to get to understand them (they are written in quite a difficult style) . . . They can be a good illustration of the *Phaedrus*." She also sent some verses on St. Francis by Dante to her friend: "seldom in poetry are there verses of such intense beauty as those on poverty: ' . . . dove Maria rimase giuso/Ella con Cristo salse en sulla croce.' "

33. During her first journey in Italy, she had written to Posternak: "Definitely, I believe that this time I shall not go to Venice. Florence and Venice at one time are too much. I do not have a heart free to love Venice, because Florence has taken it." "Cinque lettere," p. 86.

34. "Cinque lettere," p. 100 (Paris, spring 1938).

14 The Encounter

1. "Cinque lettere," p. 95 (Paris, 1937). "For instance, I cannot read the name of Giotto or think of the name of a street in Florence without emotion."

2. Ibid., p. 99 (Paris, 1937). The idea came to her "from intensely contemplating statues in Italy." It is in this same period that she showed her friend Pierre Dantu some small sculptures in clay, "not in the least uninteresting despite her total lack of instruction in this field." (From a testimonial letter which Pierre Dantu sent me on April 24, 1978.)

3. "Méditation sur un cadavre," published posthumously in *EHP*, pp. 324–27.

4. A variant of the same article in *EHP*, pp. 406–407.

5. "Méditation sur l'obéissance et la liberté," *OeL*, pp. 186–93.

6. Pétrement, 1:407.

7. "Méditation sur l'obéissance," p. 192.

8. The article, entitled, "La condition ouvrière," bears the date of September 30, 1937. *CO*, pp. 317–25.

9. This is the commission of study mentioned in chap. 12.

10. Pétrement, 2:181.

11. The words of Messali Hadj, in the broadcast dedicated to Simone Weil by French television, April 16, 1968.

12. Pétrement, 2:176.

13. "Cinque lettere," pp. 100–103 (Paris, spring 1938).

14. Pétrement, 2:186. The appeal appeared in *Feuilles libres de la quinzaine*, March 25, 1938.

15. Letter to Gaston Bergery, *EHP*, pp. 283–89.

16. "Réflexions sur la conférence de Bouché," *EHP*, pp. 279–82. Henri Bouché, a disciple of Alain and a member of the group at the *Nouveaux Cahiers*, had had a public conference on "the French problem of national defense," at the Société de géographie, March 28, 1938. Pétrement, 2:188.

17. Ibid., p. 168.

18. From my conversation with Dom Boissart in Paris, rue de la Source, in 1975. It was Elizabeth Flory-Blondel, the daughter of the philosopher Maurice Blondel (1861–1949), who brought Simone Weil to meet him. "She was a fine woman of thirty-eight years, a good mother; she had lived in a milieu of generous culture. Blondel held many receptions for scientists and philosophers."

19. Charles G. Bell, *The Half Gods* (Boston, Houghton Mifflin, 1968), pp. 296–98. Bell

terms his novel "a work of fiction" which still depends to a great extent upon "fact" and aims at "history." In it Simone Weil is a "necessary symbolic power" for which it was difficult to find an equivalent. And he goes on: "I met her at Solesmes when I was a student abroad, and (as in the novel) it was long after that I discovered the fact." He calls her Heloise Frank and explains that "it would be wrong to search here for any kind of portrait of Simone Weil . . . though I confess I would have wished, in an independent creation and at a distance, to honor one whose memory I revere." (*See The Half Gods,* introduction, pp. vii–viii.)

20. Pétrement, 2:191.
21. It was a letter in English; the draft has been published in Simone Weil, *Seventy Letters,* ed. Richard Rees (London, Oxford University Press, 1965), pp. 102–105.
22. Pétrement, 2:192. Charles G. Bell has written me in this connection, July 7, 1976: "In *The Half Gods,* Leflore, the protagonist, struggles against the disconcerting supposition that he is himself the angel messenger. For the purposes of the novel, at that time I thought that the anomaly to explain was that one . . . it is pleasant to learn that I was in reality the 'devil boy' and that the burden of the angel had to be taken on by another, whom I do not remember."
23. *AdD,* pp. 43–44.
24. *CS,* pp. 9–10.
25. *CI,* p. 264. Framed graphically, here they are: "Reading/dark night/double correlation of contraries/gravity/equilibrium/imagination/unlimited and limit/similarity between what is lowest and what is highest/upheavals/void/vertical hierarchy."
26. *CS,* pp. 9–10. Quoted by kind permission of Editions Gallimard, 1950.

15 Jaffier, or Pity

1. Pétrement, 2:204.
2. "Les nouvelles données du problème colonial dans l'empire français," in *EHP,* pp. 351–56. The article, written after the agreement of Munich, was published in *Essais et combats,* December, 1938.
3. From the synthesis of her presentation on the work of Guillaume de Tarde, *Nouveaux Cahiers,* no. 38, February 1, 1939, p. 20.
4. "Fragment" (1939?), in *EHP,* p. 293.
5. Ibid., p. 295.
6. From my conversation with Charles Flory, whom I was able to meet through Dom Boissart. The husband of Elizabeth Blondel, who died in 1973, Flory was, from around 1930, president of the Jeunesse Catholique. "By way of the *Nouveaux Cahiers* I had a personal relationship with Simone Weil, a relationship which was even closer than my wife's. In reading *La condition ouvrière,* I found again the most telling points of her interventions." He, too, is a philosopher. He has arranged a conference on Blondel in Italy.
7. Pétrement, 2:214.
8. Pétrement, 2:251.
9. Letter of Simone Weil to Edoardo Volterra, the only one left among all those Simone wrote him; the others were lost at the time of his arrest. Published in English in Weil,

Seventy Letters. This is the only collection of letters so far published; it is due to the "tireless assistance of Simone's mother" and of many of her kind correspondents. Written in an "extremely clear" hand, often they are only "accurate" copies or drafts; often they lack a date. The letter to Volterra, presumably written in 1940, is on pp. 127–29 of the collection.

10. Testimony of Edoardo Volterra (Rome 1904–1984), whom I met in December, 1976, in Rome. A university professor of Roman law since 1927, he was pensioned off in 1939 because of the Fascist laws. He then taught in Egypt, at the École française de droit, and in France, Holland and Belgium. He reentered Italy in 1940 and was arrested in 1943 for anti-Fascist activities (he had been one of the founders of the Action Party). After July 25, he participated in the war of liberation as a partisan. He was restored to his position at the University of Bologna in 1945, and for two years he served as rector-in-charge. Called to the University of Rome in 1951, he was a constitutional judge from 1973 until his death.

11. "Réflexions sur la barbarie," in *EHP*, pp. 63–65.

12. This and the preceding quotations, except where noted, are from "Quelques réflexions sur les origines de l'hitlérisme," *EHP*, pp. 11–60. The essay is divided into three parts: 1. "Permanence et changements des caractères nationaux." 2. "Hitler et la politique extérieure de la Rome antique." 3. "Hitler et le régime intérieur de l'Empire romain." The second part was published in *Nouveaux Cahiers*, no. 53, January 1, 1940. The third, already in galleys, was refused by the censors.

13. Pétrement, 2:246.

14. Ibid., p. 217.

15. Ibid., p. 220.

16. The *Bhagavad Gītā* is a Sanskrit poem of eighteen chapters, considered, by reason of its language and spirit, to be of the pre-Buddhist period, i.e., around 500 B.C. It is included in the much longer epic, the *Mahābhārata*, in eighteen books. But, if the central theme of the *Mahābhārata*, the history of a war between the forces of good and evil, has reference to historical events in the dynastic wars between the kings of India, in the *Bhagavad Gītā*, the war has a symbolical meaning. It is the spiritual struggle of the human soul (the hero, Arjuna) that interrogates its god (Krishna), on the reasons for engaging in battle for the governance of a realm, which in reality is the Realm of Heaven. The soul dreads the death of its own passions and of the body; the voice of the Eternal speaks of immortality. Achieving serenity, the soul prepares for action, no longer in time but in another dimension, Eternity, through prayers and silence, as it offers its entire life with love to the God of Love. The soul then has a vision of all things, creation and destruction, immortality and life-death, harmonized in the transcendent One.

17. Pétrement, 2:250.

18. Ibid., p. 269.

19. *CI*, p. 93.

20. Pétrement, 2:273.

21. *Poèmes—suivis de Venise sauvée—Lettre de Paul Valéry*, (Paris, Gallimard, 1968), p. 53.

22. Simone had both texts; unlike the English one, the copy of Saint-Réal has annota-

tions. These notes are found in Andrée Mansau, "Venise sauvée: Simone Weil, auteur de theatre," Association pour l'Étude de la Pensée de Simone Weil, *Bulletin,* no. 7, 1977. This is a study of the Weil manuscripts dealing with this theatrical work.

23. *Venezia salva* (Venise sauvée), trans. and introduction by Cristina Campo (Brescia, 1963), act 2, scene 4, p. 52.

24. Ibid., act 2, scene 6, p. 55.

25. Mansau, "Venise sauvée." This has to do with the first handwritten version in a note-book. Two other typed copies exist among the manuscripts preserved by André Weil; there is also a third version entrusted to Gilbert Kahn; they contain a few variants from the printed text.

26. *Venezia salva,* act 2, scene 6, p. 58.

27. Ibid., act 2, scene 16, p. 78. All the speeches of Jaffier, of which this monologue is the peak, were composed "immediately" by Simone and are "a very personal contribution" to the tragedy, which follows the course of Saint-Réal's story.

28. Ibid., act 2, scene 6, *passim.*

29. Ibid., act 2, scene 16, p. 79.

30. Ibid., introduction by Cristina Campo, p. 12.

31. *Poèmes,* pp. 49 and 104–105.

32. Ibid., p. 19; cf. also *CS,* p. 16.

33. *Poèmes,* p. 48.

34. Ibid., p. 45.

35. Mansau, "Venise sauvée," annotation to the first manuscript version.

36. Pétrement, 2:251.

37. *Poèmes,* p. 45.

38. *Venezia salva,* introduction, p. 15. Here is the entire passage: "Passing from prose to verse according to the 'rhythm of her conscience,' handling the traditional meter [alexandrine, hendecasyllable, a line of nine syllables] with a variety which is constantly imitative, with her timeless diction, which soars over all languages and does not rest in any, Simone Weil seems, upon an accurate examination, to be a poetess of exceptional wisdom."

39. *Poèmes,* p. 55.

40. Fragment of a letter to B. (Boris Souvarine?), found among the pages of the first manuscript version on Jaffier. Mansau, "Venise sauvée."

41. *Venezia salva,* act 2, scene 6, p. 59. With regard to the enthusiasm of Simone Weil for the theater, we cite again what she wrote to Posternak from Paris (1937). "Why do I not have all the existences I would need, to dedicate one of them to the theater?" A great actor, Louis Jouvet, had great "admiration for her, because of their spiritual affinity." "A man of a rich interior life, both in his way of recitation and his conception of the personality and the role of the actor, Jouvet returned repeatedly to the theme of Weil's attention. A precise trace of it remains in his book *Le comédien désincarné* (Paris, 1954), where we read (p. 206), 'Note: Attention; Simone Weil.' And then, certainly, although I do not recall the exact details, in his lessons at the Conservatoire." I was told this in 1974 by Mme. Herlin-Besson, who for years was closely associated with the work of Jouvet.

16 The Truce

1. From the draft of a letter to the Islamicist, Emile Dermenghem, following an article of his on Morocco, which had appeared in *Esprit;* it had particularly struck Simone. Pétrement does not know whether the letter in its final form was ever sent. Pétrement, 2:282.

2. From the draft of a letter of congratulation to a former comrade of the Normale, Hourcade, who was then in service at Lisbon and had made arrangements for Simone to have a visa for Portugal, a stop on the way to Morocco and England. The first two letters were written in the first month after her arrival at Marseilles. Pétrement, 2:283.

3. *CI,* p. 222.

4. After having served as a nurse during the war, Camille Marcoux was now living in Marseilles, where he would remain for twelve years, at the lycée Thiers. He says of meeting Simone again, "She spoke by herself, as though she were soothsaying." In addition to playing the violin and the piano, Marcoux, when I met him, was composing. "Some of my musical phrases definitely have a relationship with the phrases of the *Pesanteur,*" he declares. He becomes pensive and adds, "I speak of her as if with myself, and in speaking of her I am always afraid of diminishing her stature."

5. Letter from Simone to Antonio, April 22, 1941. Pétrement, 2:312.

6. From my conversation in 1976, in Paris, with Jean Lambert (Issoudun, 1914). A son-in-law of Gide, an author (*L'art de la fugue,* 1945; *Les vacances du coeur,* 1951; *Tobiolo,* 1956 . . .), a critic (*Remarques sur l'oeuvre de Jean Schlumberger,* 1942; *Gide familier,* 1958; *Les plaisirs de voir,* 1969 . . .), translator (Hermann Hesse, Thomas Mann, Alfred Hayes, William Humphrey . . .), he already had a relationship of natural intimacy and of attraction with the *Cahiers du Sud,* to which he had sent, on the eve of the war, his first article destined for print, the Gidian pastiche, "Les nourritures célestes." Now, free of military obligations, thanks to the intervention of Jean Ballard, who had passed himself off as his uncle, he had spent a time in the littered attic of the editorial offices, where he had the chance to participate "from his angle as an under-under-undersecretary" in the creation of a journal, which was becoming ever more authoritative. "A product and a symbol of their city, the *Cahiers* were truly a crossroads, where I found the fortunate conjunction of what had the greatest attraction for me, Mediterranean civilizations and the civilization of Europe."

7. With reference to her pseudonym, it was Simone herself who said, "I will sign my name this way, because of my parents." From my conversation with Marcelle Ballard, in September, 1976.

8. From my conversation with Jean Ballard, at his home in Marseilles; from the room there was a view looking out over the port. A wonderful man, sharp and kindly, he met me in March, 1973, a little before his death, which occurred the following June.

9. From my conversation with Jean Tortel, in his home on the edge of the countryside, in September, 1973. Born near Avignon in 1904 (his grandparents were farmers), he was an official in the civil administration at Gordes, Toul and, from 1938, in Marseilles. He has been living in Avignon since 1965. His latest collection of poetry, published by Flammarion (among earlier collections had been *Instants qualifiés,* Gallimard, 1973), is *Les corps attaqués.* What are its secret themes? "Limits, relationships, continuities and

ruptures, transparencies/opaquenesses between bodies attacked by themselves and by language." From 1938 to 1966 he was part of the editorial committee of the *Cahiers du Sud;* those years were for him "a daily source of irreplaceable poetry." Jean Tortel believes that "for many reasons the action caused by the *Cahiers* was important; they awakened many expressions of authorship which would otherwise never have appeared." From a letter he wrote me June 21, 1979.

10. From *Les vacances du coeur,* récits by Jean Lambert (Paris, Gallimard, 1951), p. 233.

11. From my conversation with Jean Lambert. *See* n. 6.

12. Marcelle Ballard has given me a copy of this page of the album, an unpublished document. Together with her husband, Marcelle was fully involved with the life and organization of the *Cahiers du Sud,* for which she was the administrative director. The journal came into being in 1921 at the will of Jean Ballard (by occupation an expert in the office of weights and measures), Marcel Pagnol (a private teacher of English), and Gaston Mouren, three lycée classmates, who had been called to arms as soon as they were old enough and had met again after the war. Called *Fortunio* (a character by De Musset) for five years, in 1925 it became the *Cahiers du Sud.* It ceased publication in December, 1966. On June 6, 1975, the cours du Vieux Port, where the principal entrance of the *Cahiers* faced, was renamed the cours Jean Ballard. In 1971, Robert Stoltz of the Bibliothéconomie of Lièges proposed to Jean and Marcelle Ballard that they agree to edit the essential bibliography of the *Cahiers,* beginning with 1925. "At a certain point my husband said to me, 'Look, here is your Simone.' They were the numbers 230 and 231 of December, 1940 and January, 1941, which contained her article on the *Iliad.*" This is the account given me by Marcelle Ballard.

13. This is what Jean Tortel told me, and he was right. Here is the entirety of strophe 367, in the original text:

Asses plus long, qu'un Siecle Platonique,
Me fut le moys, que sans toy suis esté;
Mais quand ton front je revy pacifique,
Sejour treshault de toute honnesteté,
Ou l'empire est du conseil arresté
Mes songes alors je creux estre devins.
Car en mon corps: mon Ame, tu revins,
Sentant ses mains, mains celestement blanches,
Avec leur bras mortellement divins
L'un coronner mon col, l'aultre mes hanches.

From Maurice Scève, *Oeuvres complètes,* texte établi et annoté par Pascal Quignard (Paris, Mercure de France, 1974), p. 196.

14. *CI,* p. 262.

15. All the "cahiers" of Simone Weil, collected in *Cahiers,* volumes 1, 2, and 3, nouvelle édition, revue et augmentée (Paris, Plon, 1970, 1972, 1974), date from the period of Marseilles, except for the "premier cahier," which seems to have been begun around 1933–34 and continued until the eve of the war (see *CI,* pp. 11–90).

16. *See* chap. 6.

17. Ibid.

18. *See* Chapter 14.
19. Ibid.
20. *CII*, p. 135.
21. Fr. Joseph-Marie Perrin (Troyes, 1905), often incorrectly cited as Jean-Marie. Struck by blindness when he was twelve, he learned braille and had a brilliant career in the lycée. He became a Dominican novice in 1922 and a priest in 1929. He has earned a licentiate in sacred theology. Assigned to the Dominican convent in Marseilles, he fulfilled several ministries: chaplain for women students, preacher during retreats for both the cloistered and the laity, inspirer of groups of ecumenical openness (especially active from 1937 in a Jewish-Christian group of bible study). In 1937, he organized a lay association which has spread to the whole world, thanks to his numerous trips (France, Europe, both of the Americas) and to his pastoral and exegetical activity. In 1942, he was named superior of the convent of Montpellier, where he would remain until the beginning of 1946; in 1943, he was arrested by the Gestapo for his manifold assistance to persons sought by the Nazis, among whom there were numerous Jews. He would continue to do this throughout the period of German occupation, at the risk of his own life. In 1960, he founded a priestly movement upon the special request of priests anxious to enrich together a specific form of spirituality.

    He has written numerous books, articles and essays, among them, *La virginité chrétienne* (Paris, Desclée de Brouwer), *L'heure des laïques* (Paris, La Colombe), and *Aujourd'hui l'Evangiel de l'amour.*
22. The letter of Perrin to Simone Weil was sent June 3, 1941. Pétrement, 2:329.
23. This was her "desire, explicit and repeated during our meetings . . . We spoke of it often and I am a witness . . . " affirms J.-M. Perrin in the preface to *Attente de Dieu* (Paris, Fayard, 1966), p. 5. "Furthermore, Simone Weil loved to express herself by letter." Fr. Perrin told me this in our conversation of 1973 in Aix-en-Provence. This correspondence was seized from him along with his other letters by the Gestapo. It was considered of no interest and left unnoticed until Perrin, upon his release, got it back. "Of the letters, one was missing," he told me.
24. Ibid., p. 11.
25. J.-M. Perrin and G. Thibon, *Simone Weil telle que nous l'avons connue* (Paris, La Colombe, 1952), p. 43.
26. Letter 4, from Marseilles, "15 mai environ," *AdD*, p. 36.
27. From the chapter, "Amitié," in the essay, "Formes de l'Amour Implicite de Dieu," *AdD*, p. 204.
28. From the contribution of Fr. Perrin to the conference of May 28, 1977 at the Sainte-Baume, organized by the Association pour l'étude de la Pensée de Simone Weil. With the title, "Mon dialogue avec Simone Weil," the text has been published in *Cahiers Simone Weil*, the quarterly published by the Association, 1(1) (June, 1978):2–11.
29. Letter 4, *AdD*, p. 51.
30. Letter 4, *AdD*, p. 45.
31. Letter 4, *AdD*, pp. 41–43.
32. From George Herbert (1593–1633), *The Temple*, here is the poem, "Love,"

Love bade me welcome; yet my soul drew back,
Guilty of dust and sin.
But quick-ey'd Love, observing me grow slack
From my first entrance in,
Drew nearer to me, sweetly questioning
If I lack'd anything.

"A guest," I answer'd, "worthy to be here."
Love said, "You shall be he."
"I, the unkind, ungrateful? Ah, my dear,
I cannot look on Thee."
Love took my hand and smiling did reply,
"Who made the eyes but I?"

"Truth, Lord, but I have marr'd them, let my shame
Go where it doth deserve."
"And know you not," says Love, "Who bore the blame?"
"My dear, then I will serve."
"You must sit down," says Love, "and taste my meat."
So I did sit and eat.

33. Letter 4, *AdD*, p. 50.
34. Letter 4, *AdD*, p. 45.
35. From the contribution of Fr. Perrin at the conference of Sainte-Baume. *See* n. 28.
36. Letter 4, *AdD*, p. 46.
37. From the contribution of Fr. Perrin at the conference of Sainte-Baume. *See* n. 28.
38. Letter 4, *AdD*, p. 51.
39. Letter 4, *AdD*, p. 50.
40. From the contribution of Fr. Perrin at the conference of Sainte-Baume. *See* n. 28.
41. Letter 1, January 19, 1942, *AdD*, p. 18.
42. Ibid., p. 21.
43. Letter 2, *AdD*, pp. 23–26. Simone Weil writes: "This is a postscript to the letter which I told you constituted a provisional conclusion."
44. Letter 1, p. 25.
45. Letter 4, *AdD*, pp. 52–53.
46. Ibid., p. 52.
47. Ibid., p. 53.
48. Ibid., p. 55.
49. Ibid., pp. 57–58.
50. Ibid., p. 58.
51. *CII*, p. 117.
52. *CII*, p. 118.
53. From the chapter, "Amour des pratiques religieuses," in the essay, "Formes de l'Amour implicite de Dieu," *AdD*, pp. 177–79.
54. From the chapter, "L'amour du prochain." Ibid., p. 144.

55. Letter 4, p. 60.
56. Letter 1, p. 16.
57. Ibid., p. 17.
58. *CII*, p. 173.
59. Letter 2, p. 28.
60. Ibid.
61. Letter 1, *AdD*, p. 22.
62. From my conversation in Paris in 1976 with the late Stanislas Fumet, a French writer. A similar description of Simone Weil in her Marseilles period occurs in the last of his numerous works, *Histoire de Dieu dans ma vie* (Paris, Fayard, 1978).
63. From my conversations with Suzy Allemand, in September 1976. At the time of her encounter with Simone, Suzy was working on a diploma in English and was active in two action groups which worked against deportation. In 1946, she received in Marseilles the first convoys of orphans who had been rescued from concentration camps and were on their way to Israel. Today she is a child psychologist and speech therapist.
64. From my conversation with Berthe Bruschi Ergas, in September, 1976. Berthe presently teaches French and philosophy to students who have psychological problems with their studies. An extremely lively person, she is very alert to the currents of evolving contemporary spirituality.
65. Together with Jean Tortel and others, Toursky was part of the editorial committee of *Cahiers du Sud*.
66. From my conversation of September 22, 1976, in her home in Paris, with Malou David, who was in charge of distributing *Témoignage Chrétien* in southern and southeastern France from December, 1941 to 1943. "Because of the great risks involved in publication, we had to be as certain as we could that every copy would reach ten or fifteen readers. So we had to be sure to reach them and this meant spending a lot of time in finding and encouraging suitable people." This was a circulation "which required great agility and profound commitment. Simone gave a certain number of copies to some friends who were suitable for circulating them (Jean Tortel and his wife); she gave some copies to others not only to bring them around but to help them convince even more persons." (From the communication of Malou David, which she felt it was "her duty" to publish in the *Cahiers Simone Weil*, 2(4) (December, 1979), Association pour l'Étude de la Pensée de Simone Weil; she was "the only one to know with accuracy the work of Simone Weil in the Resistance."
67. The whole episode of her friendship with Gustave Thibon is taken from my conversation with him in March, 1973. I was invited to spend a day at Saint-Marcel. The places have remained the same: the door of the house, the dining room, a little dark; a room has been added on the ground floor, with a long table, where Thibon works. The village is the same, as is the ancient washhouse. Other notes come from the conference, *Présence de Simone Weil*, in two parts, "Histoire d'une amitié" and "Philosophie, foi et mystique," which Thibon presented at the Club du livre civique, Paris, May 20, 1975, and from Perrin and Thibon, *Simone Weil*. Born in 1903, Gustave Thibon was a farmer before becoming a philosopher. Self-taught, he is the author of numerous works, among which is *Notre regard qui manque à la lumière* (1970). He is very active in conferences in France and abroad.

68. Letter 4, *AdD*, p. 48.

69. From the first letter Thibon received from Simone, Perrin and Thibon, *Simone Weil*, pp. 131–32.

70. Gilbert Kahn (1914), a teacher of philosophy, had been a student of Michel Alexandre, through whom he met Simone. Kahn holds that the only way to try to interpret certain "strange and surprising" aspects of her life is in the "comprehension of her thought." For Simone Weil, experience had above all an "objective value," and for this reason she wished to live it to the fullest; she did so in all phases of her life, both in her actions (work in the factory, war in Spain) and in her thought (revolutionary syndicalism). According to Gilbert Kahn, it is "in the religious world, which she both discovered and constructed, where she definitively committed herself, without any hope or desire of return." From the contribution of Gilbert Kahn to the conference staged by himself, *Vigueur de Alain, rigueur de Simone Weil*, at the Centre culturel international de Cerisy-la-Salle, July 21-August 1, 1974, published in *Simone Weil, philosophe, historienne, mystique* (Paris, 1978), pp. 9–12.

71. Letter of "Wednesday, August 6," 1941, from the *Bulletin*, no. 7, (1977), Association pour l'Étude de la Pensée de Simone Weil.

72. Quoted by Hélène Honnorat on August 22, 1962, in her comments on the "Prologue" of Simone Weil, subsequently published in *Feuilles aux Vents, Feuillets des Avents*, cahiers trimestriels, Peyrégoux, no. 1 (January, 1972), p. 15. Earlier, actually the day of her departure for Saint-Marcel d'Ardèche, Simone had written an undated letter to Pierre Honnorat, so far unpublished.

73. A letter of October 5, 1941 to Gilbert Kahn, *Bulletin*, no. 7 (1977), Association pour l'Étude de la Pensée de Simone Weil.

74. Testimony of M. and Mme. Rieu, "patrons" of Simone, to Eugène Fleuré, who has made many contributions, with his lifelong researches, to our knowledge of Simone Weil. The testimony of the Rieus was first included by Fleuré in his book *Simone Weil ouvrière* (Paris, F. Lanore, 1955) and then in *Cahiers Simone Weil*, revue trimestrielle publiée par l'Association pour l'Étude de la Pensée de Simone Weil, 1(3) (December, 1978), pp. 46–47.

75. Letter to her parents, Sunday, October 5, 1941. Pétrement, 2:375.

76. *Bulletin*, no. 7 (1977), Association pour l'Étude de la Pensée de Simone Weil. She did not speak at all about this exhaustion in the letter to her parents, that same October 5, 1941. Pétrement, 2:375.

77. First letter to Thibon, Perrin and Thibon, *Simone Weil*, p. 132.

78. *CI*, p. 159.

79. *CI*, p. 202.

80. Ibid.

81. *CII*, p. 44.

82. Ibid.

83. *CII*, p. 45.

84. *CI*, p. 202.

85. Ibid.

86. *CII*, p. 46. The italics are Simone's.

87. *CI*, p. 108.

88. From the chapter, "Amour de l'ordre du monde," in "Formes de l'Amour," p. 161.
89. Ibid., p. 161.
90. Ibid., p. 168.
91. Ibid., p. 169.
92. Ibid., p. 171.
93. Ibid., p. 172.
94. Ibid.
95. Ibid.
96. *CI*, p. 132. In the Weil text, the first paragraph, all the way to "the letters," is underlined.
97. *CI*, p. 132.
98. Honnorat, p. 19.
99. Dom Clément Jacob, whose father was Jewish and an army officer and whose mother was non-Jewish and an atheist, "grew up without any religion." Towards the end of his life (he died on February 28, 1977), he considered himself "totally Jewish, by blood and in Jesus Christ." His cousin, the poet Max Jacob, followed a religious road similar to his. (From a letter Berthe Bruschi wrote me June 1, 1978.)
100. The questionnaire was published in Simone Weil, *Pensées sans ordre concernant l'amour de Dieu* (Paris, 1962), pp. 70–72.
101. So wrote Clément Jacob in a letter of October 9, 1955 to Denise-Aimé Azam, a friend of the Honnorats and later also of Selma Weil. Pétrement, 2:402.
102. Another letter of Clément Jacob. Pétrement, 2:403.
103. This is the account of Mother Germaine Roussel, a Benedictine at Dourgne (a village where rises the abbey of Sainte Scholastique [1890]), with regard to Sr. Colombe. Before taking her vows, Germaine Roussel was a young woman of an anticlerical milieu; she was interested in syndicalism and committed to "convincing herself that God does not exist." In 1942, she knew the Honnorats at Marseilles and, indirectly, Simone. Later, her reading of *La Pesanteur et la Grâce* would be decisive for her mystical turn (see Chap. 19, n. 23).
104. Letter of January 15, 1956 of Sr. Colombe to Simone Pétrement (2:403).
105. From my conversation at the old folks home, Les Arcades, in Dourgne with Thérèse de la Marguette, in the summer of 1976. This is how she described her life: "A nurse during the First World War, in the second war, I hid people, above all women. I have lived at Dourgne for forty years. I came here because I wished to live near monasteries. At times, however, I would ask myself what I was doing." She has a very natural attitude towards religion and says: "I go to Mass and receive Communion just as I am. Simone Weil never felt that she was worthy." (Thérèse died in 1977.)
106. From "Présentation de l'homme d'Oc" by Joë Bousquet, in *Le Génie d'Oc et l'Homme Méditerranéen*, a special issue of the *Cahiers du Sud*, printed on February 28, 1943, "sur les presses de l'Imprimerie Mistral à Cavaillon," pp. 11–12.
107. These are the words of Jean Ballard. Pétrement, 2:298.
108. The letter, which by mistake bears the date January 23, 1940, instead of 1941, was published in *Cahiers d'Études Cathares*, Arc, no. 2 (April–June, 1949) and again, in the same journal, Toulouse, no. 19 (1954).

109. In Simone Weil, *Pensées sans ordre concernant l'amour de Dieu* (Paris, Gallimard, 1962), pp. 63–67.

110. The late Déodat Roché, ninety-six years of age in 1973 when I met him; like a tall wooden statue, he slowly came into the littered salon of his home in Arc; he used a stick to feel his way across the floor, since he was almost blind. And yet, his eyes still had a malicious gleam. He had been a judge at Béziers and Simone Weil intended to go there to find him. For him she has remained a girl eternally young, far distant, a little eccentric, who "during the war did not have extra ration coupons, as we all did." And he adds, while he smilingly points to a large soup tureen, "Extenuatory circumstances." Through his works (*St. Augustin et les Manichéens de son temps, Contes et Légendes du Catharisme*, and others) and his review, Déodat Roché today represents Neo-Catharism, which, for him, coincides with the anthroposophy of Rudolf Steiner.

111. The two essays appear in *Le Génie d'Oc*, pp. 99–107 and pp. 150–158. The *poème épique* to which Simone refers in the first essay is a fragment of a medieval epic poem, known as the *Chanson de la Croisade*, the work of a defender of the threatened city, Toulouse. The two essays appear also in *EHP*, pp. 66–74 and pp. 75–84.

112. All the quotations are taken from the two essays, "L'Agonie d'une civilisation" and "En quoi consiste," *EHP*, pp. 66–74 and pp. 75–84.

113. From the accounts of Jean Tortel and Suzanne André, now dead, I have taken the description of the baroque bedroom of Joë Bousquet. Born at Narbonne in 1897, the son of a military physician who lived in the milieu of vine-dressers, while still a student, he voluntarily served in an assault battalion commanded by a Jesuit, Fr. Louis Houdard. In twenty months of combat he received many honors, including the cross of the Legion of Honor. On May 27, 1918, in the battle of Vailly, he was hit in the spinal column; he would remain paralyzed in his pelvis and his legs until his death (September 28, 1950). The German battalion was commanded by Lieutenant Max Ernst, the painter. They became great friends. His works: *Traduit du silence*, 1936, his basic work, discovered by Gallimard himself, during his exodus in the Midi; *Le médisant par bonté*, 1945; *Le mal du soir*, 1953. This is how Suzanne André spoke of him to me: "Bousquet does not describe things; he evokes them through the filter of his interior life; if the reader does not have the interior life as his pivot, he will not find a center of interest in the works of Bousquet. His works should be republished according to themes." Ferdinand Alquié dedicated an issue of *Cahiers du Sud* to him: *Joë Bousquet ou le recours au langage*, nos. 362–63 (September–October 1961). In his book, *Le Meneur de lune* (Paris, 1946), Bousquet says this: "I entered into my narrow life with the soul of a voluptuary; and, although I have become ever more insensible, I have felt instead of thinking. What would have ruined my life as a man, has perhaps saved the invalid I have become. I have lived like a woman, in the desire to beget souls, to nurture them with my sensations."

114. From the preface by Jean Ballard, *Le Génie d'Oc*, p. 5. Ballard here defines his friendship with Bousquet as "the most atemporal that can be dreamed of." For him, the group around Bousquet represented a "spiritual community" of a particular character, the heritage of the civilization d'Oc, which he wanted to evoke and understand through a special issue, long dreamed of, of the *Cahiers du Sud*.

115. From the introduction of Jean Ballard to the correspondence of Simone Weil and Joë Bousquet, *Cahiers du Sud,* no. 304 (1950), 37th year, vol. 32.

116. From my conversation with the late René Nelli, a Provençal scholar, a disciple of Déodat Roché and a great friend of Bousquet. The author of important studies on Catharism and the troubadours, he considers his most important works to be *Philosophie du Catharisme* (Paris, Payot) and *Moyen-Age occitan,* 2 vols. (Paris, Phoebus). He saw Simone Weil four or five times; she came to study Catharism with him and with Roché. He found attractive in her the Platonic-Christian aspect which makes her resemble Marsilio Ficino. Simone was seeking after Catholicism, "which seemed to her a more coherent structure. From Catharism and other religions she wanted to be enlightened on some problems, that of evil, for example, which obsessed her. She was profoundly disturbed by the war, by the lot her fellow Jews and all men had to endure."

117. From my conversation with Lanza del Vasto in October, 1976, at Ontignano, Florence, near the community which was initially inspired by Arca. *See also* chap. 19, n. 17.

118. All these quotations are drawn from *Cahiers du Sud,* no. 304, cited in note 115.

119. Pétrement, 2:304–305.

120. Ibid., p. 305.

121. Perrin and Thibon, *Simone Weil,* p. 150.

122. A little later, Simone would write to Thibon: "I do not know if I have told you, with reference to my notebooks, that you can read passages from them to anyone you want but you should not let anyone have them in his possession . . . If, after three or four years, you no longer hear anyone speak of me, consider yourself their full owner. I tell you all of this so that I can leave with the most free spirit. I regret only that I cannot confide to you what I am bearing within myself but what has not yet developed." (From the introduction by Gustave Thibon to *L'ombra et la grazia, La Pesanteur et la grâce,* trans. Franco Fortini (Milan, Edition di Communità, 1951), p. 17.)

123. Pétrement, 2:414.

17 Supernatural Knowledge

1. From Perrin and Thibon, *Simone Weil,* p. 151. It is a long letter certainly begun before her departure and mailed at Oran, where the passengers could only mail letters, without landing. They got to Casablanca on May 20, 1942, as the stamp on the passports of Simone and her father shows. Pétrement, 2:417.

2. The letter to Antonio, at first dated Oran, was concluded at Casablanca. The "interzonal" card to Simone Pétrement bears the stamp of Oran, May 18 (Pétrement, 2:416–417). The Provençal scholar René Nelli has shown me a card from Casablanca by Simone; the postmark is not clear as to the name of the city and the date is illegible.

3. Letter 6, May 26, 1942, from Casablanca, the last that Simone wrote to Perrin, *AdD,* p. 74.

4. Letter 6, *AdD,* pp. 35–62.

5. Letter 6, *AdD,* pp. 68–84.

6. Cabaud, *SW,* p. 20.

7. Pétrement, 2:306.

8. Both letters of July 30, 1942 are in *EdL,* pp. 185–95.

9. The project was enclosed in her first letter to Maurice Schumann, dated New York, July 30, 1942. This and the previous quotations are drawn from *EdL,* pp. 187–95.

10. *CI,* p. 133.

11. *CI,* p. 139.

12. From Cabaud, *SW,* p. 53. Simone Pétrement, too, heard that De Gaulle "must have exclaimed" in this fashion and that others "found the project absurd." "Sans doute," Simone Weil *never* spoke with the general. Pétrement, 2:483–84.

13. Ibid., p. 428. This is a draft of a letter from Simone Weil to an English captain, July 29, 1942. Italics hers.

14. The second, shorter letter to Maurice Schumann, dated New York, July 30, 1942, *EdL,* pp. 195–97.

15. A letter that can be definitely dated to September, 1942, quoted in Pétrement, 2:431–32.

16. *CII,* p. 115. Italics hers.

17. *CII,* p. 47.

18. *CI,* p. 220.

19. *CI,* p. 221. Italics hers.

20. *CI,* p. 223. Italics hers.

21. *CI,* p. 225. Italics hers.

22. *CI,* p. 222. Italics hers.

23. *CII,* p. 164.

24. Ibid.

25. Letter 4, *AdD,* p. 59.

26. *CII,* p. 98.

27. *CII,* p. 210.

28. Ibid.

29. *CII,* p. 211.

30. *CII,* p. 56. Italics hers.

31. *CII,* p. 218.

32. *CII,* p. 230.

33. *CS,* p. 15.

34. *CIII,* p. 216. Italics hers.

35. Cabaud, *Exp.,* p. 333.

36. Letter to her parents, Pétrement, 2:432–33.

37. Letter to her brother, dated a little later. Ibid., p. 433.

38. Letter to her parents. Ibid., p. 433.

39. Ibid., p. 435.

40. This is the story told me by Eveline Weil, in our conversation, Paris, 1975.

41. This is the recollection of Alain de Possel. Pétrement, 2:440.

42. Letter to her brother, probably October, 1942. Ibid., pp. 441–42.

43. Letter to her parents from Rome, May, 1937. Ibid., pp. 441–42.

44. Draft letter to Fr. Couturier, September 15, 1942. This is the basis for the *Lettre à un religieux* (Paris, Gallimard, 1951). In the draft, the list of "presumed heresies" is pre-

sented in fifteen paragraphs, rather than the thirty-five of the *Lettre.* Pétrement, 2:436–37.

45. Letter from New York, without a date, *EdL,* pp. 197–201.

46. André Weil told me of this episode during our first conversation, in Paris, September, 1973. Today in upper Manhattan, one may visit the fascinating museum, The Cloisters, where entire structures of medieval art have been literally transplanted: there are numerous French and Spanish cloisters.

47. The preceding verses are translated from the opening canticle of the "Ascent of Mount Carmel," in which the soul expresses "its happiness in that, through the dark night of faith, it has in nakedness and purification attained union with its beloved." From John of the Cross, *Oeuvres complètes,* trans. Fr. Cyprien de la Nativité de la Vierge (Paris, Desclée de Brouwer, 1967), pp. 73–74.

48. *CI,* p. 27.

49. *CI,* p. 73.

50. In the spring of 1938, Simone wrote an enthusiastic letter on T. E. Lawrence to her friend Posternak, from Paris: "If you want to meet a prodigious combination of an authentic hero, a perfectly lucid thinker, an artist, a scholar, rounded off by a sort of saint, read his *Seven Pillars of Wisdom . . .* Never, insofar as I am aware, from the *Iliad* until today, has war been described with such sincerity, such complete lack of declamation, whether heroic or horrified . . . I know of no one, in any other epoch, who has realized to the same degree what I love to admire." *Cinque lettere,* p. 101.

51. *CI,* pp. 35–36. Italics hers.

52. *CI,* p. 28.

53. *CI,* p. 260.

54. *CII,* p. 226.

55. The *Cahiers d'Amérique* are really six notebooks, considered as seven, since the numeration goes from one to seven; in fact one of the notebooks, begun at both ends, carries two numbers, two and three. Dating them is difficult: it seems that they were begun towards the end of September, 1942, and mostly written in the following October, when Simone Weil, hoping to depart for England, rediscovered the inspiration for entrusting her thoughts again to her *cahiers.* (Pétrement, 2:442–43.) In 1950, the *cahiers* were published by Gallimard with the title, *La Connaissance Surnaturelle,* "given the frequency of this expression in the writings of Simone Weil." As a premise to the *cahiers,* there appeared for the first time in 1950, at the beginning of *La Connaissance Surnaturelle,* the two pages of the "Prologue," a title preferred by Simone to the initial one, "Commencement du livre." These two pages were reproduced in facsimile in the third volume of the *Cahiers* (Paris, 1957), and published at the conclusion of *Cahiers III* (Paris, 1974), pp. 291–92.

   Furthermore, we find in the *Cahiers* two significant indications which allow us to know, in a very precise way, Simone Weil's intentions with regard to the text of the "Prologue" and all her notebooks. They are the phrase which serves as a title, "Beginning of the book (the book destined to contain these thoughts and many others)" and the phrase at the end, "there follows an unordered mass of fragments."

56. *CS,* p. 235. As often happens, the source of the fable is not given. "Her knowledge of

folklore was inexhaustible," Aimé Patri has told me; "she interpreted fables and legends from all the countries of the world in a retrospective vision."

57. *CIII*, p. 215, italics hers.
58. *CI*, p. 258.
59. *CS*, p. 295.
60. *CS*, p. 296.
61. *CS*, p. 233.
62. *CS*, p. 250.
63. *CS*, p. 233.
64. *CS*, p. 49.
65. *CS*, p. 46.
66. *CS*, p. 49.
67. *CS*, p. 91.
68. *CS*, p. 92.
69. *CS*, p. 238.
70. Simone defines the story of the cobbler as the attempt to "translate a spiritual experience." *CS*, p. 234.
71. *CS*, p. 235.
72. *CS*, p. 234.
73. *CS*, p. 35. The same certainty is expressed in a more ample fashion in *Intuitions préchrétiennes* (Paris, 1951), p. 165.
74. *CS*, pp. 222–23.
75. *CS*, p. 49.
76. *CS*, p. 250.
77. *CS*, p. 252.
78. *CS*, p. 254.
79. *CS*, p. 97.
80. *CS*, p. 87.
81. *CS*, p. 250. The alignment of Weil's text has been preserved.
82. Ibid.
83. *CS*, pp. 43–44.
84. *CS*, p. 58.
85. *CS*, p. 224.
86. *CS*, p. 225.
87. *CS*, p. 224.
88. *CS*, p. 165.
89. *CS*, p. 37.
90. *CS*, p. 40.
91. *CS*, p. 165.
92. *CS*, p. 46.
93. *CS*, p. 47.
94. *CS*, p. 87.
95. *CS*, p. 36.
96. *CS*, p. 101. Italics hers.

97. *CS,* p. 81.
98. μεταξύ is one of the recurrent concepts in *Cahiers II.* We provide here the original wording of the French edition (Paris, 1970):

    Sur la première page de la couverture, Simone Weil a écrit: "2 (1941)".
    La page 2 de la couverture porte:
    1941, I
    μεταξύ
    analogie
    transposition
    lire

99. *CS,* p. 167.
100. *CS,* pp. 204–205.
101. *CS,* p. 206.
102. *CII,* p. 173.
103. *CS,* p. 26.
104. *CS,* p. 203.
105. Pétrement, 2:444–45.
106. From my conversation with André Weil, Paris, 1975.
107. I met Jean Wahl, an important Kierkegaard scholar, who has since died, in 1973: an octogenarian, small and fragile, with his white hair in curls, almost blind, and with words he had trouble uttering; he still had an extraordinary memory and a lively feeling for human relationships. "I saw Simone Weil twice in my life: the first time, when I met her at the presentation of the *Electre,* by Giraudoux, which she liked very much and I did not like at all; the second time, at the beginning of the war, at her home. I represented the existentialist philosopher to her. Her article on the *Iliad,* which Paulhan had me read in manuscript, pleased me without reserve."
108. Pétrement, 2:445–46. This letter also appears in *Seventy Letters,* pp. 157–61.
109. Pétrement, 2:448. Hélène Honnorat, in her August 22, 1962, comment on the "Prologue" of Simone Weil, declared: "She recommended the 'Prologue' to her mother as a sort of spiritual testament" (*Feuilles aux Vents,* p. 6). For this reason, probably, Selma Weil, who concerned herself personally with all the works of her daughter, wanted the pages of the "Prologue" to appear first in the first edition, 1950, of *La Connaissance Surnaturelle.*

18 The History of Her Social Thought

1. Letter to her parents, with the salutation, "Darlings," like all the letters from London, December 16, [1942], *EdL,* p. 218.
2. Letter to her parents, December 31, 1942, *EdL,* p. 220. *See also* Pétrement, 2:450–51.
3. With reference to *canular,* see chap. 5.
4. Francis-Louis Closon, *Le temps des passions. De Jean Moulin à la libération* (Paris, 1974), pp. 32–33.
5. Letter to her parents, December 31, 1942, *EdL,* p. 221.
6. Letter to her parents, January 8, 1943, *EdL,* p. 224.

7. Letter to her parents, March 1, [1943], *EdL*, p. 231.

8. Cabaud, *SW*, p. 38.

9. Letter to her parents, March 1, [1943], *EdL*, p. 231.

10. Letter to her parents, January 22, 1943, *EdL*, p. 225.

11. Letter to her parents, January 8, 1943, *EdL*, p. 224.

12. Cabaud, *SW*, p. 41.

13. The man involved was Guillaume Guindey, who had been a fellow student of Simone. As inspector of finances at Vichy, he was able to make the trip back and forth between Vichy and Paris. It was Adèle Dubreuil who had the idea to entrust to him the package containing the "text in prose, quite long, typed . . . very topical . . . I believe that it would be worth the effort that it not be lost." Simone had spoken to him of it in a letter from Toulouse in August, 1940. Pétrement, 2:279.

14. Letter to her mother at the beginning of July [1934]. The italics are in the text. Pétrement, 1:416.

15. From *Oppression et Liberté* (Paris, Gallimard, 1955), pp. 57–162. It is a collection of social and political writings, the principal nucleus of which is "Réflexions sur les causes de la liberté et de l'oppression sociale," written in 1934 and including 114 typed pages. We recall how Alain prized this essay. Jeanne Alexandre remarks in this connection: to her, Alain "offers the *Libres Propos,* sacrificing happily the whole band of his faithful . . . We are far beyond the pride of a teacher before his student . . . Perhaps Alain allowed here a sense of equality to peep through, a sense he never confessed except for Paul Valéry? He did not betray his feelings ever. Or did he cherish a sort of work-alliance with Simone Weil? But she had already been caught up in the whirlpool of social action and the dream had no sequel." From "Rencontre de Simone Weil et d'Alain," Alain, *Actes,* p. 194.

16. Letter of March 1, [1943], *EdL*, p. 232.

17. "Réflexions sur la révolte," *EdL*, pp. 109–25.

18. "Légitimé de gouvernement provisoire," *EdL*, pp. 58–73.

19. "Remarques sur le nouveau projet de Constitution," *EdL*, pp. 85–92. Italics hers.

20. "Idées essentielles pour une nouvelle Constitution," *EdL*, pp. 93–97; italics hers. A form of control sponsored by Simone Weil, at the basis of the structure of the government, is the *popular referendum,* which should "settle the serious disputes between the legislative and judicial powers" and, every twenty years, say whether "in relation to the imperfection of human affairs, public life is satisfactory." The referendum would always be preceded by a long period of reflection and discussion, during which all propaganda would be forbidden under the threat of serious penalties. (*See EdL*, p. 97.)

21. "Étude pour une Déclaration des Obligations envers l'Être Humain," in *EdL*, pp. 74–80. Italics mine.

22. Ibid., p. 77.

23. "Fragments et notes," *EdL*, pp. 151–52.

24. Letter to her parents, May 22, 1943, *EdL*, p. 237.

25. *CI*, p. 223. Italics hers.

26. "Étude pour une Déclaration des Obligations," *EdL*, p. 84. Here reference is made to the first of the two "fundamental conditions" for the practical application of the declaration of duties.

27. Simone gives this example: "Gide has surely always known that books like *Les Nour-ritures terrestres* and *Les Caves du Vatican* have influenced the behavior of hundreds of young people and has been proud of that . . . There is no reason, then, to place these books behind the impenetrable barrier of art for art's sake, nor to put in prison a young person who throws someone from a train while it is speeding along." (*E*, p. 38.) In April–May, 1941, Simone wrote a letter to the *Cahiers du Sud*, "Lettre sur les responsabilités de la littérature," "to champion a vision not shared by the review, to almost all of those 'with whom even she sympathized.'" At that time it was almost the official position, whether in Paris or Vichy, to blame writers for the defeat of 1940. Si-mone was convinced of this responsibility, on which hangs "the affliction (*malheur*)" of our time with regard to the whole world, inasmuch as it is penetrated by western influence. In fact, "the essential characteristic of the first half of the twentieth century is the weakening, even the disappearance, of the concept of value." The literature of the twentieth century is "essentially psychological," describing states of mind not subjected to the determination of value, as if "the tendency towards the good could somehow be absent from the thought of a man." Even though she granted that writers should not teach morality, Simone insisted that they must "express the human condi-tion. And nothing is as important for human life, for all men and at every moment, as good and evil." But note carefully: it is also true that a certain moralism is worse than amorality. "Those who at this time heap blame on famous writers are worth infinitely less than the writers . . . If the present sufferings are to bring a redressing, this will not happen through slogans, but in the silence of moral solitude." The letter was only published ten years later, in 1951, in *Cahiers du Sud*, 38th year, no. 310, pp. 426–30.

28. "Étude pour une Déclaration des Obligations," p. 83. "We have completely lost the idea of punishment. We do not know any longer that it consists in providing what is good. For us it stops at the infliction of evil. This is the reason why in modern society there exists only one thing more hateful than crime: repressive justice." (From "La personne et le sacré," *EdL*, p. 40.) The problem of making justice testify to our *attention* on the human creature, of making it a sign of the respect we owe human sensibility and our aspiration for what is good, had kept Simone occupied for a time. *See* "L'amour du prochain," part of the essay, "Formes de l'amour implicite de Dieu," *AdD*, pp. 124–46.

29. This and all preceding quotations, except where otherwise noted, are taken from *E*, pt. one, "Les besoins de l'âme," pp. 9–57. Italics mine.

30. "Étude pour une Déclaration des Obligations," p. 83.

31. "Fragments et notes," *EdL*, p. 170. Italics hers.

32. "Étude pour une Déclaration des Obligations," pp. 83–84.

33. Because what is not authentic is harmful. We recall what she wrote Thibon on the sense of nature as a "reality" and not as "scene or setting": (*see* chap. 16) "the earth gives herself only to those who have deserved her . . . to those who have given her their lives." As authentic testimony of this, Simone was, perhaps, thinking of the book by Emile Guillaumin, *La vie d'un simple* (Paris, 1934), which she had given to Marcel Lecarpentier.

34. This and all the preceding quotations, except where otherwise noted, are taken from *E*, part two, "Déracinement ouvrier" and "Déracinement payan," pp. 61–129. Italics mine.

35. The reference arises spontaneously, although the episode from Gide's tale of criminal madness occurred during the second half of the nineteenth century and the trial was not completed until November 20, 1901. See André Gide, *La séquestrée de Poitiers* (Paris, Gallimard, 1930).

36. This is a problem upon which Simone Weil was already reflecting in the autumn of 1934, as Simone Pétrement confirmed in her letter to me of January 12, 1978.

37. The idea of *new life* is an allusion to "Idées essentielles pour une nouvelle Constitution," *EdL*, pp. 93–97.

38. This is the second of the two "fundamental conditions" for the practical implementation of the Declaration of Duties.

39. This and all the preceding quotations, except where otherwise noted, are taken from *E*, pt. two, "Déracinement et nation," pp. 129–233. Italics mine.

40. "Fragments et notes," *EdL*, pp. 151–52.

41. Simone adds: "And, something of even greater interest, embryos, seeds, sketches of organizations in their course of development." (*E*, p. 270.) These were the only forms of association which she trusted. On March 30, 1941, the JOC (Jeunesse Ouvrière Chrétienne) organized two meetings at Marseilles, one in the heart of the working quarter. Simone wrote for the *Cahiers du Sud* (no. 234, April 1941) that this movement seemed young in the positive sense, inasmuch as it was not galvanized by "collective inebriation, magnetism, words of the day, obsession with power, adulation of youth." She held that in the JOC there found expression "the pure Christian spirit. Politics does not enter there; religion itself only exists insofar as it is translated." And she affirmed: "The JOC only is concerned with the misery (*malheur*) of young workers; the existence of such an organization is perhaps the only sure sign that Christianity is not dead among us." (*E*, p. 87.) She spoke to Schumann of the Témoignage Chrétien as of "what there is of the best today in France" and of an ambience to which she was bound "by a lively and profound friendship." (Letter without date, from New York, *EdL*, p. 198.)

42. *CII*, p. 117. This is a reference to the Darwinian notion of *condition of existence*, which guided Simone Weil in her study of the development of society in *Oppression et Liberté*. Italics hers.

43. This and all the preceding quotations, except where otherwise noted, are taken from *E*, pt. 3, pp. 238–380. Italics mine.

44. *CS*, p. 165.

45. "We note all the same that, in the new "Declaration of the rights of man and the citizen," published by the press of the Free French Forces on August 14, 1943 . . . there is also a list of duties. Perhaps, to some degree, some attention had been paid to Simone's ideas." Pétrement, 2:465.

46. She wrote to her friend, because "practically," it was difficult to be able "to speak together at our ease." The letter says, at the beginning, "I am astonished to see how

many pages I have written you without noticing it. It's only a question of personal matters. It is all without any interest. Read this letter only if and when you really have time to waste." Letter from London, without a date, *EdL*, pp. 201–202.

47. Letter to her parents, January 22, 1943, *EdL*, p. 226.
48. Postscript to the letter to Francis-Louis Closon. Pétrement, 2:509. Often, in her letters to her parents, Simone calls Closon a good, a true *"copain."*

19 The Meaning of a Woman's Life

1. Letter to her parents, July 28, 1943, *EdL*, p. 253.
2. Pétrement, 2:511.
3. From an unpublished document on Simone Weil, given to me in 1973, and later published in the volume, *La mort née de leur propre vie* (Paris, 1974). "As you know, my contribution to the knowledge of the message of Simone Weil is nothing other than a testimonial-interpretation of her death." This was how Maurice Schumann (Paris, 1911) began his paper at the gathering, "Vigueur d'Alain, rigueur de Simone Weil" (Cerisy-la-Salle, July 21–August 1, 1974); it is also now part of *La mort née de leur propre vie,* a sort of evocation-meditation on Péguy, Simone Weil, and Gandhi. It is considered "his most notable work." The letters which Simone wrote him from New York and London are among the most revealing on her spiritual journey; we find there her conception of death, her consciousness of herself as an instrument useful for men in the propagation of truth, and the "project" of practical and symbolic significance. In London, where he had rejoined De Gaulle, after a very risky escape from his status as a prisoner of war, Schumann was the spokesman for Free France on the radio. A teacher of philosophy, a journalist of varied experience (he had been co-director of the Havas Agency, the foreign policy editor of *Sept,* the Dominican journal, the political director of *L'Aube,* a writer (*The Good Nazi*), he played an active political role between 1951 and 1973 as minister for the safeguard of the territory, as minister for scientific research and as minister of social welfare. Among his principal goals: freedom of instruction, which, because of his adherence to Christianity, coincided for him with the desire to accord citizenship to believers, in a France which was then extreme in its laicism; an effective recognition of the family dimension in social policy. In foreign affairs, the reconciliation of France and Germany and the support of the rights of man in the European assembly of which he was a part. Elected to the Académie Française in 1974, he was vice-president of the senate in 1981.
4. *See* chap. 16, n. 63.
5. Letter that can be dated between May and June. Pétrement, 1:409.
6. From Malcolm Muggeridge's interview with André Weil, *GtG*, p. 149.
7. *CI*, p. 262.
8. From the introduction by Gustav Thibon to *La Pesanteur et la Grâce.*
9. From the presentation by Maurice Schumann, "Simone Weil et la présence de Dieu," for "Recherches et experiences spirituelles," Notre-Dame, Paris, November, 1973 (later published as a booklet, p. 3).
10. *CS*, p. 13.

11. Letter 4, *AdD*, p. 37.

12. Note the following passages: "Only the unconditioned brings one to God." "Love is supernatural when it is unconditioned." "There are only two unconditioned loves: love for God and anonymous love for one's neighbor." *CS*, pp. 75–76.

13. The phrases quoted come from the preface to *CO* (pp. 14–16) or from my conversation with Albertine Thévenon in her house at Saint-Étienne, in September, 1973. I underline the expression, "perfect coherence," because of the strong value Albertine gives to it.

14. Duperray, "Quand Simone Weil passa chez nous," pp. 96–98.

15. Cabaud, *Exp.*, p. 276.

16. Letter of testimonial, April 15, 1978, of L. O., who has allowed me to give only her initials.

17. From my conversation with Lanza del Vasto, in September, 1976. Giuseppe Giovanni Lanza del Vasto (San Vito dei Normanni, Apulia, 1901–Murcia, Spain, 1981), after attending the lycée Condorcet in Paris, received his doctorate at the Scuola Normale Superiore in Pisa with a thesis on the "trinitarian vision of man and the world." At the center of his life is the agitation of 1936, the need to lodge against the destructiveness already appearing a "positive counterrevolution"; for this purpose he decided to go to India, to Gandhi, to "learn to become a better Christian." From this he drew the inspiration for founding his Order of Nonviolent Labor, where oriental asceticism and Christian doctrine flow together; he gives the name "Arche" to it (the Ark in the face of the deluge). A true ashram transplanted to Europe, precisely to Borie Noble (Hérault-Languedoc), the Arche has, since 1948, begun the reconstruction, in the style of the region, of "an entire village abandoned since the First World War."

    In addition to being a writer and a poet, Lanza was a sculptor in wood, an engraver of ivory, and a student of popular music (in the special number of the *Cahiers du Sud*, dedicated to "Le Génie d'Oc," he presented and translated *La Baronessa di Carini*). Among his numerous works there has recently been republished in Italy the story of his first trip to India, *Pellegrinaggio alle sorgenti* (Milan, 1978). In our conversation, Lanza told me that he had finished the history of his order, from its first inspiration in 1937 to 1948. In 1942, when he met Simone Weil, it was to her that he recounted the development of that idea, which had been within him for five years. Simone said, "What a beautiful diamond, with all its faces corresponding." Lanza replied, "It has only one fault: it does not exist." Simone answered with certainty, "It will."

18. From the testimonial letter sent me by Fr. Jacques Loew from Freiburg, November 16, 1976. He had helped to found l'École de la Foi there. Jacques Loew, formerly an attorney in Nice and then a Dominican friar, became in July, 1941, the first worker-priest in France. He narrates his experience in *Journal d'une mission ouvrière* (Paris, Editions du Cerf, 1959). They are notes made month by month, with introductory pages for every chapter.

    The École de la Foi began in 1969, above all with the intention of allowing "men and women, religious and lay, to share together in the reconstruction of a human or Christian fabric where they live, through the implantation of communities, in a human way."

19. From a letter of April 24, 1978, in which Anne Reynaud-Guérithault synthesized and completed what she first told me in our first meeting of 1973. After living in Rome from 1946 to 1960, where she taught at the Centre d'Études Supérieures of the lycée Chateaubriand, she taught classics until a short time ago at the lycée Alain in Le Vésinet, a little city near Paris, where the philosopher, teacher of Simone Weil spent the last years of his life.

20. From the letter of testimonial of Pierre Dantu, April 24, 1978.

21. From my conversation with Jacques Redon, in August, 1976.

22. From my first conversation with Marcelle Ballard, in Marseilles, in September, 1973.

23. From my first conversation with Guillaume de Tarde in 1972. What was *La Pesanteur et la Grace,* the anthology that Gustave Thibon created out of the notebooks Simone left with him with such trust? Let us listen to Thibon himself. "It is a sad task for me to offer to the public the extraordinary work of Simone Weil. Until now I have shared with only a very few friends the joy of knowing her person and her thought; and I now have the bitter impression of letting out a family secret. My only comfort is the thought that through the inevitable profanation of publicity her testimony will reach some soul, some sister of hers." After hesitating between "printing the thoughts of Simone Weil one after another in the order of their composition or arranging them," he chose arrangement. "Here it is not a question of philosophy, but of life. Instead of pretending to construct a personal system, Simone Weil wanted with all of her power to be absent from her work. Her only desire was not to be a screen between God and men . . . She was heard; some of her texts attain that impersonal resonance that is the sign of supreme inspiration." He was assisted and encouraged in his work, by, among others, Fr. Perrin, Lanza del Vasto, Hélène and Pierre Honnorat, and Gabriel Marcel (preface to *L'ombra e la grazia*).

   Mother Germaine Roussel (see chap. 16, n. 103) also feels that Simone is experienced through "our own inner selves"; in her opinion it was not a mistake to publish all of the notes and unfinished writings; it is interesting, in fact, "to see her in conflict." Pierre Honnorat gave her *La Pesanteur et la Grâce,* just after its publication, as a Christmas present in 1947. Somewhat later, Pierre would give her an unpublished letter of Simone (which we have reproduced in the illustrations). "The fire, the absoluteness of that true interior dimension marked me deeply; I was not an intellectual . . . I came to En-Calcat on a tourist visit with Hélène (I was twenty-eight at the time); something incredible happened: I felt myself literally seized by the hair by a decision stronger than I was. And with my anticlerical feet joined together, I leaped over my personal difficulties. I entered the monastery a year and a half later, in October of 1948. I was the only daughter of unbelievers; for four years they did not want to see me." From Simone, she says she learned "to look at obstacles in the face, to grasp them and to wait, until ever so slowly the difficulties disappear." She adds, "Simone Weil is *a poet;* she would surely have become sweeter."

24. Pétrement, 2:209.

25. From my conversation in the summer of 1974, at her home on Lake Geneva, with Alida de Jager, who has since died. Despite being over eighty years of age and hindered in her movements, speech, and writing by a recent stroke, she was rich in her interests and very much up to date in the field of social and political sciences, attentive

to revolutionary movements in the world (she was in correspondence with Ivan Illich). Alida, who called herself "a soldier without chevrons in the international workers' movement," met Simone at Montana in 1934. An article written by Simone and translated into Dutch had impressed her; she had written "Révolution proletarienne," in the belief that she was an aged syndicalist; in happy wonder, she saw in front of her a young girl. Alida, her two daughters, and the Weils became fast friends. "I have known many persons, but rarely have I been able to know someone as well as her. And we were certainly very different. We spoke of the Greeks, Athens, the polis, and then Florence and the cities of Italy. Simone was interested in the past to understand better the evolution of the world." In 1974, Alida published *La Commune vivante* (Paris, Les Editions Syndicalistes): "the world described in these pages does not presuppose new inventions . . . but the reasonable use of existent possibilities." For a monetary unit she suggests the gam (general activity measure), corresponding to an hour of standard labor; this topic too, they discussed at length, Alida, her mathematician brother, and Simone Weil.

Alida's daughter, Elisa de Jager, resembles her mother in her gestures and inflections. She recalls, "I was nine years old in 1934, but I remember her very well. Then, between 1936 and 1940, the Weils gave us their house in the country, La Guinguette; then we were in England and Mexico. It was there I learned of her death; I wept desperately. Why had Simone allowed herself to die in that way? The absurdity and folly of wanting to be pure; we must tame the 'gross animal' for our own welfare, but not die; we do not have the right, in the face of the world and ourselves. I wept above all in sorrow that I could hold no further conversations with her. Endless conversations, on history, for example. She soared like an eagle, then gradually she would set essential problems, which she alone knew how to set, with absolute rigor."

26. In our conversation, in Marseilles in 1976 (*see* chap. 16, n. 64), Berthe Bruschi Ergas told me these words of Pierre Honnorat (Salon-de-Provence, 1903–Marseilles, 1971). A graduate of l'École Normale Supérieure, a teacher of mathematics, he was a comrade of André Weil and knew Simone in Paris. When he met her again in Marseilles, around Christmas of 1940, he was dumbfounded by the strength of her convictions and found her "more tied to the Church than I would have believed, and more authentic than thousands and thousands of others." It would be Pierre who would preserve the papers and books which Simone could not carry with her to New York. To Denise-Aimé Azam, in fact, he would turn over a file with copies of her manuscripts ("even the least scribble of her handwriting" in letters for Pierre and his sister), the originals of which would be deposited in the Bibliothèque Nationale.

What was the story of Pierre? We reconstruct it from the *Cahier des Avents,* no. 1 (January, 1972) and from the paper by his friend, the mathematician Jean Coulomb, in the *Annuaire des Anciens Élèves de l'École Normale Supérieure.* His father, a very honest civil servant, wanted him to have a religious education, but his mother, who had a keen sensibility, was both a nonbeliever and anticlerical. For his whole life, Pierre would suffer an interior conflict between a rare spiritual sensibility and his inability to belong to the Catholic Church with full consciousness. His sister Hélène would refine and filter her own faith in contact with the loyal objections of her brother.

What mattered for Pierre Honnorat? The role of feeling, nature and man bound together, reading, the importance of religions. He would read and reread the *Bhagavad Gītā.* On March 21, 1971, he wrote in his diary, "A point that interests me . . . is the convergence, or the radical divergence, between western mystics and Buddhists . . . Even admitting my immense ignorance, I would bet on the convergence."

27. From the interview with Marie-Magdeleine Davy in *Elles étaient cent et mille-femmes dans la resistance,* by Marianne Monestier (Paris, Fayard, 1972), p. 203. The italics are mine, given the emphasis that M.-M. Davy, a student of mystics and religious thinkers, from the Middle Ages to our own day, places on the concept of wandering, established as an image.

28. From my conversation with Fr. J.-M. Perrin in 1973 and from Perrin and Thibon, *Simone Weil,* pp. 122–23. The letters-dialogue of Simone Weil to Fr. Perrin, published in *Attente de Dieu,* have served as a route for many nonbelievers to the Dominican in the exercise of his apostolate to the laity of the entire world.

29. Perrin and Thibon, *Simone Weil,* pp. 195–97.

30. Maurice Schumann, "Simone Weil et la présence de Dieu," pp. 7–8.

31. Denise-Aimé Azam, the author of many publications, among which is a brilliant biography of Géricault, had brought the works of Simone Weil to the attention of the apostolic nuncio, Angelo Roncalli, the future John XXIII. Although she attended the classes of Alain around 1930, she had not met Simone, but she knew her thought later, either through her parents or the Honnorats, with whom she had become very friendly, or the reading of *La Pesanteur et la Grâce,* which Thibon had sent her in galleys. A Jew with roots in Paris and Passy ("three sources which seal you," as she remarks, she became a Catholic in 1939. In the attitude of openness shown by the nuncio Roncalli towards Jews, she sensed "an enlargement of her own spiritual ideas." She spoke to him of the Weils, of Dr. Bernard, in his secularism baffled by the spiritual evolution of his daughter, of Selma, destitute of all comfort in her sorrow. Roncalli immediately evinced a desire to write them and did so in 1952. As Thibon had wished, Denise had been an intermediary with the Weils, so that they would not be disturbed by the success of *La Pesanteur* among Catholics, so now, too, she was an intermediary between the apostolic nuncio and the Weils, who were very much surprised by his letter. When they understood the reason he had written, Roncalli became for the Weils "someone who seems to be really fond of our daughter." (This is taken from *L'extraordinaire ambassadeur,* by Denise-Aimé Azam (Paris, La Table Ronde, 1967) and from a conversation with the author in 1973.)

32. "A woman . . . who knew that she was not attractive, who understood that she spoke too much and was too intense; this caused her great sorrow, because she knew well that all of this drove others away from her. But her only reply was to become even more intense." I was told this in August, 1975, by the English author Leslie Paul, who had known Simone Weil since 1938, through an article appearing in an independent labor monthly. "I had walked the same road; so after the war I felt deeply close to her. And on February 6, 1957, I bought her grave for twelve pounds." At the beginning of 1948, Leslie Paul organized a committee which included the philosopher Frederick Tomlin, who had written a monograph on Simone, Richard Rees, who had translated several of her works, T. S. Eliot, the author of the preface to the English edition of

L'Enracinement, and Herbert Read, poet, art critic, and pacifist philosopher. In agreement with the Weil family, the committee placed a tombstone at Ashford, very sober, and modeled upon the commemorative stone dedicated to the fallen of the Resistance in the Luxembourg gardens of Paris. The ceremony of dedication took place on May 1, 1958. The little green marker with the verses was added years later by no one knows who. Leslie Paul sees Simone as completely isolated from her contemporaries. "To those of her generation (Sartre, Simone de Beauvoir), her ascetism seemed an absurdity, a neurosis. Camus was attracted to her by their common moral passion." Leslie Paul dedicated to Simone a poem with the title, "Lady whose grave I own." It appears in a collection, *Journey to Connemara* (Walton-on-Thames, Outposts Publications, 1972). The poet grasps Simone in her "heroic stature," an enormous load for a woman to bear. Here are the last verses:

And so, Simone, lady whose grave I own,
The migraine, the nausea without cessation,
The Solesmes masses beating on the brain,
The iron will to shrug off so much suffering—
    This we know.
But tell us, godly Simone,
Of the waiting till the Saviour came again.
Was this the real affliction,
The cross you had to bear,
That you were simply what you were?

33. *Poèmes,* p. 48.
34. *CIII,* p. 68. This idea, which matured in Simone Weil with the development of her interior exercise and experience, is at the heart of her pedagogy, expressed in "Réflexions sur le bon usage des études scolaires en vue de l'amour de Dieu," which she composed in 1942 and sent to Fr. Perrin from Casablanca for his "indirect relations with the *jécistes* of Montpellier." *AdD,* pp. 85–97. (Jéciste comes from Jeunesse Étudiante Catholique.)
35. *CS,* p. 325.
36. *CII,* p. 113.
37. "Cette guerre est une guerre de religions," *EdL,* pp. 100–102.
38. *See* chap. 18, especially the introduction to *L'Enracinement.*
39. *CI,* p. 236.
40. *CS,* p. 98.
41. "Fragments et notes," *EdL,* pp. 169–70.
42. Letter to her parents of July 18, 1943, *EdL,* p. 250.
43. "When a society is rushing irresistibly towards falsehood, the only consolation of the noble heart is the rejection of privileges. We shall see in *L'Enracinement* the depth of this rejection in Simone Weil. With nobility she bore her taste, or rather her madness for truth . . . This madness allowed Simone Weil to understand, beyond her most natural prejudices, the illness of her epoch and to discern the remedies. In any case, it seems impossible to me to imagine a rebirth for Europe which does not take account of the exigencies defined by Simone Weil in *L'Enracinement.* Here lies the entire

importance of this book . . . Grand but not despairing, such is the virtue of this author. So she is still solitary. But this time it is a question of the solitude of precursors, charged with hope." These are the words with which Albert Camus introduced *L'Enracinement,* for its first edition of May 31, 1949, in the *Gallimard Bulletin* of June, 1949. It was Gilbert Kahn, as he wrote me in a letter of June 30, 1979, who presented to Brice Parain and Albert Camus the manuscript, to which Parain gave the title, *L'Enracinement.* During this period Camus set up for Gallimard the series Espoir, in which were published "Essais philosophiques," most of Simone's works. The series was intended to be "an inventory" of the illness of the age, nihilism, to "find its cure." The works to be published would be diverse, either by intention or inspiration; sometimes they would exalt nihilism, sometimes they would attempt to overcome it. "They would constitute a common conscience, they would testify to the same effort to define and overcome the deadly contradiction in which we are living. The time for choice has arrived; this necessity is itself a step forward."

44.   *CS,* p. 328.

20 Her Testimony

1.   See chap. 1, p. 9.
2.   Letter (1955) of Abbot René de Naurois to Simone Pétrement. Pétrement, 2:494–96.
3.   Letter 5, from Casablanca, sent to Solange B., who acted as secretary to Fr. Perrin, *AdD,* p. 65.
4.   Ibid., p. 66.
5.   *CIII,* p. 67.
6.   Letter 6, May 26, 1942, from Casablanca, *AdD,* p. 72.
7.   Letter to Maurice Schumann, from London, without a date, *EdL,* p. 213.
8.   *CS,* p. 177.
9.   From the essay "Cette guerre est une guerre de religions," *EdL,* p. 105. In *CII,* p. 306, Simone Weil speaks of a religious order, "without habit or insignia," of men and women who have pronounced "implicit" vows rather than explicit ones of "poverty, chastity, and obedience within the limits compatible with the orders received by way of the conscience."
10.   *CS,* p. 266.
11.   From a letter sent to me by the archiepiscopal curia of London, June 9, 1976, with a copy of a letter by Fr. Gilligan of June 4, 1976. According to Miss Iris Woods, he was already dead in 1975. His letter to the archiepiscopal curia, June 4, 1976, demonstrates the contrary, and proves conclusively that Simone Weil had not been baptized. During my visit to Ashford in August, 1975, furthermore, I was able to consult the registers of the Parish of St. Teresa of the Child Jesus and was able to determine the absence of any record, as Fr. Gilligan attests in his letter.
12.   The "last pages" of Simone Weil (from *Pensées sans ordre concernant l'amour de Dieu* (Paris, Gallimard, 1962). This "Dernier texte," to use the French phrase, was found thanks to Frs. Florent and Le Baut, Dominicans. The former had received it, at the end of 1944 or the beginning of 1945, from a girl whose name he has forgotten; she had entrusted it to him as the writing of a friend (whom she did not name), on which

she sought his opinion. Florent had judged it "of great interest" and when the girl did not return, he kept it with great care. Later, he had spoken of Simone Weil in Algiers with Fr. Le Baut and seen some facsimiles of her writing. "Struck by the similarity of thought, style and writing with the document he had kept, he was persuaded, not without reason, that this text was by Simone Weil." It was Selma Weil who dated it with certainty from London "by certain words and inflections of the writing, altogether similar to the last letters of Simone." The Dominican then offered the text to the Bibliothèque Nationale, where the other manuscripts are preserved. This was 1960. (Denise-Aimé Azam, *L'extraordinaire ambassadeur,* [Paris, Le Table Ronde, 1967], pp. 117–118.)

13. Pétrement, 2:516.

Bibliography

Works of Simone Weil

Articles

"L'agonie d'une civilisation vue à travers un poème épique" (signed "Emile Novis"). *Cahiers du Sud*, vol. 20, no. 249 (August–October 1942): 99–107. Also in a special issue of *Cahiers du Sud* (entitled *Le Génie d'Oc et l'homme méditerranéen*), vol. 21 (February 28, 1943): 99–107; and in *Écrits historiques et politiques*, pp. 66–74.

"L'Allemagne en attente (impressions d'Allemagne: août et septembre)." *La Révolution prolétarienne* 138 (October 25, 1932): 6/314–12/320. Also in *Libres Propos*, new series, vol. 6, no. 10 (October 25, 1932): 526–32 and no. 11 (November 25, 1932): 583–90; and in *Écrits historiques et politiques*, pp. 126–42.

"Après la mort du Comité des 22." *L'Effort* 288 (January 2, 1932): 1–2.

"Après la visite d'une mine." *L'Effort* 299 (March 19, 1932): 1.

"Le capital et l'ouvrier." *L'Effort* 298 (March 12, 1932): 1.

"Cinque lettere a uno studente e una lettera a Bernanos." *Nuovi Argomenti* 2 (May–June 1953): 80–103.

"Conclusions" (unsigned article). *Nouveaux Cahiers* (November 15, 1937). Also in *La condition ouvrière*, under the original title "La condition ouvrière" and with the date of the writing (September 30, 1937), pp. 317–25.

"De la perception ou l'aventure de Protée." *Libres Propos*, new series, vol. 3, no. 5 (May 20, 1929): 237–41.

"Du temps." *Libres Propos*, new series, vol. 3, no. 8 (August 20, 1929): 387–92.

"En quoi consiste l'inspiration occitanienne?" *Cahiers du Sud*, vol. 20, no. 249 (August–October 1942): 150–58. Also in a special issue of *Cahiers du Sud* (entitled *Le Génie d'Oc et l'homme méditerranéen*), vol. 21 (February 28, 1943): 150–58; and in *Écrits historiques et politiques*, pp. 75–84.

"L'Iliade ou le poème de la force" (signed "Emile Novis"). *Cahiers du Sud*, vol. 19, no. 230 (December 1940); vol. 20, no. 231 (January 1941).

"Les modes d'exploitation." *L'Effort* 298 (January 30, 1932): 1.

"Ne recommençons pas la guerre de Troie (Pouvoir des mots)." *Nouveaux Cahiers*, vol. 1, nos. 2–3 (April 1 and 15, 1937): 8–10, 15–19. Also in *Écrits historiques et politiques*, pp. 256–72.

"Les nouvelles données du problème colonial dans l'empire français." *Essais et combats* 2–3 (December 1938): 6–7. Also in *Écrits historiques et politiques,* pp. 351–56, and, as a variant on pp. 408–409.

"Perspectives: allons-nous vers la révolution prolétarienne?" *La Révolution prolétarienne* 158 (August 25, 1933): 3/311–11/319. Also in *Oppression et liberté,* pp. 9–38; a rough draft appears on pp. 257–63.

"Quelques remarques sur la réponse de la MOR (Tribune de discussion)." *L'École émancipée,* vol. 23, no. 31 (May 7, 1933).

"Réflexions sur la guerre." *La Critique sociale* 10 (November 1933): 153. Also in *Le Travailleur,* nos. 98–101 (February 3, 10, 17, 24, respectively): 3; *Libres Propos* 8 (August 31, 1935): 364–72; *Le Libertaire* 465 (October 4, 1935): 2; and *Écrits historiques et politiques,* pp. 229–39.

"Réflexions sur les origines de l'hitlérisme, II: Hitler et la politique extérieure de la Rome antique." *Nouveaux Cahiers* 53 (January 1, 1940): 14–21. Also in *Écrits historiques et politiques,* pp. 23–40.

"Le sang coulé en Tunisie." *Feuilles libres de la quinzaine,* vol. 3, no. 33 (March 25, 1937): 75–76. Also, as a variant of the same article, in *Écrits historiques et politiques,* pp. 336–38.

"La situation en Allemagne." *L'École émancipée,* vol. 23, no. 10 (December 4, 1932): 146–48, no. 12 (December 18, 1932): 178–80, no 15 (January 8, 1933): 235–37, no. 16 (January 15, 1933): 249–51, no. 18 (January 29, 1933): 284–85, no. 19 (February 5, 1933): 300–301, no. 20 (February 12, 1933): 315–16, no. 21 (February 19, 1933): 329–32, no. 22 (February 26, 1933): 347–48, no. 23 (March 5, 1933): 363–65. Also in *Écrits historiques et politiques,* pp. 146–94.

"La vie et la grève des ouvrières métallos (sur le tas)" (signed "S. Galois"). *La Révolution prolétarienne* 224 (June 10, 1936): 4/149–8/152. This article also appears under the title "Sur le tas. Souvenirs d'une exploitée" in *Cahiers de Terre Libre* 7 (July 15, 1936).

"La vie syndicale: en marge du Comité d'études." *L'Effort* 286 (December 19, 1931): 2.

Books

Attente de Dieu. Preface by J.-M. Perrin. Paris: Fayard, 1966.

Cahiers. 3 vols. Revised and expanded editions. Paris: Plon, 1970, 1972, and 1974, respectively.

La condition ouvrière. Foreword by Albertine Thévenon. Paris: Gallimard, Collection Idées, 1951.

La Connaissance Surnaturelle. Paris: Gallimard, Collection Espoir, 1950.

Écrits de Londres et dernières lettres. Paris: Gallimard, Collection Espoir, 1957.

Écrits historiques et politiques. Paris: Gallimard, Collection Espoir, 1960.

L'Enracinement, prelude à un déclaration des devoirs envers l'être humain. Paris: Gallimard, Collection Idées, 1968.

Intuitions pré-chrétiennes. Paris: La Colombe, Editions du Vieux Colombier, 1951.

Leçons de philosophie. (Roanne 1933–1936.) Transcribed and introduced by Anne Reynaud-Guérithault. Paris: Plon, Collection 10/18, 1959.

Lettre à un religieux. Paris: Gallimard, Collection Espoir, 1951.

Oppression et liberté. Paris: Gallimard, Collection Espoir, 1955.

Pensées sans ordre concernant l'amour de Dieu. Paris: Gallimard, Collection Espoir, 1962.

La Pesanteur et la grâce. Excerpts from *Cahiers,* vol. 1–3. Introduction by Gustave Thibon. Paris: Plon, Collection L'épi, 1947.

"Poèmes" suivis de "Venise sauvée; Lettre de Paul Valéry." Paris: Gallimard, Collection Espoir, 1968.
La Source grecque. Paris: Gallimard, Collection Espoir, 1953.
Sur la science. Paris: Gallimard, Collection Espoir, 1966.

English Translations

First and Last Notebooks. Translated by Richard Rees. New York: Oxford University Press, 1970.
Formative Writings, 1929–1941. Edited and translated by Dorothy T. McFarland and Wilhemina Van Ness. Amherst: University of Massachusetts Press, 1986.
Gateway to God. Edited by David Raper. Glasgow: Collins, Fontana Books, 1974.
Gravity and Grace. Translated by Arthur F. Wills. New York: G. P. Putnam's, 1952.
Intimations of Christianity Among the Ancient Greeks. Edited and translated by Elisabeth C. Geissbuhler. London: Routledge and Kegan Paul, 1957.
Lectures on Philosophy. Translated by Hugh Price. Cambridge: Cambridge University Press, 1978.
Letter to a Priest. Translated by Arthur F. Wills. London: Routledge and Kegan Paul, 1953.
The Need for Roots. Translated by Arthur F. Wills. London: Routledge and Kegan Paul, 1952.
The Notebooks of Simone Weil. Translated by Arthur F. Wills. London: Routledge and Kegan Paul, 1956.
On Science, Necessity, and the Love of God. Translated by Richard Rees. London: Oxford University Press, 1968.
Oppression and Liberty. Translated by Arthur F. Wills and John Petrie. London: Routledge and Kegan Paul, 1958.
Selected Essays, 1935–1943. Translated by Richard Rees. London: Oxford University Press, 1962.
Seventy Letters. Edited and translated by Richard Rees. London: Oxford University Press, 1965.
The Simone Weil Reader. Edited by George A. Panichas. New York: David McKay, 1977.
Venise sauvée. Translated and adapted by Richard Rees. BBC Third Programme, broadcast January 28 and 29, 1957; R.P. ref. no. TLO 20677.
Waiting on God. Translated by Emma Craufurd. London: Routledge and Kegan Paul, 1951.

Works About Simone Weil

Of the massive amount of critical material relating to Simone Weil, the following biographical works are most helpful: J.-M. Perrin and G. Thibon, *Simone Weil telle que nous l'avons connue* (Paris: La Colombe, 1952); new edition, (Paris: Fayard, 1967); J. Cabaud, *L'expérience vécue de Simone Weil,* containing considerable unpublished material (Paris: Plon, 1957) and *Simone Weil à New York et à Londres: les quinze derniers mois (1942–1943)* (Paris: Plon, 1967); S. Pétrement, *La vie de Simone Weil,* 1, *1909–1934, avec des lettres et d'autres textes inédits de Simone Weil* (Paris: Fayard, 1973) and *La vie de Simone Weil,* 2, *1934–1943, avec des lettres et d'autres textes inédits de Simone Weil* (Paris, 1973); M.-M. Davy, *Simone Weil* (Paris: Editions Universitaires, 1961); F.-L. Closon, *Le temps des passions. De Jean Moulin à la libération 1943–1944* (Paris: Presses de la Cité, 1974).

For an extensive bibliography, see J. Little's *Simone Weil, a Bibliography* (London: Grant & Cutler, 1973) and *Supplement no. 1* (1979). A. Marchetti, *Simone Weil, con una bibliografia sistematica*, is taken from the *Atti della Accademia delle Scienze dell' Istituto di Bologna* (Bologna: Tipografia Compositori, 1977).

On the vast theoretical debate inspired by the thought of Simone Weil, the basic contributions come from the proceedings of the conference "Vigueur d'Alain, Rigueur de Simone Weil," directed by Gilbert Kahn (Cerisy-la-Salle, July 21–August 1, 1974), published as *Alain, philosophe de la culture et théoricien de la démocratie* (Paris: Association les amis d'Alain, 1976) and *Simone Weil, Philosophe historienne et mystique* (Paris, 1978). Another work on Weil's thought is the *Bulletin de liaison de l'association pour l'étude de la pensée de Simone Weil* (nos. 1–10, May, 1974–January, 1978); since June 1978, it has appeared as the *Cahiers Simone Weil*. Finally, there is the presentation of Maurice Schumann, "Simone Weil et la présence de Dieu," for the group "Recherches et expériences sprituelles," at Notre Dame, Paris, November 17, 1974.

Index